Praise from his peer
Nelson Eddy

David Bispham: "Nelson Eddy, the coming baritone – or I miss my guess." [1920]

Maria Jeritza: "Nelson sang the part of Jochanahan [in **Salome**]. He was in good voice and was very well received. I was much impressed by his ability, especially his musicianship, because he had memorized his role with only eight days' notice. This was not easy, because Strauss' music is not child's play and Mr. Eddy had to do most of his studying on trains, as he was on a concert tour. I have heard Mr. Eddy sing on other occasions and always believed that he could have made a fine success in opera if he had chosen that field of music. Opera, however, is exacting and if he had devoted all his time to it, his millions of fans might not have had the chance of seeing him in so many singing films."

John Charles Thomas: "He is a serious high-minded chap, who places his artistic attainments above all else, and who remains unspoiled through the years of acclaim that have been heaped on him."

Rose Bampton: "Nelson was the handsomest young man and doing some wonderful singing, you know. I think we all felt he had star potential. I don't know that we were thinking about movies at this time. We were certainly thinking about opera. From 1928 to '32 there were many roles that he sang at that time, and he was very much in the forefront as a leading baritone."

Mario Lanza: "The thing which keeps Eddy in demand is, I think, his magnetism. Whether you see him in films, hear him in concert, over the air waves or on records, that quality is always there."

Rise Stevens: "Nelson was an exceptional man. He was a big man, very tall, very impressive looking. I really thought he could have made a fantastic opera career. When I heard him [sing], even then, I said to him, 'What a damned shame, what a loss to the opera world.' In a way I don't blame him, you get much better known in films, and there's more money – but he could have, because there was a magnificent organ."

Jeanette MacDonald: "No other man on the screen gives such an impression of eagerness and sincerity as Nelson Eddy. He is unique in this respect. It is this boy-like quality which appeals to most women – the quality of unsophisticated eagerness in a mature and attractive man. He is exactly the same on the screen as off ... anxious to please ... the least theatrical artist I've ever known. There's not an ounce of affectation in him. He was destined for stardom from the beginning."

And... Ezio Pinza on Jeanette MacDonald: "I loved singing with Jeanette. Those damn fools expected a grand diva rendition of Juliette. Jeanette sang her role as though she were fourteen years old entranced by love! As to her voice being thin and small I say bunk! It was beauty to the ear and to the eye an enchanting performance."

Other books in print by Sharon Rich:

Sweethearts: The Timeless Love Affair – on screen and off – between Jeanette MacDonald and Nelson Eddy

Jeanette MacDonald and Nelson Eddy: Interactive CD-Rom Biography

The hardback edition of *Sweethearts* was a selection of the Movie/Entertainment Book Club. Praise for *Sweethearts:*

"The star-crossed love affair of the century. Sharon Rich paints a story of love so passionate, volatile and ultimately futile, even Shakespeare's frustrated lovers pale by comparison. At least Romeo and Juliet solved matters in less than a week. The account is anything but sugar-coated. Ms. Rich's book certainly contains much to raise the eyebrows. She names names and pulls no punches. Still, this is not a sensational expose; one comes away feeling sorry for the protagonists, and wishing that their story could have had a happier resolution. Further, Ms. Rich appears to have scrupulously documented each element of her narrative. Nelson's own letters, and the frequent comments of Jeanette's older sister, Blossom Rock, give credibility to an amazing story." –Rob Ray, *Past Times*

"One of Hollywood's least well-kept secrets. Rich affords a long, exciting, revealing look at two of the most important screen personalities of the 1930s. Vital reading to anyone interested in film history, Hollywood, or popular culture." –Mike Tribby, *Booklist*

"A surprisingly interesting look at two people so wrapped up in make-believe that they began taking it seriously."—Harry Bowman, *The Dallas Morning News*

"A bonanza for MacDonald/Eddy fans, a pan full of nuggets for aficionados of Hollywood and MGM." – *Kirkus Reviews*

"This book rings true. Fans will love it." –John Smothers, *Library Journal*

Praise for *Interactive CD-Rom Biography:*

"Better than a Movie of the Week!" –E.G., via email

"The truth is out there. Or rather, right here on this CD-Rom. Listening to Nelson discuss his temper or cry when he talks about Jeanette's death tells the story better than written words ever could. The many candid photos and documents add more verification. You are to be congratulated for compiling this massive project. Read this book and then watch 'This is Your Life' and you have the whole story." – E.T., via email

Nelson Eddy

The Opera Years

1922-1935

With a bonus chapter on the opera career of Jeanette MacDonald

Nelson Eddy

The Opera Years

1922-1935

With a bonus chapter on the opera career of Jeanette MacDonald

by
Sharon Rich

Bell Harbour Press
New York

Published by Bell Harbour Press, www.bellharbourpress.com

Printed in the United States of America

ISBN 0-9711998-0-9

Copies of *Nelson Eddy: The Opera Years* may be ordered directly from Bell Harbour Press. Discounts are available for bulk orders. To contact the author directly or for a current catalog of the MacDonald/Eddy items mentioned in this book, please contact:

Mac/Eddy Club
Dept. S
PO Box 1077
New York, NY 10002

Author's Note

Before he became a movie star, Nelson Eddy was an opera star. For eleven years, from 1922 until 1933, this young baritone worked tirelessly to make a name for himself in his chosen profession. He sang wherever possible, not only in opera, but oratorios, concerts and radio. He was a man driven by ambition, with the talent and looks to match.

Hollywood beckoned in 1933. The initial lure was money and the hope that he'd find a larger audience for his concerts and operas. The next two years found Nelson juggling his previous hectic schedule with the demands of his new venture. He didn't want to drop his "serious singing" but in the end, Hollywood won out. Nelson sang his last live opera in 1935 but unlike any other movie star before or since, he continued his very active concert career plus maintained a weekly radio show (often singing operatic arias) throughout his MGM years. He became the highest paid singer in the world, a title he firmly held for many years until the arrival of Frank Sinatra.

Was he a great opera singer? The answer can be found in the hundreds of reviews that follow, written by those who observed him firsthand. Critics are by nature a jaded lot; they've heard it all and seen everything. It takes someone special to startle and impress them into enthusiastic adjectives. After reading a few pages of Nelson's reviews, you'll get the idea. It was a very rare occurrence for Nelson Eddy not to get a rave. Almost one for one, reviewers in cities far and wide praised his looks, his stage presence, his perfect diction in any language, his beautiful legato tones, his thoughtful and vivid interpretations, his ability to hold his audience's attention rapt and his sheer stamina – sounding as fresh and exuberant after singing five, ten or even fifteen encores! Occasionally someone voiced a minor complaint, but the number of outright bad reviews could probably be counted on the fingers of one hand.

Nelson's contemporaries agreed that they were witnessing something special. Many boldly called him the greatest American baritone of his generation – and they were talking about a singer still in his twenties.

Opera's loss was Hollywood's gain. There were many who grumbled that Nelson sold his soul by remaining in films after the success of *Naughty Marietta.* His friends tried to persuade Nelson to return to the opera stage until he was in his fifties. When he began a nightclub career instead, purists were horrified.

After Nelson's death Max de Schauensee, one of his old friends from the early days, wrote in the Philadelphia *Evening Bulletin:* "It is well known that in later years Nelson rather laughed off his films and secretly hoped that people would not forget that at one time he was a fine opera singer."

In celebration of Nelson's centennial year, it is fitting to honor his achievements in opera and to make certain that people do not forget. After all, the beloved movie star was first and foremost -- in the words of the critics -- one of the great voices of the twentieth century.

Sharon Rich
New York City
June 2001

For my mother

Frances Rich

Table of Contents

Introduction

In this book I break tradition by simply bolding all names of operas, oratorios and films in the text. This is to help the reader easily locate titles of the major works Nelson appeared in.

About 85% of the reviews were gathered from Nelson's personal scrapbooks housed at USC. So right here I want to Ned Comstock for allowing me unlimited access to them. The balance of the reviews and clippings came from personal scrapbooks or collections kept by fans over the years, or from various newspaper morgues around the country. My thanks to everyone who has sent in clippings over the last twenty years, and especially to Ann Argo for doing a lot of footwork for me with the newspapers. Even more thanks are due to Dorothy Dillard for giving me access to vital personal letters and for accompanying me as we "tramp, tramp, tramped" across the country, interviewing key people who knew Nelson and/or Jeanette.

I've excerpted the reviews, giving only the comments pertaining to Nelson unless the reviewer made other observations of interest. If a review said nothing noteworthy, I skipped it. The dates and performances should be fairly complete, since for the first few years Nelson was mostly singing in Philadelphia. If the event wasn't reviewed, however, we might not know about it. Whenever possible, I have differentiated between the actual singing date and when the review was published.

The clippings with Nelson's hand-written notations are from his own scrapbooks. They have been slightly reduced in size to fit the page. He began his first scrapbook in 1922. It actually was a black, loose-leaf student's notebook. Nelson eventually purchased and filled eight of these, dating and identifying the clippings on each page. He also sometimes made comments in the margins.

The opera and concert programs reproduced here were gathered from various sources. Thanks to Dorothy Dillard, Barbara Gill, Anna May Ryder and the many others who shared their collections.

The photos are from my own collection. Thanks to my daughter Juliet McIntyre for doing the scanning, layout and the cover artwork. Thanks also to my sister Julie for her help with graphics, my sister Arlene for her general assistance and my husband Jake for his editorial input. This book was truly a family affair!

When Nelson began touring in the late 1920s, he used clipping services to gather reviews for him. His scrapbooks were still pretty thorough until he hit it big in Hollywood. Around that time, new large scrapbooks were utilized, stuffed with reviews and movie magazine articles. Due to the multitudes of press he received worldwide in the 1930s and '40s, it would be nearly impossible for Nelson's scrapbooks from that period to be complete.

During these years, Nelson's mother Isabel was in charge of organizing the scrapbooks, and her large scrawl occasionally added headings or annotations. In his later years, Nelson returned to writing comments again. For his last scrapbook, the front page had pasted on it the record cover of himself and Jeanette from the "Favorites in Hi-Fi" album. He devoted 14 pages of this scrapbook to her obituaries.

To put Nelson's early career in perspective, one must remember that movies were still silent and a young singer couldn't become an overnight media star. To build a singing career took hard work and persistence. According to family friend Zepha Bogart, Isabel Eddy instilled in her son an optimistic philosophy: If he were mentally prepared for success, success would come to him. But no one could have predicted that after a decade of "paying his dues" he would suddenly be the most famous singer in the world, a star whose face and voice was known and cherished planet-wide.

This is the story of his rise to stardom.

Biography

"That young man ought to make a fine singer!" said the doctor who delivered Nelson Eddy, according to family legend.[1] Assuming the statement was true, the loudly yelling infant must have been listening because he certainly took the good doctor's comment to heart.

Nelson Ackerman Eddy was born in Providence, Rhode Island, on June 29, 1901. His mother was redhaired Isabel Kendrick, a Southern gal. His father, William Darius Eddy, was a confirmed Yankee. The two met during the Spanish-American War, when Bill Eddy was wounded and Isabel nursed him. Like many wartime romances, theirs wasn't destined to last. But by the time they came to that unhappy realization, they were married and had a young son.

"Bricktop" Eddy, boy soprano.

Bill Eddy developed a drinking problem and couldn't hold down a job.[2] The family was forced to move frequently, but remained in the Rhode Island – Massachusetts area. About the only thing Isabel and Bill had in common was their love of music. Both were singers and came from musical families. (A 1903 recording exists of Nelson's grandmother, Caroline Kendrick, singing "The Last Rose of Summer." Isabel Eddy sang with her son on two of his 1940s radio shows.[3])

Nelson started singing at a young age. A boy soprano, he made the rounds singing in local church choirs, learned Gilbert and Sullivan from his mother and opera from listening to records on the Victrola. He was a sturdy, plain-featured boy, with unruly red hair and dark blue eyes. Childhood photos show him as a serious kid who wore glasses for nearsightedness.

In 1915, Bill Eddy walked out on his family. Isabel gathered up her son and fled to Philadelphia, where they stayed with her mother until they could make it on their own. Nelson dropped permanently out of school to go to work. While helping to support Isabel, he also continued educating himself at night with correspondence courses. Lacking funds for voice lessons, he taught himself as best he could. "I bought records of Campanari and Scotti and Ruffo and Amato and sat listening until I had learned the aria and then I would bawl out the notes at the top of my lungs," he later said. "Of course I recognized the difference in my handling of the song and the way Caruso would have done it. But then I tried very hard to learn from the masters who sang from the little wax discs. I was used to teaching myself things, after so many years of studying without any outside help. I had a good range and plenty of volume – and I would sing to the phonograph accompaniment when guests would visit. And when I'd get to a part of the aria where the difference between my technique and Campanari's was too obvious, I'd merely stick out my chest and take a long breath and drown Campanari out. It was very effective."[4]

Those years of poverty scarred Nelson. Once he found people would pay him to sing, he would seek out gigs that also had a free meal thrown in. He still thought of himself as "very poor" and "a very shabby lad."[5]

Nelson lied about his age and experience to land stable employment, mostly writing for newspapers. It's true that he was fired occasionally for singing on the job. But by 1920 he and Isabel were solvent enough to start affording voice lessons for Nelson. He approached the Met's retired baritone, David Bispham, who agreed to take him on as a student. After Bispham died in 1921, Nelson went through eleven more voice teachers until he found one he liked.

Nelson made his professional debut on January 21, 1922 at the Philadelphia Academy of Music, in a revue called **The Marriage Tax**. He played the King of Greece but by some lucky error, there was a question mark instead of his name next to his character's name on the program. Now everyone had to know the identity of this talented young mystery man. And not surprisingly, his first newspaper review in the *Public Ledger* was typical of the multitudes that would follow: "He has great talent as an actor and a voice that thrilled because of its perfect control, clear resonant tone and exceptional quality."

In May of the same year Nelson sang with a Gilbert and Sullivan troupe, the Savoy Company. He eagerly took any job that came his way, singing at weddings, funerals, bar mitzvahs, "sewing circles, Rotary Clubs or anyone else who desired a burst of melody between the cabinet pudding and 'Our Honored Speaker.'" Nelson bluntly added, "I followed the job that paid the most."[6]

It didn't hurt that in adulthood Nelson was, in the words of one reviewer, "a blond Adonis." He was now six feet tall with movie star looks. His hair had turned prematurely white, giving it the appearance of being blond. According to him, he was so scared about playing Tonio in his first **I Pagliacci** that his hair turned white overnight.

On May 18, 1923, Nelson made his operatic debut in **Aida**. It was the final performance of the Philadelphia Operatic Society, and Nelson once again stood out, as evidenced by this review in the *Philadelphia Record:* "Nelson Eddy, as Amonasro, had an electrifying effect on the audience. A young singer, scarcely 20 years of age, with that indefinable gift so seldom seen of arresting the auditor's interest and holding it continuously, Mr. Eddy was a star from the moment he appeared on the stage."

The opera company regrouped as the Philadelphia Civic Opera Company in 1924, with Nelson on its roster. He sang two roles with them that first season, his above-mentioned debut as Tonio in December 1924, and a repeat of Amonasro in February 1925. Of his Tonio, the *Public Ledger* commented: "Nelson Eddy fairly swept the audience off its feet with his rendition of the Prologue, and from that moment the high standard of performance never dropped. Mr. Eddy's characterization of the difficult role was so excellent throughout that it looks as though the Civic Opera Company might already have justified its existence by the discovery of a real operatic talent."

During 1924-5, Nelson made his radio debut and sang at various events and concerts in the Philadelphia area. In between times he coached with Alexander Smallens, director of the Civic Opera, studied languages and learned repertoire.

The Civic opened their 1925-6 season again with **Aida** and according to the *Philadelphia Inquirer,*

"Nelson Eddy, previously seen as Amonasro, was even better in the part last night. Although still quite youthful, he exhibits a baritone voice of breadth and beauty, and acts with authority." Nelson sang five other roles that season, Alfio in **Cavalleria Rusticana**, Bustamente in **La Navarraise**, the title role in **Gianni Schicchi**, Abimélech in **Samson et Delilah** and Wolfram in **Tannhäuser** -- the season's finale. His Wolfram proved to be the biggest success yet, as noted by the *Evening Bulletin:* "Mr. Eddy's baritone was of beautiful lyric quality, his enunciation was clear, his inflection sure and he displayed unusual command of tone color. His efforts stirred his hearers to continued hand-clapping which subsided only after he had 'stepped out of character' in order to bow two or three times. Horrified Wagnerites trembled for fear that there might be an attempt to force an encore in violation of all tradition." Many felt that Wolfram was Nelson's best operatic role and the one most suited to his voice.

As Amonasro in **Aida.**

In 1926 Nelson made his first recording, a song he'd written called "The Rainbow Trail."[7] He also sang in oratorios and gave more concerts.

On opening night of the 1926-7 opera season, Nelson repeated his Wolfram. Also in November 1926, he sang his first Sharpless in **Madama Butterfly** and in December, his first Mercutio in **Romeo et Juliette**. At year's end he wrote a Christmas pageant called **Manifestation** and it was performed at the Overbrook Presbyterian Church. In January 1927 he repeated **Gianni Schicchi** and in February, **Aida**. In March he sang his first Marcello in **La Boheme** and the Herald in **Lohengrin**. In between these performances he continued singing oratorios, operatic scenes as well as concerts. In February, he began his first weekly radio show, the Newton Coal Hour.

Nelson's following in Philaelphia was growing, but he wasn't satisfied. He was still cycling through teachers, including Ludwig Schmidt-Fabri, Rebecca Van Conway, Henry Scot and Horatio Connell. His dissatisfaction with his voice stemmed from a problem noted by the *Evening Bulletin* reviewer, commenting on **Tannhäuser**: "His voice seems more mellow and richer than ever, with its 'luscious' quality, and when he has learned to use his high tones as well as he does those in the middle and lower part of his fine voice, and has extended its range somewhat, he may be expected to accomplish great things."

Nelson also struggled for the high A-flat in **I Pagliacci**. A lyric baritone, he'd once hoped to ease into dramatic tenor roles, as Caruso and Melchior did. Both of them had started as baritones. But without the high notes, that goal was impossible to achieve. The reader will note while studying Nelson's reviews that in the 1920s, he often sang bass-baritone roles. This sometimes drew criticism from reviewers who thought his voice too light for them. Yet he also sang some dramatic tenor roles that were no effort for him, as long as he didn't have to sing at the very top of the range. (In the movie **Phantom of the Opera** (1943), the sharp listener will hear Nelson singing a few lines here and there, both as an "off-screen" tenor and bass during the "opera" scene just before the chandelier falls. In Disney's **Make Mine Music** (1946) he sang all the roles of Willie the Operatic Whale -- soprano, tenor, baritone and bass.)

***As Wolfram in* Tannhäuser**

By the 1926-7 opera season, Nelson was discouraged about his voice. "I was pretty rotten for a long while," he said. "One day Edouard Lippe, a well-known Philadelphia singer, told me right out I didn't know how to sing. That might have made me mad, but the truth was I knew it as well as he. So I just asked him what to do. He came over to my house every day and gave me lessons. Then he sent me to William W. Vilonat, who had been his teacher. Vilonat taught me how to sing."[8]

In July 1927, Nelson borrowed money and went to Dresden for the summer. He lived with a German family and learned to speak the language fluently, which would prove useful when he did government work during WWII. At the end of Nelson's studies there, he was offered a contract with the Dresden Opera. He turned it down, preferring to make his fame at home. He would make other summer trips to Europe for more voice training, but each opera season found him back in Philadelphia. In December 1927, he was part of the ensemble for the American premiere of Strauss' **Feuersnot**. Also in December he sang Count Gil in **Secret of Suzanne** and Marcello in **La Boheme**.

Nelson's idol was Feodor Chaliapin; he adopted many of the great basso's songs and arias as his own. So it was no surprise to find Nelson singing standards like "The Blind Ploughman" in his concerts, or singing the Czar's arias in **Boris Godunov**[9]. In December 1927, Nelson sang his first **Boris** selections in concert version for the Reading Choral Society. According to the *Reading Times:* "It was absolutely faultless – every tone was sung true to pitch and with a voice clear and resonant as a bell…. It was one of the best performances of this or any other season."

In January 1928 Nelson sang Manfredo in **L'amore dei tre re**, a huge success for him, then repeated his roles in **Lohengrin** and **Madama Butterfly**. February found him singing another Amonasro; in March he sang Silvio in **I Pagliacci**, thus avoiding the troublesome A-flat. He also continued his popular Newton Coal radio show.

After spending the summer abroad, Nelson returned for the 1928-9 opera season. It opened in October with the ever-popular **Aida**. Nelson apparently had an off night, with the *Bulletin* commenting on his effort with some high notes. On November 1, he fared better singing the Wigmaker and Arlecchino in the American premiere of Strauss' **Ariadne auf Naxos**. A young Helen Jepson sang Echo. Nelson continued the season singing Kothner in **Die Meistersinger**, a repeat of Marcello and Silvio, then his debut as Lescaut in Puccini's **Manon Lescaut**.

January 1929 found Nelson still on the Newton Coal Hour while reprising his operatic roles in **Tannhäuser** and **Madama Butterfly**. The *Daily News,* in discussing Nelson's latest Wolfram, posed this question: "What more can be said about the ability of the favorite Nelson Eddy? It has not been a week since we said: 'He has to but open his mouth, warble a few notes, and the audience is his. That goes again. His voice discloses improvement every time it is heard. He can hold any group enraptured with his personality. It is high time that Eddy starts off for broader fields."

In March 1929, Nelson sang his debut Count Almaviva in Mozart's **Marriage of Figaro**. The *Ledger* commented: "Nelson need never fear. Two or three years hence will find him in higher operatic circles."

Nelson received rave reviews in April 1929 for his singing of Simeon in Debussy's **L'Enfant Prodigue** which was co-billed with Gluck's **Orfeo ed Eurydice**. The opera season closed that month with **Samson and Delilah**, and Nelson received his usual good notices.

As Manfredo in L'amore dei tre re.

The critics who had watched Nelson's career unfold were quite vocal about the fact that he was ready to move onward and upward. And indeed, at this time the pace of Nelson's career picked up dramatically. He had signed with concert manager Arthur Judson of Columbia Concerts, and had a permanent accompanist, Theodore Paxson. He now was promoted as the "leading baritone of the Philadelphia Opera Company," knew 28 operatic roles, 11 oratorios and hundreds of songs. During 1929 he began his own concert series at the Warwick Hotel, utilizing a different guest at each concert. He also began singing in more oratorios. The next year he made his New York City debut; in 1931 and '32 Arthur Judson sent him out on tour around the East Coast. Then in early 1933 Nelson ventured out to California and we know the rest of the story!

But back to May 1929. After singing the leads in more oratorios -- **Odysseus** by Max Bruch, **Elijah**, and Brahms' "Four Serious Songs," Nelson changed gears and made his vaudeville debut. For one week he appeared at the Stanley Theater, singing Escamillo in a scaled-down scene from **Carmen** (which obviously included the "Toreador Song"). His "act" preceded **A Man's Man** starring William Haines and Josephine Dunn.

For the 1929-30 opera season, Nelson repeated Mercutio in **Romeo et Juliette**, then took part when the Civic Opera presented the full Wagner "Ring" cycle. He sang the small role of Donner in **Das Rheingold** on November 21 and played Gunther in **Götterdämmerung** on January 16, 1930. In between he sang Valentine in **Faust**, Peter in **Hansel and Gretl**, another Amonasro, the more important role of the High Priest in **Samson and Delilah** and Papageno in **The Magic Flute**. There was quite a furor over **Hansel and Gretl** due to Nelson tottering onstage with a flask, even though he didn't drink from it. In this era of Prohibition, it was inevitable that protesting letters were written by the local temperance league!

In February 1930, Nelson added another new role to his repertoire, Belcore in **L'elisir d'amore**. He had two more performances with the Civic Opera in **Marriage of Figaro** and **Die Meistersinger**, then the season ended and Philadelphia Civic Opera Company folded due to lack of funds. The stock market crash of '29 was the culprit, but several of the Civic Opera's singers – Nelson included – were invited to join the Philadelphia Grand Opera Company.

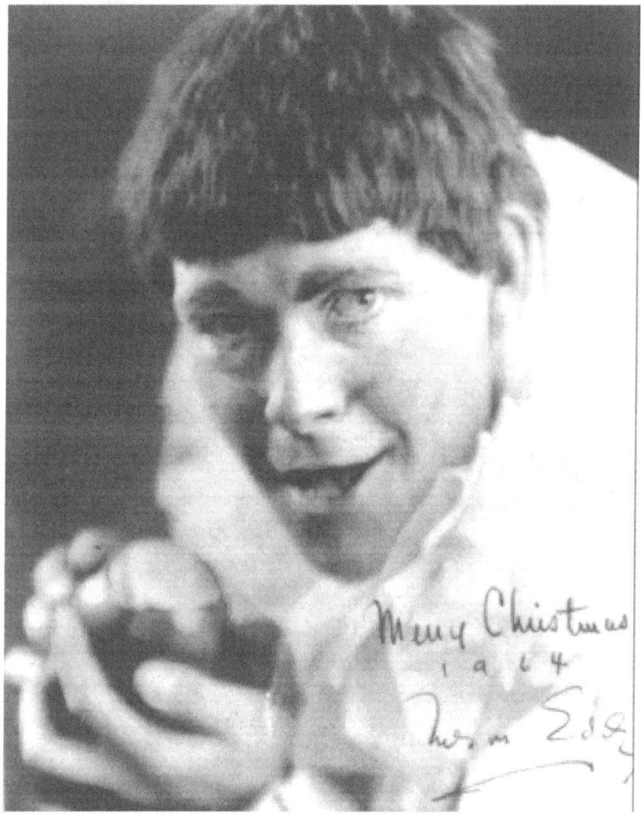

During the spring of 1930, Nelson busied himself with oratorio work, his popular Warwick Hotel concerts, his radio show and other guest appearances in which he usually sang operatic excerpts. Instead of going to Europe, the summer found him in New York City. He sang in Verdi's **Requiem** and the bass role in Beethoven's Ninth Symphony at Lewisohn Stadium (an outdoor theater). He then returned to Philadelphia to sing in their outdoor theater, Robin Hood Dell, where he was obliged to repeat both his numbers – and 600 extra chairs had to be added to accommodate his fans!

As Tonio in **I Pagliacci.**

In the fall he started another series of Warwick Hotel concerts, started a new radio series for Atwater Kent and continued on with his normal busy schedule. In a November 1930 interview he said, "I worked, worked and worked. And it's a constant grind even today. I don't believe anyone realizes how hard I work because I try to make it all look easy. It might detract from their enjoyment of the songs if they knew that I stayed awake nights, pulling my hair and chewing my fingernails trying to learn them."

"The Depression enabled me to get good engagements," he explained in another interview. "The giants of the old days were refusing to cut their fees. The public desired recitals but just couldn't pay the old prices. By being cheap, I became 'the popular young baritone.' There are plenty of young singers with better voices than mine, but I've worked harder than most of them and gotten further. If I heard that someone was going to give an opera I got the score and learned it and then when they wondered who to get, I would say, 'Why not me? I know it.' And I'd get the job. All the other singers who hadn't studied would say, 'Lucky dog! He gets all the breaks!' And I wasn't lucky at all. I'm not very quick at learning scores, either. Many's the time I've propped myself up with black coffee and gone over and over a score trying to get it through my head. It hasn't been easy for me, so consequently I've had to work harder."[10]

One of Nelson's friends at that time was Malcolm Poindexter, a bass. Despite Poindexter's beautiful voice he had trouble getting singing engagements because he was black. Poindexter approached Nelson for helping in finding a voice teacher who would coach him. As he recalled some sixty years later: "[Nelson] responded by telling me to come sing with him, which I did. Then he and his own voice teacher, Dr. Edouard Lippe, agreed to take me as a student. I had an afternoon teaching position which allowed me time in the morning to practice with Nelson, and on some days Dr. Lippe would be there, too. He had his own studio on Locust Street.

"At the time I was studying with Nelson I was so poor that I had to carry the music I had wrapped up in newspaper. Much of the music I did have was given to me by Nelson. So one day Nelson called me on the phone to ask me to come meet him at the corner of Thirteenth and Locust streets. He had just returned from a singing engagement in Toronto, Canada, and he said that he had something for me. When I arrived at the appointed place, there was Nelson waiting to present me with a beautiful genuine leather case in which to carry my music. He had bought it in Toronto with some of the money he had made singing there. As he handed it to me he said, 'Now Malcolm, I don't want to see you with your music wrapped in newspaper anymore.' .... This was long before I or anyone else could know he was to become a world celebrity. He was a wonderful friend in so many ways."

Poindexter described Nelson's other attempts to help him. "Occasionally when he would get a call to sing at Conwell's church and other places too, he would call them close to the time he was to perform and tell them he couldn't make it, but he would send a replacement singer. He told them that they must pay his substitute the same amount as they were to pay him. I was that substitute vocalist. This was Nelson's way of trying to help me get a break."

Malcolm Poindexter did land a concert in Ethical Hall. "This particular night the hall was filled. Nelson also sang there and the people who came to hear my concert also knew Nelson. When Nelson arrived to hear me sing, he didn't like the placement of the piano on the stage. So he asked, 'Who's in charge here?' Since it was the first time the place was let out to a Negro singer, everybody who had to do with the management of the place was afraid to admit who was in charge. So Nelson went over to a man who appeared to be in charge and said, 'I want that piano moved. This man can't sing with it in that position.' The man said, 'We don't have anybody to do that.' Nelson then asked, 'But is it all right to move it?' The man indicated that it was and with that Nelson jumped up on the stage and moved the piano around himself to where he wanted it to be. Well, the place came down. This is just one example of the kind of caring and unselfish person Nelson was."[11]

Nineteen thirty-one found Nelson spending more time in New York, and he apparently took an apartment there. In July, he repeated Verdi's **Requiem** and Beethoven's Ninth at Lewisohn Stadium. September found him back in Philadelphia for his first role with the Philadelphia Grand Opera Company, that of Orestes in **Elektra**. Nelson received raves, as he did for his next opera in November, **Madama Butterfly**. "The best Sharpless seen here for many seasons," was the consensus. On November 24, Nelson was back in New York to sing the dramatic tenor role of the Drum Major in **Wozzeck**. This production was held at the New York Metropolitan Opera, with Stokowski conducting.

That same year, Nelson started another series of Warwick Hotel concerts. He repeated **Gianni Schicchi** and **Hansel and Gretl**, then starred in Mendelssohn's **Elijah** and sang bass in Handel's **Messiah**.

In 1932, Nelson was back on the radio with the Hoffman Hour. He finished his opera season with **Lohengrin**, **Elektra** and **Secret of Suzanne**, in which his co-star was Helen Jepson.

On March 16, 1932, Nelson sang at Carnegie Hall in New York, in an important world premiere of Resphighi's **Maria Egiziaca**, conducted by the composer. The performance was repeated the following two evenings, to great acclaim.

In April, Nelson headed out on concert tour. "Crowd holds baritone an extra hour at concert," noted one newspaper. "Nelson Eddy... stands with Lawrence Tibbett and John Charles Thomas as one of the three

The world premiere of **Maria Egiziaca** *at Carnegie Hall*

best baritones in America," asserted another. "He created a furor," wrote a Cincinnati critic, calling Nelson "one of the greatest, most justly famed of American singers."

On April 26, 1932, Nelson was in Hartford to sing the bass solo in Verdi's **Requiem**. On June 21, he sang Tonio at a Robin Hood Dell **I Pagliacci**. It was the first opera ever presented there and Nelson breezed through the high A-flat, singing "superbly" according to *Musical America*. In July he returned to New York for another Beethoven's Ninth at Lewisohn Stadium.

On November 9, 1932, Nelson returned to New York's Metropolitan Opera. The occasion was a condensed version of Strauss' **Salome**, with Fritz Reiner conducting and Maria Jeritza starring. This was a benefit for the Musician's Symphony Orchestra. Nelson sang Jochanahan and *Musical Courier* commented: "The richness and perfect evenness of his voice as well as the intelligence he displays in his singing have made him within a period of only a few seasons one of the outstanding and yet most promising of the American list of singers."

February 1933 found Nelson singing in California for the first time. He'd already agreed to substitute for Lotte Lehman in Los Angeles, probably in mid-January (the program is proof of this), but how much advance notice he had we'll never know. The point is, his San Diego concert on February 27 was a triumph. He sang at least 14 encores and according to the *San Diego Sun*, "He sings so easily that at the end of two hours singing, his voice was as fresh and rich as when he began."

The morning of February 28, the phone wires were burning between San Diego and Los Angeles. The studios had been tipped off about Nelson's impact in San Diego, so representatives were sent to the L.A.

The Philharmonic Review

THE OFFICIAL PROGRAM

Behymer Artist Courses

JOSE ITURBI
January 29

DON COSSACK CHORUS
February 14

Vol. XXIX — JANUARY-FEBRUARY, 1933 — Nos. 8-9

BEHYMER CALENDAR

(Philharmonic Auditorium)

Jan. 29—Jose Iturbi, Spanish pianist—Sunday matinee.

Feb. 12—Don Cossack Russian Male Chorus—Sunday matinee.

14—Don Cossack Russian Male Chorus—Tuesday evening.

21—Josef Hofmann, Polish pianist.

28—Nelson Eddy, American baritone.

Mar. 12—Walter Gieseking, German pianist—Sunday matinee.

14—Josef Szigeti, Hungarian violinist.

Apr. 18—Paul Robeson, colored baritone.

May 2—Yehudi Menuhin, violinist.

THE GODOWSKY MASTER CLASS

Beginning July 17th, Leopold Godowsky is planning to come to Los Angeles for a five weeks' Master Class in the study of piano literature. Active students will be limited to twenty, at a fee of $200, for the class. Four hours daily, for four days a week, will give eighty hours class work in five weeks. A deposit of $50.00 is required for registration through the office of L. E. Behymer, 705 Auditorium Building, balance to be paid before the commencement of the Course.

In case Mr. Godowsky decides any active pupil is not far enough advanced for the Master Class, he reserves the option of transfering him to the Listeners Class, with three private lessons in addition.

The number of auditors, or listeners, will be unlimited, and the fee will be $100 for five weeks. A registration of $25.00 will be required, balance payable before commencement of the class.

In addition to the above, Mr. Godowsky is planning a class of five weeks' duration, (for the fifth day of each week), for the study of his own compositions, of which there are now several hundred published. For this class the active students will be limited to ten, at $75.00. Auditors unlimited, at $25.00 for the five weeks. This class would consist of twenty hours' study, or four hours weekly.

Circulars will be ready for distribution later but registration may be made at any time.

Mr. Godowsky has had many noted artists among his pupils, among them Issay Dobrowen, conductor of the San Francisco Symphony Orchestra; Terresita Carreno, Vladimar Shavitch, conductor of the Syracuse Symphony Orchestra; Manna Zucca, composer, George McManus, Marvin Maazel, Olga Steeb, Bertha Wilbur, Fannie C. Dillon, and a number of other Los Angeles teachers.

USE YOUR

LOTTE LEHMANN Tickets for NELSON EDDY

TUESDAY EVENING, FEBRUARY 28

It is not necessary to change them at the Boxoffice.

The program announcing Nelson's Los Angeles debut.

Philharmonic to check him out that night. The Los Angeles concert was equally successful with another 14 encores and 32 curtain calls! Afterwards, he received offers from three studios for a movie contract.

Nelson decided to sign with RKO on Saturday night, March 4th and was told his first film would be **Maiden Cruise** (later released as **Melody Cruise**). On Monday, March 6th, this fact was verified by a columnist in the *Hollywood Citizen News.* However, that same day Nelson learned that all studio actors had been put on half-pay (due to the fact that the studio had gone into receivership). Nelson left RKO, saying, "I'm not an actor, I'm a singer. I went into movies for the money. Nothing except the money will keep me in them." He had already sent telegrams to the remaining seventeen concert dates on this tour, regretfully canceling them. Now he wired again that he would fulfill the dates, and continued his cross-country tour.[12]

With his Parsifal *co-star, Rose Bampton*

March 31, 1933 found Nelson back in Philadelphia for an important event, the American broadcast premiere of Wagner's **Parsifal**. The uncut opera was sung over a period of three days. Stokowski conducted and the cast included Rose Bampton and Robert Steel. Nelson sang the bass role of Gurnemanz to rave reviews.

MGM continued to hound Nelson to sign a contract. He was promised four months off each year to continue his concerts, and would be allowed to finish the current tour as well. Nelson still hesitated, then said later in an interview, "I didn't know whether to sign it or not, but while I was thinking about it my agents practically did it for me." His MGM screen test was apparently awful. He acted a scene from **The Barretts of Wimpole Street** with Maureen O'Sullivan, directed by Felix Feist. After 58 takes, Feist finally suggested that Nelson stop trying to act and just look into the camera and sing "On the Road to Mandalay." According to newspaper reports, it wasn't until April 22, 1933 that Nelson finally signed on the dotted line. He reported to the studio in June to start his new life.

Once the novelty of meeting movie stars wore off, Nelson found himself with little to do. After all the grandiose promises, MGM had no projects for him. He tested for a minor role in **Queen Christina** that he didn't get. Now he was expected to take acting lessons and play golf. This didn't go over well with Nelson, which in turn angered his boss, Louie B. Mayer. The two were destined never to get along.[13]

Nelson stuck it out at MGM for six months. He was ready to walk when his option ended at the end of 1933. But by then fate intervened, and his life would never be the same.

Up to this point, Nelson's private life had never interfered with his career. He had never allowed any romance to get serious enough distract him. His original plan in signing with MGM was to make a movie or two just to interest more people in attending his concerts. He never wanted to "go Hollywood."

But then he met and fell hard for Jeanette MacDonald, long before they made a film together.[14] "She was stunning and startlingly beautiful," he said of their first meeting. "She would take your breath away."[15] He proposed to her within a week of their first date, was crushed when she turned him down.[16] But she talked Mayer into letting him co-star with her in **Naughty Marietta**, and the rest is history.

With his voice teacher, Dr. Lippe, who played the Innkeeper in the film that made him a movie star, **Naughty Marietta**

With Kathryn Meisle

Nelson refused a contract from the Metropolitan Opera to stay in Hollywood, and refused again on subsequent years--to the despair of his opera crowd. But he had not totally abandoned opera. On August 24, 1934, he sang a concert version of **Carmen** at the Hollywood Bowl, with costars Nina Koshetz and Tandy Mackenzie. On November 6 he starred in **Secret of Suzanne** with Doris Kenyon and Edouard Lippe. On November 26 and December 8, 1934, he sang Wolfram in a San Francisco Opera production of **Tannhäuser**, with a stellar cast that included Lauritz Melchior, Elisabeth Rethberg and Ezio Pinza. On May 30, 1935, he sang the Second Puritan in the world premiere of Howard Hanson's **The Merry Mount**, in Ann Arbor, Michigan. (Nelson's role was minor; the stars were Rose Bampton and John Charles Thomas.) For his final opera appearance he returned to San Francisco for **Aida**, on December 11, 1935. His costars were Elisabeth Rethberg, Kathryn Meisle, his final opera review mirrored the gushing approval of his very first one. "Beautifully, nobly sung was the Amonasro of Nelson Eddy," praised the *San Francisco Examiner.*

It apparently wasn't a conscious decision on Nelson's part to stop singing opera. According to one his mentors, in the early days he and Jeanette discussed doing operas. Jeanette was persuaded that he could still make the transition to dramatic tenor and to the mentor's disgust, Jeanette set about trying to "change" Nelson's voice. After a short period of time Nelson abandoned the idea, telling her, "I'm a baritone, and that's that."[17]

On a date with Jeanette, visiting Charlotte Cushing after an L.A. Civic Opera production of **Maytime.**

But because of Jeanette, he stayed in Hollywood permanently. Many of his opera friends never forgave her for that.

In 1935, Nelson fitted his living room with top-of-the-line recording equipment. His "Hollywood" parties usually included any of the famous opera names that happened to be in town, such as Ezio Pinza or Rosa Ponselle. Nelson's night wasn't complete unless they'd made home recordings of famous duets, trios or quartets. For one Christmas, he recorded the **Faust** trio with himself, Jeanette and Allan Jones. Copies of this priceless treasure were given out to their friends as Christmas gifts!

Nelson continued his vocal studies with teachers such as Douglas Stanley[18], Dr. Lazar Samoiloff and Herbert Wall. He also studied the books of English voice coach E. Herbert-Caesari (who had taught Gigli), including *The Voice of the Mind.*[19]

In the mid 1940s Nelson and Jeanette talked again of leaving Hollywood and doing Broadway or opera. Nothing panned out for them together but Jeanette went on to make a successful opera debut and have a short-lived career.

It was not out of character for Nelson to romance his leading lady. He'd had lengthy relationships with Maybelle Marston and Helen Jepson.[20] He also admitted to a fling with Grace Moore, which was his later excuse for not wanting to make a film with her.[21] Eleanor Steber offered up the tidbit that her relationship with Nelson was the reason for their cutting a record album together.[22] Rïse Stevens denied to this author a romance during the filming **The Chocolate Soldier**, but contemporary correspondence indicates that Jeanette was very suspicious at the time. Stevens told this author in 1982: "I heard [they had a romance] and when I met Jeanette, there was a slight friction there, like 'hands off, he's mine.' I was unaware of what it was at the time, just that she was nervous about Nelson working with me."[23]

If Jeanette was so territorial about Nelson, why didn't she marry him? It certainly wasn't for his lack of trying.

Though many a female fan would think Jeanette crazy, she had her reasons. First, Nelson wanted to settle down with a wife who would keep his home and raise his children. This meant Jeanette giving up her career or at least semi-retiring, which he was insistent upon and which she refused to do. Second, Nelson suffered from periods of depression and sometimes irrational rages, which Jeanette felt ill-equipped to deal with. Third, she worried that he would not or could not curb his wandering eye.[24]

An operatic moment their public never saw: Nelson and Jeanette in the second act of* Tosca. *It was filmed for the "first"* Maytime *and then discarded.

Valid as her concerns may have been, in retrospect her decision didn't turn out for the best. Jeanette married Nelson Eddy lookalike Gene Raymond in 1937 but her marriage – though it lasted – had its own peculiarities. Nelson married Doris Kenyon's friend, Ann Franklin, on the rebound in January 1939. She was an older woman, like Maybelle Marston, and also a divorcée with a son. They eloped to Las Vegas and shortly after, left together on his yearly concert tour. Within weeks, Nelson sent Ann home and she never toured with him again. It wasn't long after that the papers were hinting that this marriage was headed for the divorce courts. All through the 1940s, newspaper blurbs leaked out about their various separations, but the sticking point seemed to be the millions of dollars Ann was demanding for Nelson's freedom. What didn't hit the papers was the threatened scandal that Ann also held over his Nelson's head, since he had resumed his relationship with Jeanette.[25]

The reason for mentioning Nelson's personal life here is that it had such a dramatic impact on him professionally.

According to Nelson's mother, Jeanette coached her son on his concert selections before he set off each year. With the exception of the 1937 and 1939 tours -- when they were not on speaking terms – her handprint was on everything he sang. Nelson even went so far as to have her sing his intended repertoire to him, so he'd have the memory of her in mind when he sang "their" songs.[26]

Maudlin as this may sound, it was their *modus operandi* for many years. In April 1944, Jeanette was hospitalized in El Paso with food poisoning. Nelson had a Carnegie Hall recital but wasn't certain he could go on. He did, and got through the first set of numbers without mishap. On the second set, he was scheduled to sing "Who is Sylvia?" This song had been noted in a

"Like an old married couple," commented one fan at seeing Nelson and Jeanette together in the mid '40s.

contemporary letter as being particularly significant for them (although it's not explained why). Nelson was so shaky singing it that the *Herald-Tribune* critic made a point of describing how "vocally uneven" the first two sets were, "characterized by sentimentality of style which reached its nadir in a treacly, dragged version of Schubert's 'Who is Sylvia?'"

At intermission, Nelson was handed a telegram that had been sent to his hotel; Jeanette's condition was much improved. Now he went out and sang in suddenly excellent voice. When it was time for encores, he stepped up to the front of the stage, held up his hand to quiet the audience and said, "If you don't mind I am going to sing a song that is very dear to me," and he sang "Indian Love Call."

Singing the Porter Song from **Martha** *for* **Phantom of the Opera.**

For better or worse, her effect on him cannot be denied

In 1942, with only one film left under his MGM contract, Nelson bought his freedom from Louie B. Mayer. He was tired of Mayer's interference in his personal life, and disgusted with the mediocre scripts of the last two MacDonald-Eddy films. During WWII, he did government work under the auspices of the OSS.[27] He was sent overseas on a singing tour in late 1943 but actually had a few tense moments in Cairo when he was forced to kill a man to protect his cover. Lawrence Tibbett, Jr., told this author that his dad did similar work, as singers who spoke German were a valuable commodity.[28]

After the war, Nelson floundered professionally. He kept up his weekly radio show while dropping out the annual concert tours. He wanted to return to films with Jeanette but for a variety of reasons, none of their projects got off the ground-- though she did sing with him on radio. Baritone Theodor Uppman knew Nelson during this period and told this author: "I know that he was very unhappy with his marriage and she [Ann] was a difficult person about things for him. He was terribly frustrated and knew that he was not going to be able to get away from his marriage that easily. And I knew Jeanette had been involved. I understood it was a very intense love affair."[29] At Nelson's lowest point, he felt he had nothing left to give the world and was ready to quit singing altogether. Luckily, this didn't happen; he resumed touring in the late '40s and in the '50s he reinvented his career in nightclubs.

His fans hated seeing Nelson in such a setting, but they turned out in droves anyway – it was better to see him that way than not at all. As with his first two careers, Nelson was a smash hit in supper clubs and worked nonstop for the last fourteen years of his life. He handled his marriage by never being around, preferring instead to return to the nomad existence of his youth. He spent forty weeks a year on the road with his new singing partner, the young, buxom blond, Gale Sherwood. Most fans were careful not to notice that he and Gale stayed in the same hotel suite.[30] Nor had he cut the umbilical cord with Jeanette; there were periods of reconciliation both personally and professionally. In 1958 Nelson and Jeanette

Nelson Eddy, concert star. In his prime years, his superstardom was on a par with today's rock stars. He had screaming women rushing at the stage, hiding under the bed in his hotel room, mentally unbalanced stalkers, bodyguards and police escorts for his concerts and while he traveled on tour. "I'm still the same guy I was before," he complained, observing the fickleness of "overnight" success.

Far left: singing onstage.

Left: Backstage afterwards, ready to sign autographs for his (mostly) female admirers.

Below: with his accompanist of many years, Theodore Paxson.

Nelson sang with many opera singers during his career, both on radio and in recordings.

Left, with Rïse Stevens, his co-star in The Chocolate Soldier.

Below left, with Nadine Connor, one of his radio series co-stars.

Below right, with Dorothy Kirsten, his co-host on "The Kraft Music Hall."

He never co-hosted a series with Jeanette because no sponsor could afford their combined salaries. But she guest-starred on his programs.

Nelson was a regular on the Edgar Bergen "Chase & Sanborn Hour" – a major factor in that show's phenomenal ratings. The show became #1 after he joined it. Even when he had his own series, he returned as a guest over the years.

His opera friends included Rosa Ponselle, Nino Martini and Gladys Swarthout. Bottom left: With Salvatore Baccaloni, who later co-starred in a '50s TV movie of The Desert Song. *Bottom right: With Amelita Galli-Curci.*

With Lotte Lehman, whose cancelled concert led to Nelson being seen and heard by the movie studios in 1933.

cut a record album together, "Favorites in Hi-Fi," that quickly went gold.

Nelson had written at least two movie treatments for himself and Jeanette but was unsuccessful in getting the projects off the ground. It would, however, be accurate to call him a true Renaissance man. Not only did he write screenplays, treatments, poetry and elegantly spiritual prose, but he scripted the comedy for his nightclub act. He was also a talented sculptor and artist, though he felt his paintings suffered from lack of proper training. This high-school dropout also wrote and re-wrote translations to arias and songs, composed a few numbers himself and wrote romantic, impassioned lyrics. A whole study could be done of his musical writings; suffice to say that the theme usually running through these works was a sexually charged love for a woman who no longer with him. His obsession with this subject doesn't quite fit the picture of a supposedly happily married man.[31]

After Jeanette's early death from a heart condition in 1965, Nelson aged overnight. That he blamed himself for her lonely last years was evident; his once-handsome face was etched with sadness. Reporters who interviewed him described him as "bitter," "lonely," "sad," and "a broken man, beaten by life."[32] Even though

A later shot of Nelson and Jeanette goofing around at a party honoring Lauritz Melchior (right).

he was drinking, his voice remained virtually untampered by time. At worst, what one hears in a recording of his live nightclub act is apathethic sloppiness and the sense that he's doing this on automatic.[33] That he could continue singing his movie hits such as "Indian Love Call" and "Will Your Remember" night after night, year after year -- when one thinks of the personal connotations these songs had for him – was a testament to his sheer will and professionalism. But occasionally at these performances he would push the microphone away and sing an aria or one of his standard concert numbers, just to show that his magnificent voice was still intact and could fill the rafters.

In the end, Nelson Eddy had no life except his music. He told reporters he would sing until he dropped, and he did just that. The night of March 5, 1967, he suffered a massive stroke onstage in Miami and died early the next morning. For a man who had once been the epitome of boundless energy and health, and whose father outlived him (nearly making it to 93), Nelson's death at 65 was painfully premature. He had outlived Jeanette MacDonald by only two years.

Certainly Nelson inspired the generation of singers that followed him. Mario Lanza, for example, named Nelson as his inspiration and auditioned for him when he was just starting out. Thankfully, through the legacy of Nelson's recordings, radio shows and films, his voice will continue to inspire.

Reviews

Philadelphia Evening Ledger, 1922: "They had the first dress rehearsal of **The Marriage Tax** last week, and it's really going to be dandy. The costumes are as pretty as can be, and the dancing is fine, too. Nelson Eddy is to sing in it, and if you have ever heard Nelson Eddy sing you will want to go for that alone, for that young man has a most gorgeous voice, let me tell you. I have only heard him once, but me I want to hear him again and often."

January 22, 1922. *Public Ledger,* by Hester Rawley: "The staid old Academy was filled to capacity Tuesday night, when the much-talked-of **Marriage Tax** was given. It seemed as if all the members of the younger set had some sort of a part or other, even if it was merely to walk across the stage, and all the fond relatives were there to applaud.... Jane Maule McIver, who had the leading role, was admirable, but the outstanding character of the entire play was the young man who played opposite her and who appeared on the program merely as 'The King of Greece.' So many persons have asked me who he is that I hasten to tell them his name is Nelson Eddy, and quite agree with them that he has great talent as an actor and a voice that thrilled because of its perfect control, clear resonant tone and exceptional quality." [Note: Tuesday night was January 17, 1922.]

March 10, 1922, *Public Ledger:* Opening performance of **This and That,** vaudeville show. "I went up to the Plays and Players last night to see the opening performance of **This and That,** a show which is being given the rest of the week and three days next week with Mrs. Hiram B. Eliason as manager. The show was given by practically the same people who gave **Why Not?** for two years, but was vaudeville and not a musical comedy as formerly. There were a great many good acts, including dancing, impersonations, fencing, songs and a clever monologue by Miss Jacquelyn Green, who also wrote the lyrics. The show opened with a charming 'sampler' song and dance by Miss Ethel France and the good-looking Nelson Eddy..."

Undated clipping: "Rehearsals have begun for this year's production of **Why Not?**, a sequel to that clever musical travesty that was written and produced by a number of society folks last year. At first it was rumored the title would be 'What Not by the Why Nots?' but I am told the season's production will simply be called 'Why Not 1922?' The performance will be given for a week with two matinees at the Little Theatre, beginning April 24. Most all the clever boys and girls who took part in last year's affair will be stars again this year. A newcomer will be Nelson Eddy, who was the hit in Mrs. Dixon's **Marriage Tax,** given a couple of months ago at the Academy. It will be remembered he took the part of the king in this production and was among those most warmly received by the audience. The proceeds, as last year, will go the University Settlement house." NOTE: Nelson wrote a note under this clipping, "Did not do this"

No date, *Philadelphia Record:* "A musicale will be given at the Universalist Church of the Restoration on Wednesday. Nelson Eddy will be the barytone."

The Record: "One of the features of the patriotic meeting to be held at the Academy of Music Sunday afternoon, April 9, at 3:00 by the Belleau Wood Memorial Association, will be the singing of 'In Flanders Field' by Nelson Eddy. Another feature will be a short concert by the Orpheus Club. Tickets are free..."

May 25, 1922, Nelson sang in **Iolanthe**. *North American,* May 26, 1922: "A large audience last night applauded the Savoy Company's performance of **Iolanthe** at the Broad Street Theater. The performance will be repeated this evening and again tomorrow night, the opera being given for the benefit of the Alfred Reginald Allen Memorial Fund in the Department of Fine Arts at the University of Pennsylvania." This is the twenty-second production by this troupe of Gilbert and Sullivan operas, and it is easily the best effort... Nelson Eddy, who played Strephon, and Charles Francis Ward, the Lord Chancellor, were easily the stars of the cast. The performance by these two could not be improved; they do better than many a professional in these parts."

May 26, 1922, *Philadelphia Inquirer:* "The production as a whole would have done credit to any company. In

Evening Phila. Public Ledger

THEY had the first dress rehearsal of "The Marriage Tax" last week, and it's really going to be dandy. The costumes are as pretty as can be, and the dancing is fine, too. Nelson Eddy is to sing in it, and if you have ever heard Nelson Eddy sing you will want to go for that alone, for that young man has a most gorgeous voice, let me tell you. I have only heard him once, but me I want to hear him again and often. Jack Whiting, of "Why Not" fame, is teaching the dancing, and altogether it's going to be great.

Evening Public Ledger

OF COURSE, every one is looking forward to the "Marriage Tax" tonight, which is to be given in the Academy of Music. Have you heard that the Richards girls are to be the little boy twins of the show. A wee bird saw them at the rehearsal, and she told me she never had seen anything cuter than their costumes.

There's a pretty sub-deb chorus that we will all be interested in, and some charming Quaker maids. And did you know that Deborah Seal is going to lead a party of Cook's tourists through the show. I'll wager that part of the performance will be a riot, if nothing else. Uytendale Caner is in it, you know, and Nelson Eddy, and Jane Maule and nearly all our leading lights in Amateurdom. That's a good word, don't you think? I'm rather taken with it myself.

Phila. Public Ledger, Jan. 22, 1922.

By Hester F. Rawley

THE staid old Academy was filled to capacity Tuesday night, when the much-talked-of "Marriage Tax" was given. It seemed as if all the members of the younger set had some sort of a part or other, even if it was merely to walk across the stage, and all the fond relatives were there to applaud. The house was so crowded that it was necessary to put chairs down in the orchestra pit, all of which proves a goodly sum was taken in to help swell the coffers of the Seamen's Church Institute, in whose benefit the affair was given. If, however, one anticipated seeing a play such as last year's "Why Not?" they were sadly mistaken. The "Marriage Tax," while entertaining, lacked the go and pep of last year's performance. Jack Whiting, who was one of the hits in "Why Not?" did not have an opportunity this year to show his decided talent, and the few songs which were allotted to him were not up to the mark.

Jane Maule McIver, who had the leading role, was adorable, but the outstanding character of the entire play was the young man who played opposite her and who appeared on the program merely as "The King of Greece." So many persons have asked me who he is that I hasten to tell them his name is Nelson Eddy, and quite agree with them that he has great talent as an actor and a voice that thrilled because of its perfect control, clear, resonant tone and exceptional quality.

The costumes were lovely and in many cases strikingly original. Particularly smart were the young girls who danced in the chorus of "Girls From Quakertown." Peggy Thayer was the leader of the chorus, and it is said from her appearances in other amateur affairs she has attracted the attention of one of the country's best-known producers, who has offered to put Peggy on the legitimate stage. Her sister Polly, who plays the violin so well, has received a like offer, but we will all hope they remain with us—just the Thayer girls.

costumes and scenery it was adequate. The chorus did some admirable singing, though once or twice the men members of it failed in the attack. The women were better throughout than the men, though this is not to say that both did not deserve praise. No doubt there will be an improvement in the remaining performances. **Iolanthe** is by no means an easy opera. But the Savoy Company has mastered its difficulties surprisingly.... No individual in the cast did better work than Mr. Nelson Eddy as Strephon. He has an excellent voice, which he uses with skill. and his stage presence is attractive." *Evening Bulletin:* "Of the male members of the cast. a notable success may be credited to Nelson Eddy, who, as Strephon, the hapless shepherd--half fairy, half mortal--has none of the crudeness or uncertainty of the amateur, either as actor or singer. Easy, graceful and showing an excellent understanding of all that he has to do, Mr. Eddy fills his part without effort, and not in a long time has there been revealed a baritone voice of greater beauty, of fresh, sympathetic quality, excellent volume and range, and evidently of great possibilities." *The Ledger:* "The part of Strephon... was well played by Nelson Eddy."

May 26, 1922, *Evening Ledger:* "Do you remember Nelson Eddy, who took the part of the King in **The Marriage Tax** at the Academy in the early winter? Well, Nelson, I hear, will take an important part in **Iolanthe,** the Gilbert and Sullivan opera which will be given on Thursday, Friday and Saturday at the Broad Street Theatre, and from all I am told about this year's production it will be far superior to those of previous years, for more technique has been introduced than ever before. Mr. Eddy will enact the role of Strephon, son of Iolanthe, and will, I wager, be the hit of the show, as he was in **The Marriage Tax**."

[Note: A clipping from May 1923 states that Nelson also sang the romantic lead (a tenor role) in **The Pirates of Penzance** with the Savoy Company in 1922, although there are no newspaper reviews of it in Nelson's scrapbook. The Savoy Company was for about 25 years Philadelphia's leading amateur organization for light opera.]

June 4, 1922, by Hester F. Rawley: "The opera in which I told you Nelson Eddy was to take the leading part... Well, Mr. Eddy lived up to all expectations and was without doubt the "hit" of the show. I went the first night which of course is always the most trying, but, as in **The Marriage Tax**, Mr. Eddy was a composed and finished character in the play. All about me every one was talking about this young singer, his wonderful voice and acting so that the Savoy Company should indeed be proud to have him as one of their members." **Iolanthe** review, *Evening Ledger:* "Nelson Eddy made a hit as the handsome hero."

May 3-5, 1923: Nelson sang in **The Pirates of Penzance** for the Savoy Company, at the Broad Street Theater. *Public Ledger,* May 6, 1923: "The Savoy Company came across with a stunning performance of **The Pirates of Penzance** last night. And when I saw Sara Baily I did not wonder that Cecil De Mille had wanted her in a picture. She is beautiful.... You never would have recognized Nelson Eddy all done up with whiskers and a uniform, but when he sang you knew him all right and his voice was glorious." Unlabeled clipping: "The chorus numbers 60. Many were in last year's production. Mrs. Millington and Nelson Eddy have turned tables. Last year she was his mother in a production. This year she is his daughter." *Public Register:* "Last year he had the romantic lead [in **The Pirates of Penzance**], this year, the Major General."

May 11, 1923, more performances of **The Pirates of Penzance**: *Evening Bulletin:* "While it is difficult to pick out from the generally able cast any one for particular praise, perhaps that honor should go to Nelson Eddy, for his work in the exacting part of the Major General. Not only did Mr. Eddy sing well, but his enunciation was a model for many professionals." *Philadelphia Inquirer:* "Nelson Eddy was seen as the Major General, and he showed to fine advantage in this his first definite character role." *Philadelphia Record:* "Nelson Eddy as the major general was quite the best bit of humor in the whole thing." *Public Ledger:* "The men were equally capable, outstanding performances being contributed by Nelson Eddy, who is generally seen in juvenile roles, but who last night essayed the hard part of the Major General." *North American:* "Perhaps the palm for all-round acting, singing and, being a Gilbert and Sullivan opera, elocutionary ability should go to Nelson Eddy..."

Public Ledger: "The Philadelphia Operatic Society is preparing to give an elaborate performance of **Aida** on

"Aida" by Operatic Society

The Philadelphia Operatic Society is preparing to give an elaborate performance of "Aida" on Thursday evening, May 17, at the Academy of Music. There will be a ballet of forty especially trained by Ethel Quirk Phillips. Margaret Cook is the prima ballerina. There will be a special dance by Miss Phillips, and Odetta Kellarmann, niece of the famous Annette Kellermann, will appear as one of the Moorish slaves. This will be the sixty-first production by the society and it is to be the last under the present title of the organization, which, in the autumn, is to become the Philadelphia Civic Opera Company.

The important role of Ameris will be taken by Clair Eugenia Smith, a distinguished concert singer, formerly of this city. Mme. Smith made her professional opera debut three years ago with the Philadelphia Opera Company as Laura in "La Gioconda." The Aida, Marie Wilkins, is a young soprano who resides at Wallingford and who is under the tutelage of Henri Scott. The role of Radames will be sung by the well-known tenor, George Rothermel, who for two years was soloist at the famous Grace Church of New York. Eleanor Emeline Starkey, Nelson Eddy as Amonasro, Dr. Andrew Knox as Ramfis, J. Burnet Holland as the King and Howard Haug complete the cast.

Nelson Eddy—ACADEMY

Public Ledger

The Philadelphia Operatic Society is preparing to give an elaborate performance of "Aida" on Thursday evening, May 17, at the Academy of Music. For instance, there will be a ballet of 40, especially trained by Ethel Quirk Phillips. Margaret Cook is the prima ballerina, although there will be a special dance by Miss Phillips and Odette Kellermann, niece of the famous Annette Kellermann, will appear as one of the Moorish slaves. This will be the sixty-first production by the society, and it is to be the last under the present title of the organization, which in the autumn is to become the Philadelphia Civic Opera Company.

The announcement is made that for the important role of Amneris there has been enrolled Clair Eugenia Smith, a distinguished concert singer, formerly of this city, but now of New York. Mme. Smith made her professional opera debut three years ago with the Philadelphia Opera Company as Laura in "La Gioconda." Since that time she has been studying in Europe, and it is her intention, following a concert in New York with a symphony orchestra under direction of Wassili Leps, to make a concert tour of Europe. She is intending later to establish her own opera house. She, of course, is a volunteer singer, as are all the members of the Philadelphia Operatic Society cast and chorus.

The Aida, Marie Wilkins, is a young soprano who resides at Wallingford and who is under the tutelage of Henri Scott. The role of Radames will be sung by the well-known tenor, George Rothermel, who for two years was soloist at the famous Grace Church of New York, to which city he went every week-end.

Eleanor Emeline Starkey, Nelson Eddy as Amonasro, Dr. Andrew Knox as Ramfis, J. Burnet Holland as the King and Howard Haug are in the cast. The chorus is large and has been well trained by Karl Schroeder on stage work, and by Wassili Leps, general director of the society, in the score. The opera is one of the outstanding events of Music Week, and the presentation is under auspices of the Music League as sponsor for presentations in that period.

Wassili Leps, general director of the Philadelphia Operatic Society, having just returned from an European tour, has resumed conduct of rehearsals of the Philadelphia Operatic Society for the performance to be given during the Music Week in May. "Aida" will be sung, under auspices of the Music League, and the performance will be at the Academy of Music on Thursday evening, May 17. The cast is now complete, and is announced as follows: Aida, Marie Wilkins; Amneris, Marie Stone Langston; Priestess, Eleanor Emeline Starkey; Radames, George Rothermel; Amonasro, Nelson Eddy; Ramfis, Dr. Andrew Knox; King, A. H. DeBuest; Messenger, Howard Haug.

Thursday evening, May 17, at the Academy of Music. There will be a ballet of forty especially trained by Ethel Quirk Phillips. Margaret Cook is the prima ballerina. There will be a special dance by Miss Phillips, and Odetta Kellermann, niece of the famous Annette Kellermann, will appear as one of the Moorish slaves. This will be the sixty-first production by the society and it is to be the last under the present title of the organization, which, in the autumn, is to become the Philadelphia Civic Opera Company." The Amneris is Clair Eugenia Smith, the **Aida** is Marie Wilkins, the Radames is George Rothermel."

May 1923, undated, *Philadelphia Inquirer:* "Nelson Eddy is to be the Amonasro. He is a young baritone who has recently been heard in a number of concerts and he has appeared with the Savoy Company, which also is to have him this spring in the cast of **The Pirates of Penzance."**

May 18, 1923, *Philadelphia Record* **(Aida** was given by the Philadelphia Operatic Society): "The Philadelphia Operatic Society, singing its final performance under that famous name, gave a production of Verdi's **Aida** in the Academy of Music last night that was a brilliant climax to a career of 17 seasons of valuable propaganda for opera in English and also a culminating exhibition of just what Philadelphia talent has been able to accomplish... Nelson Eddy, as Amonasro, had an electrifying effect on the audience. A young singer, scarcely 20 years of age, with that indefinable gift so seldom seen of arresting the auditor's interest and holding it continuously, Mr. Eddy was a star from the moment he appeared on the stage. His enunciation alone was a distinguishing mark, every syllable being easily understood, while his acting was spontaneous and natural. Vocally he was also pleasing, although his voice has by no means attained maturity." *Evening Bulletin:* "One of the real successes was that of Nelson Eddy, an excellent young baritone, who, in addition to a voice of beautiful quality, sings with rare ease and intelligence and has the natural aptitude for operatic work that bespeaks for him a notable stage career. His Amonasro, while naturally lacking matured poise and dramatic power, had fervor and expressiveness, and vocally was so good as to be full of rich promise." *Evening Public Ledger:* "Of the male roles, Nelson Eddy was perhaps the best as Amonasro, his diction being perfect throughout, every word being easily understood. His voice was excellent and his action very good." *Philadelphia Inquirer:* "The Amonasro of Nelson Eddy was a revelation in the way of clean-cut, sharply chiseled enunciation." *Public Ledger:* "Wilson (sic) Eddy made the most of his chances as Amonasro, and suited action to lyric diction in a way that gave him front-rank rating in the cast. No better work was done during the evening than his delivery of his first aria."

Nelson sang at a rally for W. Freeland Kendrick running for Mayor, Sept 14, 1923: "Nelson Eddy's encore was something about a rainbow trail, and the baritone went over big when he changed it on the finale to 'The Kendrick Trail.' The audience wanted some more from Eddy, but Eddy and Judge Patterson pulled Kendrick from the stage. Three thousand people were at the show.

Nelson sang the role of an American newspaper correspondent at Mrs. Dixon's **Which Turn?** May 29, 1924, *Public Ledger:* "Love and laughter combined to make an interesting little melodrama at the Plays and Players club. One playlet presented **Which Turn?** comes from the pen of Mrs. George Dallas Dixon... **Which Turn?** is costumed in the period of 1898. The scene is laid on a sugar plantation. There is a Cuban insurrect, admirably portrayed by Harvey T. Sayen, and an American newspaper correspondent, the role taken by Nelson Eddy."

First mention of Nelson on radio, 1924. He sang at 9:25, on WOO recital, with Josephine McCulloh, soprano, Nelson Eddy, baritone, Harriette G. Ridley, accompanist.

Philadelphia Ledger quotes Mrs. Henry M. Tracy, president of the Philadelphia Civic Opera Company: "We're proud of the Philadelphia singers we've engaged—among them Nelson Eddy, baritone..."

[Note: "The Met" mentioned in the following review and future reviews refers to Hammerstein's Metropolitan Opera House on Broad Street in Philadelphia, not the Metropolitan Opera of New York City, unless otherwise noted.]

THE PHILADELPHIA RECORD, SATURDAY, MAY 12, 1923

AL LEADERS HOPE TO AR

PRINCIPALS IN OPERATIC SOCIETY'S "AIDA"

BURNETT HOLLAND, "THE KING"

MARIE WILKINS, "AIDA"

NELSON EDDY, "AMONASRO"

ELEANOR EMELINE STARKEY, "HIGH PRIESTESS"

CLAIR EUGENIA SMITH, "AMNERIS"

December 11, 1924: Nelson sang in **I Pagliacci** in duo bill with **Cavalleria Rusticana**. *Public Ledger,* December 12, 1924: "The Civic Opera Company of Philadelphia gave the most brilliant and successful as well as the finest performance of its short but meteoric existence, when the double bill, **Cavalleria Rusticana** and **I Pagliacci** was presented last night to an audience that filled the Metropolitan Opera House. The performance of both operas met the highest professional standards in every way, and the immense audience expressed its delight with both works... Nelson Eddy, as Tonio, fairly swept the audience off its feet with his rendition of the Prologue, and from that moment the high standard of performance never dropped. Mr. Eddy's characterization of the difficult role of Tonio was so excellent throughout that it looks as though the Civic Opera Company might already have justified its existence by the discovery of a real operatic talent... Too much credit cannot be given to Alexander Smallens for the marvels which he has achieved with chorus, local singers and professional principals in the splendid rendition of these two operas. His direction was authoritative, the tempi correct in every detail and he has the secret of obtaining actual dynamics from a nonprofessional chorus--which is almost the last word in operatic training and directing." *Philadelphia Evening Bulletin:* "Mr. Eddy did not wear the usual clown make-up nor attempt to give the character much in the way of grotesque manner or comic antics, but his acting nevertheless had a touch of originality and cleverness. His voice is of rare beauty in the mellow richness of its quality, particularly in the middle and lower tones, and while he was not wholly equal to the demands of the Prologue at its climax, he sang this favorite number in a sympathetic and expressive manner, winning enthusiastic applause." *The New York Times:* "Nelson Eddy, as Tonio, gave a remarkably beautiful rendition of the prologue. Mr. Eddy's performance of the difficult role throughout was so excellent that it looks as though the Civic Opera Company had already justified its existence by the discovery of a real operatic talent as well as a remarkable voice." *Musical America:* "Nelson Eddy electrified his audience with the intensity of his Tonio."

December 26, 1924: Nelson on WOO, a Philadelphia radio station.

January 29, 1925: Nelson sang at the Met, at a benefit of the Columbus Italian Hospital. The program included **I Pagliacci,** preceded by a concert. *Public Ledger:* "Nelson Eddy made the usually rather inconspicuous role of Silvio stand out, singing the part excellently... Alexander Smallens gave a notably fine reading of the score." [Note: Smallens was Nelson's voice coach at that time.]

Feb 11, 1925: Nelson sang in **Aida** at the Met, produced by the Philadelphia Civic Opera Co. This production was noted as the most successful performance, on both sides of the footlights, in the history of the organization. *Evening Bulletin,* February 12, 1925: "A most satisfying performance of **Aida,** scenically, musically and dramatically, was given at the Metropolitan last night by the Philadelphia Civic Opera Company before an enthusiastic audience that packed the great auditorium to the doors... The principal roles were all in the hands of singers capable of doing them justice and the result was an evening wherein it would be difficult to pick single outstanding performances... Nelson Eddy's singing of the part of Amonasro, the Ethiopian king, proved to be one of the revelations of the evening. He displayed unsuspected power and dramatic fire in a voice of beautiful texture, which has been in the past considered best in the lyric mood. The charm was there, but there was strength and emotional color as well. Mr. Eddy posses to an unusual degree the faculty of making a character come to life. His Amonasro was a turbulent, wild-eyed savage hating his enemies vigorously and stopping at nothing to win his ends. Vocally he displayed clear diction, uniformly fine tone production and a keen sense of the shifting moods of the music." *Musical Digest:* "Nelson Eddy's voice is admirably suited to the part and he acted the role to perfection." *The American:* "Nelson Eddy sang and acted the part of Amonasro with fire and finish, so that the city can claim, not merely acknowledge him, as its own." *Philadelphia Ledger:* "Nelson Eddy carried off the honors in the difficult and elaborate role of Amonasro. His voice is admirably suited to the part and he acted the role to perfection."

February 13, 1925: Nelson began radio broadcasts on WIP.

Nelson sang at the Gimbel's Department Store auditorium on a Saturday afternoon, in March or April 1925.

May 6, 1925: The Matinee Musical Club had its spring concert in the Elks' new auditorium. The second act from **Martha** was performed. *Evening Bulletin:* "Nelson Eddy, as Plunkett, sang and acted in his usual finished and artistic manner." *Philadelphia Ledge:* "The Matinee Musical Club closed a brilliant season last night with an exceptionally interesting entertainment given in the Elks' Auditorium before an audience which completely filled to large hall... .The second act of **Martha** was presented last evening with the assistance of the club orchestra and with scenery and costumes, the solo parts being sung by Hilda Reiter as Martha, Ruth Montague as Nancy, Charles Cline as Lionel and Nelson Eddy as Plunkett. It was admirably sung and acted throughout under the skillful direction of Mr. Smallens."

June 3, 1925: The Philadelphia Music League produced the second act of **Aida.** Nelson sang Amonasro for an audience of 35,000 people. At the end of concert, John Philip Sousa mounted the stage and led a number of bands win "The Stars and Stripes Forever." *Evening Bulletin:* " The excerpt from the Verdi opera was on an extensive and elaborate scale, and while there is little solo work in this scene, such as there is was admirably done by the all-Philadelphia cast, including Bianca Saroya, prima donna of the San Carlo Opera Company (formerly Miss Alma Weisshaar) as Aida; Marie Stone Langston, as Amneris; Royal P. MacLellan, as Radames, Nelson Eddy, as Amonasro… the elaborate ballet in this scene being arranged and directed by Caroline Littlefield."

August 1925: Nelson sang at Lemon Hill with the Fairmont Park Symphony Orchestra. He performed "Evening Star," "En Tu" from **The Masked Ball.** Alexander Smallens conducted. *Public Ledger:* "Nelson Eddy, baritone of this city, was the first soloist of the season at the Lemon Hill concerts last evening... .The usual crowd was in attendance, filling the seats and overflowing into the woods behind the auditorium. Nelson Eddy was in splendid voice and sang two operatic selections, the 'Evening Star,' from **Tannhäuser,** in the first half, which was obliged to repeat, and 'En Tu,' from Verdi's **The Masked Ball in** the second half."

October 3, 1925: Nelson sang 4 numbers on WIP for the Gimbal Brothers' show.

November 5, 1925: The Philadelphia Civic Opera season opened with **Aida**, at the Met. The stars were Bianca Saroya, Thomas Muir, and Nelson. *Public Ledger,* November 6, 1925: "The Civic Opera Company of Philadelphia opened its third season at the Metropolitan Opera House last evening with a generally excellent performance of **Aida.** The house was filled almost to the doors and the enthusiasm of the immense audience increased as the opera progressed, reaching its first climax at the close of the second act, the scene before the gates of Thebes. This was beautifully staged, an exceptionally large and well-trained ballet directed by Caroline Littlefield adding much to the vivid picture... Nelson Eddy was an excellent Amonasro, displaying his beautiful voice and faultless intonation in both acts in which he appeared and doing the dramatic parts well." *Evening Bulletin:* "Mr. Eddy shows considerable talent for stage work and his acting of Amonasro is intelligent and spirited, keeping him well in the picture." *Philadelphia Inquirer:* "Nelson Eddy, previously seen as Amonasro, was even better in the part last night. Although still quite youthful, he exhibits a baritone voice of breadth and beauty, and acts with authority."

November 17, 1925: A clipping notes that the Matinee Musical Club concert featured **The Lady of Shalott**, by Charles Bennet, with Nelson Eddy singing. *Evening Bulletin:* "With a delightful and well-balanced program, and an attendance that entirely filled the ballroom of the Bellevue-Stratford, the Matinee Musical Club yesterday afternoon observed Federation Day, featuring The **Lady of the Shalott**, a cantata by Charles Bennett... With the usual large and well trained chorus, assisted by Lodo Goforth, soprano, and Nelson Eddy, baritone, the cantata fulfilled all expectations."

October 3, 1925: WJP featured an operatic program from The Philadelphia Civic Opera. Seven numbers were sung in the hour show. Nelson sang a **La Boheme** duet with Royal P. MacLelland, tenor, and a solo, "Evening Star."

[Note: Nelson also sang frequently at Overbrook Presbyterian Church in their choir of Negro Spirituals.]

December 31, 1925: Nelson sang in **Cavalleria Rusticana** and **I Pagliacci** at the Met. *Evening Bulletin:* "The Philadelphia Civic Opera Company ended the old year auspiciously with its fourth performance of the season, at the Metropolitan Opera House last evening. The audience was little short of "capacity" and was in a receptive mood and generous in its applause. There was considerable worth applauding, too, in both operas.... Mr. Eddy has won success in several important roles with the Civic Company, and always there is much to admire in his work. If his Alfio was somewhat lacking in robustness and authority, and his rich, sympathetic baritone did not seem heavy enough for some of the music, he nevertheless gave an intelligent and competent portrayal." Nelson then sang Silvio. "Mr. Eddy again appeared, having the role of Silvio, the lover of Nedda. . . .Here he was at his best, acting well and disclosing the rare beauty of his luscious baritone in the scene with Nedda." *Public Ledger:* "**Cavalleria** came first, as it always does, and the performance moved with a spirit and snap not often met with in professional companies... Elizabeth Bonner and Nelson Eddy took the roles of Lola and Alfio, respectively, and both met all the vocal requirements, although neither was especially impressive dramatically.... The great performance of the evening was **I Pagliacci,** and few companies have ever given in Philadelphia a presentation of this opera, which equaled that of the Civic Opera last evening. This was chiefly due to the superb interpretations of the role of Tonio by Ivan Ivantzoff and that of Nedda by Irene Williams."

January 14, 1926: Nelson sang in two one-act operas, **Gianni Schicchi** and the role of Bustamente in **La Navarraise.** *Evening Bulletin,* January 15, 1926: "What may be called a severe test of the resources of the Philadelphia Civic Opera Co., in the performance of two operatic works of strongly contrasting character, was very successfully met, at the Metropolitan Opera House last evening, in the presentation of a double bill including **La Navarraise**, by Massenet, and **Gianni Schicchi**, by Puccini. The first is tremendous tragedy, the second sprightly comedy, and it is greatly to the credit of Alexander Smallens, the splendidly efficient musical director of the organization, and Alexander Puglia, the skilful stage director, as well as the performers, that both works were given in a manner that provided first a succession of thrills and then a veritable feast of laughter... **La Navarraise.** . .is not especially notable musically....In last night's performance the Civic Opera Co. had an excellent cast.. Julia Claussen (as Anita), Mischa Leon (Araquil) Henri Scott (as General Garrido), and admirable also were Reinhold Schmidt, as Remigio, Bernard Poland, as Ramon, and Nelson Eddy, as Bustamente... Gianni Schicchi... was filled entirely by Philadelphia singers. Nelson Eddy was capital as Schicchi, catching the buoyant spirit of the part with a clever touch of buffo comedy, which, in the making of the will, fairly roused the audience to shouts of laughter. His sympathetic baritone also suits the part and he sang very beautifully the 'Farewell, Dear Florence' aria, which is one of the few outstanding numbers." *Daily News:* "Nelson Eddy in the title part showed the audience that he is not only a capable singer, but a splendid actor." *Public Ledger:* "Nelson Eddy, in the title role, revealed (as he did as Bustamente in **La Navarraise)** a high order of ability for comedy dramatic work, being always very funny, but never overdoing the role--a mistake which it would have been very easy to make. His enunciation was very clear, especially in the scene in which the new will is made. Mr. Smallens had apparently laid great stress upon clearness of enunciation, and except when he allowed the large orchestra to overpower the voices, virtually every word could be heard." *Philadelphia Inquirer:* "Nelson Eddy, in the part of Gianni, undoubtedly gave the best performance of his career, he not only meeting every requirement of the vocal, but also grasped the full humor of the part."

February 5, 1926: Nelson sang at the first of three concerts at the Crystal Ballroom of the Benjamin Franklin Hotel, at an event hosted by the Women's Symphony Orchestra. *Public Ledger:* "One of the most interesting experiments in our musical life, the founding and developing of an orchestra, manned, so to speak, entirely by women and known as the Women's Symphony Orchestra of Philadelphia, has certainly proved a valuable asset to music in this city, as the orchestra demonstrated at a concert in the ballroom of the Ben Franklin Hotel last night... .The soloist was Nelson Eddy, baritone, whose fine voice showed to excellent advantages in an aria ['Cantabile de Rysoor'] from Paladilhe's **Patrie** and later in a group of songs with piano accompaniment--'Over the Steppe,' by Gretchaninoff, 'When the King Went Forth to War,' by Koeneman and Leoni's 'Tally-ho.' Mr. Eddy was obliged to respond with encore numbers after each appearance." *The Record:* "The soloist was Nelson Eddy, baritone, who has a remarkably good voice, which apparently has by no means reached its fullest maturity. His singing is enjoyable and was enthusiastically received by the audience. The number of musicians present last night would indicate great interest in this growing organization, as well as in the singing of Eddy, who is one of the favorite singers of the Civic Opera Company." *Philadelphia Inquirer:* "Mr. Eddy's beautiful voice was in superb condition, and he showed himself to be a recitalist of importance, in addition to his well-known excellent operatic work." *Evening Bulletin:* "Nelson Eddy, baritone soloist, whose recent appearances both in opera and concert have gained for him a well-deserved admiration for a voice that seems continually to improve.... His tones were exceptionally clear and flexible last night."

February 17, 1926: *Philadelphia Ledger* noted that Nelson sang yesterday at the 22nd charter luncheon of the

Philomusician Club in the Ritz-Carlton Hotel. Nearly 400 women were present. Nelson sang "Evening Star", the Porter Song from **Martha,** and other operatic numbers. The same paper on the same date noted that Nelson had sung at another lunch of the Matinee Musical Club at the Bellevue. "A very effective number, which also had to be repeated, was the painting representing the first singing of the Marseillaise. It was sung by Nelson Eddy...." *The Record:* "An exceptionally attractive program..." *Philadelphia Ledger:* "The Matinee Musical Club yesterday gave one of the most interesting and beautifully staged entertainments of the season at its bi-weekly meeting at the Bellevue. One of the largest audiences of the season was present. The program was partly musical, partly ballet, and partly tableaux, the latter being a series of famous paintings represented by living figures, strikingly arranged by Frank B.A. Linton. The ballet was under the direction of Caroline Littlefield... Very effective...."

February 18, 1926: Nelson sang Abimélech in **Samson and Delilah** at the Met. *Evening Bulletin,* February 19, 1926: "That talented and growing young artist, Nelson Eddy, added to his list of successes with the Civic Company, as Abimélech, acting intelligently and making such good use of his fresh, sympathetic baritone that the Satraps' first-act demise at the hands of the strong man was the more to be deplored." *Philadelphia Inquirer:* "Another triumph was added to its already long list by the Philadelphia Civic Opera Co. The statuesque Julia Claussen was the Delilah... Paul Althouse, a too much neglected tenor, was the Samson... Nelson Eddy as Abimelech added another portrait of distinction to his already large collection." *The Record:* "Nelson Eddy did a splendid short score as the Satrap."

March 25, 1926, Nelson sang at the Met in **Tannhäuser**. *Evening Bulletin,* March 26, 1926: "The 1925-26 season of the Civic Opera Company came to an end in the Metropolitan Opera House last night, with a highly creditable performance of **Tannhäuser**... An audience that filled the big theatre to capacity applauded with enthusiastic vigor... The biggest individual hit of the evening, judging by the audience's applause, was scored by Nelson Eddy, in his delivery of Wolfram's love song in the second act. Mr. Eddy's baritone was of beautiful lyric quality, his enunciation was clear, his inflection sure and he displayed unusual command of tone color. His efforts stirred his hearers to continued hand-clapping which subsided only after he had 'stepped out of character' in order to bow two or three times. Horrified Wagnerites trembled for fear that there might be an attempt to force an encore in violation of all tradition." *Ledger:* "Civic Opera Gives Fine **Tannhäuser: "**Nelson Eddy as Wolfram was probably the star of the cast. He was in magnificent voice and possessed a tone quality of the greatest beauty, besides delineating the role very finely in its pathos and nobility. After the song in the Wartburg scene, the audience nearly stopped the opera with its applause. The 'Song to the Evening Star,' in the third act, was another unusually fine bit of singing. His enunciation (the opera was sung in English) was exceedingly clear." *The Record:* "How rapidly Nelson Eddy is developing into a real personality on the stage! He not only sings well but has a grace and distinction, a gift for characterization unique in an amateur. His impersonation of Wolfram was a fine piece of work to which his distinct enunciation gave additional charm." *Philadelphia Inquirer:* "To Alexander Smallens must be given the greatest praise for the finest achievement attained by the Philadelphia Civic Opera Company in its three years of history, that is the performance of Richard Wagner's immortal music drama, **Tannhäuser,** at the Metropolitan Opera House last evening. It was the last of the season's scheduled performances and was the crowning occasion of a year that has been replete with results never before attained by such an organization. Conductor Smallens never arose, at least in this city, to such heights as he did in his guidance of the orchestra, principals and chorus last evening.... An excellent cast had been assembled for this final performance of the season... Nelson Eddy, who seems to grow at every appearance with this company, was the Wolfram, and his rich baritone was heard to advantage throughout the opera, he having done nothing better than the singing of the Song to the Evening Star." [Note: the *Philadelphia Gazette Democrat* from March 28 had a review in German.]

April 5, 1926, *Public Ledger:* "A large audience assembled at the Penn Athletic Club last evening to hear the Easter Sunday concert. Nelson Eddy was soloist... Mr. Eddy was in good voice and scored a great success. Some of his principal numbers were 'Hosanna,' 'As There the Tulip,' from Lehmann's **A Persian Garden**, 'I

THE EVENING BULLETIN—PHILADELPHIA, SATURDA

THE EVENING BULLETIN—PHILADE]

AN EVENING OF SONG

Operatic Selections and Other Numbers on Interesting Program

A program of unusual diversity and considerable interest was presented by a number of young women singers, under the direction of Mrs. Phillips Jenkins, before an audience which filled the ballroom of the Penn Athletic Club, last evening.

These talented singers had the good fortune to have the support of William Sylvano Thunder at the piano, and to his brilliant and sympathetic playing is due a large share of the credit for a highly successful concert. Florence Haenle, violinist; Blanche Hubbard, harpist, and Effie Irene Hubbard, violoncellist, also gave able assistance in several numbers.

Nelson Eddy, the popular young Philadelphia baritone, gave a finished portrayal of Rigoletto in the duet scene from the second act of Verdi's opera of that name, with Hilda Reiter, well-known coloratura soprano, singing the part of Gilda. Miss Reiter was also heard in the familiar Bell Song from Delibes' "Lakme."

In a program of such length and variety, it is impossible to note all the numbers, but among those deserving special mention are Katherine Eimermann's singing, in costume, of the difficult Doll Song from Offenbach's "Tales of Hoffman;" the excellent rendition of the quartette from the second act of Meyerbeer's "Les Huguenots" by Hilda Reiter, Jane Butterworth, Mildred Baily and Winifred Clark; Jeanne Davis, whose pleasing soprano was heard to advantage in Hummel's "Halleluja"; Viola Hull, whose rich contralto gave good expression to "O Mio Fernando" from Donizetti's "La Favorita"; Louise Street, whose clear soprano won approval both in her solo number and in two trios, which were well sung by Miss Street, Helen Bussinger and Albertine Hindertmark. Miss Bussinger was also heard to advantage in Schubert's "Ave Maria" with the chorus, displaying a mezzo-soprano of rare sweetness.

One of the best numbers on the program was the aria "Ritorna vincitor," from "Aida," sung by Mildred Warner Baily, who has a dramatic soprano voice of excellent quality and sings artistically and with feeling. The program closed with an aria and chorus from "Semiramide," by Rossini, the solo being sung by Mary Schwartz, coloratura soprano. Others who aided in the evening's entertainment were Louis Kolp, Genevieve Barowski, Natalie Roth, Charlotte Bentley, Betty Gibson, Edith House, Minerva Crossan, Ruth Wier, Alma Wagener, Katherine Rappold and Constance Harding.

5-13-26

Must Down to the Sea Again,' 'The Rainbow Trail' [a song written by Nelson] and, as encore number to his second group, 'Tally-ho.'"

April 25, 1926: Nelson gave a concert with the Monday Musicales. *Doylestown Daily Intelligencer,* April 26, 1926: "Nelson Eddy's pleasing personality, wedded to the sustained control and fine lyric tone of his voice, evoked the full resources of the several creations whose expression he essayed."

May 12, 1926: The artists and advanced pupils of Mrs. Phillips Jenkins gave an recital at the Penn Athletic Club last evening, with Nelson as guest. *Public Ledger,* May 13, 1926: "A scene from the second act of **Rigoletto** in costume was also given by Hilda Reiter and Nelson Eddy." *Evening Bulletin:* "Nelson Eddy, the popular young Philadelphia baritone, gave a finished portrayal of Rigoletto in the duet scene from the second act of Verdi's opera of that name, with Hilda Reiter, well-known coloratura soprano, singing the part of Gilda." [Note: Nelson never sang in the complete opera of **Rigoletto**; in fact, **Aida** was the only Verdi opera he starred in.]

[Note: by 1926 Nelson had studied voice with David Bispham, Ludwig Schmidt-Fabri, Rebecca Van B. Conway, Henry Scott, and Horatio Connell.]

May 25, 1926, Nelson sang with the Octave Club for its closing concert. *Norristown Register,* May 26, 1926: "The rich baritone voice of Nelson Eddy has a depth, a resonance, and a flexibility, together with finished musicianship, that makes hearing him a real pleasure.... Theodore Paxson was accompanist for Mr. Richardson and for the chorus, and his support was invaluable Mr. Eddy was heard in two groups, all of his selections being pleasing and of sufficient variety to show his versatility. His numbers were 'Pauvre Martyr Obscur,' from the opera **Patrie**, 'When the King Went to War,' and 'Tally Ho,' followed by an encore, 'Cargoes.' His later songs were a selection from the song cycle, 'In a Persian Garden,' 'Sea Fever,' and two Negro spirituals, 'I'm Troubled,' and 'Joshua Fit de Battle of Jericho,' and his final encore being 'The Rainbow Trail.'" *Norristown Times-Herald:* "Mr. Eddy, whose popularity as a Civic Opera Star and concert singer has gained him wide prominence as a baritone lived up to all expectations. He possesses a voice of great depth and feeling and excellent range, and his audience received all his numbers with spontaneous enthusiasm."

June 6, 1926: Nelson sang at Bucknell University. *Lewisburgh Saturday News,* June 12, 1926: "Wonderful Rendition of **St. Paul** by Talented Baptist Choristers.... Nelson Eddy, the baritone, of Philadelphia, Pa., has a rich powerful voice, intelligence to capture the fervent eloquence of arias, phrasing that graphically exposed the musical outline, a diction of unusual clarity. Mr. Eddy sang in a manner that stamped him immediately as an unusual vocalist."

September 25, 1926, *Philadelphia Ledger:* "An interesting performance of a rarely heard oratorio, **The Fall of Babylon**, by Spohr, was given in the Auditorium of the Sesqui-Centennial last evening by eight combined choral societies... The united chorus consisted of approximately 600 voices.... Mr. Hartzell had selected an unusually competent solo quartet, or rather quintet, in Emily Stokes Hagar and Emma Zuern as sopranos; Katherine Noll, contralto; Dr. John B. Becker, tenor, and Nelson Eddy, baritone. These singers did splendid work, both in solo and ensemble numbers."

October 26, 1926: Nelson recorded his own song, "The Rainbow Trail" for Columbia Records.

November 11, 1926 was opening night of the Philadelphia Civic Opera, at the Philadelphia Metropolitan Opera House. **Tannhäuser** was the opera. *Public Ledger:* "Nelson Eddy, as Wolfram, and Elsa Feiskey, as Venus, scored the greatest vocal successes of the performance. Mr. Eddy, specifically, was in beautiful voice and not only sang the pathetic role of Wolfram very finely, but also acted it admirably, doing his best work in the 'Song to the Evening Star' and in the contest of the singers in the second act... The enunciation of all the singers was nearly perfect, that of Miss [Helen] Stanley and Messrs. [Paul] Althouse, Patton, Wizla and Eddy being so clear that every syllable could easily be distinguished. Mr. Smallens led with his usual skill and, considering the immense difficulties of the opera, gave an astonishingly fine reading." *Philadelphia Inquirer:* "It was doubly to the

"MANIFESTATION" OFFERED IN PAGEANTRY AT CHURCH

Uplifting Effect of Christmas Depicted at Overbrook Presbyterian

"Manifestation," a pageant presenting the uplifting effect of the Christmas spirit, was given last night at Overbrook Presbyterian Church, Lancaster avenue and City Line.

The pageant was written and directed by Nelson Eddy, baritone, in the Civic Opera Company and a member of the church choir. It was presented by members of the Sunday School, of which Delbert B. Gray, Jr., is superintendent.

The Christmas spirit made itself manifest by transformation of dispositions of the characters in the play, the change occurring only when the Light of Christ, for which the clergyman fervently prays, has fully dawned in each individual consciousness.

The Christmas spirit was emphasized by the voices of the carolers, who sang "Adeste Fideles" and other carols. About 200 persons were present.

Public Ledger
12-23

What Do You Think of It?

Five Persons Are Asked a Question of Timely Interest.

The Question

..*Is Classical Music Gaining in Popularity Over Jazz?*

Where Asked

Central part of the city.

The Answers

Dr. Charles S. Hirsh, 900 Spruce [illegible]harmonic Society: "I think that without a doubt classical music is becoming almost as popular as jazz. This is proved by the tremendous increase [illegible] the attendance [illegible] the symphony [illegible]ts. Those who [illegible]he modern [illegible] instinct-[illegible]cal and [illegible]ould [illegible] few [illegible] the [illegible]

lighter pieces of the classical composers."

5.—Nelson Eddy, baritone, 13th and Spruce sts.: "Months of study would be required to answer this question definitely. I throughly enjoy the highest forms of music and in recreating the finest music, but on the other hand I can enjoy hearing a good snapappy jazz band. The appeal of good music never fails. Contrary to [illegible]e opinions of some musicians, I do not think jazz is a throwback to the savage strains of the jungle, but is an art in itself. I don't believe the apex of the beauty of jazz has yet been reached, but it is developing a beauty distinctly it's own."

Tomorrow's Question—*Should a Man Remove His Hat When Riding In an Elevator With Ladies?* (Suggested by Howard Stout).

Awful rot.

didn't say this!!

Eve. Bulletin 1-6-27

credit of the company that among the finest impressions made were the efforts of Philadelphians, including Nelson Eddy as a Wolfram of splendid bearing, notably beautiful voice, and strikingly sincerity in acting." *Evening Bulletin:* "The singing of Nelson Eddy in the role of Wolfram was such as to make a real impression, this talented and promising young baritone scoring another success. His voice seems more mellow and richer than ever, with its 'luscious' quality, and when he has learned to use his high tones as well as he does those in the middle and lower part of his fine voice, and has extended its range somewhat, he may be expected to accomplish great things. He put much feeling into Wolfram's song in the hall, though he seemed somewhat too conscious of the effect he was producing upon the audience, singing 'I gaze around upon this fair assembly' of 'dames and maidens fair' directly to the ladies in the body of the house instead of to those in the scene whom he was supposed to be addressing." *The Record:* "The Philadelphia Civic Opera Company auspiciously opened its fourth season last night at the Metropolitan Opera House with a splendid performance of **Tannhäuser**. Cut off from the municipal appropriation by a taxpayers' suit, the large audience showed that the company could count upon generous public appreciation for its support.... Perhaps the most pleasing role was sung by Nelson Eddy as Wolfram."

November 16, 1926, *Doyletown Intelligencer:* "Music lovers of Doylestown and vicinity last night enjoyed another one of the Monday Musicale's judiciously and charmingly arranged programs... The Doylestown musical clientele enthusiastically welcome Leon (sic) Nelson Eddy's return. The poise and charm of Mr. Eddy's concert manner were expected by those who have heard and seen him before, but it seemed that he has attained and added verve and dramatic power where these are required. Both in classical numbers and in songs of a less exalted character Mr. Eddy was very effective. Some of the audience were particularly delighted to hear for the first time John Masefield's fine 'Cargoes' set to appropriate music."

November 18, 1926: Nelson sang with the Philadelphia Opera Company in **Madama Butterfly** at the Met. November 19, 1926 reviews: "Nelson Eddy was the Sharpless. His interpretation was good, besides having virtually perfect enunciation." [Helen Stanley was the Butterfly.] *Philadelphia Inquirer:* "Nelson Eddy has had the good fortune to have, in succession, two of the most beneficent of baritone parts, and last night made his Sharpless as sympathetic as his Wolfram had been one week before. This young Philadelphia singer not only has a voice of singular beauty, but the taste and intelligence in acting as well as singing which should insure him a notable career, as he gains in maturity." *The Record:* "Nelson Eddy was a joy, his enunciation, voice and manner being a decided asset." *Evening Bulletin:* "In sheer competence, vocally and histrionically, Eddy and Miss Stanley carried off the honors of the evening. His beautifully modulated baritone, clear enunciation and finely restrained vocalization made this one of the best of his roles." *Musical America:* "There was a first-rate Sharpless in that dependable and fast developing artist, Nelson Eddy."

December 16, 1926: Nelson sang in **Romeo et Juliette** at the Met with Philadelphia Civic Opera Company. *Evening Bulletin,* December 17, 1926: "It is worth noting that some of the best singing of the performance was done by Philadelphia members of the cast. Nelson Eddy seemed quite 'at home' as Mercutio, his stride and his acting showing ease and self possession, and again was heard the rich quality of his splendid baritone." *Public Ledger:* "Nelson Eddy.... showed his decided operatic talent as Mercutio." *The Record:* "'A rose by any other name' may be just as sweet, but a production of the Gounod **Romeo et Juliet** without a soprano capable of singing the beautiful music written for the romantic heroine lacks the most essential element of success.... Whether Rosa Low, who endeavored to sing the role, was tone deaf, unable to hear the orchestra or simply suffering from a bad attack of stage fright, is a question, but with a singer of her type there was no possibility of making the production anything but uninteresting and more or less of an endurance test.... The Romeo, Ralph Errolele, was a satisfactory, if not brilliant, member of the cast... Nelson Eddy, who is always one of the assets of the Civic Opera, was far from his best form, suffering from laryngitis and being unable to sing to his fullest capacity… Eddy's acting in the role of Mercutio was enjoyable and he would have been an outstanding figure had he been in good voice." *Philadelphia Inquirer:* "Nelson Eddy, whose beautiful baritone and eloquence of acting set some femininity a-flutter..."

December 23, 1926, *Public Ledger:* "Nelson Eddy wrote a Christmas pageant called **Manifestation** given last

PHILADELPHIA CIVIC OPERA CO.

FOURTH SEASON — *METROPOLITAN OPERA HOUSE*

THURSDAY EVG., FEB. 17, at 8 P. M.

AIDA

With ALL-STAR CAST

"AIDA," . . . . PERALTA (Metropolitan Opera Co.) | "AMNERIS," MATZENAUER (Metropolitan Opera Co.)

"RADAMES," PAUL ALTHOUSE; "AMONASRO," NELSON EDDY; HIGH PRIEST, FRED PATTON

Conductor, ALEXANDER SMALLENS. Orchestra—45 Members of Phila. Orchestra

ALL PHILADELPHIA BALLET

FLORENCE COWANOVA, Ballet Mistress and Premiere Danseuse

Tickets, 50c to $2.50, at 1600 Walnut St., Room 807; Metropolitan Opera House and Weymann's, 1108 Chestnut St.

AIDA IS PRESENTED BY CIVIC OPERA CO.

Admirable Performance of Verdi's Composition Given at Metropolitan OperaHouse

Aida, Verdi's melodious opera selected by the Philadelphia Civic Opera Company for presentation at the Metropolitan Opera House last evening, marked a high water mark in the many splendid achievements of this increasingly valuable local musical organization. Rarely, even with much more pretentious professional organizations has such a splendid cast been assembled and even still more rarely has each member of such a cast appeared to the very best advantage. The performance last night was one of exceptional merit, whether the viewpoint be orchestral, vocal or scenic investure and all connected with the Civic Opera Company should be congratulated.

Outstanding in the list of principals was Margaret Matzenauer, who sang the role of Amneris. Impressively regal in appearance and with an oppulence of tone and an increasing artistry of usage, that makes one wonder this great contralto easily won the laurels of the evening, her singing in the third act being of especial brilliance. Frances Peralta was the Aida and her conception of the part was also one of much merit, even if at times she did seem to bring a little too much stress on her production of volume in tone.

The always dependable Paul Althouse was the Rhadames and he, spurred by the surrounding cast, fairly outdid himself, his singing of the big aria in the first act being received with an ovation, although he really shone to much better advantage in the final scene. Nelson Eddy, who grows in artistic stature with each appearance, was Amonasro, and displayed a beauty of tone, which reminded one of the days of Hammerstein and the velvety voice of Sammarco. Fred Patton was very good as Ramfis and Rheinhold Schmidt displayed a sonorous voice as the King of Egypt. The ballet was as usual with this organisation a thing of delight. The scenery was more adequate if exception might be noted to the peculiar celestial apparition representing a moon in the Nile scene.

PHILADELPHIA CIVIC OPERA CO.

Metropolitan Opera House

FOURTH SEASON

Thursday Evening Feb. 17, at 8 P. M.

AIDA

With ALL-STAR CAST

"AIDA" . . . . Peralta (Metropolitan Opera Co.)

"AMNERIS" . . Matzenauer (Metropolitan Opera Co.)

"RADAMES," PAUL ALTHOUSE
"AMONASRO," NELSON EDDY
HIGH PRIEST, FRED PATTON

Conductor, ALEXANDER SMALLENS. Orchestra—45 Members of Phila. Orchestra

ALL PHILADELPHIA BALLET

FLORENCE COWANOVA, Ballet Mistress and Premiere Danseuse

Tickets, 50c to $2.50 at 1600 Walnut St., Room 807; Metropolitan Opera House and Weymann's, 1108 Chestnut St.

FEBRUARY 18, 1927

CIVIC OPERA GIVES 'AIDA' WTH 'STARS'

Peralta and Matzenauer, of Metropolitan, Get Ovation as Slave and Princess

ALTHOUSE IS GOOD RADAMES

The Civic Opera Company scored another great success last evening when it presented an excellent "Aida," with two Metropolitan Opera Company stars in the cast. Frances Peralta sang the title role and Margaret Matzenauer was the Amneris.

The "well-balanced cast with no stars" idea of opera may be all right in theory, but the house was entirely sold out last evening, and it may be inferred that the presence of Mesdames Peralta and Matzenauer had something to do with it.

The performance went through with plenty of spirit. Miss Peralta sang better than she ever has done before in Philadelphia, especially in the closing parts of the first and second acts and in the Nile scene, which was one of the high spots of the opera. Despite the fact that her intonation was not entirely impeccable at all times and that she showed an occasional tendency to drag the tempo, her performance was very successful with the public. Her characterization and acting were excellent.

Mme. Matzenauer, who made a most regal-looking Princess, was at her best in the great trial scene at the beginning of the last act. It seldom has been sung or acted better than she did it. She was called before the curtain many times at the close of the scene.

The male characters of the opera were fully as good as the Metropolitan singers. Paul Althouse demonstrated that Radames is one of his best roles. He was in fine voice and acted splendidly. The very difficult tenor part of the Nile scene was superbly done from every standpoint, as was the popular "Celeste Aida," although Mr. Althouse got better and better in voice and action as the opera progressed.

Nelson Eddy displayed his fine voice and clear enunciation in the role of Amonasro and Fred Patton was impressive as the High Priest, while Reinhold Schmidt did very excellent work as the King. The lesser roles of the Priestess and the Messenger were well taken by Sara Murphy and Pierino Salvucci.

The performance was the best "Aida" the company has given. The chorus made a splendid showing in tone quality, volume and intonation. The ballet, led by Miss Cowanova, scored a great popular success. Mr. Smallens conducted with energy and spirit, and Mr. Puglia did admirable work as stage director, especially in the third act, which was most attractively set.

The highest points of the opera were the scene before the gates of Thebes, the Nile scene and the trial scene, although the standard of performance throughout was exceedingly high.

S. L. L.

night at Overbrook Presbyterian Church, 200 people were present.

January 8, 1927: Nelson sang in **Gianni Schicchi.** *Philadelphia Inquirer,* January 9, 1927: "Mr. Eddy proved himself to be a capital comedian as well as a superb singer--although he is still somewhat youthful for a role of this type, a circumstance considerably offset, however, by his Cyrano-like makeup." *The Record:* "Nelson Eddy did a splendid piece of characterization as the clever, crafty 'Schicchi' quite surpassing in skill and power his many laudable efforts with the Civic Company." *Evening Bulletin:* "Mr. Eddy's acting of Gianni was a splendid piece of comedy worked, judged by any standards. Nelson Eddy again showing genuine talent as a comedian and singing well in the title role." [Note: this was a matinee. Nelson's friend Reinhold Schmidt sang Simon the Sheriff.]

February 18, 1927, *Philadelphia Ledger:* "The Civic Opera Company scored another great success last evening when it presented an excellent **Aida,** with two Metropolitan Opera Company stars in the cast. Frances Peralta sang the title role and Margaret Matzenauer was the Amneris… Nelson Eddy displayed his fine voice and clear enunciation in the role of Amonasro." *Philadelphia Inquirer:* "Nelson Eddy, who grows in artistic stature with each appearance, was Amonasro, and displayed a beauty of tone, which reminded one of the days of Hammerstein and the velvety voice of Sammarco." *The Record:* "Nelson Eddy, whose voice is of exceptional quality but who does not have the volume to compete with the grand opera singers of the professional stage in last evening's cast, makes an admirable Amonasro. It is a role that he has given before." *Evening Bulletin:* "Mr. Eddy again made a good impression as Amonasro, a part which shows his beautiful baritone to excellent advantage." *Musical America:* "Nelson Eddy, ever a pillar of strength to the Civic troupe, won deserved distinction for an impressive performance as Amonasro, conceived in the right dramatic key. His fresh and well-trained baritone lent compelling tonal charm to the second and third acts."

February 23, 1927: Nelson began a new radio series, the Newton Coal Hour on WIP. It aired on Saturday nights from 9:00 pm to 10:00 pm. Nelson sometimes had a guest artist singing with him, but not always. On this first program, Nelson sang "Evening Star" and "Largo al factotum."

March 10, 1927, Nelson sang in a **La Boheme** at the Met. *Bulletin,* March 11, 1927: "The Civic Opera Company gave one of the best performances of its existence at the Metropolitan Opera House last evening in a presentation of Puccini's tragic opera, **La Boheme**… The cast was so exceptionally well balanced and the work was generally so good that it is difficult to pick any outstanding member... The Bohemians were very fine--Nelson Eddy, as Marcello, Reinhold Schmidt as Schaunard, and Sigurd Nilssen, a newcomer in the Civic Opera Company, as Colline. Mr. Eddy displayed his fine voice and unusually clear enunciation in the role of the painter and did some excellent dramatic work, both comic and tragic, in what is perhaps the most diversified even if one of the lesser roles of the opera." *The Record:* "**La Boheme**… was a splendid success. In voice, in acting ability, in general artistry, it was a triumph difficult to surpass... Nelson Eddy, singing Marcello, had a glorious baritone, coupled with an engaging personality." *Evening Bulletin:* "Marcello... was sung with ease and smoothness of rich tone by Nelson Eddy." *Philadelphia Inquirer:* "Nelson Eddy won still more laurels as Marcello, both his acting and singing being irresistibly excellent."

March 20, 1927: Nelson and Elizabeth Harrison sang on radio on the Public Ledger Sunday concert.

March 22, 1927: Nelson sang on the Newton Coal Hour.

March 24, 1927: Nelson sang in **Lohengrin** at the Met. *The Ledger:* "The last performance of the fourth and most successful season of the Philadelphia Civic Opera Company took place last evening at the Metropolitan Opera House, when Wagner's **Lohengrin** was presented in English before a house almost completely sold out... The cast was unusually good and extremely well balanced... The comparatively lesser roles of the King and the Herald were very finely done by Henri Scott and Nelson Eddy. Both of these singers are remarkable for their splendid enunciation and every word could be distinctly heard… Mr. Eddy sang very beautifully, the role giving him little opportunity for dramatic display." *The Inquirer:* "Nelson Eddy gave outstanding interest to

WOMEN'S SYMPHONY IN AN AMBITIOUS CONCERT

Nelson Eddy Soloist With Unique Local Orchestra in Closing Concert of Season

Quite the most ambitious programme yet tackled by the Women's Symphony Orchestra was presented before a large and appreciative audience in the crystal ballroom of the Benjamin Franklin Hotel last night under the direction of J. W. F. Leman, and with Nelson Eddy, that finely equipped baritone of the Civic Opera Company, as soloist. The concert was the organization's last of the season, and was given to help raise the guarantors' fund of $10,000 to further its educational work.

In all its history, the Women's Symphony Orchestra has not undertaken more exacting numbers than the slow movement of the Tchaikovsky Fourth Symphony and the Vorspiel to Wagner's "Lohengrin," which were featured last night. The concert began with the Beethoven "Prometheus" Overture, and also included a movement, "La Danse," from Massenet's "Neapolitan Scenes," a version of the G minor prelude of Rachmaninoff, and the ballet music from Gounod's "Faust," not the customary Kermesse waltzes, but excerpts from the rarely heard Walpurgis scene. Mr. Eddy, whose beautiful voice and admirable art gave outstanding interest to his singing, was heard in an aria from "Hans Heiling," a little-known old German opera, by Marschner, with more popular appeal in selections from "Countess Maritza," a ballad encore, and there were Strauss and Woodforde-Finden numbers.

The seventy members of the Women's Symphony Orchestra achieved quite an ample volume of tone, and played with the zeal of true devotion as well as some novel effects of intonation and rhythm, especially in the Wagner and Tchaikovsky numbers.

WOMEN'S SYMPHONY GIVES THIRD CONCERT OF SEASON

Nelson Eddy Is Soloist—J. W. F. Leman Conducts Orchestra

The Women's Symphony Orchestra of Philadelphia, J. W. F. Leman conducting, gave the third concert of its second annual series last night at the Benjamin Franklin before a large audience.

The soloist was Nelson Eddy, baritone, who sang several numbers, accompanied by Miss Mildred Ackley, pianist.

The program given by the orchestra included overture to "Prometheus," Beethoven; second movement of Tschaikowsky's Fourth Symphony; prelude to Wagner's "Lohengrin"; "Scene Napolitaine," Massenet; "Prelude in G Minor," Rachmaninoff, and ballet music from Gounod's "Faust."

Newton Coal Hour

9-10 Tonight, WFI

Artists:

Mildred Faas—soprano. For nine years soloist with Bethlehem Bach Choir; special soloist at St. Luke's of the Epiphany.

Nelson Eddy—baritone. With Philadelphia Civic Opera Company, and formerly of Savoy Opera Company.

Mr. Chas. A. Johnson will continue his answers to heating questions.

All-Phila. Program

"All-Philadelphia" Hour

In another all-Philadelphia hour the George B. Newton Coal Company will continue its radio forum from WFI, 9 to 10 o'clock tonight. Mildred Faas, soprano, and Nelson Eddy, baritone, both of Philadelphia, will sing solos and in duets.

Mildred Faas is special soloist at St. Luke and the Epiphany and was for nine years soloist with the Bethlehem Bach Choir. She sang Bach's St. Matthew's Passion with Willem Mengelberg and the New York Symphony Orchestra and next week will take a solo part in Bach's Mass in B minor with the New York Oratorio Society.

Nelson Eddy has sung with the Philadelphia Civic Opera Company in German, Italian and English opera and formerly sang Gilbert and Sullivan roles with the Savoy Opera Company.

Charles A. Johnson, president of the George B. Newton Coal Company, will continue his "Answers to Heating Questions" for about ten minutes of the hour.

The program follows:

"Ombra Mai Fu," from "Xerxes" . Handel
"Pauvre Martyr Obscur," from "Patrie," Paladilhe

Nelson Eddy

"Beautiful Blue Danube" (waltz) . J. Strauss

Mildred Faas

"Baigne d'eau tes Mains," from "Thaïs," Massenet
"La Ci Darem la Mano," from "Don Giovanni" . . . . Mozart

Duets

"Desir de l'Orient" . . . . Saint-Saens
"Italian Lullaby" . . . . Gadero
"The Piper of Love" . . . . Carew

Miss Faas

"Will the Red Sun Never Set?" Woodforde-Finden
"The Light I Love Best" . . . . Hopkins
"The Two Grenadiers" . . . . Schumann

Mr. Eddy

"Belle Nuit," from "Tales of Hoffmann" Offenbach

Duet

the very important role of the Herald." *The Record:* "Nelson Eddy as the Herald was another singer who knew how to make every syllable heard." *Musical America:* "A conspicuously good Herald in Nelson Eddy."

April 7, 1927, *The Ledger:* "The Matinee Musical Club gave its annual spring concert in the ballroom of the Bellevue-Stratford last evening before an audience which virtually filled the auditorium... The concert began with a scene from **Don Pasquale** of Donizetti. Elizabeth Harrison took the role of Norma and Mr. Eddy that of Dr. Malatesta... The third number consisted of episodes from **Deep River,** of which Nelson Eddy gave the prologue." *The Bulletin:* "Nelson Eddy as Dr. Malatesta... did a clever bit of acting, as well as singing with fine flexibility, good round tone and a general air of ease... Mr. Eddy had an entirely different role in the Prologue from **Deep River** and a solo which brought out the resonance of his voice with fine effect." *The Inquirer:* "Nelson Eddy gave the prologue with haunting beauty." *The Record:* "The scene from Donizetti's **Don Pasquale**... was well managed and extremely well sung."

Undated clipping from April, 1927: "The Women's Symphony Orchestra of Philadelphia will give its final concert on Thursday in the ballroom of the Ben Franklin. Nelson Eddy will be soloist." *The Record,* April 7: "Mr. Eddy's first number was the aria from Hans Heiling' **An jenen Tag**. He has a very clean, very pleasing voice which completely won his audience, even in his encores, which, unfortunately, were of a very mediocre quality, not worthy of his talents... Mr. Eddy's second and last selections included 'Will the Red Sun Never Set?' by Woodforede-Finden; Strauss,' 'All Souls Day,' and Kalman's 'Play Gypsies, Dance Gypsies' from **The Countess Maritza."** *Inquirer:* "Mr. Eddy, whose beautiful voice and admirable art gave outstanding interest to his singing..."

April 16, 1927: Nelson sang on Newton Coal Hour, with Mildred Faas, soprano. It was an 'all—Philadelphia hour.'

April 17, 1927, *Norristown Times-Herald:* "Commemorating the 100th anniversary of the death of Beethoven, the Octave Club of Norristown, at its March meeting yesterday afternoon at the Elks Auditorium, featured the master composer's musical classics in an artistic program. Nelson Eddy, baritone, was the assisting artist of the day. He is a member of the Civic Opera Company, and possesses a voice of good range and volume. His shading and sympathetic interpretation was particularly notable in his first solo 'Adelaide' by Beethoven, which he sang with dramatic expression. His second well sung group included 'Will the Red Sun Never Set' by Woodford-Finden and 'The Light I love Best' by Hopkins. Theodore Paxson effectively played Mr. Eddy's piano accompaniments."

April 20, 1927: the Savoy Company performed **Iolanthe** at the Academy of Music, with Maybelle Marston in the cast along with Nelson. "Although the cast as a whole is deserving of praise, honors for the evening were easily won by Nelson Eddy, young baritone, who has won acclaim for his work with the Civic Opera Company, in the role of Strephon. The part is not strange for Eddy, who played it five years ago, but since that time his voice has become much surer and its range greater. Gilbert and Sullivan devotees had the surprise of their lives last evening when Mr. Eddy sang the second-act solo, 'Fold Your Flapping Wings,' which has been cut out of virtually all American productions of the opera. The strain is melancholy and not, perhaps, in keeping with the spirit of the rest of the piece, but both music and lyrics are noteworthy, and Eddy did justice to both. His acting of the role was highly satisfactory... Maybelle Beretta Marston sang well the role of the Fairy Queen, winning one of the best and most deserved hands of the evening on the 'Oh, Foolish Fay' number." *Record:* "Eddy's fine baritone and his dignity and poise made the role of Strephon, the shepherd, of due importance." *Bulletin:* "Mr. Eddy's voice retained its beauty and smoothness of tone but his histrionic treatment of the part lacked the simple joyousness that marked his previous appearance. There was a touch of the grand manner which was depressing." *Inquirer:* "Mr. Nelson Eddy's Strephon was well sung." *Musical America:* "Mr. Eddy's admirable voice was heard to special advantage in the second act number 'Fold your Flapping Wings,' a solo, which is generally omitted from productions of **Iolanthe."**

April 26, 1927: Nelson sang at the Merion War Tribute House before an audience of 350. The concert was a

, MAY 8, 1927

NELSON EDDY—"Iolanthe"
Savoy Company—Academy of Music, May 20 and 21

Savoy Will Offer 'Iolanthe' May 20

Gilbert and Sullivan Opera Will Be Repeated on 21st at Academy

Rehearsals are progressing splendidly for the Savoy Company's production of Gilbert and Sullivan's "Iolanthe," which it will present at the Academy of Music on the evenings of May 20 and 21st.

An important change in the cast has just been announced, Anna Deans Remont replacing Sara Bailey Heberton in the role of Iolanthe. Miss Remont has just been singing the same role with the Rose Valley Chorus. She is a prominent social leader in Media, and her experience in light opera work of this character is expected to make her portrayal of Iolanthe noteworthy.

Six members of the University of Pennsylvania band will be used for the famous Entrance of the Peers number which requires sounding brasses on the stage as well as in the orchestra. The famous U. of P. drum-major, whose height always attracts attention at football games, will lead the band. As was the case last year, twenty-eight members of the Philadelphia Orchestra will accompany the presentation.

Today Edward Jacoby, who plays the important role of Private Willis, is entertaining members of the cast and chorus at his home in Radnor, and a rehearsal is to be held on the lawn.

"Iolanthe" is the twenty-seventh annual production of the Savoy Company, and was chosen this year because of the tremendous success the same light opera has had in New York, where it has been offered professionally for almost an entire season.

The Savoy Company has selected its cast with great care. The difficult role of Strephon, the Arcadian shepherd, will be taken by Nelson Eddy, who has won for himself a splendid reputation in grand opera through his appearance with the Civic Opera Company here. Robert V. Bolger will play the Earl of Mountararat; Walter Antrim will be Earl Tolloller, and Mr. Jacoby will appear as the philosophic Private Willis. In the comedy part of the Lord Chancellor, Albert W. Zimmerman will be seen.

Maybelle Beretta Marston will essay the difficult part of the Fairy Queen. Marie Zara Randall, also a favorite with Savoy audiences, will take the role of Phyllis. The three fairies, Celia, Leila and Fleta, will be portrayed by Phyllis Newgeon, Christine Kendrick and Mary Carroll Rolin.

Public Ledger 5-8

Savoy Opera Co. To Give 'Iolanthe' Twice This Week

Nelson Eddy Heads Unusually Strong Cast for Annual Production

THE Savoy Opera Company, which gives an annual production of a Gilbert and Sullivan opera, will present "Iolanthe" at the Academy of Music next Friday and Saturday evenings. This is the twenty-seventh annual performance, and the cast is one of the strongest that the company has ever had.

Nelson Eddy will take the role of Strephon, with Anna Deans Remont in the title role and Marie Zara Randall as Phyllis, the Arcadian sheperdess. Others in the cast will be Albert Zimmerman, as the Lord Chancellor; Edward Jacoby, as Private Willis; Robert V. Bolger, as the Earl of Mountararat; Walter Antrim, as the Earl of Tolloller; Maybelle Beretta Marston, as the Fairy Queen, and Phyllis Newgeon, Christine Kendrick and Mary Carroll Rolin as Celia, Leila and Fleta, respectively.

There will be the usual large chorus, and the famous Entrance of the Peers will be accompanied by a brass band from the University of Pennsylvania. The stage director is Joseph Craig Fox; the musical director, J. W. F. Leman, and twenty-eight members of the Philadelphia Orchestra will supply the accompaniment. The opera is being staged for the benefit of the Major Alfred Reginald Allen Memorial Fund for the School of Music at the University of Pennsylvania.

Inquirer 5-15

ment at the Tourraine, 1520 Spruce street.

Mr. Nelson Eddy, of the Lenox, will sail the latter part of July for a two month's European trip.

Miss Faith Biddle Fitler, daughter of Mr. and Mrs. N. Myers Fitler, of

P. Ledger

SEASON

Nelson Eddy's Rise

When the Gilbert and Sullivan opera "Iolanthe" is offered by the Savoy Company at the Academy of Music on Friday and Saturday evenings of this week, the important role of Strephon, the Arcadian shepherd, will be played and sung by Nelson Eddy, who, in the last couple of seasons has come forward here to the position of one of the best of the younger singers of this city.

NELSON EDDY

Eddy is no stranger in the Savoy productions. Five years ago he sang the role of Strephon for them, and made a profound impression, and the following season he assumed the part of the Major General in the same company's presentation of "The Pirates of Penzance." Since that time he has won a splendid reputation for himself in the field of grand opera, and right now he is recognized as a leading baritone with the Philadelphia Civic Opera Company.

Among the important roles he has taken of late have been that of Marcello in "La Boheme," Sharpless in "Madame Butterfly," Gianni in "Gianni Schichi" and Mercutio in "Romeo and Juliet." He has won high praise for his work in "Aida," "Tannhauser," "Pagliacci," "Cavalleria" and "The Secret of Suzanne."

Public Ledger 5-15

benefit for the Philadelphia Home for Incurables. Elizabeth Harrison, soprano, also sang. *Bulletin,* April 27, 1927: "An early Italian love song and a lost stanza of comedy in the fine recital given in the Merion Tribute House, last evening, by Nelson Eddy and Elizabeth Harrison. The amorous words of the song came to a sudden end. Miss Harrison could not find the spot in her folio where the encore continued. She leaned forward and peeked into the book of her fellow singer. Shyly, an arm, quite in keeping with the spirit of the music, crept around her waist, the lost spot was found and the song continued to its end--with the arm in its place. The byplay brought amusement to the audience, which responded with noisy applause. Mr. Eddy's singing was very acceptable, with a noticeable improvement in the higher tones. His best selection was his first, the 'Ombra Mai Fu' of Handel, better known as 'Largo.' Another song, 'No Prophet I,' by Rachmaninoff was also suited to his baritone register."

May 26, 1927 clipping: "The spring concert by the orchestra of the Symphony Society of Frankford will be given in Frankford High School on the 26. Admission is free and no tickets are required." (Review on opposite page.).

Clipping: "The Fifth Annual Spring Music Festival will be presented by the Philadelphia Music League in the Arena, June 4-7, the biggest municipal music event of the year. Over 1000 trained choristers (sic) will take part. Nelson Eddy will be soloist. Caroline Littlefield will feature her Littlefield Ballet." It was further explained that Littlefield had trained 300 dancers [note: her parents ran a dance school and had trained youngster Jeanette MacDonald to dance.] The audience was expected to number 9000. *Inquirer,* June 5, 1927*:* "The high point, musically, of the chorus, was the fine and finished presentation of the Gounod Mass, with Mae Ebrey Hotz, Royal P. MacLellan and Nelson Eddy as the well-equipped soloists… Mr. Eddy distinguish[ed] himself among the soloists." *Record:* "Despite the dampness, which is unsympathetic with tone, the soloists had no trouble with their voices." *Bulletin:* "Mae Ebrey Hotz, soprano, and Nelson Eddy, baritone, distinguished themselves both in their individual solos and in the trios wherein their voices were heard in the pauses of the choral singing. It speaks volumes for their fine vocalization that they were able to sustain the proportions of the music in the immense auditorium after the great outpouring of tone by the choir."

June 12, 1927 clipping: "Woman's symphony orchestra will give their third concert of the season at the Grove next Tuesday. Nelson Eddy will be soloist." This concert was postponed by rain to June 15. *The Record,* June 16, 1927: "Nelson Eddy...scored a decided hit with an audience of several hundred at the music auditorium of Willow Grove Park, first night The popular soloist apparently had no difficulty in covering the open auditorium without sacrificing the mellow, unaffected tone which has brought him enthusiastic accord, and his offerings were well received. His 'Chanson du Toreador,' from Bizet's **Carmen**; 'Will the Sun Never Rise,' of Woodforde-Findefl, and 'The Light I Love Best' of Hopkins, sung as an encore, are worthy of special mention in his selections of the evening." *Ledger:* "Mr. Eddy sang very well... .All the numbers, whether orchestra or vocal, were enthusiastically received, and the concert proved to be one of the most enjoyable and best performed of the season."

June 27, 1927, unidentified clipping: "Last Sunday evening, Professor Paul Stolz, director of Music at Bucknell University, gave the best entertainment by way of a musical program ever enjoyed in Lewisburg… Mr. Eddy introduced... 'In the Beginning God Created the Heaven and the Earth' in **Creation** Oratorio. Nelson Eddy has an excellent voice particularly in the upper register, of rich, expressive quality, with the requisite poise and routine. He was able to show individuality in his work. He delivered 'Rolling in Foaming Billows' with an opulence of tone, with facility and clearness in treatment, and a virile style that moved the audience to acclaim him."

July 1927: Nelson left for Dresden to study opera. He lived with a German family and was offered a contract with the Dresden Opera, which he turned down. He felt that as an American singer, he should find his success at home. Later he said in an interview: "After my return from abroad, my first singing netted me about $3,000 the first year, $6,000 the second year and after that from $15,000 to $30,000 a year."

Savoy Ready to Be Heard

"Iolanthe" With Cast of Well-Known Singers Will Have Two Performances.

The Savoy Company, famous for yearly productions of Gilbert and Sullivan operas, will present "Iolanthe" at the Academy of Music on Friday and Saturday nights of this week. This will be the company's twenty-seventh annual production. Nelson Eddy, who has won praise for his work with the Philadelphia Civic Opera Company for the last two seasons, will sing the role of Strephon. Anna Deans Remont will be heard in the title role. She has been singing it with great success with the Rose Valley Chorus. Marie Zara Randall, who has been associated with the Savoy company in a number of offerings, will sing the role of Phyllis, the Arcadian shepherdess. Albert Zimmerman, another Savoy favorite, will be seen as Lord Chancellor, a role which he has played before with success. Edward Jacoby, also a Savoy veteran, will play the role of the philosophic Private Willis. The roles of the Earl of Mountararat and the Earl of Tolloller will be taken, respectively, by Robert V. Bolger and Walter Antrim, both experienced in Gilbert and Sullivan. Maybelle Beretta Marston will sing the role of the Fairy Queen, and Phyllis Newgeon, Christine Kendrick and Mary Carroll Rolin will be seen as Celia, Leila and Fleta, respectively. There will be the customary large choruses of men and women, and the "entrance of the peers" will be accompanied by a brass band of six pieces from the University of Pennsylvania, led by the stately drum-major whose height always attracts attention at Franklin Field. As usual, the musical accompaniment will be supplied by members of the Philadelphia Orchestra—28 men in all.

Nelson Eddy.

As was the case last year, the stage director for the performance is Joseph Craig Fox, and the musical director J. W. F. Leman. The beneficiary is the Major Alfred Reginald Allen Memorial Fund for the School of Music at the University of Pennsylvania.

C LEDGER—PHILAD

NELSON EDDY STAR OF SAVOY 'IOLANTHE'

Young Baritone Shines in Fine Production of Gilbert and Sullivan Opera

SINGS SELDOM-HEARD SOLO

As its twenty-seventh annual production of Gilbert and Sullivan opera, the Savoy Company last evening presented "Iolanthe" at the Academy of Music, and it was generally agreed that the performance ranked among the best of the organization's efforts in recent years, second, possibly, only to "The Gondoliers" of 1924 in felicitous casting, ensemble work and the tempo.

Although the cast as a whole is deserving of praise, honors for the evening were easily won by Nelson Eddy, young baritone, who has won acclaim for his work with the Civic Opera Company, in the role of Strephon. The part is not strange for Eddy, who played it five years ago, but since that time his voice has become much surer and its range greater.

Gilbert and Sullivan devotees had the surprise of their lives last evening when Mr. Eddy sang the second-act solo, "Fold Your Flapping Wings," which has been cut out of virtually all American productions of the opera. The strain is melancholy and not, perhaps, in keeping with the spirit of the rest of the piece, but both music and lyrics are noteworthy, and Eddy did justice to both. His acting of the role was highly satisfactory.

Playing opposite him as Phyllis, ward of chancery, was Marie Zara Randall, also familiar to Savoy audiences, who both sang and acted her role splendidly, especially in the "None Shall Part Us" duet and in her songs with the stately peers.

Albert W. Zimmerman, as the Lord Chancellor, was remarkable for his clarity of diction. Every word and syllable of the famous Nightmare song was clear and distinct to the last row. Mr. Zimmerman's comedy values were excellent and he gave the role all the unction it requires.

Maybelle Beretta Marston sang well the role of the Fairy Queen, winning one of the best and most deserved hands of the evening on the "Oh, Foolish Fay" number. Anna Deans Remont was also vocally satisfactory and did justice to her beautiful last-act solo. Robert V. Bolger and Walter Antrim capitally performed the roles of the Earl of Mountararat and Earl Tolloller, and although their voices might have been stronger in such difficult numbers as the famous "Blue Blood" of the first act, they were generally satisfactory.

Edward C. Jacoby was the stiff and gallant Private Willis of the occasion, and Phyllis Newgeon, Christine Kendrick and Mary Carroll Rolin were excellent as the three fairies.

The chorus work was up to the high standard of the company and the performance went smoothly with one or two exceptions. At times the orchestration erred in the direction of too much leisureliness. The performance was directed by Joseph Craig Fox and J. W. F. Leman conducted the orchestra. "Iolanthe" will be repeated tonight.

WILLOW GROVE ILLUSTRATED NEWS, SATURDAY, JU[illegible] 11, 1927

POPULAR BARITONE IS SOLOIST

NELSON EDDY IS THE SOLOIST WITH SYMPHONY

Women's Symphony Orchestra of Philadelphia Concert at Willow Grove Park, June 14

The Women's Symphony Orchestra of Philadelphia, under the direction of J. W. F. Leman, will give the third concert of the First Willow Grove Music Festival, under the auspices of the Philadelphia Music League, at 8.15 P. M. Tuesday, June 14, in the Music Auditorium at Willow Grove Park.

Philadelphia is indeed very proud of this famous musical body which has served as an example for other large cities in the organization of women's orchestras.

The Women's Symphony Orchestra of Philadelphia is the largest in the world composed entirely of women players. There are [illegible] and no [illegible] in the organization.

The famous Symphony was founded by Mabel Swint Ewer in [illegible] and since then, it has, under the able direction of J. W. F. Leman, won unstinted praise from both press and public.

Those who enjoy the finest orchestral music, as well as the novel and unique, will have such an opportunity on Tuesday night when they hear the Women's Symphony Orchestra of Philadelphia render one of its most pretentious programs.

That a large audience will be present in the Auditorium for the occasion is assured.

Nelson Eddy to Sing

Nelson Eddy, distinguished baritone of the Philadelphia Civic Opera Company, will be the soloist with the orchestra for this concert and that fact, alone, constitutes an outstanding feature of the event.

The triumphs of this gifted singer are too recent and too well known to need any elaboration and patrons of the Women's Symphony Orchestra concert on Tuesday night, June 14, may expect a musical treat.

The facilities at Willow Grove [illegible] and the delightful [illegible] of this type. [illegible]

[illegible] Festival series follows:

Women's Symphony Orchestra
J. W. F. Leman, Conductor
Soloist
MR. NELSON EDDY

Music Auditorium
Willow Grove Park
8.15 P. M. Tuesday, June 14

Part 1

1—Overture, "Prometheus" ... Beethoven
2—Largo from "The New World Symphony" ... Dvorak
3—Baritone Solo: Chanson du Toreador, "Carmen" ... Bizet
Mr. Nelson Eddy
4—Scene Napolitaine, "La Danse" ... Massenet
Tarantelle-like movement from a Neapolitan festival of characteristic pieces by the modern French composer.

Part 2

5—Tannhauser ... Wagner
The song of the Pilgrims. The Evening Star. Excerpts of the Ballet. March and Venus Music.
6—(a) A Round of Old-Fashioned Dances ... Schmid
[illegible]
(b) Intermezzo, "Whispering Willows" ... Herbert
7—Songs for Baritone:
(a) "Will the Red Sun Never Set" ... Woodforde Finden
(b) "Cargoes" ... Dobson
(c) "The Prophet, I" ... Rachmaninoff
Mr. Nelson Eddy
Miss [illegible] at the piano.

COMING EVENTS At WILLOW GROVE

NOW—CAPTAIN HUGO
Sensational High Diver
4 Times Daily

Beginning Monday, June 13
THE GREAT CURRAN

Sat., June 11—
INTERNATIONAL PHILHARMONIC BAND
S. A. Sama, Conductor
[illegible]
St. Paul's Ref. Epis. S. S.

Sun., June 12—
INTERNATIONAL PHILHARMONIC BAND
S. A. Sama, Conductor
DOYLESTOWN HIGH SCHOOL BAND
[illegible] BOYS
Prof. Luigi Valerio
Conductor

Mon., June 13—
Corpus Christi S. S.

Tues., June 14—
WOMEN'S SYMPHONY ORCHESTRA
With Nelson Eddy

NELSON EDDY, BARITONE

The triumphs of the distinguished baritone of the Philadelphia Civic Opera Company are too well known to need repeating here. He will sing with the Women's Symphony Orchestra on Tuesday, June 14.

Postponed, because of rain, to the following night.

EVENING PUBLIC LEDGER—PHILADE

LOCAL CIVIC OPERA STAR ON AIR AT 9

Nelson Eddy, Baritone, Sings Solo Selections During Newton Hour Over Station WIP

NAVY DAY PROGRAM AT 10:30

A group of all-Philadelphia artists will broadcast during the Newton Coal Radio Forum tonight at 9 over WIP.

The program features Nelson Eddy, baritone of the Philadelphia Civic Opera Company, whose roles include German, Italian and English opera. The Philadelphia Trio, consisting of Sascha Jacobinoff, violinist, Josef Wissow, pianist, and Emil Flogman, cellist, of the Philadelphia Orchestra, will be an additional feature of the hour.

The program follows:

Philadelphia Trio—
"Two Russian songs .... Glinka
"Tango" .... Albiniz
"Andante Cantabile" .... Tchaikowsky

Solos by Nelson Eddy—
"Lascia Ch'io Pianga," from "Rinaldo" .... Handel
"La Cennamella" .... Rosselini
"When the King Went Forth to War" .... Koeneman
"Drink to Me Only With Thine Eyes" .... Koeneman

Philadelphia Trio—
"Adagio" .... Beethoven
"By the Brook" .... Boisdeffre
"Nina-Pergolisi" .... Kreisler
"The Old Refrain" .... Kreisler

Solos by Nelson Eddy—
"Wotan's Farewell to Brunnhilde," from "Die Walkure" .... Wagner
"Kashmiri Song" .... Woodforde-Finden
"No Prophet I" .... Rachmaninoff

Evening Public Ledger Radio Tin

ALL SCHEDULES IN EASTERN STANDARD TIME

WEATHER FORECAST

1:30—WFI.
2:00—WJZ.
6:00—WIP.
7:55—WLIT.

TIME

11:55 A. M.—**WOO**: Time signals.
7:00—**WJZ**: Correct time announced.
9:00—**WEAF, WEEI, WJAR, WFI, WWJ, WSAI, WCAE, WTAM, WGY, KSD, WRC, WDAF**: Correct time announced.
9:00—**WABQ, WIAD.**
9:55—**WOO, KDKA, WGY, WRC**: Time signals.
10:00—**WJZ, WBZ - WBZA, KDKA, KYW, WHAM, WJR, WTMJ**: Correct time announced.

Stations Reserve Right to Change Programs Without Notice

Local Broadcasts

10:00 A. M.—**WIP**: Menu.
10:15—**WFI**: Market reports.
10:30—**WFI**: "Pies for Autumn Desserts."
11:00—**WLIT**: Talk on "Household Commodities."
WOO: Grand organ.
12:00 noon—**WOO**: Golden's Crystal Tearoom Orchestra.
WLIT: Almanac; Stanley Theatre organ recital.
WCAU: Lansdowne Theatre organ recital by Arthur Hinett.
12:20 P. M.—**WLIT**: Religious service by the Rev. James Ramsey Swain, pastor Woodland Presbyterian Church.
12:30—**WLIT**: Benjamin Franklin Hotel Concert Orchestra.
1:00—**WFI**: Strawbridge & Clothier Tearoom Ensemble.
WIP: Gimbel Tearoom Orchestra.
1:30—**WFI**: Market reports; ensemble continued.
2:00—**WLIT**: Arcadia Concert Orchestra.
2:[illegible] ... Abigail F.

Local Opera Star

NELSON EDDY

Baritone of the Philadelphia Civic Opera Company, who will broadcast a program of French and English songs during the Newton Coal Radio Forum over WIP at 9 o'clock tonight

ty, October 27

Features

7:30 P. M.—**WCAU**: Snellenburg Symphony Orchestra.
8:00—**WFI, WEAF**: Half Hours With Great Composers; Arcadie Birkenholz, violinist.
WIP: Lord Calvert Hour of Music.
WJZ: R. C. A. Radiotrons.
8:30—**WFI, WEAF**: Hoover Sentinels.
9:00—**WIP**: Nelson Eddy, baritone.
WFI, WEAF: Clicquot Club Eskimos.
WJZ: Morley Singers.
9:30—**WJZ**: Spotlight Hour.
10:30—**WFI, WEAF**: Navy Day program. Speakers, Secretary of the Navy Curtis D. Wilbur, Commander Richard E. Byrd, Admiral Hilary Jones.

7:30—**WLIT**: Pe[illegible] business conditions.
WOO: Dinner music by the WOO Trio.
WCAU: Snellenburg Symphony Orchestra.
7:45—**WABQ**: Bernard Feuerstein, tenor; Josef Myerov, pianist.
WIAD: B. B. Todd piano period.
8:00—**WFI, WEAF**: Half hours with great composers; Arcadie Birkenholz, violinist.
WIP: Lord Calvert hour of music.
WCAU: Blue Anchor Sailors at "The Halloween Party."
WABQ: Felin's I. X. L. Frolicers.
WIAD: Talk on Africa by the Rev. Alfred J. Lewis.
8:15—**WIAD**: Lou Herscher and Jack Dichter, songs.
8:30—**WFI, WEAF**: Hoover Sentinels.
WABQ: Oakland-Pontiac Pathfinders.
WIAD: Elizabeth Overbeck, soprano.
9:00—**WFI, WEAF**: Clicquot Club Eskimos; "Dog Night."
WIP: Newton Coal Radio Forum; Nelson Eddy, baritone.

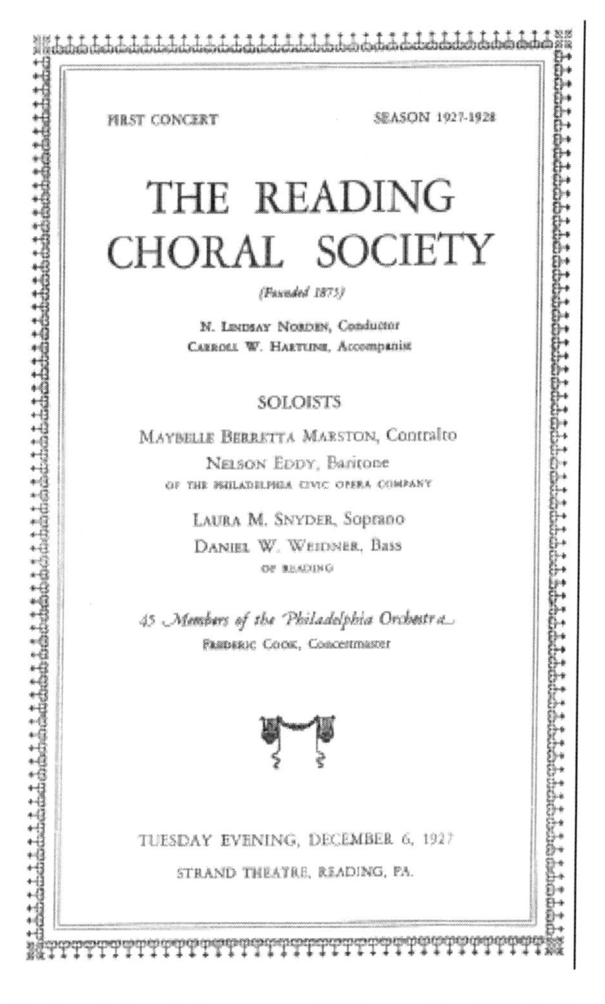

FIRST CONCERT SEASON 1927-1928

THE READING
CHORAL SOCIETY

(Founded 1875)

N. Lindsay Norden, Conductor
Carroll W. Hartline, Accompanist

SOLOISTS

Maybelle Berretta Marston, Contralto
Nelson Eddy, Baritone
of the Philadelphia Civic Opera Company
Laura M. Snyder, Soprano
Daniel W. Weidner, Bass
of Reading

45 Members of the Philadelphia Orchestra
Frederic Cook, Concertmaster

TUESDAY EVENING, DECEMBER 6, 1927
STRAND THEATRE, READING, PA.

October 27, 1927, clipping: "Nelson Eddy sings French and English songs during Newton Coal Radio Forum on WJP at 9:00."

November 1, 1927: Nelson sang at Matinee Musical Club of Philadelphia. *Record:* "Nelson Eddy, baritone, accompanied by Helen Boothroyd Buckley at the piano, entertained with song selections including 'No Prophet I,' by Rachmaninoff, 'Tally-Ho!' by Leoni, 'Will the Red Sun Never Set?' by Woodforde-Findene, 'The Crying of Water' by Campbell-Tipton and 'At the Last' by Bax. Mr. Eddy made a hit from gallery down to parquet floor." *Public Ledger:* "A second group of songs, sung with vibrant richness and dramatic fire by Nelson Eddy..." *Bulletin:* "Mr. Eddy sang especially well." *Musical America:* "Nelson Eddy, young baritone of fine achievement and even finer promise, sang with suave tone and great verbal clearness."

December 1927: "The Young Men and Young Women's Hebrew Association announces that, owing to a sudden death in her family, Rosa Low, soprano, has been obliged to postpone her appearance in the concert of the association this evening. Nelson Eddy, baritone, who was to have appeared later in the season, will take Miss Low's place in the concert, with Willem van den Burg, violoncellist." Nelson sang on December 6. *Record,* December 7, 1927: "Nelson Eddy... was received with enthusiasm that was justified by his performance. The singer rarely disappoints, and last night he displayed the power of rich tone for which he is noted to more than usual advantage." [Ven Den Gurg was cellist.] *Musical America:* "Mr. Eddy was in sonorous voice and sang with vigor and taste. 'Where'er You Walk' and 'Ombra Mai Piu' were finely projected. Nelson also sang an aria 'Suonatal l'ora.' from Montemezzi's opera **L'Amore dei Tre Re**, and a group of lyrics made up of Speaks' Hungarian 'Bludgeon Song,' 'At the Last' by Arnold Bax, and Walter Golde's 'Love Was With Me Yesterday.'" *Public Ledger:* "As a closing number, Mr. Eddy and Mr. Van den Burg united in Massenet's 'Elegie' for baritone voice with violoncello obligato. Isadore Freed was an efficient accompanist for both soloists, each of whom was obliged to respond with an encore number after each group."

December 1, 1927: the Philadelphia Civic Opera at the Met presented the American premiere of a double bill, in German, of **Die Maienkoenigin by** Gluck and **Feuersnot** by Strauss. *Bulletin,* December 2, 1927: "A representative audience which filled the Metropolitan Opera House last evening, including Mayor and Mrs. Kendrick, members of the German and Austrian Embassies, music critics and distinguished guests from other cities, added distinction to an unusually interesting musical event, the American premiere of two operas. Preparations for the production have been going on for months, under the ardent and artistic guidance of Alexander Smallens. " Nelson was mentioned as one of the "able members of the cast." Another clipping noted: "Nelson Eddy made the most of [his] limited opportunities."

December 6, 1927: Nelson sang in concert with Maybelle Marston for the Reading Choral Society. *Reading Times,* December 7, 1927: "Overwhelming applause was given the chorus of 200 voices, at Reading Choral

TIMES PHONE 6101 THE READING TIMES

Things Musical In Reading

By WILLIAM WOOD BRITTON

CHORAL SOCIETY THRILLS CROWD

Great Applause Accorded 200 Voices at Concert in Strand Theatre

Overwhelming applause was given the chorus of 200 voices, the orchestra, and the conductor of the Reading Choral society, N. Lindsay Norden, at the close of one of the best of many good concerts given by this organization, in the Strand theatre last night. It was so good in every respect that even the hypercritical reviewer would be at a loss to find a reasonable basis of complaint.

The chorus was large, the volume of tone magnificent, its quality of tone good, and the balance equally good. The orchestra of 43 players of the Philadelphia orchestra gave an ideal accompaniment with a sonorous support of the chorus that furnished a substantial base for the great choral superstructure. Norden conducted with his accustomed ability, and with an authority that kept singers and accompanying instrumentalists on the alert throughout the entire performance.

The performance was uniformly good, but there are certain parts which gave a greater thrill to the large audience by reason of the character of the works sung, as the two Brahms' works, "Nanie" (text by Schiller) and the "Rhapsodie" for alto solo and male chorus. These were sung with intelligence, with feeling, with good phrasing and splendid attention to dynamics, and with an impressive precision in attack and release, and they were splendid performances of great and noble music. But the thrill was not felt by the audience, because the appeal was to the musical mentality of the auditors, and there was nothing to stir the emotions.

Work of Soloist Excellent

The singing of the "Coronation Music" from "Moussorgsky's "Boris Godounoff" thrilled the audience because the imposing volume of tone of combined orchestra and voices, themselves stirred by the grandeur of the music and text, was overwhelming, and made a direct appeal to the mind and the feelings. The work of the soloist in this number, Nelson Eddy, was worthy of emphatic praise. His voice is a splendid resonant baritone, pure in quality, uniform throughout its ample register, and it was used with an ease and freedom from offensive mannerism that was decidedly pleasing.

The "Scena and Prayer" from Mascagni's "Cavalleria Rusticana" was given with fine effect, and with a real fervor that pleased and impressed. The general effect produced by this work was that of evident appreciation of the work of the singers, players, and Conductor Norden. There was a finish to the performance of this music, as well as of the "Nanie and the "Rhapsodie" of Brahms.

The Verdi "Te Deum" was the largest number on the program, and the longest. Sung in Latin as was indisputably appropriate, it would have been helpful to many of the audience to have had the Latin text printed at length on the program. As it was, the audience could catch the musical tones but could only partly catch the Latin text, and to the real enjoyment and appreciation of any choral work, it is absolutely essential that the words as well as the music be intelligible. It must, however, be regarded as a good performance because the intonation was good, the dynamic effects impressive and appropriate, the unanimity and unity in attack and throughout the performance, splendid, and the response to the conductor, immediate. It was a fine work, and musically was a mighty good performance.

"Tune True To Pitch"

Eddy put himself in immediate and hearty rapport with his audience, by his magnificent delivery of the declamatory "Monologue of Boris Godounoff," called commonly the "Czar's Song," from Moussorgsky's opera. It was absolutely faultless—every tone was sung true to pitch and with a voice clear and resonant as a bell, and with a distinctness of verbal utterance that could be easily understood in every part of the large theatre. It was one of the best performance of this or any other season.

Maybelle Berretta Marston, contralto, sang her alto solo in the "Rhapsodie" correctly and with a fluent delivery, and her textual enunciation was intelligible. There was, however, to the writer, something lacking in her voice although the general effect of her work was fair. Her singing of the "People Victorious" from Parker's "Hora Novissima" was better, but there was the same lack of warmth, of fire, of what the French term "elan," and her performance was not satisfying.

Reading Singers Please

Miss Laura M. Snyder, a Reading soprano, sang her solo in the Mascagni work smoothly, clearly, and sweetly, and deserves praise; and the same must be said of the singing of Daniel W. Weidner, bass, also a Reading singer. He sang his small but important part clearly, in good voice, and appropriately. The male chorus in the "Rhapsodoie" sang well, with good intonation, distinctly, and effectively.

The performance by the orchestra of the "Finlandia" of Sibelius, was emphatically first class. It is a work that can be easily muddled in performance, and it is one that requires cleanness and clearness in every section of the orchestra or the result will be a musical nightmare. The performance of the members of the Philadelphia orchestra, under Norden, delighted and impressed the audience, the largest yet seen at a choral society concert in recent years.

The work of the chorus gave substantial evidence of the ability of its director, and of his painstaking care in preparation during rehearsals.

Society. It was so good in every respect that even the hypercritical reviewer would be at a loss to find a reasonable basis of complaint. The singing of the 'Coronation Music' from Mussorgsky's **Boris Godunoff** (sic) thrilled the audience because the imposing volume of tone of combined orchestra and voices, themselves stirred by the grandeur of the music and text, was overwhelming, and made a direct appeal to the mind and the feelings. The work of the soloist in this number, Nelson Eddy, was worthy of emphatic praise. His voice is a splendid resonant baritone, pure in quality, uniform throughout its ample register, and it was used with an ease and freedom from offensive mannerism that was decidedly pleasing... Eddy put himself in immediate and hearty rapport with his audience, by his magnificent delivery of the declamatory Monologue of **Boris Godunoff**, called commonly the Czar's Song... It was absolutely faultless--every tone was sung true to pitch and with a voice clear and resonant as a bell, and with a distinctness of verbal utterance that could be easily understood in every part of the large theatre. It was one of the best performances of this or any other season... Maybelle Berretta Marston, contralto, sang her alto solo in the 'Rhapsodic' correctly and with a fluent delivery, and her textual enunciation was intelligible. There was, however, to the writer, something lacking in her voice although the general effect of her work was fair. Her singing of the 'People Victorious' from Parker's **Hora Novissima** was better, but there was the same lack of warmth, of fire, of what the French term 'élan,' and her performance was not satisfying." *Reading Eagle,* December 7: "Mr. Eddy's finely developed voice was first heard in the monologue number... The dramatic style in which he sang the number thrilled the audience. His apparent ease of manner in singing and the fact that his voice at all times was under control captivated his hearers. This was also typical of Mrs. Marston's singing. Mrs. Marston has a richly toned voice and of a quality not often noted in contraltos. Her singing of the aria from **Hora Novissima** won the admiration of everyone present... Mr. Eddy [also] did excellent work in the coronation scene."

December 8, 1927: Nelson sang Marcello in **La Boheme** at the Met. *Inquirer,* December 12, 1927: "It may safely be said that the Civic Opera Company's performance of **La Boheme** last Thursday night at the Metropolitan more successfully captures the essential atmosphere of the opera than the Metropolitan Opera Company's recent presentation of the same work in the Academy... The Marcello of Nelson Eddy, also, was far more effective than the Marcello of Giuseppe Danise with the Metropolitan." *Musical America:* "The large audience responded warmly to the vocal charm and irresistible comedy touches which marked the role of Nelson Eddy as Marcello, Pauline Lawn as Musetta. Both artists have not only a youthful beauty of face and voice, but a vibrant magnetism that wins the sympathies of the audience." [Note: Irene Williams sang the role of Mimi.]

December 9, 1927 clipping: "Second double bill in two weeks of the Philadelphia Civic Opera Company, **Secret of Suzanne,** by Wolf-Ferrari, and **Cavalleria Rusticana.**" *Public Ledger:* "The delightful **Secret of Suzanne**, by Wolf-Ferrari, exceedingly well done, and the best rendition of **Cavalleria Rusticana** the company has given in the nearly five seasons of its existence.... **Suzanne** was ideally cast, the three principals being Irene Williams as the Countess Suzanne, Nelson Eddy as Count Gil, and Joseph Craig Fox as Sante, the deaf and dumb servant. All of these fitted perfectly into their respective roles in every respect, vocally, in stage appearance, in enunciation and in dramatic action... Both Miss Williams and Mr. Eddy were perfect in their diction, very fine in the serious musical numbers of the opera and absolutely convincing in their comedy delineation. The rage of the Count was splendidly done by Mr. Eddy, and Miss Williams was no whit behind his standard of performance in action and in voice." *Daily News:* "Nelson Eddy played the husband. He has a scintillating baritone which Philadelphians enjoy. He seldom has difficulty in 'pulling down the house.' Last night was no exception. And too, when he began to break the dishes, throw bric-a-brac, hurl books to the wall, the audience was convulsed." *Inquirer:* "Irene Williams and Nelson Eddy were agreeable and ingratiating as the only audible members of the triangular cast, completed with comedy competence by Joseph Craig Fox as the tongue—tied servant. Miss Williams' voice, while not powerful, is of pleasing quality, and Mr. Eddy's enunciation was conspicuously clear, while his voice was fine and flexible." *Bulletin:* "Mr. Eddy also sang admirably, the music requiring nothing to which his rich baritone is not equal, and he put much spirit into his impersonation of Count Gil."

December 15, 1927: Another **La Boheme** at the Met. *Public Ledger,* December 16, 1927: "The opera had

Two Operas Are Given Here

Civic Offers Fine "Love of Three Kings"; Philadelphia Company Presents "Butterfly"

By SAMUEL L. LACIAR

Italo Montemezzi's operatic masterpiece, "The Love of Three Kings," was presented last evening at the Metropolitan Opera House by the Philadelphia Civic Opera Company. It is one of the most opulent scores that has been given to the world by an Italian composer and one of the relatively few ones which shows unmistakeable signs of becoming a member of the permanent repertoire; it is also one of the most difficult operas on the stage today.

In a good many ways Montemezzi has followed the Wagnerian precedent by placing most of the melody in the orchestra, using it to develop the emotional elements of the various situations and creating an orchestration at times almost overpowering in its volume.

Considering the enormous difficulty of the opera, last evening's performance was exceedingly good. The dramatic and pathetic role of Archibaldo, the aged blind king, was taken by Adamo Didur, who created the role in the United States, and who probably has sung it more frequently than any other basso, as well as having set the standard interpretation, at least in this country. Mr. Didur's work last evening was very fine.

Helen Stanley the Heroine

Helen Stanley took the role of Fiora, singing it very well and acting accordingly. She did her best vocal work in the duets with the other chief characters, notably with Manfredo in the second act and with Avito in the first and the second. Her best dramatic work was in the scene with Archibaldo in the second.

Paul Althouse was the Avito, and sang very well throughout, but especially so in the great tenor vocal number of the last act.

The singing honors of the performance, however, were carried off by Nelson Eddy as Manfredo, his splendid voice showing to excellent advantage in the long solo at the beginning of the second act, one of the most beautiful and melodious numbers of the opera.

The smaller roles of Ancella and Flaminio were admirably taken by Ruth Cornett and Albert Mahler, respectively.

The Civic Opera chorus covered itself with glory in the unaccompanied dirge over the casket of Fiora in the last act—the only place in the opera requiring a chorus. Some of the details of the stage settings, however, left something to be desired, although excellent in the final act. Alexander Smallens conducted a spirited performance, but sometimes let his orchestral enthusiasm get the better of his sense of balance.

Debut Features "Butterfly"

Takane Nambu, formerly a member of the Japanese Imperial Theatre at Tokio, made her Philadelphi debut last evening with the Phil phia Grand Opera Company Academy of Music as C pathetic heroine of " dama Butterfly."

The diminu the audien

PHILADELPHIA CIVIC OPERA STARS TO BE HEARD THIS WEEK

Above is Helen Stanley, who will sing the role of Fiora in "L'Amore dei Tre Re," to be presented at the Metropolitan Opera House by the Philadelphia Civic Opera next Thursday evening. At the right is Nelson Eddy, who sings the part of Manfredo on the same programme.

NELSON EDDY, baritone, with the Philadelphia Civic Opera Company, who will give a recital in the Academy of Music foyer, Monday evening

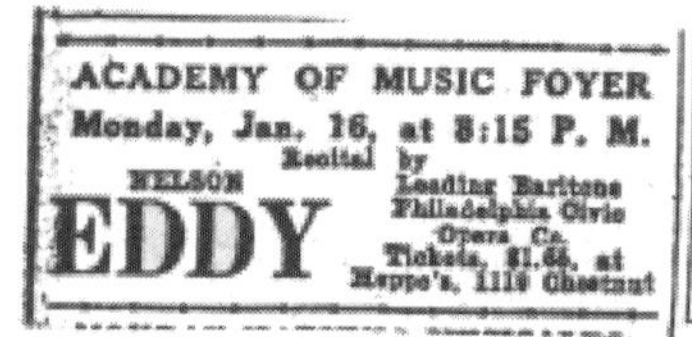

ACADEMY OF MUSIC FOYER
Monday, Jan. 16, at 8:15 P. M.
Recital by
NELSON
EDDY
Leading Baritone
Philadelphia Civic
Opera Co.
Tickets, $1.65, at
Heppe's, 1119 Chestnut

NELSON EDDY GIVES CHARMING RECITAL

Youthful Baritone Scores Success in Academy Foyer

Nelson Eddy, one of the most brilliant of the younger baritones of this city and who has done much excellent operatic work with the Philadelphia Civic Opera Company, gave a recital in the foyer of the Academy of Music last evening before an audience which virtually filled the auditorium and received the young singer with enthusiasm.

Mr. Eddy's splendid voice was shown to excellent advantage. The recital began with Francis Hopkinson's "Ode from the Poems of Ossian," which was especially well sung, followed by a French group—"Les Hiboux" and "L'Attente" by Laparra and the aria "Gloire a Vanna" from Fevrier's opera "Monna Vanna." As an encore Mr. Eddy sang the "Song to the Evening Star," from "Tannhauser," in English.

He did fine work in the German lieder which came next. There was "Der Traum" of Rubinstein, "Der Schwann" by Grieg and the expressive "Allerseelen" of Richard Strauss, with the same composer's "Zugeignung" as an encore. After a vivid rendition of the monologue of Boris from Moussorgsky's "Boris Godounoff," Mr. Eddy closed his regular program with four songs in English by Campbell-Tipton, Golde, Bax and Keel.

NELSON EDDY IN RECITAL

Baritone Cordially Received in Academy of Music Foyer

Nelson Eddy, who for the past two or three seasons has been making a name for himself in leading roles with the Civic Opera Company, appeared in recital last evening, in the Academy of Music Foyer, and proved that he is capable of holding his own and keeping an audience thoroughly interested without stage surroundings or the aid of operatic costume and action. Assisted ably and sympathetically by Sherwood Johnson as accompanist, at every point of his varied and interesting program, Mr. Eddy at once ingratiated himself with his large and receptive audience.

His voice retaining all of the oft-mentioned "luscious" quality, Mr. Eddy is acquiring the style and authority of a real artist, putting more virility into his tones and singing with added ease and pliancy and with more skill in modulation and phrasing. There is a firmer "grip" on his higher tones and more freedom than last season, although the middle and lower ones are by far the best and it is these that are used with the most assurance and expression.

Beginning with Ode from Ossian's Poems, by the old-time Francis Hopkinson, Mr. Eddy next sang a group of two songs in French, by Lappara, and, with a demonstration of his flair for operatic music, "Gloire a' Vanna," from Fevrier's "Monna Vanna." After this, as an encore, was given, with much smoothness and rich beauty of well-sustained tone, the Largo of Handel. Then came a group of three songs, by Rubinstein, Grieg and Richard Strauss, with another by Strauss and "Song to the Evening Star," from "Tannhauser," Wagner—sung in English with considerable poise and depth of feeling—as encores. "I Have Achieved the Highest," the monologue of Boris from Moussorgsky's opera, the next number, was well done, but the great Russian music is not yet entirely within the young singer's power and scope. There was a Rachmaninoff song as an encore after this, and, finally, an attractive group in English by Campbell-Tipton, Golde, Bax and Keel.

attracted an audience that almost filled the big opera house, and the performance was marked by a warmth and friendliness... that occasioned frequent and prolonged applause. Alexander Smallens, who directed, moved a dynamic baton... Nelson Eddy sang a more than satisfactory Marcello." *Bulletin:* "Eddy, whose baritone voice has earned him so much praise during the past few years, continues to stand out as one of' the most capable handlers of operatic comedy on an stage, and his subtle treatment given to the burlesque minuet caused more than one to chuckle." *Inquirer:* **"**Nelson Eddy made an excellent Marcello -- and was made up to look like Shakespeare.**"** *Daily News:* **"**Nelson Eddy, as Marcello, was deserving of better than passing mention. He sang the role of the starving artist with a warmth of feeling." *Record:* "Nelson Eddy was a capital Marcello."

January 5, 1928, clipping: "Nelson sings tonight at 9, over WIP, for Newton Coal Serenaders, with an orchestra of selected stars from the Philadelphia Orchestra. This is a new series. The program includes: 'In questa tomba' by Beethoven, 'Ich Liebe Dich' by Grieg, 'The Eriking' by Schubert and 'All Souls' Day' by Strauss."

January 12, 1928. Nelson sang in **The Love of Three Kings** performed at the Met by the Philadelphia Civic Opera Company. *Public Ledger,* January 13, 1928: "It is one of the most opulent scores that has been given to the world by an Italian composer... it is also one of the most difficult operas on the stage today... The singing honors of the performance, however, were carried off by Nelson Eddy as Manfredo, his splendid voice showing to excellent advantage in the long solo at the beginning of the second act, one of the most beautiful and melodious numbers of the opera." *Bulletin:* "Nelson Eddy... distinguished himself in the battlement scene with his singing of 'suonata e 1'ora,' one of the few melodious vocal arias of the great tragedy. Mr. Eddy was not recognized by even his close friends when he made a dashing entrance last night. A black wig and some skillful work on the part of a makeup artist seemed to transform him completely." [Note: Helen Stanley co-starred.] *Record:* "A thoroughly convincing Manfredo, dramatically true and vocally beautiful, by Nelson Eddy." *Inquirer:* "Nelson Eddy, as the mere husband, cut a far more romantic figure and sang far more admirably than did Paul Althouse as Avito. Mr. Eddy's make-up effected so complete a transformation, with a synthetic nose and dark wig, that he became a new personality, and sang with beauty and line and freedom of style." *Musical America,* January 28, 1928: "Nelson Eddy, who was exceptionally successful in getting under the surface of his role, appeared as Manfredo." *Musical Courier,* January 26. 1928: "Nelson Eddy, as Manfredo, made a lasting impression with the use of his beautifully toned, smooth baritone, proving himself admirably suited to the part, and arousing a keen interest as to his future career in the music world."

January 13, 1928, Evening *Ledger:* "Nelson Eddy will give a recital in the Academy of Music foyer, Monday, January 16, 1928." *Public Ledger:* January 17, 1928: "Nelson Eddy, one of the most brilliant of the younger baritones of this city and who has done much excellent work with the Philadelphia Civic Opera Company, gave a recital... before an audience which virtually filled the auditorium and received the young singer with enthusiasm. Mr. Eddy's splendid voice was shown to excellent advantage." [NOTE: for the program, see opposite page.] *Bulletin:* "Nelson Eddy, who for the past two or three seasons has been making a name for himself in leading roles with the Civic Opera Company, appeared in recital last evening... and proved that he is capable of holding his own and keeping an audience thoroughly interested without stage surroundings or the aid of operatic costume and action. Assisted ably and sympathetically by Sherwood Johnson as accompanist, at every point of his varied and interesting program, Mr. Eddy at once ingratiated himself with his large and receptive audience. His voice retaining all of the oft-mentioned 'luscious' quality, Mr. Eddy is acquiring the style and authority of a real artist, putting more virility into his tones and singing with added ease and pliancy and with more skill in modulation and phrasing. There is a firmer 'grip' on his higher tones and more freedom than last season, although the middle and lower ones are by far the best and it is these that are used with the most assurance and expression." *Inquirer:* "Nelson Eddy... offered a varied programme carefully chosen and intended to display the full powers of his rich and resonant voice. The result was very pleasing to the audience, which occupied every available seat in the small auditorium. Of particular note was Mr. Eddy's singing, as an encore, the 'Evening Star' from Wagner's **Tannhäuser.** He sang this difficult number with great ease and, consequently, was enabled to put into it a warmth of feeling which made it a lovely evening." *Daily News:* "Rich and vibrant was the voice of Nelson Eddy... This pleasing vocalist of the Philadelphia Civic Opera Company used care in the choosing of his program, offering only those numbers which he was able to render with

PUBLIC LEDGER—P

NOTED PHILADELPHIA VOCA

LEDGER SUNDAY CONCERTS BEGIN

Nelson Eddy and Helen Buchanan Hitner, With Arcadia Orchestra, Open Series

ON AIR OVER STATION WLIT

Beginning today, Station WLIT will broadcast a series of Sunday afternoon concerts, sponsored by the PUBLIC LEDGER, morning and evening.

Today's initial offering will be presented by two outstanding local vocalists, Nelson Eddy, baritone of the famous Philadelphia Civic Opera Company, and Helen Buchanan Hitner, soprano. The Arcadia Concert Orchestra will present a special orchestral program and will play at each of the succeeding concerts, when different guest artists will be presented.

The programs will begin at 2 o'clock each Sunday.

The make-up of the programs will be entirely in keeping with the dignity of the day and will be arranged to present the best in music without emphasizing the ultra-classical element, though such selections will, of course, be included.

This afternoon Mr. Eddy's solo numbers will be the aria, "C'est ici, le berceau de notre liberte," from "Patrie," by Paladilhe; the "Pilgrim's Song," by Tschaikowsky; the old Irish song, "Believe Me if All Those Endearing Young Charms," and "Tomorrow," by Keel.

Miss Hitner will present as solos "Erin Traum," by Grieg; the "Gi-rometta," of Sibella; Leoni's "The Birth of Morn," and the great soprano aria, "Voi la sapete," from "Cavalleria Rusticana," by Mascagni.

Miss Hitner and Mr. Eddy will be heard in two duets, selections from "Samson and Delila," by Saint-Saens, and "O Tell Me, Beloved," from "The Secret of Suzanne," by Wolf-Ferrari.

The radio audience will also be treated today to two cello solos by Peter Wenner, of this city, who will play two of his own compositions, "Elegie" and "Gavotte No. 1."

IN FIRST PUBLIC LEDGER CONCERT

Helen Buchanan Hitner, Philadelphia soprano, and Nelson Eddy, baritone of the Philadelphia Opera Company, who will be heard this afternoon during the first Public Ledger Concert Period over Station WLIT at 2 o'clock. The Arcadia Concert Orchestra will present a musical program

The complete program for this afternoon follows:

Overture, "Egmont" .... Beethoven
Baritone aria, "C'est ici, le berceau de notre liberte," from "Patrie," Paladilhe
Waltz, "A Summer Evening" ... Waldteufel
Soprano Soli—
(a) "Ein Traum" .... Grieg
(b) "Girometta" .... Sibella
(c) "The Birth of Morn" .... Leoni
"Rondo Capriccioso" .... Mendelssohn
Cello Solos by Peter Wenner
(a) "Elegie" .... Wenner
(b) "Gavotte No. 1" .... Wenner
Duet
Selection from "Samson and Dalila," Saint-Saens
Baritone Soli—
(a) "Pilgrim's Song" .... Tschaikowsky
(b) "Believe Me, If All Those Endearing Young Charms" .. Irish Air
(c) "Tomorrow." .... Keel
"Hungarian Rhapsodie No. 6" .... Liszt
Soprano aria, "Voi lo sapete," from "Cavalleria Rusticana" ..... Mascagni
"Symphonette Spirituelle," Green-Warren-Lange
Duet, "O, Tell Me Beloved," from "Secret of Suzanne" ..... Wolf-Ferrari
Selection from "The Red Mill" .... Herbert

superior ability. His first rendition, that of the 'Ode from Ossian's Poems,' was perhaps, the best of the evening. Sherwood Anderson gave a capable accompaniment." *Musical America,* February 1, 1928: "Nelson Eddy's concert in the Academy Foyer January 16 revealed the varied art of this brilliant young baritone of the Civic Opera Company. He was dramatic in arias from Fevier's **Monna Vanna** and Mussorgsky's **Boris Godunov,** and gave lyric vocality to Strauss and other lieder." *Musical Courier,* February 2, 1928: "Nelson Eddy... created an excellent impression."

January 26, 1928: Nelson sang in **Lohengrin** at the Met, in English. "Mr. Eddy gave a well executed performance of the Herald, a difficult part in itself, inasmuch as he is a sort of a master of ceremonies through all the opera." *Public Ledger:* "Nelson Eddy was remarkably efficient in vocalization and enunciation as the Herald." *Daily News:* "Popular Nelson Eddy sang The King's Herald." *Record:* "Some of the best singing of the evening was done by Nelson Eddy, who gave new but not undue importance to the part of the Herald. His diction is quite the clearest in this organization." *Musical Courier,* February 2, 1928: "Nelson Eddy, as the King's Herald, was excellent, as he has been in whatever role he has essayed... A capacity audience recalled the artists again and again, with spontaneous enthusiasm."

Amonasro in Aida *was one of Nelson's most popular roles. It was his first operatic part and ironically would also be his last.*

February 1, 1928: Nelson starred in **The Secret of Suzanne** at the Matinee Musical Club. *Evening Bulletin:* "Nelson Eddy gave a clever interpretation of the role of Count Gil, creating considerable mirth with his acting."

February 5, 1928: Nelson broadcast with the Acadia Concert Orchestra, sponsored by the *Public Ledger,* broadcast over WLJT, 2 pm.

February 9, 1928: Nelson sang in **Madama Butterfly** at the Met. Helen Stanley was his co-star. *Bulletin:* "Nelson Eddy... sang the role of the consul with that same ease and distinct articulation that have distinguished his work in the past." *Public Ledger:* "Mr. Eddy possesses a voice of much charm." *Inquirer:* "Nelson Eddy, again doing splendid work, vocally and dramatically, as the kindly consul. While both Mr. Eddy and Mr. Davies (Pinkerton) used English with ease and authority in the first-act toast, it was apparently Scotch that they used with equal ease and authority as the beverage. At least it was a very realistic Scotch bottle, and the enforcement boys might have found it of interest to sniff the contents of the glasses that Mr. Davies quaffed with gusto and Mr. Eddy sampled somewhat more gingerly, perhaps suspicious of the champagne glasses used." *Record:* "Nelson Eddy's tones were full and clear, and his diction was about impeccable." *Musical Courier,* "Nelson Eddy, as Sharpless, was excellent in every particular. Whenever he appears, in any role, his popularity is immediately evident, and this gave ample scope for his splendid vocal and dramatic talents. Especially noteworthy were his acting and singing in the difficult 'letter scene.'" *Musical America:* "Nelson Eddy was a Sharpless who looked the part and enhanced the charm of his clear baritone equipment with diction good enough to be favorably comparable with that of George Meader in Mr. Gatti's troupe."

February 17, 1928: Nelson sang in **Aida** at the Met with the Philadelphia Civic Opera Company. *Public Ledger,* February 18, 1928: "The feature of last evening's performance of **Aida** by the Civic Opera Company was the superb performance of the title role both vocally and dramatically by Florence Austral, who made her first appearance in opera in this city, although she has been heard before as a concert singer... The Amonasro of Nelson Eddy was also very good and both in the closing scene of the second act and in the third (the Nile scene) he sang with fine vocalization and perfect enunciation and acted exceedingly well. On the other hand, the Radames of Edward Papania, a tenor who made his debut here in last evening's performance, was disappointing..." *Inquirer:* "Mr. Nelson Eddy's Amonasro was another fine piece of work. His voice easily compassed the music and his stage presence was admirable; he has grown greatly in ease and technical skill of late." *Bulletin:* "Of course, Nelson Eddy was the Amonasro--a part with which he is quite familiar, having sung it no less than four times with this company, and he seems to improve with every performance." *Musical America,* February 24: "Nelson Eddy's Amonasro was of notably high quality, vocally and histrionically." *Record:* "Nelson Eddy grasped with apparent ease the conspicuous but not especially numerous opportunities of the part of Amonasro."

February 19, 1928, clipping: "Nelson Eddy and Helen Buchanan Hitner sing on WLJT."

February 23, 1928, clipping: "Nelson Eddy sings on WIP, and Newton Coal Serenaders sings 'Famous Operatic Overtures and Melodies' tonight."

March 9, 1928, *Record:* "Frankford Symphony Orchestra gave its second concert of the season last night in the auditorium of Frankford High School... Nelson Eddy was soloist. Mr. Eddy was in excellent voice and sang with a clear depth and fidelity to tone that merited the applause and encores received. In the Toreador's Song, from Bizet's **Carmen,** the orchestra shifted key for a few measures, but even in spite of this his voice carried on. His voice retains its fullness of volume and tone beauty throughout the entire range, even up into the tenor sections of the scale.... Sherwood Johnson accompanied Mr. Eddy, first on the organ, and then on the piano." *Musical America,* March 24: "Nelson Eddy, a rising young baritone of the Civic Opera Company, tonally dramatized his operatic arias and sang an English group with the intelligence and intelligibility for which he has become noted." [Note: Nelson sang Handel's "Largo" with organ accompaniment, and "Drink to Me Only with Thine Eyes" as an encore. Then songs in English: "Captain Stratton's Fancy," "Trade Winds," and "Tally-Ho." He also sang "La Maison Grise" by Messager.] *Frankford Gazette:* "Nelson Eddy was the soloist, a baritone whose operatic experiences of a few years have decisively tested his mettle and found it not wanting either in vocal beauty or dramatic efficiency. Indeed, as a singer, his big (and broad) voice has notably matured to a degree that ranks him among the not nearly too many vocalists whose tonality satisfyingly bridges the gap between bass and tenor. To Mr. Eddy nature has given a fortune in voice and a generous competency in dramatic action; moreover, she has bestowed, if not an essential, at least an extremely advantageous gift -- namely a fine physique for the housing of a fair personality."

March 13, 1928: Nelson was soloist for the Society for Contemporary Music concert, at the Academy of Music foyer. *Ledger,* March 14, 1928: "It lasted an hour and a half and before it was over even the most hardened modernist had received sufficient to last until the next concert, although no casualties were reported... The concert was admirably performed, Nelson Eddy doing the Blitzstein and the Whitehorne vocal works most artistically." *Evening Bulletin:* "'The Society for Contemporary Music,' said a member of the audience as he left the Academy of Music Foyer last night, 'is at least performing one useful service by increasing our respect for Bach.' Nelson Eddy, baritone, of the Civic Opera Company and Marc Blitzstein, pianist, next presented 'Two Coon Shouts' by Blitzstein. All of Eddy's vocal skill was insufficient to make the songs come to life. This singer, who has charmed so many audiences, might have been mistaken for a talented 'old clothes' man." *Daily News:* "The feature of the evening was 'The Grim Troubadour,' by Emerson Whithorne, which was played publicly for the first time. Nelson Eddy sang the three songs... Blitzstein also played his 'Two Coon Shouts,' which was delightfully rendered by Eddy. Here he was well-nigh perfect. His rich voice boomed at the

NELSON EDDY ON AIR IN LEDGER CONCERT

Shares Honors With Elizabeth Harrison, Soprano, in Today's Program Over Station WLIT

ARCADIA ORCHESTRA PLAYS

Nelson Eddy, baritone, and Elizabeth Harrison, soprano, both of this city and both of whom need no introduction to Philadelphia radio fans and music lovers generally, will present the vocal portion of today's Sunday afternoon concert, at 2 o'clock over Station WLIT.

This is the sixteenth concert of a series sponsored by the PUBLIC LEDGER, published morning, evening and Sunday, the orchestral portions of each concert being presented by the Arcadia Concert Orchestra, Feri Sarkozi, conductor, and the vocal programs being presented each Sunday by different vocalists.

Mr. Eddy will sing as his first number "The Legend of the Brush," from "The Juggler of Notre Dame," by Massenet, and, among other numbers, the "Cabal Cotta Zingaresca Seismit," of Doda, and the popular "Captain Stratton's Fancy," by Deems Taylor. He will sing a total of six solos.

Miss Harrison will present as her first number, "Pleurez, Pleurez, mes Yeux," from "Le Cid," by Massenet, and among other numbers Szulc's "Claire de Lune." She will sing six solos in all.

Mr. Eddy and Miss Harrison will also be heard in the following duets, "Pronta io son," from Donizetti's "Don Pasquale"; "Answer," by Terry; "Swans," by Kramer, and "Delight," by Luckstone. Miss Alice Wightman, pianist, will be the accompanist for the vocalists throughout the concert.

Feri Sarkozi will play the following cymbalum solos: "Hungarian Airs," by Danko, and "Negro Spiritual," by Burleigh. The orchestra will present, among other numbers, "Selections from the Tales of Hoffmann," by Offenbach, and Saint-Saens' "Danse Bacchanale."

The detailed program follows:

Overture, "Ruy Blas" .... Mendelssohn
Orchestra
"Pleurez, Pleurez, Mes Yeux" ("Le Cid") .... Massenet
Elizabeth Harrison, soprano
"Valse de Concert" ("Magic of Love") .... Venis
Orchestra
"Legend of the Brush" ("The Juggler of Notre Dame") .... Massenet
Nelson Eddy, baritone
"Entr'acte Gavottee" .... Gillet
Orchestra
"Clare de Lune" .... Szulc
"Chanson Norwegienne" .... Foudrain
Elizabeth Harrison, soprano
Hungarian Airs .... Danko
Negro Spiritual .... Burleigh
Cymbalum soli, Feri Sarkozi
"Cabal Cotta Zingaresca Seismit" .... Doda
"La Maison Grise" .... Messager
"Liebesfeier" .... Weingartner
Nelson Eddy, baritone
Selections from "Tales of Hoffman" .... Offenbach
Orchestra
Duet—"Pronta io son" ("Don Pasquale") .... Donizetti
Elizabeth Harrison, soprano
Nelson Eddy, baritone
"Adoration" .... Borowsky
Orchestra
"Answer" .... Terry
"Swans" .... Kramer
"Delight" .... Luckstone
Elizabeth Harrison, soprano
"Scherzo—Fandango" .... Marquara
Orchestra
"Serenade" .... Carpenter
"Captaine Stratton's Fancy" .... Deems Taylor
Nelson Eddy, baritone
"A Tear" .... Moussorgsky
Orchestra
"Danse Bacchanale" .... Saint-Saens
Orchestra

Concert Stars

Nelson Eddy, Philadelphia operatic baritone, and Elizabeth Harrison, concert soprano, also of this city, will present the vocal portion of the Sunday afternoon concert today over Station WLIT, beginning at 2 o'clock. This concert, the sixteenth of a series sponsored by the Public Ledger, published morning, evening and Sunday, will also feature the Arcadia Concert Orchestra, with Feri Sarkozi, cymbalum player, as instrumental soloist. The concert lasts until 4 o'clock

Public Ledger I

SUNDAY

BASEBALL SCORES

7:00—WFI, WJZ.
7:25—WEAF.

TIME SIGNALS

10:55—KDKA, WGY, WRC.

CORRECT TIME ANNOUNCE

7:00—WJZ.
8:00—WCAU.
9:45—WEAF, WFI, WRC, WGY.
10:00—WJZ, KDKA, WBZ.
11:00—WCAU.

Local Broadcasts

2:00—P. M.—WLIT: PUBLIC LEDGER Sunday concert: Arcadia Concert Orchestra; Elizabeth Harrison, soprano; Nelson Eddy, baritone; Alice Wightman, pianist.
WFAN: Herbert's Orchestra from WMCA.
2:30—WOO: Bethany Sunday school musical services.
3:00—WCAU (WOR chain): Symphonic hour; United Symphony Orchestra; Victor Bay, violinist.
3:30—WFAN: Program from WMCA.
4:00—WCAU (WOR chain): Cathedral hour.
WLIT: Lit Brothers' Chorus, Henry Hotz, director; Alice Wightman, pianist.
6:00—WOO: Organ recital, by Rollo Maitland.
WFI (WEAF chain): Stetson Parade with the Weymouth Post, American Legion Band, "Gold Rush of '49."
WFAN: Program from WMCA.
6:15—WCAU: Golden Dragon Concert Orchestra.
6:30—WCAU: Pabl J. Devitt Orchestra.
7:00—WFAN: McAlpin Orchestra.
WCAU: To be announced.
7:05—WFI (WEAF chain): Hans Barth, pianist.
7:30—WCAU: One Hour [illegible]

adio Timetable

MAY 20

Features

2:00—WLIT: Public Ledger Sunday concert; Arcadia Concert Orchestra; Elizabeth Harrison, soprano; Nelson Eddy, baritone.
3:00—WCAU, WOR: Symphonic Hour; Victor Bay, violinist.
3:30—WJZ: Music of the Masters; Devora Nadworney, contralto; Mathilde Harding, pianist.
4:00—WLIT: Lit Brothers Chorus; Henry Hotz, director.
6:00—WFI, WEAF: Stetson Parade, with the Weymouth Post (American Legion) Band; "Gold Rush of '49."
WOO: Organ recital by Rollo Maitland.
6:30—WJZ: Cook's travelogue; "In the British Isles."
7:05—WFI, WEAF: Hans Barth, pianist.
9:00—WCAU, WOR: Dan Voorhees Concert Orchestra.
9:15—WFI: Pipe organ recital by David C. Souder.
WEAF: Atwater Kent Hour; William Simmons, baritone.
9:30—WCAU, WOR: La Palina Casino program.
9:45—WFI, WEAF: Biblical drama, "Diana of the Ephesians."
WJZ: High Spots of Melody.
10:15—WCAU, WOR: United Military Band.

Pub. Ledger 5-20-28

audience. They liked it, too." *Inquirer:* "Mr. Eddy sang as though he imagined himself on the stage of the Metropolitan, the result being that only a lightning calculator could have counted all the echoes that submerged his usually excellent enunciation. Mr. Blitzstein pounded the piano in a way that suggested the desirability of an S.P.C.A. for the protection of defenseless pianos." *Musical America,* March 31, 1928: "Nelson Eddy...did as well by them as might be."

March 16, 1928: Erich Korngold's **Der Ring des Polykrates** and **I Pagliacci** were performed at the Met. Nelson was Silvio. *Ledger,* March 17, 1928*:* "Mr. Eddy's popularity with Civic Opera Company audiences was strikingly shown when, after not appearing with the three principals at the first few curtain calls at the close of the first act, he came out with the others and was most enthusiastically received." *Bulletin:* "He was truly a handsome Silvio who sang well... Six curtain calls were taken by the clown and Nedda, when another demonstration of appreciation was given Nelson Eddy. Several minutes elapsed before the applause ceased." *Inquirer:* "Mr. Eddy's Silvio won instant and deserved appreciation." *Daily News:* "Nelson Eddy, the now-worshiped baritone, sang the ill-fated Silvio with feeling that is seldom equaled." *Musical America:* "Nelson Eddy took the part of Silvio as well as he has the other numerous roles in which he has appeared. At the close of the opera all of the principals except Eddy appeared before the curtain several times, and when Mr. Eddy did appear, it was quite evident what the audience had been waiting for, as the applause increased very noticeably. Mr. Eddy's excellent work with the Civic Company more than merits his popularity."

March 22, 1928: Nelson sang on WIP radio station. Clipping, *Daily News:* "Nelson Eddy is considered by musical circles of Philadelphia to be destined for a glorious career. Due to his thorough training, both here and abroad, his voice has become one of exquisite tone."

March 23, 1928: Final concert of Society for Contemporary Music; Nelson and Irene Williams sang. *Record:* "The bill opened with an atonal farce with alleged music by the German modernist, Paul Hinemuth, Irene William, Nelson Eddy, Edouard Lippe, Albert Mahler, Sidney Stucliffe, Margaret Scott Oliver and Peggy Oliver. The two last-named did not sing… Nelson Eddy splendid as the husband."

March 24, 1928: Nelson gave a concert at Witherspoon Hall for the benefit of Women's' Medical College Alumnae fund. In the March 26 'Social Wheeze,' *Public Ledger* called Nelson "that fearfully good-looking baritone." *Public Ledger,* March 30, 1928: "Nelson sang yesterday in Hannah Penn House, at Republican Women's Club, at 3:00 tea."

March 29, 1928: In the evening, Nelson sang with the Woman's Club chorus, in **The Highwayman**, a cantata. *Swarthmore News:* "Mr. Eddy was very generous with his encores and was recalled many times by a large and appreciative audience." [Note: Nelson sang "Largo," Rubenstein's "Der Traum," Grieg's "Em Schwan," Weingartner's "Liebesfeier," then later "Evening Star," "Will the Red Sun Never Set?" "Capt. Stratton's Fancy," "Tally Ho" and "Highwayman."] *Chester Times,* March 30: "Nelson Eddy... sang the solo passages of the cantata, and gave two groups of songs. His clear and resonant voice was heard to good advantage."

April 15, 1928, *Public Ledger* society column: "At 2:30 on Thursday [April 19] we'll all be found, beyond a doubt, at the Charlotte Cushman club benefit in the Erlanger Theater. It is one of the things we look forward to every year, and the program for this one is extremely intriguing… Nelson Eddy is going to sing. If no one else were going to do anything at all, we'd go on just that account."

May 8, 1929: Nelson and Ethel Righter Wilson, soprano, sang in the Brahms Festival for the reading Choral Society.

May 11, 1928: Orpheus Club presented their spring concert last night in the Schubert Playhouse. *Wilmington Evening Journal:* "Nelson Eddy… was generously applauded by the audience for his solo numbers. Choosing the 'Largo al Factotum' from the **Barbiere di Siviglia**, by Rossini, as his opening number, Mr. Eddy carried his audience by storm, and was forced to encore with an aria from **Xerxes,** by Handel. He was soloist with the

Season 1928 – 29

Penna News

Musical Season for Penn A. C. Has Sixty-one Noted Artists

GERTRUDE KAPPEL

NELSON EDDY

The subscription lists for the 1928–1929 season of the Penn Athletic Club Musical Association will be opened next month, when 2000 members will be sought for the forthcoming series of seventeen Sunday evening concerts in the Club.

The Association this year is offering an unusual, even a phenomenal opportunity, for its program lists sixty-one artists, many of whom are of international note and who can be heard on a season ticket costing only $15. Heretofore the Association, which is non-profit-making, has been compelled to operate at a deficit and this year may be its last.

The names of those who will appear this winter follow: Feodor Chaliapin, basso; Gitta Gradova, pianist; Lucrezia Bori, soprano; Tito Schipa, tenor; Sophie Braslau, contralto; Richard Crooks, tenor; Vladimir Horowitz, pianist; Andres Segovia, guitarist; Sylvia Lent, violinist; Nelson Eddy, baritone; Gertrude Kappel, soprano; Lawrence Tibbett, baritone; Cornelia Otis Skinner, in her character sketches; The Philadelphia Chamber String Simfonietta; Paul Whiteman and his orchestra of twenty-five; The Revelers, a male quartet, and Newman's Travelogues.

Strollshc

THE coincidence of cinema surrounds an incident concerning Nelson Eddy, of the Philadelphia Civic Opera Company and a Philadelphia matron whose name shall be kept secret.

While abroad Mr. Eddy began practicing one evening—it is the custom of singers to practice—and was interrupted by a voice across the areaway of the hotel. "Bravo!" said the feminine voice, "but that's about all of that we can stand this evening, thank you."

Eddy returned home and visited friends. He met an altogether charming lady. They both talked of Paris and the numerous Americans there this summer.

"Many rowdy parties, too," said Eddy.

"Oh, yes," the matron returned. "Imagine, some American in our hotel insisted on singing late at night. I stopped him."

"I had almost the same experience," said Eddy. "I was practicing and some rowdy American woman shouted across the areaway."

It was at this moment that the matron began to blush and both realized the coincidence. The mutual explanations that followed provided a little chagrin for the principals and some amusement for the rest of those present.

Evening Ledger 9-28-28

club in the next selection, 'The Sacrifice of the Aryan Rose' by Cadman." *Wilmington Morning News:* "Mr. Eddy... immediately won his audience with the quality of his tone and range, and personality."

June 6, 1928, Doylestown *Daily Intelligence:* "To speak technically of Mr. Eddy's superb voice would be to mar the effect of an organ so rare and a personality so charming, that in combination they seem almost beyond praise. He has all those qualities which enter into the making of a really great singer, and to these he adds a simplicity of manner and a genuineness which seldom is met with. The range of his program was sufficiently exacting to bring out true virtuosity, and his rendition of these numbers reveal the full scope of artistry wedded to deep humanism."

September 23, 1928: Nelson sang on WLIT, with Marie Stone Langsont-List, contralto. They performed the duet "Death to Samson" from **Samson et Delilah**. Nelson's solos were, "Is Not His Word Like a Fire" from **Elijah** by Mendelssohn, "Blich'ich Umber" from **Tannhäuser**, another duet, "Break, Divine Light" by Allitsen, and solo Australian Bush songs by William G. James.

September 23, 1928: Nelson sang on the Newton Coal Hour. His guest was Maria Stone.

September 25, 1928: Nelson did a radio broadcast from the Academy, details unknown.

October 2, 1928, *Wilmington Evening Journal:* "Nelson Eddy to broadcast on WDEL tomorrow night at 7, then will give a concert at Wilmington Furniture Company Store."

No date: Nelson on Coal radio show again, sang "Duna" by McGill, "Less than the Dust" by Woodforde-Findenthen; on the second part of the show he sang, "Love Goes a-Riding," by Bridge, "Starry Night" by Densmore, "Drink to Me Only With Thine Eyes" by Jonson.

October 7, 1928: *L'Opinione* had a picture of Nelson as Amonasro, advertising him in opening production.

October 13, 1928: Nelson apparently sang a radio recital, details unknown.

October 18, 1928: **Aida** opened the season at the Academy of Music, the new home of the Civic Opera Company due to the Met being sold. Emily Roosevelt made her Philadelphia debut at this performance. *Bulletin*, October 19, 1928: "The Amonasro of Nelson Eddy again enabled the popular young Philadelphia baritone to display to advantage some of the beautiful tones in his voice, as well as to show his ease and forcefulness as an actor, but it also served to indicate that Mr. Eddy has not all the power and endurance necessary for dramatic roles and that he cannot safely continue to force his tones beyond their natural scope. The high tones last night showed effort and lack of control, in marked contrast to the genuine beauty of those in the middle and lower parts of his really fine voice. Comedy, after all, seems to be Mr. Eddy's forte and the lighter roles his métier. In evidence, his deft and wholly admirable **Gianni Schicchi** in past seasons." *Inquirer:* "Honors of the evening were won by Nelson Eddy for his finely effective and beautifully sung Amonasro. Mr. Eddy continues to grow in ease and artistry. His singing and acting are admirable, and his diction might well be emulated by most operatic artists." *Record:* "Nelson Eddy sang with much tonal beauty as Amonasro whenever he permitted his admirable lyric gifts to overcome a reprehensible tendency to overact the part. Too much has been made, of late years, of the ferocity of Amonasro. It is not necessary to bite the scenery in interpreting the character." *Ledger:* "Nelson Eddy repeated his former successes in the role of Amonasro."

November 2, 1928, *Ledger:* "Richard Strauss' opera, **Ariadne auf Naxos**, had its first American performance in the Academy of Music last night. The performance was the fourth American premiere of German operas given by the Civic Company." Helen Jepson played Echo, in one of her first roles. Nelson was the Wigmaker in the Prologue and Arlecchino in the succeeding opera. *Inquirer:* "Nelson Eddy and Albert Mahler were notably good in the comedy quartette." *Bulletin:* "Nelson Eddy, as the wigmaker, had an opportunity to do some of the comedy work in which he excels and to use his fine baritone voice effectively." *New York Times:* "Among the

PUBLIC LEDGER'S 2D CONCERT HEARD

Program Is Broadcast Over Station WLIT From 2 to 4 in Afternoon

ARCADIA ORCHESTRA AIDS

A two-hour concert which ranged in character from the religious nature of Mendelssohn's oratorio "Elijah" to the gayety of Gruenfeld's "Romance" was presented yesterday by the Arcadia Concert Orchestra and assisting singers as the second of this season's PUBLIC LEDGER radio concerts. The program was broadcast from 2 to 4 o'clock over Station WLIT.

Nelson Eddy, baritone, who appeared in the first and also the last concert in last season's series, and Marie Stone Langston-List, contralto, who has also been heard before in the PUBLIC LEDGER concerts, were yesterday's vocal soloists.

The Arcadia Concert Orchestra, which alternates with the Benjamin Franklin Orchestra in the presentation of the instrumental portion of the program, opened the program with the popular "Overture to William Tell" of Rossini.

Feri Sarkozi, conductor of the orchestra, played two cymbalum solos, Mosart's " Menuetto in E Flat" and Dango's "Hungarian Air."

Duet Is First

Mr. Eddy and Mrs. Langston-List sang as their first number a duet from Saint-Saens' "Samson et Delila" entitled, "Death to Samson." The orchestra then played the beautiful "Valse des Fleurs" of Tschaikowsky, which was followed by Mrs. Langston-List's first solo group.

She sang 'Gleeson's "The Little Hills," Bach's "Ah, Love, But a Day," and "Here Awa', There Awa'," by Gilchrist. The orchestra next played Boldi's "Chanson Bohemienne" and Dvorak's "Slavonic Dance No. 3."

A feature of the concert was the presentation by Nelson Eddy of a group of six "Australian Bush Songs," by William G. James, which he brought here from London for their Philadelphia premiere.

Massenet in Second Group

Mrs. Lanston-List included in her second group Massenet's "Oh! Si Les Fleurs Avaient des Yeux," Wekerlin's "Mignonette" and Saint-Saens' "La Cloche." She and Mr. Eddy sang as a second duet Allitsen's "Break, Divine Light."

The song which Wolfram sings in the prize contest in Wagner's "Tannhauser," "Blick, ich umher," was another solo number sung by Mr. Eddy.

Mrs. Langston-List's third group included three songs in German the "Sapphische Ode" of Brahms, a "Cradle Song," by Hans Hermann, and "Waldeinsamkeit," by Max Reger.

The spirited "Marche Militaire" of Schubert, played by the Arcadia Concert Orchestra, closed the group.

Public Ledger Sept 24

URNAL, WILMINGTON, DEL

NOTED BARITONE ON WDEL TOMORROW

NELSON EDDY

Mr. Eddy, leading baritone of the Philadelphia Civic Opera Co., will broadcast a recital from WDEL tomorrow night at 7 o'clock, and immediately following will give another concert at the Wilmington Furniture Company store, which is celebrating it. 28th anniversary this week.

Mr. Eddy, who was enthusiastically received as soloist with the Orpheus Club last May, needs no introduction t Wilmington audiences. The Philadelphia Civic Opera Company will open their season on October 18 with a performance of Verdi's Opera "Aida." Mr. Eddy will have the leading baritone role of "Amonasro." The public is cordially invited to visit the Wilmington Furniture Co. store each evening this week.

Wilmington Morning Journal Oct 12.

group of four clowns was to be noticed the fine voice of Nelson Eddy, the Arlecchino." *Musical Courier,* November 8, 1928: "Nelson Eddy, a polished baritone, was of marked excellence as Arlecchino."

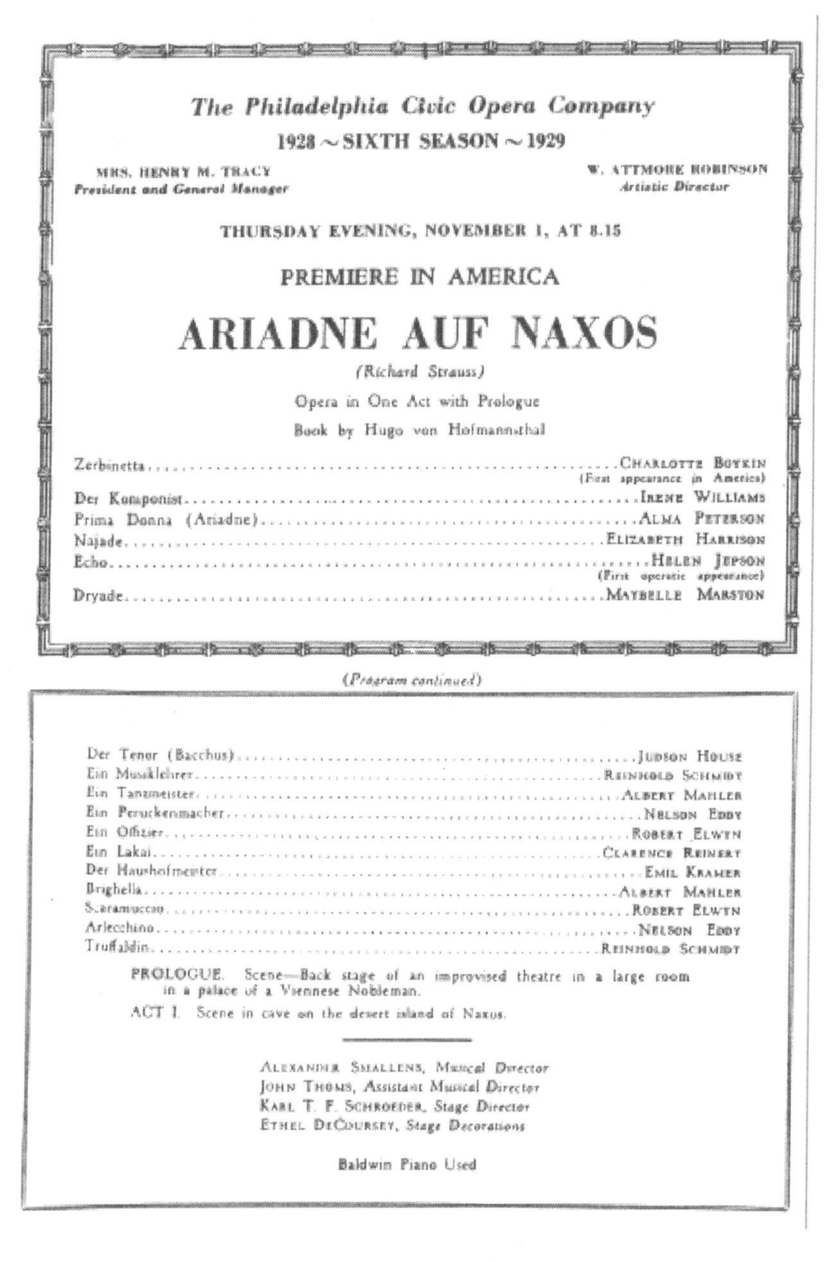

The Philadelphia Civic Opera Company

1928 ~ SIXTH SEASON ~ 1929

MRS. HENRY M. TRACY
President and General Manager

W. ATTMORE ROBINSON
Artistic Director

THURSDAY EVENING, NOVEMBER 1, AT 8.15

PREMIERE IN AMERICA

ARIADNE AUF NAXOS

(Richard Strauss)

Opera in One Act with Prologue

Book by Hugo von Hofmannsthal

Zerbinetta.......Charlotte Boykin
(First appearance in America)
Der Komponist.......Irene Williams
Prima Donna (Ariadne).......Alma Peterson
Najade.......Elizabeth Harrison
Echo.......Helen Jepson
(First operatic appearance)
Dryade.......Maybelle Marston

(Program continued)

Der Tenor (Bacchus).......Judson House
Ein Musiklehrer.......Reinhold Schmidt
Ein Tanzmeister.......Albert Mahler
Ein Peruckenmacher.......Nelson Eddy
Ein Offizier.......Robert Elwyn
Ein Lakai.......Clarence Reinert
Der Haushofmeister.......Emil Kramer
Brighella.......Albert Mahler
Scaramuccio.......Robert Elwyn
Arlecchino.......Nelson Eddy
Truffaldin.......Reinhold Schmidt

PROLOGUE. Scene—Back stage of an improvised theatre in a large room in a palace of a Viennese Nobleman.

ACT I. Scene in cave on the desert island of Naxos.

Alexander Smallens, *Musical Director*
John Thoms, *Assistant Musical Director*
Karl T. F. Schroeder, *Stage Director*
Ethel DeCoursey, *Stage Decorations*

Baldwin Piano Used

November 8, 1928: **La Boheme** at the Academy of Music, with Irene Williams. *Musical Courier:* "Nelson Eddy was at his best in the part of Marcello." *Ledger.* "Of the masculine roles, Nelson Eddy as Marcello and Reinhold Schmidt as Schaunard were the best, both in voice, enunciation and action. Mr. Eddy showed that beautiful enunciation which always characterizes his work and his acting grows better with each performance." *Inquirer:* "Nelson Eddy gives outstanding interest to Marcello, singing splendidly and acting with unflagging zest." *Daily News:* "The popular male vocal star of the year, who has made his personality and ability attractive, Nelson Eddy, created the evening's sensation as Marcello." *Record:* "Nelson Eddy, under vocal and histrionic conditions that suit him admirably, scored deservedly as Marcello." *Bulletin:* 'Nelson Eddy interpreted the part of the painter Marcello with spirit and feeling and his flexible baritone voice is well adapted to the lyric passages... .His singing was richly beautiful." *Musical America:* "Nelson Eddy gave his best performance this season as Marcello."

November 22, 1928, Philadelphia Civic Opera Company did **Die Meistersinger** at the Academy of Music. *Record:* "Good vocalism by Nelson Eddy." *Inquirer:* "Nelson Eddy gave humorous accent to the reading of the rules as Kothner." *Ledger:* "The comic work of Mr. Eddy, as well as his enunciation, being very good, although certain features of his make-up suggested a stage Irishman rather than a Nuremburg Meistersinger." *Bulletin:* "Nelson Eddy's delightful baritone was used to good effect in the part of Kothner whom he made a Falstaffian figure. His very inflection of the line 'Der Sanger Sitzt' (The Singer Sits) was enough to bring sounds of

PHILADELPHIA ATTRACTS THE SPOTLIGHT WITH AN AMERICAN PREMIERE

THE Philadelphia Civic Opera Company's recent production of "Ariadne auf Naxos" represents the second Strauss opera to be introduced to this country via this enterprising organization. ("Feuersnot" had an initial performance a year ago last fall.)

In the top row (left to right) are: Irene Williams who, as Komponist, gave one of the most convincing performances of her career, vocally and histrionically; Conductor Alexander Smallens, to whom chief credit for the general excellence of the production is due; and Alma Peterson, the Ariadne, whom reviewers found admirably suited to her part. In the scene pictured are Judson House, who sang the leading tenor rôle of Bacchus, Nelson Eddy, baritone, and other members of an able supporting cast

merriment from the audience." *Daily News:* "Nelson Eddy, one of the season's popular idols, was singing." *Musical America:* "Nelson Eddy scored decisively as Kothnew." *Musical Courier:* "Of the local artists who took part, Maybelle Marston as Magdalene, Albert Mahler as David and Nelson Eddy as Kothnew, were especially fine."

November 23, 1928: Nelson and Helen Stanley sang for the Medical College Fund. *Bulletin:* "The singers, both in good voice, after appearing in leading roles with the Civic Opera Company in **Die Meistersinger** the night before, seemed anxious to please and had no difficulty in doing so, as the cordial manner in which they were received amply testified... .New were the Six Australian Bush Songs, by William G. James, which Mr. Eddy gave as his next number -- new, very interesting and admirably done. Especially beautiful were his mezzo voice tones in 'Bush Silence' and 'Comrades of Mine,' the latter sung with appealing pathos." *Public Ledger:* "The audience took on an air of critical expectancy when Mr. Eddy announced his selections. 'I picked them up in London,' he said, 'and I like them. I hope you will, too.' With the completion of the first selection, 'The Land of Who Knows Where,' sung in a dialect peculiar to the bush country of Australia, the audience burst into applause. The other numbers were equally well received."

December 6, 1928, Providence, R.I. *Bulletin:* "Nelson Eddy, baritone, will appear in his first concert in his native state since his appearance in opera tomorrow night at the concert of the Newport Philharmonic." *Newport Herald,* December 8, 1928: "Mr. Eddy made an instantaneous success. He is one of the best baritones heard here. His diction is extraordinary, while his breath control is apparently perfect. He sings with intelligence and evident joy in his work. Some of his sustained notes are wonderfully stirring."

December 8, 1928: This was the opening of 33rd season of Philharmonic Society at the Rogers High School Hall. "Mr. Nelson Eddy sang baritone solos, to the delight of all… Mr. Eddy also gave great enjoyment by his unusually fine voice and the fine way of using it. It is classed as a baritone, and is of manly, rich quality, with well-balanced upper register, full and sweet. His songs were all full of life, the words were clearly heard, and had an important part in the enjoyment, too. He seemed to like 'sea songs,' and gave them with much enjoyment to his listeners... There was a tremendous encore, and Mr. Eddy sang 'Smilin' Through.' The audience desired more, but he smiled and bowed, when recalled again."

December 10, 1928: Academy of Music presented **Cavalleria Rusticana** and **I Pagliacci.** "Nelson Eddy was Silvio, in which role he also figured in last year's performance; he was also fine indeed, his beautiful, smooth baritone blending perfectly with Miss Williams's voice." *Ledger:* "Nelson Eddy was very fine as Silvio, singing the one important number of the role, the duet with Nedda, with beautiful voice and blending perfectly with that of Miss Williams." *Bulletin:* "Nelson Eddy, of course, was a handsome young Silvio and performed in his usual capable manner." *Inquirer:* "Mr. Eddy's Silvio was finely sung." *Record:* "Nelson Eddy a notably good Silvio."

December 21, 1928: Nelson sang in **Manon Lescaut** at the Philadelphia Academy of Music. *The Ledger:* "The Civic Opera Company last evening added another to its long list (for an organization only in its sixth season) of operatic triumphs, when it added Puccini's **Manon Lescaut** to its repertoire in a performance of remarkable vividness, which at certain times, such as the dramatic close of the third act, positively was brilliant. The... cast was particularly well balanced, and under the inspiring leadership of Alexander Smallens, gave an extremely convincing performance dramatically as well as a fine one from the musical end… Nelson Eddy added another to the roles which suit him best in the difficult one of Lescaut and in every way gave a fine interpretation of the scapegrace (sic) brother of the unfortunate heroine." *Daily News:* "Nelson Eddy, in an all-too brief role, was in superb form, as usual." [Stars of this production included Pauline Lawn and Reinhold Schmit] *Bulletin:* "It is surprising how easily Nelson Eddy fits into a variety of operatic roles. After successfully portraying one of Richard Wagner's Master Singers not long ago he last night essayed the part of Manon's drunken soldier-brother and made the character real and convincing. His singing in the second act was particularly effective with well-placed tones and good volume seemingly achieved without effort. The entire second act, as a matter of fact, was particularly well done." *Record:* "Nelson Eddy was an excellent Lescaut." *Inquirer:* "Mrs. Henry M.

Local Company Does Meistersinger

MA 2-8

Effective Performance Given by Philadelphians

By H. T. Craven

PHILADELPHIA, Nov. 26.—The Philadelphia Civic Opera Company attained a new plane of achievement on Thursday night, with a performance of Die Meistersinger in the Academy of Music.

The production exhibited the resources of the local organization even more strikingly than the Strauss novelties with which it has won national distinction. There are accepted standards for Die Meistersinger that are much more exacting than in the case of works receiving a first hearing in this country. The New York Metropolitan has usually met these demands with success. It was this seasoned organization, therefore, which the Civic management, in a sense challenged, in last week's notable presentation.

Effective Performance

A spirited attempt won notable justification in a highly effective performance, in the main well sung, rightly keyed to the subject matter and generously and enthusiastically patronized. A capacity audience was in attendance.

For the balance, authority and splendid cohesion of the production, Alexander Smallens, directing the orchestra and, with characteristic zeal, the singers, too, was unmistakably responsible. He gave an inspiring reading of the score. The augmented chorus, with recruits from the Philadelphia Choral Society, the Fortnightly Club and the Snellenburg Chorus, covered itself with glory in the ensembles.

Several obstacles were encountered in assembling the cast. Karl Jorn, formerly of the Metropolitan, was enlisted for the role of Walther when Paul Althouse, a familiar figure in the Civic performances, was prevented by illness from appearing. Jorn, who, until now has not been in America for five years, presented a Walther with all his old charm and sense of romantic values and sang with a wealth and beauty of tone not equalled by the Metropolitan's present contingent of German tenors. Only in the Prize Song did Mr. Jorn's voice exhibit any signs of wear, and even here these indications were slight and in no wise alarming. The admirable artist inspirited the entire production from the outset.

Robert Ringling of the Chicago Company, booked for Beckmesser, developed laryngitis on the day of the performance. Arnold Gabor of the Metropolitan was reached by telephone and arrived an hour and a half before the curtain rose. His Beckmesser proved rather surprisingly dignified and not sharply accented in humor, but it was an extremely creditable interpretation, nonetheless, satisfactory vocally and, considering the lack of rehearsals, a heroic accomplishment.

A Radiant Eva

Aside from Mr. Jorn's portion the individual vocal honors of the evening went to the radiant Eva of Helen Stanley. She was in brilliant voice.

(*Continued on page* 16)

Local Company Does Meister-singer

(*Continued from page* 9)

Fred Patton's Sachs lacked a certain breadth of treatment, both vocally and dramatically in the first two acts; but, with his first rate endowment of lyric resources, he warmed up to his responsibilities in the Wahn, Wahn and throughout the balance of the opera.

Nelson Eddy scored decisively as Kothner and there was a particularly attractive Magdalena in Maybelle Marston and an engaging David in Albert Mahler. Other roles were well taken by Herbert Gould, Robert Elwayn, Clyde Dengler, James Montgomery, Reinhold Schmidt, Paul Towner, Sydney Sutcliffe. Sheldon Walker's determination to be comical as the night watchman was executed at the expense of accuracy of vocal pitch.

But in the glamor and charm and musical effulgence of the performance as a whole, a few slips in detail left but a fleeting impression on a delighted throng. The rounds of applause after each act testified both to the popular appeal of Die Meistersinger and to the tonic excellence of this production, the first one which the master musical comedy has ever received here at the hands of a local organization. So many persons were turned away from the sold-out Academy on Thursday night, that consideration is now being given to a plan for a repeat performance some time later in the season.

Musical Courier

iladelphia Civic Opera Gives Die Meistersinger

iladelphia Civic Opera Company presented Wag- stersinger at the Academy of Music, Philadelphia, ber 22. The performance proved to be the most s of the season, so far, requiring, as it does, the gree of efficiency, orchestrally, dramatically and It might easily be said that the highest honors go to Alexander Smallens, conductor, for his splendid work in bringing out the detailed beauty of the wonderful score, as well as leading the principals and chorus through the intricate action of the opera. It was gratifying to note the evident appreciation of the audience of Mr. Smallen's work, in the prolonged applause which greeted him at each appearance on the conductor's stand and also when he appeared before the curtain with the principals.

Many high spots were reached, however, throughout the opera. Helen Stanley as Eva was eminently suited to the role, both singing and acting it beautifully. Karl Jörn, as Walther, was excellent in every respect, while the work of Arnold Gabor as Beckmesser was marvellous, as he substituted at the last minute for Robert Ringling, who was suddenly taken ill on the afternoon of the day of the performance. Permission was given by the Metropolitan Opera Company for Mr. Gabor to come over and "save the day." So, with no rehearsal, Mr. Gabor stepped upon the stage and gave one of the most convincing interpretations of the evening. The humorous features of the part were splendidly portrayed, while he was equally good as to voice. Fred Patton, as Hans Sachs, was excellent both vocally and dramatically.

Of the local artists who took part, Maybelle Marston as Magdalene, Albert Mahler as David and Nelson Eddy as Kothner, were especially fine, although the other parts were also very well done as follows: Herbert Gould (Pogner); Robert Elwyn (Vogelgesang); Clyde Dengler (Zorn); James Smith (Moser); James Montgomery (Eisslinger); Clarence Reinert (Nachtigal); Reinhold Schmidt (Ortel); Paul Towner (Foltz); Sydney Sutcliffe (Schwartz); and Sheldon Walker (Night Watchman).

The scenery and stage effects were most attractive under the expert management of Karl T. F. Schroeder.

M. M. C.

Philadelphia Civic Opera Gives Boheme

The Philadelphia Civic Opera Company gave an unusually fine performance of La Boheme in the Academy of Music, Philadelphia, on November 8. All of the principals were in excellent voice, with Irene Williams heading the cast as Mimi. She was a success both vocally and histrionically, her beautiful voice showing to particular advantage in the solo and in the duet with Rodolfo in the first act. Pauline Lawn did some fine singing and acting in the role of Musetta and shared with Miss Williams the triumph of the evening. Nelson Eddy was at his best in the part of Marcello, while Rheinhold Schmidt's portrayal of the role of Schaunard left little to be desired. Good work also was done by Norberto Ardelli and Sigurd Nilssen, the other two members of the famous quartet of Bohemians. Others in the cast were Albert Mahler as Benoit; Burnett Holland, Alcindoro; Pierino Salvucci, Parpignol, and Virgilio Cossovel, as the customs officer. There was perfect unity and balance between voices and orchestra throughout the performance of the opera, much of which was due to the masterly directing of Alexander Smallens.

MC 11-22

Musical Courier 11-22

Artists of Distinction in Musical Offerings of the Week

NELSON EDDY—
Civic Opera

Record 1-13-29

Wagner's "Tannhauser" Capably Presented By Philadelphia Civic Opera Company

To aim high, in operatic circles, is only expected. But to exceed all expectations is indeed miraculous. Yet, that may be the proud boast of the Philadelphia Civic Opera Co., because of its gorgeous presentation of Wagner's sometime's boring "Tannhauser," last night, in the Academy of Music. Crowded to the doors, with seats unavailable, even at a price, the listeners gave enthusiastic vent to their admiration for the accomplishments of this troupe. And down in the orchestra pit, Alexander Smallens, musical director of the company, and doubtlessly most responsible for the success of the performance, took but a few bows, and hastened to the wings.

"Tannhauser," even by the great Metropolitan Co., calls for every form of precision and vocal courage. It insists that absolute rhythm and coloring be accorded it. Mrs. Tracy's company gave what can be rightfully acknowledged one of the best operatic performances that any local company has afforded its patrons. Everything was correct to the dot. The voices of the participants were inimitable. The chorus could not have been improved. The costuming was colorful and elaborate. The settings were in perfect taste. And . . . the house was sold out!

It was Paul Althouse, notable songster, who was entrusted with the title role. During every appearance, he evinced perfect voice and diction. Althouse is no novice at this singing business. He knows his notes and his inflections. He knows the temper of the music, and does not make attempt to overshadow it. Althouse was given many opportunities during the course of the rather lengthy presentation to display his true qualities. He hesitated little in execution. With little gusto and less showmanship, he portrayed the role of the damned Tannhauser as it has seldom been visualized on a local platform.

Emily Roosevelt, who made her debut with this company last year, did notably as the pitied Elizabeth. She has made a great stride forward during the last year. It was in her appearance then, when we predicted a bright future for this soprano. That day is rapidly approaching.

What more can be said about the ability of the favorite Nelson Eddy? It has not been a week since we said: "He has to but open his mouth, warble a few notes, and the audience is his." That goes again.

Albert Mahler and Reinhold Schmidt, the "Gold Dust Twins" of this company, exhibited their capabilities in good fashion. Herbert Gould, James Montgomery, Ralph Jusko, Leone Kruse and Florence Irons all played important roles nicely. The four pages, Pauline Snyder, Edna Zanzinger, Ruth Cornett and Edna Wood, also won applause. Incidental dancing was executed under the eagle eye of Alexandre Gavrilov and Valentina Koshuba.

News 1-18

Tracy, president of the company, confided that throat-spraying was the pastime practiced by most of the principals in intermissions. Nelson Eddy, however, showed no hint of a cold in his singing as Lescaut, which he also acted efficiently." *Musical Courier:* "Of marked excellence, also, was the first part of Act 2, where Nelson Eddy as Lescaut, holds with his sister a domestic scene..."

[Note: Nelson signed with concert manager Arthur Judson of Columbia Concerts. He now was promoted as the "leading baritone of the Philadelphia Opera Company," knew 28 operatic roles, 11 oratorios and hundreds of songs.]

January 13, 1929, clipping: "Nelson and Sylvia Lent, violinist, will be on the program for Penn Athletic Club Musical Association this evening." *Ledger,* January 14, 1929: "A recital notable for good taste and artistic worth... Nelson Eddy's superb clarity of diction added much to the enjoyment of his group of 'Australian Bush Songs.'" *Daily News:* "No matter what he sings he is sure of 'his public.' They will applaud any one of his vocal endeavors. And then he played up to them. When he announced that an encore would be 'Believe Me If All Those Endearing Charms' the 'oh's' and 'ah's' of his female admirers could be heard all over the place. But Eddy is one of our favorites. His work with the Philadelphia Civic Opera Company places him in an enviable position." *Bulletin:* "Mr. Eddy revealed exceptional clarity and ability in the numbers selected and all of them were given with a richness of tone which was marked." [Note: Nelson filled in an open date caused by illness of Chaliapin.]

January 17, 1929: Nelson sang in **Tannhäuser** at the Academy of Music. *Daily News,* January 18, 1929: "What more can be said about the ability of the favorite Nelson Eddy? It has not been a week since we said: 'He has to but open his mouth, warble a few notes, and the audience is his.' That goes again. His voice discloses improvement every time it is heard. He can hold any group enraptured with his personality. It is high time that Eddy starts off for broader fields." *Ledger:* "Nelson Eddy is exactly suited to the role of Wolfram and his splendid voice has never shown to greater advantage than in the song of the second act, '0 Himmel, lasst dich jetzt erflehen,' in which the virtuous minstrel extols the benefits of idea love, and in the pathetic quality of the 'Song of the Evening Star' in the third. Neither of these songs have been more effectively rendered in Philadelphia for many seasons, either in quality of voice or in emotional rendition." *Inquirer:* "Especially fine work was done by Nelson Eddy as Wolfram. His lyric baritone is ideally suited to Wolfram's benign and dignified measures, and his enunciation was refreshingly clear. His simulation of harp playing was worthy of a synchronized sound film." *Record:* "The voices of all the principals reached a commendably high plane of excellence. Nelson Eddy is ideally suited to the role of Wolfram. He sang it beautifully, scoring, of course, with the Evening Star romanza." [Note: Emily Roosevelt again starred along with Paul Althouse.] *Bulletin.* "The real praise of the evening, however, would seem last night to belong to the men of the cast. Nelson Eddy, in the role of Wolfram, displayed a magnificent resonance of tone, seeming to have conquered any undue forcing of high notes, and singing at all times with a feeling and tenderness that made the part truly noble. His work was so consistent that a selection of his songs is difficult. In the minstrel hail his song of love was beautifully done, while the Evening Star in blended shading of tone, and restrained climax was another triumph for the young baritone. The work of Althouse and Eddy in all of their scenes together was also of note, their final scene before the shrine reaching an impassioned climax in which both soloists were vocally excellent." *Musical Courier:* "Nelson Eddy as Wolfram was well cast. His smooth, rich and vibrant voice is always a joy, and his acting is equally good. His singing of the well-known Evening Star in the last act was one of the high points of the performance.".

January 23, 1929: Nelson sang on the Newton Coal Hour, with guest Maria Stone.

January 30, 1929: Nelson was soloist for The Woman's Symphony Orchestra. *Atlantic City Press-Union:* "Mr. Eddy sang the 'Ballad of Adamastor' from the opera **L'Africaine** with excellent effect, and a group of six Australian bush songs, to which he brought a craftsmanship that gave each one its individual color. Mr. Eddy revealed a voice coating sonority with smoothness and directed by clear musical intelligence. He should be highly entertaining in a recital of his own here."

LARGE AUDIENCE HEARS FINE CONCERT

Nelson Eddy, Baritone, Wins Acclaim; Fine Playing by Russian String Quartette

RECITAL by the RUSSIAN STRING QUARTET, members of the Philadelphia Orchestra, and NELSON EDDY, baritone, of Philadelphia, at the Lamberton auditorium, auspices of the Musical Arts Club.

Program

I

American Quartet .... Dvorak
Allegro ma non troppo
Lento
Molto vivace
Finale Vivace ma non troppo.
Russian String Quartet

II

"Largo al factorum" from the "Barber of Seville" .... Rossini
Mr. Eddy

III

Theme and Variations "Londonderry Air" .... Bridge
Russian String Quartet

IV

a. Roadways .... Densmore
b. Trade Winds .... Keel
c. Cargoes .... Doban
d. I Must Go Down to the Seas Again .... Densmore
(All from poems of John Masfield)
Mr. Eddy

V

a. Praeludium and Allegro Pugnani-Kreisler
b. Ave Maria .... Schubert-Wilhelmj
c. Theme and Variations Corelli-Kreisler
Mr. Simkin

VI

a. Sarabande .... Liadow
b. Courante .... Glazounow
(Arranged by Mr. Joel Belov)
c. Molly on the Shore .... Grainger
Russian String Quartet

VII

a. Will the Red Sun Never Set? Woodforde-Finden
b. The Cloths of Heaven .... Dunhill
c. Nocturne .... Curran
d. Love Was with Me Yesterday Golde

Mr. Eddy
Clarence Fuhrman
At the Piano

We are indebted to the ladies of the *Musical Arts Club for some most* delightful musical entertainment on Tuesday night, the occasion being the first of a series of three concerts sponsored by the club. The artists on this occasion were Mr. Nelson Eddy, baritone, and the Russian String Quartet. Although they were stated the other way around on the program, we here place Mr. Eddy first, for we believe the large audience will agree that fine as was the string quartet, the baritone proved to be the star attraction of the evening. We might easily call it an Eddy recital.

Carlisle, which has heard Bispham and Werrenrath, and others in recent years, never enjoyed any baritone more than it did Mr. Eddy. He has a wonderful voice in every particular; it has quality, range and power, and along with his vocal accomplishments he signs with a captivating manner that adds greatly to the pleasure of the audience. He sings as if he meant it and as if he likes to sing, and that is the way we like to see a singer perform. Mr. Eddy did not come here entirely unheralded, but yet we were not prepared to meet in him as colorful and accomplished an artist as we did.

Mr. Eddy's fine performance, however, should not allow us to detract anything from the very proficient playing of the Russian String Quartet. This form of music is enchanting when well played, and it was well played last night. The members individually are artists of high rank—Mr. Simkin showed that in his solo number—and their ensemble work further showed their ability. They are from the Philadelphia Orchestra. The four instruments are particularly adapted, as was shown in the numbers last night, to express all the moods the human mind can frame—light and gay, or solemn, or mirthful, or fiery and spirited. Each instrument as it brought out its part in the hands of these skilled players, seemed like an individual voice, yet all harmonized and blended perfectly. We can thank the quartet for another fine demonstration of the delights of this chamber music—we hear too little of it.

The opening number of the quartet was probably its best on the program—the suite of four movements by Dvorak. In the Finale was given a good idea of the spirit and dash which is one of the chief delights of the string quartet playing. Another popular number was Grainger's "Molly On the Shore." This was followed by an encore, "Old Black Joe," which, while selected no doubt to represent something that everyone knows, nevertheless did not appear as very striking on these string instruments, although the familiar plaintiveness was all there.

Mr. Simkin, who played the second violin in the quartet, played three pieces as solo numbers. He demonstrated masterful technique and control of his instrument, playing the most difficult passages with precision and apparent ease. In "Ave Maria" he had a chance to bring out the tones of his violin in this beautiful melody. Liberal applause greeted him and he played an encore with a muted instrument very appealingly.

From the very first Mr. Eddy captured his audience with the selection from Rossini's "Barber of Seville." He showed wonderful diction and ability as an actor, which he is. As an encore he sang the well-known "Elegie," made popular in these times by Caruso and Kreisler and others. The haunting melody will probably remain with the thousand auditors for days to come.

Evening Sentinel
Carlisle, Pa.
2-6-29

Of the second brace of four songs the best proved to be "I Must Go Down to the Seas Again," Densmore. The encore this time was "Tally-ho," a very spirited selection.

A number which demonstrated Mr. Eddy's superior dramatic talent was the first of the last brace, "Will the Red Sun Never Set?" We can hear him now say the word 'swift" at the end of the phrase. "Love Was With Me Yesterday" also was most liberally applauded, having been sung with gusto. Even then the soloist did not spare his voice, but appeared for an encore to sing "The Road to Mandalay." After this the audience was still more reluctant to leave, and the continued applause brought a second encore, "The Volga Boat Song," a fitting climax to the evening.

More than a word is to be said of the very satisfactory work of Mr. Clarence Fuhrman at the piano. His playing was most sympathetic, as that of an accompanist should be, and added greatly to the rendition of the songs. His fine technique was appreciated by the pianists in the audience, just as the violinists present took particular enjoyment in the quartet, and vocalists in *Mr. Eddy*.

It was an evening long to be remembered. The large auditorium was filled almost to capacity, the main floor being practically all filled and the gallery about half filled. Fears that the room would not be sufficiently heated proved groundless, for it was very comfortable in that respect. The next concert in the series, on April 2, will be by Carlisle artists, and another fine program is anticipated.

T. E. S.

February 6, 1929, *Evening Sentinel,* Carlisle, Pennsylvania: "We are indebted to the ladies of the Musical Arts Club for some most delightful musical entertainment on Tuesday night, the occasion being the first of a series of three concerts sponsored by the club. The artists on this occasion were Mr. Nelson Eddy, baritone, and the Russian String Quartet. Although they were stated the other way around on the program, we here place Mr. Eddy first, for we believe the large audience will agree that fine as was the string quartet, the baritone proved to be the star attraction of the evening. We might easily call it an Eddy recital. Carlisle, which has heard Bispham and Werrenrath, and others in recent years, never enjoyed any baritone more than it did Mr. Eddy. He has a wonderful voice in every particular; it has quality, range and power, and along with his vocal accomplishments he sings with a captivating manner that adds greatly to the pleasure of the audience. He sings as if he meant it and as if he likes to sing, and that is the way we like to see a singer perform. Mr. Eddy did not come here entirely unheralded, but yet we were not prepared to meet in him as colorful and accomplished an artist as we did.... The soloist did not spare his voice, but appeared for an encore to sing 'The Road to Mandalay.' After this the audience was still more reluctant to leave, and the continued applause brought a second encore, the Volga Boat Song, a fitting climax to the evening."

February 13, 1929: Nelson sang on the Newton Coal Hour. [Note: Each week Nelson would sing songs starting with a particular letter. This week was the "G" week.]

February 27, 1929: Nelson was on Newton Coal Hour again.

February 28, 1929: the Symphony Society gave a concert and Nelson was soloist. *Frankford*: "Nelson Eddy... reiterated the merits of his natural and acquired equipment for chamber, concert and opera music; and both his program number and his encore to it with the orchestra revealed an advance in his already notable progression toward eminence as a baritone singer. He has gained in plasticity of tonal modulation in facile transition from one to another mode or (which is more significant) interpretative mood. This last-named qualification had marked accentuation in the differing appeal of the Adamastor (Meyerbeer) and the familiar 'Elegie' of Massenet." Nelson gave three encores.

March 7, 1929: **Madama Butterfly** at the Academy of Music, starring Helen Stanley as Butterfly, with Paul Althouse and Nelson Eddy. *Ledger,* March 8, 1929: "Nelson Eddy again gave an admirable presentation of the role of Consul Sharpless. His enunciation was perfect, as usual--as indeed was that of most of the members of the cast -- and he sang beautifully all the numbers assigned to the character." *Inquirer:* "Nelson Eddy's fine lyric baritone gave interest to the Consul's music, and his acting was smoothly efficient." *Record:* "The three leading artists, Helen Stanley as the Butterfly, Paul Althouse as Pinkerton and Nelson Eddy as the Consul acquainted themselves with distinction dramatically and vocally. They caught the spirit of the work, its romance and its poignancy, as did Alexander Smallens in his interpretation of the score." *Bulletin:* 'Nelson Eddy was at ease and missed none of the rather limited opportunities afforded by the part of Sharpless to display the rich quality of his voice and to do some creditable singing." *Musical Courier,* March 21, 1929: "Nelson Eddy made an excellent Sharpless, both vocally and dramatically. His splendid baritone was heard most pleasurably in all the music assigned to him. His clear diction was a noticeable and praiseworthy feature of his singing."

March 8, 1929: The Brahms Chorus of Philadelphia performed Bach's **The Passion According to St. John** with a chorus of one hundred. "The solo voices were impressive and superbly handled." Nelson was listed as a bass. *Bulletin,* March 9, 1929: "Mr. Eddy interpreted with great artistry the bass aria 'Haste, Ye Deeply Wounded Spirits.'" [Note: This was the first Philadelphia presentation of **Passion**.]

March 21, 1929: The Academy of Music presented **Marriage of Figaro**. It was "sparklingly" done. "Nelson Eddy singing smoothly as the Count, investing the role with the right touch of debonair artificiality." *Record,* March 22, 1929: "The contribution of Nelson Eddy, the Count Almaviva, must, moreover, take rank as a Mozart portrayal of the first order, lyrically refined and subtle." *Bulletin:* "Nelson Eddy has had parts better suited to him than that of the Count, but he entered into it with characteristic earnestness. His acting was good and his vocalism easy, at times showing to advantage the well-known beautiful quality of his middle and lower

Musical Arts Club Series Is Opened Auspiciously

The first of the series of concerts under the auspices of the Musical Arts Club was presented Tuesday night before a large and appreciative audience in the high school auditorium.

The Russian String Quartet, composed of Joel Belov, violin; Jack Simkins, violin; Sam Rosen, viola; and Benjamin Gusikoff, cello; members of the Philadelphia orchestra, gave as their first number the American Quartet by Dvorak which was characterized not only by its breadth of delivery, but also by its dash and warmth of expression. The lento movement and the finale with its delicate hints of negro melody were especially charming. While their whole program was delightful, possibly the Dvorak Quartet, themes and variations by that ancient of the violin Corelli, played by Mr. Simkin as a solo, and Schubert's Moment Musicale played with muted strings by Mr. Simkin as an encore, were best received by the audience. Sarabande by Tiadow and the Courante by Glazounow, two gems arranged for string quartet by Mr. Joel Belov, charmingly executed, enchanted the listeners by their delicacy and grace.

The skillful playing and artistic interpretation of each member, both in individual and ensemble works, proved them masters of their particular instruments.

Nelson Eddy, baritone, well known in operatic circles and on the concert stage, gave as his first number the famous "Largo al Factotum" from Rossini's opera "The Barber of Seville."

Mr. Eddy's robust well rounded tones are splendidly fitted for that role. But numbers which found their way to the hearts of his audience were his songs of the sea from poems of Masefield and the song of the Volga Boatman sung as an encore.

His rich resonance of voice, excellent diction and interpretation in song merit especial commendation.

Both the quartet and Mr. Eddy were most gracious in acceding to many requests by the audience for encores.

The accompanist, Mr. Clarence Fuhrman, showed superlative skill in that difficult and usually unappreciated art.

Altogether, the occasion was filled with bright promise, not only for the remaining concerts of the season, but for other seasons to come.

Evening Sentinel
Carlisle, Pa.
2-6

"Go Down, Moses" to Be Sung Tonight By Nelson Eddy in Newton Coal Hour

2-13

NELSON EDDY, popular baritone and operatic figure, will feature the Newton Coal Forum concert tonight through WIP from 9 to 10.

Eddy has distinguished himself in vocal circles throughout this country and abroad, where he has been engaged in a concert tour. He will sing several solos, including "Ganymede," by Schubert, and the old spiritual "Go Down Moses."

This concert is one in a series of Newton Alphabetical hours. Tonight's program contains selections or composers whose names start with the letter "G."

A galaxy of musical "G's" will be played by the Newton Coal Orchestra, under the leadership of Clarence Fuhrman, the prominent composer. Old and new favorites are among the selections, including Gensler's "Queen High" music, "Turkeys in the Straw," by Gulon, and Grieg's "Peer Gynt Suite." The members of the Newton Orchestra are composed of first-rank musicians from the Philadelphia Orchestra and the Victor Recording Orchestras.

The program follows:

"Newton Coal March" .... Fuhrman
Selection from "Queen High" .... Gensler
Gavotte .... Gossec
Tango Jealousie .... Gade
Soloist: Nelson Eddy, Baritone
"Ganymede" .... Schubert
"Calf of Gold," from "Faust" .... Gounod
"Unfold, Ye Portals," from "Redemption" .... Gounod
"Turkey in the Straw" .... Gulon
Russian Slumber Song .... Gretchaninow
Peer Gynt Suite .... Grieg
Soloist: Nelson Eddy, Baritone
"Go Down, Moses"—Spiritual
"Goin' Home" .... Dvorak
"Three Dances," from "Henry VIII." .... German

News 2-13

2-13

NELSON EDDY GOES ON THE AIR TONIGHT

Is Featured Artist on Newton Forum Hour, WIP, 9—Gold Strand Hour, WLIT, 10:30

LATTER IS NEW SERIES

Nelson Eddy, Baritone; Newton Radio Forum (WIP, 9). Nelson Eddy, Philadelphia operatic baritone, will feature the Newton Coal Forum concert tonight. He will sing several solos, including "Ganymede," by Schubert, and the old spiritual, "Go Down, Moses." This concert is one in a series of "Alphabetical Hours." Tonight's program contains selections or composers whose names start with the letter "G." The Newton Coal Orchestra is under the leadership of Clarence Fuhrman.

"Newton Coal March" .... Fuhrman
Selections from "Queen High" .... Gensler
Gavotte .... Gossec
"Tango Jealousie" .... Gade
Soloist, Nelson Eddy, Baritone
(a) "Ganymede," by Schubert
(b) "Calf of Gold," by Gounod, from "Faust"
"Unfold, Ye Portals," from "Redemption" .... Gounod
"Turkey in the Straw" .... Gulon
Russian Slumber Song .... Gretchaninow
"Peer Gynt" Suite .... Grieg
Soloist, Nelson Eddy, Baritone
(a) "Go Down, Moses," Spiritual
(b) "Goin' Home," by Dvorak
"Three Dances," from "Henry VIII." .... German

E. Ledger 2-13

Nelson Eddy in Newton Coal Hour (WIP, 9). Nelson Eddy, noted operatic and concert star, will be presented on the Newton Coal Radio Forum tonight. This is the "I" hour in the series of Newton Alphabetical Hours. All the names of numbers and composers in this recital begin with the letter "I."

Mr. Eddy will sing Beethoven's "In Questa Tomba" and "Ia Nie Chotchou," the latter an infrequently heard Russian composition which Eddy learned in Paris under the tutelage of the great Manonkoff. A varied program of musical "I's" will be played by the Newton Coal Orchestra, directed by Clarence Fuhrman.

"Newton Coal March" .... Fuhrman
"Procession of the Sardar" .... Iwanow
"Invincible Eagle" .... Sousa
"In a Chinese Temple Garden" .... Ketelbey
Soloist, Nelson Eddy, Baritone—
(a) "In Questa Tomba" .... Beethoven
(b) "Invictus" .... Huhn
"Ich Liebe Dich" .... Grieg
"Iolanthe" selection .... Sullivan
"'S Wonderful" .... Gershwin
Soloist, Nelson Eddy, Baritone—
(a) "Sea Fever" .... Ireland
(b) "Ia Nie Chotchou" .... Levina
"In a Monastery Garden" .... Ketelbey
"I'd Love to Call You My Sweetheart" .... Ash

E. Ledger 2-27

tones." *Ledger:* "Nelson Eddy as the Count scored another great success." *Daily News:* "Nelson Eddy, the blond baritone, played the count. He, too, is one of the local satellites. Eddy need never fear. Two or three years hence will find him in higher operatic circles." *Musical Courier,* April 6, 1929: "Nelson Eddy scored a success as the Count.... Mr. Eddy's work was splendid in portrayal, and vocally of a very high order. His voice is increasing in depth but losing none of that smooth and real musical timbre for which it is becoming noted."

April 4, 1929: The Academy of Music presented Gluck's **Orfeo ed Eurydice** with co-bill **L'Enfant Prodigue** by Debussy. *Inquirer,* April 5, 1929: "Nelson Eddy accomplished an astonishing transformation in his make-up as the father..." *Bulletin:* "Nelson Eddy sang with richness of voice and a lyricism in keeping with the music." *Record:* "The admirable Nelson Eddy as Simeon, the father." *Ledger:* "Neither Mr. Mahler nor Mr. Eddy has done better singing since their connection with the company... Mr. Eddy's work was consistently good throughout." *Daily News:* "Our favorite, Nelson Eddy, did a swell job of the father's portion."

April 11, 1929: Nelson sang at the Woman's Club Chorus of Swarthmore spring concert at the Swarthmore Club house. "Mr. Eddy, who is a favorite with Swarthmore audiences, possesses a voice of beautiful quality and evenness, handles it well and presents his songs in a genuinely artistic manner." [This clipping is from an unnamed Swarthmore newspaper, April 12, 1929.]

April 18, 1929: The Academy of Music featured **Samson and Delilah** to close the season. *Bulletin,* April 19, 1929: "Nelson Eddy sang well in his brief scene as Abimélech, whom Samson slays in the first scene." *Inquirer:* "Mr. Eddy was excellent in his single scene as Abimelech." [Margarete Matzenauer and Paul Althouse had the title roles.] *Ledger:* "Nelson Eddy was a very capable Abimelech." *Record:* "Although Nelson Eddy's part, as Abimelech, was very small (meeting with his fate early in the first act) he portrayed the character with his usual puissance."

April 24, 1929: Nelson sang on the Newton Coal Hour. This week he sang numbers starting with letter Q.

April 28, 1929: Nelson sang in the afternoon with Philadelphia Boys' Harmonica Band, broadcast on the radio. Review, April 29, 1929: "Among Mr. Eddy's contributions, sung in his dependably fine style and in very good voice, were 'Music of Hungary,' by the Philadelphia composer Celeste Heckscher; Martin's 'Come of the Fair,' two compositions by Manning; 'In the Luxembourg Gardens' and 'The Lamplighter;' 'Captain Stratton's Fancy' by Taylor, and 'Faites Silence,' from Debussy's **L'Enfant Prodigue.**"

April 29, 1929: Philadelphia Choral Society gave its spring concert in Witherspoon Hall with the cantata **Odysseus** by Max Bruch. *Ledger,* April 20, 1929: "Mr. Eddy took the role of Odysseus, and his fine voice and perfect diction were heard to great advantage in both parts of the cantata." *Bulletin:* "The title role of the unhappy wanderer from the Trojan Wars was sung by Nelson Eddy, whose operatic training was evidenced in the ringing resonance of such solos as Odysseus' vow of revenge against Penelope's suitors. Mr. Eddy's tone quality throughout was flawless. Once he erred in his liens by failing to include all the syllables of the word 'Odysseus.' It was a minor slip in the general excellence of his interpretation." *Inquirer:* "Of the soloists, Nelson Eddy in the title role was naturally outstanding, his clear enunciation and beautiful baritone voice giving unflagging interest to his music." *Record:* "Nelson Eddy... contributed his usual brilliant performance."

May 2, 1939: Sixty-one male voices sang at Schubert Playhouse, presented by the Orpheus Club of Wilmington. Nelson was the soloist. *Wilmington, Delaware Morning News:* "Especially pleasing to the audience were the solo numbers carried by the rich baritone voice of Nelson Eddy, who was encored consistently." *Wilmington Evening Journal:* "Fully 700 music lovers last night attended a concert presented by the Orpheus Club of Wilmington in the Schubert Playhouse. The club, consisting of 61 male voices, presented what was probably the finest program they had offered in the twelve years of the club's existence. Nelson Eddy, baritone, gave an especially pleasing performance, and he received enthusiastic applause from the audience, following his solo numbers."

May 3, 1929: Nelson sang with the Tioga Choral Society and the Germantown Choral Society, comprising

St. John Passion Is Sung Here by Brahms Chorus

Great Throng at Recital Given in First Presbyterian Church.

Although constructed on lines less monumental than the "Passion According to St. Matthew" and the colossal "Mass in B Minor," Bach's "St. John Passion" is second to none of the composer's achievements in symmetry of proportions and fineness of musical craftmanship.

It was this noble work, profoundly moving both as a pattern of artistry and as an expression in oratorio form of the devotional spirit of the Leipsic titan, which engaged the attention of the Brahms chorus, under N. Lindsay Norden, at the First Presbyterian Church last night.

So rich is the "St. John Passion" in strokes of polyphonic mastery, so pregnant with musical values, still unmatched in their field and scope, and so ideal is the fusion of text and score that a performance of this work conveys the impression of inspiration functioning uninterruptedly and according to a predetermined plan from introduction to closing bars.

But Bach combined the perception of a critic with his superbly original endowment as a composer.

The "St. John Passion" underwent several stages of revision by the master during the great productive period as Leipsic Cantor, organist and music director of the Thomaskirche and Nicolaikirche.

Not only was the Brockes text favored for religious compositions of the day, transfigured and glorified in adapting it for the nonscriptural portions of this "Passion," but several musical numbers were excised for use elsewhere and in some instances replaced with still more exquisite substitutes before the work reached its final form of poignant and eloquent beauty. It is thus a product of prayerfully considered taste standards as well as an exhibit of the composer's instinctive genius.

As far as ascertained, this was the first performance of this work here. The orchestration, played by members of the Philadelphia Orchestra, was the original—strings, flutes, oboes, organ and the piano substituted for the cembalo.

The chorus, which is in its fourth year, gave definite evidence of its development and displayed adequate artistic finish in its conception and delivery of this tremendous contrapuntal masterwork.

The score is largely solo recitative, interspersed with intricate although melodic choruses. The soloists rose splendidly to their opportunities with appreciable tones and shadings.

The soloists were Elizabeth Harrison, soprano; Maybelle Marston, alto; Frank Oglesby, tenor; Nelson Eddy, bass, and Lester R. Paton, bass. Rollo F. Maitland played the organ and Roma E. Angel the piano.

The increasing popularity of the Brahms Chorus was evidenced by its large attendance.

Record 3.9

BRAHMS CHORUS

Singing Society Gives Difficult Bach Passion Music

The Brahms Chorus of Philadelphia, under the direction of N. Lindsey Norden, was heard last night in an inspiring rendition of Bach's "Passion According to St. John," by an appreciative audience that filled the First Presbyterian Church, Locust st. above 15th.

The soloists were Elizabeth Harrison, soprano, Maybelle Marston, alto, Nelson Eddy and Lester R. Paton, bassos, and Frank Oglesby, tenor. The instrumental parts were played by an orchestra composed of players from the Philadelphia Orchestra, Roma E. Angel at the piano and Rollo F. Maitland at the organ.

"The Passion According to Saint John" is one of the greatest examples of ecclesiastical music extant. Recitatives, arias, choruses and chorales, all in the most elevated mood, follow each other in an unbroken flow of beautiful melody and involved contrapuntal development. The solo voices, supported by obbligatos by flute, oboe or English horn, give comments upon the narrative recitatives of the tenor. Mr. Oglesby last night sang the arduous tenor part with expression and great beauty of tone. In the arias "Ah My Soul, Whither Wilt Thou Fly?" and "My Heart, Behold How All the World," he did notable work. Mr. Eddy interpreted with great artistry the bass aria "Haste, Ye Deeply Wounded Spirits," the chorus punctuating its intricate pattern with the questions "Come Where? and Fly Where?"

This was the first presentation of "Passion According to Saint John," in Philadelphia, and it is certain that the Brahms Chorus was the organization best fitted by training and traditions to present it. Mr. Norden brought out all the sincere simplicity of the chorales, the significant and difficult chorus passages in a way that made the performance one of the outstanding musical events of the season.

The co-ordination was perfect between the voices and the orchestra, whose instrumentation, the original one, consisted of flutes, oboes, organ, piano (in place of the obsolete cembalo), and the usual strings. English horns took the place of the oboe da caccia, an obsolete oboe in A.

Before the Passion music, Mr. Maitland gave the "Oh, World, I E'en Must Leave Thee," by Johannes Brahms, as a tribute to the memory of S. Wesley Sears, organist at St. James Episcopal Church.

Bulletin 3.9

BRAHMS CHORUS SINGS "ST. JOHN'S PASSION"

3.9

Organization Is Augmented by Soloists and Philadelphia Orchestra Men

In line with ambitious earlier presentations of the Brahms Chorus, this choral society presented last evening in the First Presbyterian Church as its second offering for the season Johann Sebastian Bach's "Passion According to Saint John" before a capacity audience whose reverent appreciation and interest was eloquent testimony of the finished performance that was given. In what was the first hearing in Philadelphia of this profoundly beautiful work, the first of Bach's attempts at Passion music, the Brahms' Chorus, under the leadership of N. Lindsay Norden, equaled, if it did not surpass, the high quality of its performance of the "St. Matthew Passion" last year.

Assisted by musicians from the Philadelphia Orchestra, with Rollo F. Maitland, organist, and Roma E. Angel, pianist, the chorus interspersed its dramatic outbursts and contemplative chorals among the meditative arias and recitatives, assigned the task of narrating the story, which were sung by soloists including Elizabeth Harrison, Maybelle Marston, Frank Oglesby, Nelson Eddy and Lester R. Paton. Of these, Mr. Paton, who sang the role of Jesus, was the most outstanding, both for the rich quality of his fine bass and the compelling character of the music written for his part.

The other vocalists, likewise, proved admirable in their singing of the florid and frequently arduous arias which occupied the greater part of the music. The chorus of one hundred voices blended with admirable enthusiasm and discipline in the fleeting and dynamic choruses in which it stimulates the angry mob of the story, while singing of a subtle and stirring richness was manifest in the old Lutheran chorales, simple and poignant for all the webb of splendid harmony in which Bach invested them.

Many of the faults of past concerts have been overcome, and the performance last night indicated a great stride forward inthe artistic accomplishments of this organization.

40 Inquirer 3.9

* meaning – Mr. Eddy – permission given to change – by L. Martin.

nearly 200 singers, plus members of the Philadelphia Orchestra. They performed **Elijah** at Simon Gratz High School and there were more than 1200 people in the audience. *Ledger,* May 4, 1929: "Mr. Eddy's fine gifts as an interpretative singer were enthusiastically received, while in narrative and in ensemble all the soloists gave outstanding performances." *Bulletin:* "The solo parts were taken by Nelson Eddy, baritone, who brought his operatic experience to the role of Elijah and sang it with force and understanding."

May 8, 1929: Reading Choral Society's All-Brahms program with 200 singers. "Mr. Eddy sang gloriously the 'Four Serious Songs,' written with Biblical context. He has a great voice of natural beauty and accompanying it is a fine command of his vocal resources and an innate sense of musical interpretation. He immediately repeated his success as soloist with the choral society several years prior." *Ledger:* "The solo work... was very well done by Mrs. Wilson and Mr. Eddy." *Reading Eagle,* May 9, 1929: "The soloists were Mrs. Ethel Righter Wilson, soprano, and Nelson Eddy, bass, both of Philadelphia; both prominently identified in choral and operatic circles. Their singing proved a big factor to the success of the concert."

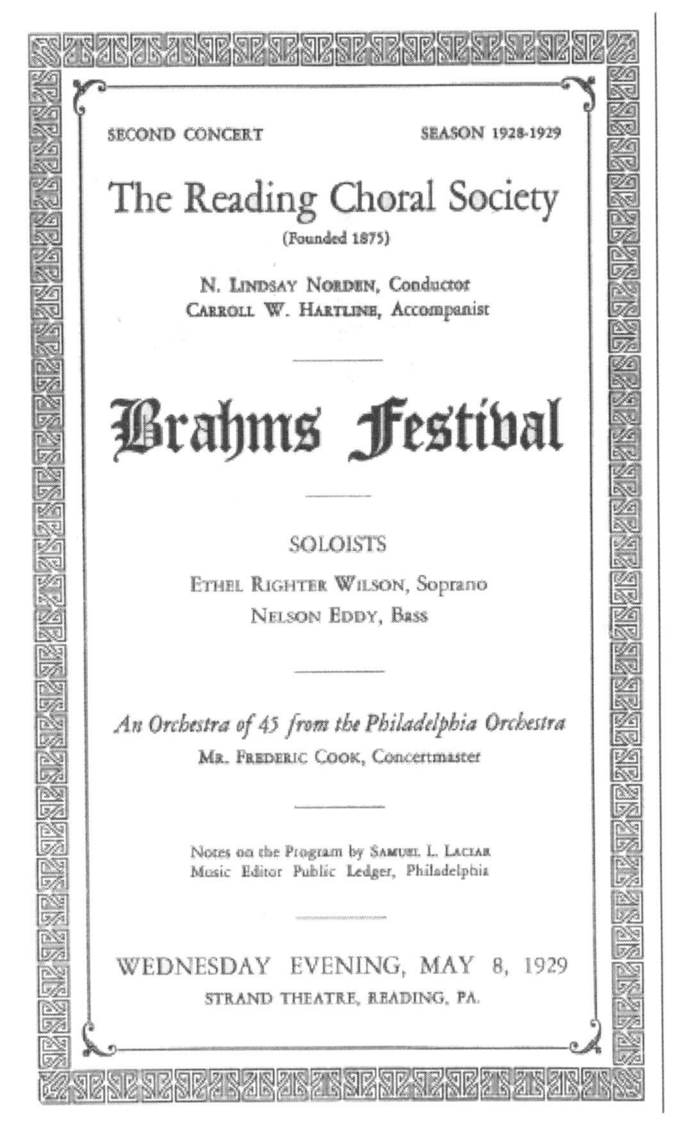
SECOND CONCERT SEASON 1928-1929

The Reading Choral Society

(Founded 1875)

N. Lindsay Norden, Conductor
Carroll W. Hartline, Accompanist

Brahms Festival

SOLOISTS

Ethel Righter Wilson, Soprano
Nelson Eddy, Bass

An Orchestra of 45 from the Philadelphia Orchestra
Mr. Frederic Cook, Concertmaster

Notes on the Program by Samuel L. Laciar
Music Editor Public Ledger, Philadelphia

WEDNESDAY EVENING, MAY 8, 1929
STRAND THEATRE, READING, PA.

May 9, 1929: The Haddon Heights Male Chorus of the Fathers Association gave its final concert of the season in the Haddon Heights High School. *Bulletin,* May 10, 1929: "A delighted audience numbering about 800, insisted upon one encore after another by the combined choruses and by Mr. Eddy, and the concert was pronounced the most delightful ever heard in the town."

May 15, 1929: Nelson sang on Newton Coal Hour, this week it was "T" numbers.

May 21, 1929: Nelson sang "W" numbers on Newton Coal Hour.

May 24. 1929: A May Festival of Music was held at the Baptist Temple, chorus of about 500 voices. *Ledger:* "Mr. Eddy gave splendid renditions of the aria 'Monne Vanna,' of Fevrier, and a group of songs by Koeneman, Manning and Deems Taylor… Mr. Eddy was accompanied by Theodore Paxson." *Bulletin:* "Nelson Eddy did excellent work."

May 26, 1929: "Nelson Eddy will be heard this week at the Stanley Theater as a special stage artist. Nelson sings 'Toreador Song,' Helen Jepson, Micaela's aria, and the Littlefield Ballet will appear. Nelson has just received an offer by cable to sing for the Staats Opera of Dresden." [Note: Soprano Ethel Righter Wilson was mentioned in the reviews rather than Helen Jepson.] Nelson sang prior to the screening of **A Man's Man** starring William Haines and Josephine Dunn.

May 28, 1929: *Inquirer* noted in its review of **A Man's Man:** "A Carmen Fantasy is offered colorfully if in a somewhat scrambled manner with Micaela wandering into the Inn scene in search of no one in particular. Nelson Eddy, turned dark and dashing, sang the famous Toreador aria agreeably."

May 28, 1929: Nelson sang Newton Coal; this was the "W" hour. Also, Theodore Paxson is announced as Nelson's regular accompanist.

June 28, 1929, *Doyletown Daily Intelligencer*: "Nelson Eddy delights large audience here. In one of the most delightful concerts ever heard in Doylestown, The Monday Musicale, last night at the high school auditorium, presented Nelson Eddy… and Theodore Paxson."

No date: Nelson sings tomorrow over WIP, Ted Paxson accompanying him for the Mastbaum Radio Hour. This will be recorded before a screening of Warner Brothers' **The Gamblers**, a new talkie starring H.B. Warner, Lois Wilson, Jason Robards. Nelson Eddy is the soloist, and per one paper "sings remarkably well." Catherine Littlefield dances. "A novelty was the presentation of 'Poet and Peasant.' Charles Previn directed the orchestra, while on the stage, grouped with artistry was a large chorus. Nelson Eddy, romantic in appearance and with a fine voice, was the soloist."

September 9, 1929, *Morning Ledger*: "At the musicale last Sunday evening the guests and cottagers had the pleasure of hearing Nelson Eddy, the popular baritone of the Philadelphia Civic Opera Company, in a well-chosen program... He was accompanied by that talented young pianist, Theodore Paxson, of Norristown, and it was really the outstanding artistic event of the season."

No date: The musical season of Asbury Methodist church will come to a close Sunday evening. "This church choir has presented for the past six seasons some of the best opera, oratorio and concert singers in the country and this season has been a busy one for the strictly volunteer choir of the church. It opened the season in September with Nelson Eddy...He, making an excellent impression, has been requested to return next season."

October 27, 1929, *Inquirer*. "The popularity on the air of Nelson Eddy, principal baritone of the Philadelphia Civic Opera Company and guest artist on many of the broadcasting hours from Station WIP, is exemplified in the hundreds of requests received by this artist from his many radio admirers. On Friday at 9:30 Nelson Eddy will present a recital of requests: 'Bella Mia' by Pergolossi, 'Claire de Lune' by Saure, 'At Night' by Rachmaninoff, 'Verschwiegene Lieg' (Silent Love) by Wolf, 'Song of the Flee' by Mussorgsky and 'Sea Rapture' by Coates."

November 3, 1929, *Record:* "Nelson Eddy, baritone, will give a series of six musicales, one a month, in the new ballroom of the Warwick Hotel, 17th and Locust St. Mr. Eddy will sing on each of the six programs and in addition, other artists will be presented at each concert, eleven in all." [Note: Allan Jones was included in this group. The dates were: November 14, December 18, and in 1930: January 23, February 20, March 12 and April 10. About 100 women were patronesses for the series.]

November 3, 1929: Nelson sang an all-request program on WIP radio.

November 8, 1929, *Record:* "Civic Opera Group is Unimpressive in **Romeo et Juliette**; Irene Williams and Nelson Eddy Among Few High Spots in Cast." [This was sung at the Academy of Music.] "As Mercutio, Nelson Eddy again gave evidence of his increasing powers both as an actor and as a baritone. His performance was superb and lent a dash of color to the entire production." *Ledger*: "Nelson Eddy as Mercutio was excellent, singing the Queen Mab aria of the first act with splendid tonal quality and acting with his usual artistic delineation of role." *Inquirer:*

A Phila. Baritone

Nelson Eddy, leading baritone with the Civic Opera Company, will be heard this week at the Stanley Theatre as a special stage artist. Mr. Eddy is among the foremost operatic artists, and he has a high reputation for achievement in concert work. Moreover, he is a Philadelphian. He is a pupil of William W. Vilonat, of New York, and he studied in France and Germany as well as in this country. His European training is evident in the poise of his interpretations in opera, and he sings in foreign tongues expressively and with excellent diction. Radio audiences know him well, and he is always a welcome addition to a radio program. He makes his home in this city, and he is heard at the Presbyterian church in Overbrook as bass-baritone soloist.

NELSON EDDY

Pub Ledger 5-26

Record 11-10

MONTHLY CONCERT GIVEN

Nelson Eddy and Irene Williams Appear at Warwick

Nelson Eddy, baritone, and Irene Williams, soprano, were the entertainers last night at the monthly concert given at the Warwick Hotel. They were accompanied by Theodore Paxson, pianist.

Among the patronesses for the concert were Mrs. Edward T. Stotesbury, Mrs. George Horace Lorimer, Mrs. Sidney Thayer and Mrs. George W. Elkins.

The next musical was announced for Monday evening, December 18, when Alan Jones, tenor, and Mr. Eddy will be the features.

11-15

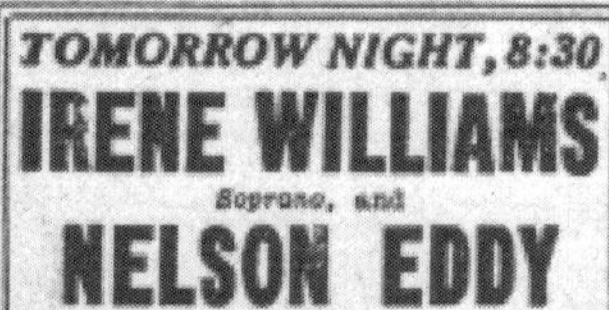

OVEMBER 15, 192

TWO SINGERS IN RECITAL

Nelson Eddy and Irene Williams in Varied and Interesting Program

Two of the leading singers of the Philadelphia Civic Opera Company, Nelson Eddy, baritone, and Irene Williams, soprano, were heard in an interesting program of solos and duets, in the attractive new ballroom of the Warwick Hotel, last evening. This was the first of six recitals in which Mr. Eddy is to appear, each time with a different assisting artist. The program, in the presentation of which Theodore Paxson was the able accompanist, except for two groups of solos was made up of selections from the operas of Mozart, beginning with the duet, "La dove prende amor ricetto," from "Il Flauto Magico" (The Magic Flute), after which Mr. Eddy sang "Non piu andrai," from "Le Nozze di Figaro" (The Marriage of Figaro), and Miss Williams, "Batti, batti," from "Don Giovanni," and "Deh, vieni, non tardar," from "Le Nozze di Figaro," these being followed by the duet, "Crudeli perche finora," from the same opera. All of these were done in a felicitous manner. After the last named, the singers sang with an engaging touch of intimacy and piquant humor, the old favorite "Madame, Will You Walk with Me?"

Mr. Eddy then changed the mood of the recital with a group of songs in English and the modern style, first the Negro Spiritual, "Water Boy," by Robinson, into which he put real feeling. The rich, smooth quality of the baritone's voice was displayed to special advantage in his sympathetic delivery of Manning's "In the Luxembourg Gardens," and its power of climax in the more dramatic "Sea Rapture" of Coates, the last in this group. Then, as an encore, again displaying his happy faculty for discovering unusual and interesting songs, Mr. Eddy sang "The Kentucky Volunteer," the composition of "A Lady of Philadelphia" and published in this city in 1794.

After Miss Williams again used with skill and expressiveness her pure soprano in three songs, "La Belle du Roi," Holmes; Massenet's familiar "Crepuscle," this with lovely pianissimo tones, and "A Dream," by Grieg, there was, as the concluding number, another Mozart duet, "La ci darem la manoi," from "Don Giovanni," which, in response to enthusiastic applause, was repeated. "Because," said Mr. Eddy, "we did not expect to be received so politely and have no more duets with us." The second recital in the series will be given on Wednesday evening, December 18, when Mr. Eddy will have the assistance of Allan Jones, tenor.

Bulletin 11-15

SIX MUSICALES

IN THE NEW BALLROOM OF

THE WARWICK

LOCUST STREET AT SEVENTEENTH

WITH

NELSON EDDY

BARITONE

AND THE FOLLOWING ARTISTS:

THURSDAY, NOVEMBER 14
IRENE WILLIAMS
SOPRANO

WEDNESDAY, DECEMBER 18
ALLAN JONES
TENOR

THURSDAY, JANUARY 23
RUSSIAN
STRING QUARTET
AND
THEODORE PAXSON, PIANIST

THURSDAY, FEBRUARY 20
ALMA PETERSON
SOPRANO

WEDNESDAY, MARCH 12
RONALD O'NEIL, PIANIST
AND
THEODORE PAXSON, PIANIST

THURSDAY, APRIL 10
BIANCA SAROYA, SOPRANO
AND
DIMITRI ONOFREI, TENOR

SUBSCRIPTIONS $15.00
SINGLE TICKETS $3.00

Evenings 8.30

OVERLEAF: Handwritten correspondence from Nelson regarding his Warwick Concert Series.

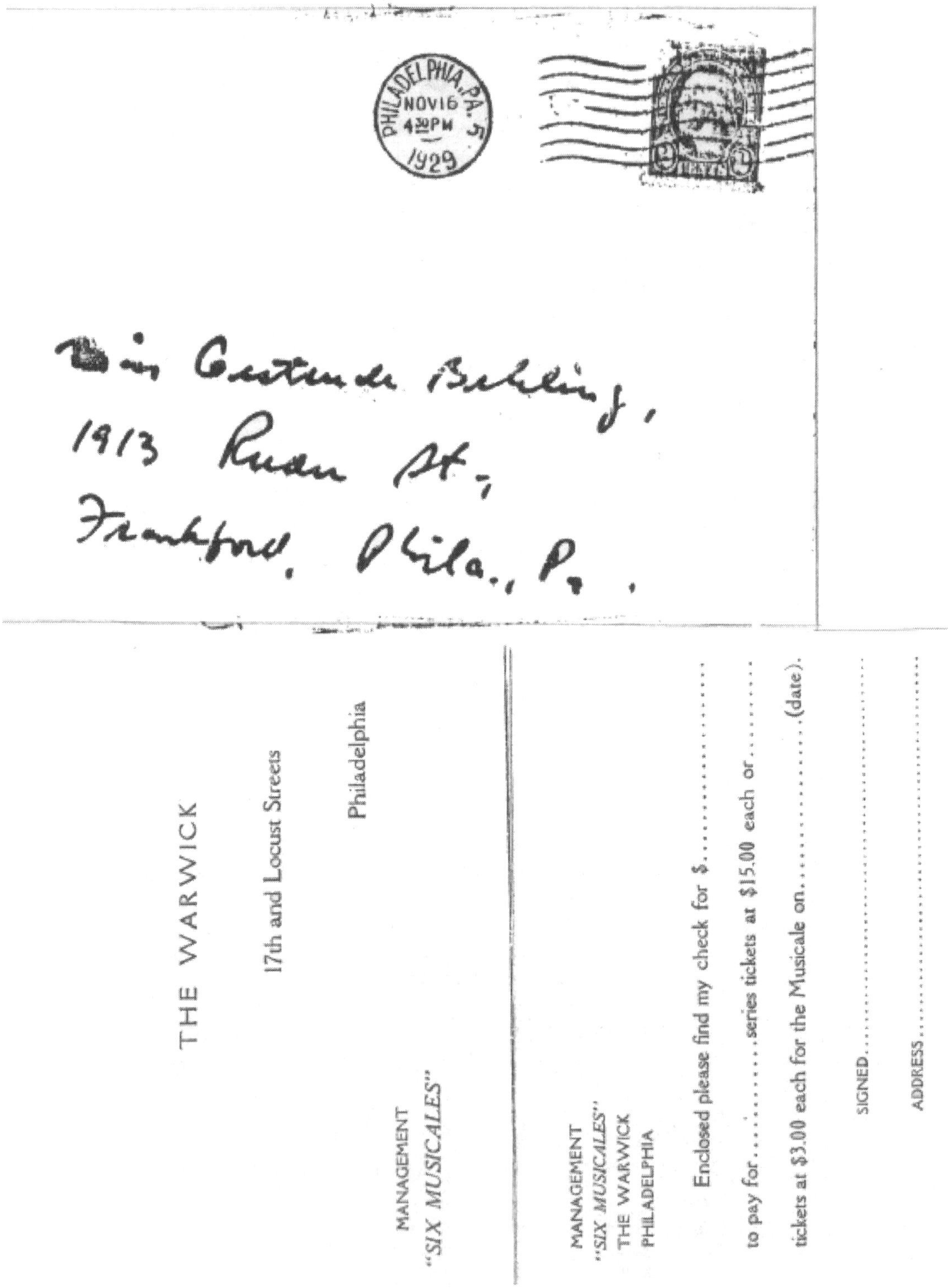

PHILADELPHIA, PA. 5
NOV 16
4:30 PM
1929

Miss Gertrude Belling,
1913 Ruan St.,
Frankford, Phila., Pa.

THE WARWICK

17th and Locust Streets

Philadelphia

MANAGEMENT
"SIX MUSICALES"

MANAGEMENT
"SIX MUSICALES"
THE WARWICK
PHILADELPHIA

Enclosed please find my check for $..........................

to pay for............series tickets at $15.00 each or..........

tickets at $3.00 each for the Musicale on.....................(date).

SIGNED..

ADDRESS..

NELSON EDDY
1112 PACKARD BUILDING
PHILADELPHIA, PA.

November 15, 1929.

Miss Gertrude Behling,
1913 Ruan Street,
Frankford, Philadelphia, Pa.

Dear Miss Behling:-

I regret that your letter addressed to Radio Station WIP was not forwarded to me until yesterday - too late to let you know about my first concert at The Warwick.

I am sending you separately one of the announcements that went out several weeks ago. The series rate, $12.50, will be accepted for the remaining five concerts, or $10.00 if you wish to subscribe to only four. I am enclosing two complimentary tickets for the next concert on December 18, and hope you will be able to use them.

Best wishes,

Nelson Eddy

Dec. 18
8.30 P. M.
2

"SIX MUSICALES"
THE WARWICK — PHILADELPHIA
SEASON 1929-1930
NELSON EDDY ALLAN JONES

"Nelson Eddy made a vigorous Mercutio, and his richly resonant baritone made the most of the limited vocal opportunities of the part."

November 14, 1929: Nelson did his first Warwick Hotel concert of the new series, with Irene Williams. [Note: A single ticket cost $3; the subscription price for the series of 6 was $15.] *Musical America,* November 25, 1929: "The program was Mozartean in aspect. Both singers had made a distinguished contribution late last season to **Le Nozze de Figaro**, as given by the Civic Company. Their voices blended beautifully in **The Magic Flute** duet, La dove Prende, and later in Crudele perche Finora, and the La ci Darem. Mr. Eddy's suave and finely handled baritone was heard to advantage in the Non piu Andrai."

November 21, 1929: Nelson sang at the Academy of Music in **Das Rheingold**. Co-stars included Arnold Gabor, one of the leading Met baritones. *Bulletin,* November 22, 1929: "Nelson Eddy used his fine voice effectively so far as he had opportunity, as Donner." *Daily News:* "Nelson Eddy is still the artist he has always been. Although his was not a long nor important bit, he evinced talent and voice." *Ledger:* "Nelson Eddy an excellent Donner, singing the great number near the close of the work in a beautiful voice." *Inquirer:* "Nelson Eddy's makeup as Donner was a vivid picture of a thunderclap, ready to commit a hammer murder any minute, and his voice enhanced the fine breadth of the music." *Musical America,* December 15, 1929: "Nelson Eddy's excellent baritone lent distinction to the role of Donner." *Musical Courier,* January 30, 1930: "Nelson Eddy, as Donner, was in beautiful voice and altogether convincing as the part."

November 25, 1929: The Choral Society of Philadelphia presented its first concert of its season at Drexel Institute. Nelson Eddy was soloist, with a chorus of 125 voices. More than 1000 people attended. *Record,* November 26, 1929: "Eddy's splendid sense of drama and his fine rich voice were especially adapted to 'An Old Witch Within That Wood Doth Dwell' from **Hansel and Gretl**. Other selections for Eddy's solo program included: 'Where'e'r You Walk,' Handel: 'Even Bravest Heart May Swell, Gounod, Starry Night, O, That It Were So' and 'The Open Road.'" *Bulletin:* "Nelson Eddy...was greeted with prolonged applause. Mr. Eddy was again notable for the excellence and skill of his singing, the beauty of his tonal quality, and an exceptionally pleasing personality."

November 27, 1929: Nelson sang at University of Pennsylvania's Glee Club. *Ledger,* November 28, 1929: "Nelson Eddy... guest soloist of the club, sang selections of Mozart, Bizet and Cadman as well as five love ditties in as many different languages." *Bulletin:* "The club was at its best in the sacred 'Seraphic Song' by Rubinstein, in which it was assisted by Nelson Eddy, guest soloist of the club, who was in exceptionally fine voice. His rich baritone, blended with the voices of the chorus, gave the large and enthusiastic audience the full beauty of the song."

December 5, 1929: Nelson sang in **Faust**. *Bulletin,* December 6, 1929: "The Civic Opera Company gave its best vocal performance this season last night, presenting **Faust**.... For consistent dramatic presentation, as well as excellent execution of vocal requirements, the honors went to George Baklanoff, as Mephistopheles, and Nelson Eddy, in the role of Valentine.... Nelson Eddy took the role with ease and looked the part to perfection. He was in excellent voice last night, singing the 'Farewell' in the second act with a tender simplicity and pathos not over-sentimentalized, and enacting the death scene in a convincing manner." *Record:* "Nelson Eddy, looking very young and quite handsome as Valentine, gave, as usual, a splendid account of himself, especially in the first act." [Anne Roselle was Marguerite] *Inquirer:* "Nelson Eddy was a sincere but underkeyed Valentine." *Daily News:* "And then there was our favorite, Nelson Eddy, the swashbuckling dueling brother, who gives his life to keep his sister's good name. Nelson still sends the local opera-goers into throes of enthusiasm." *Ledger:* "Nelson Eddy was an entirely adequate Valentine." *Musical America*, December 25, "Nelson Eddy gave a stirringly romantic performance."

December 15, 1929, clipping: Nelson will sing his second Warwick concert on December 18 with Allan Jones, including duets from **La Boheme** and **La Forza del Destino**. *Daily News,* December 16, 1929: "Nelson Eddy, the idol baritone of local operatic circles, took another step toward fame when he sang the second of a series of recitals in the Warwick's ballroom last night. Once again he displayed his inimitable voice in a charming manner, proving that he can accomplish wonders on the concert platform in as big a way as he does before the opera footlights.... It was with Allan Jones, the Gotham tenor who had his beginnings up Scranton way, that blond Eddy sang duets

NELSON EDDY
Who will sing in concert at the Hotel Warwick on next Wednesday evening

Pub. Ledger 12-15

Nelson Eddy, baritone, will present Allan Jones, tenor, of New York, in the second of his series of six musicales at the Warwick next Wednesday evening. They will sing duets from "La Boehme" and "La Forza del Destino." Mr. Jones will sing arias from "L'Africaine" and "Rigoletto," an Italian and an English group. Mr. Eddy will sing songs by Beethoven, a Russian group and a new Chinese cycle by Bantock. Theodore Paxon will be the accompanist.

VOCALISTS IN RECITAL

More Than 300 Hear Jones and Eddy at Warwick Hotel

Allan Jones, tenor, and Nelson Eddy, baritone, last night divided honors at a well received recital given at the Warwick Hotel. More than 300 persons attended.

Mr. Eddy and Mr. Jones presented selections from works of Beethoven, Tosti, Tschaikowsky, Bantock, Giannini and Warford. PL 12.19

Ledger 12-19

Inquirer 12-19

TENOR IN DEBUT HERE

Allen Jones in Recital With Nelson Eddy, Local Baritone

Allen Jones, tenor, of New York, made his Philadelphia debut last night on the programme of Nelson Eddy, well-known Philadelphia baritone, who presented the second of his series of recitals at the Warwick, Seventeenth and Locust streets. Jones, a former Scranton choir boy, was the winner of the tenor solo competition at the National Welsh Eisteddfod, at the Academy of Music here several years ago.

The lengthy programme covered a wide range of composers including Beethoven, Rachmaninoff, Tschaikowsky, Puccini, Meyerbeer, Bantock, Dunn, Verdi, Protheroe and others. Outstanding selections were the duet from "La Boheme," "O Mimi tu piu non torni"; an impressive Chinese cycle by Bantock, to which Mr. Eddy lent fine interpretation, and a group in English by Mr. Jones: "Under the Greenwood Tree", Dunn; "Tell Me, Oh Blue, Blue Sky", Giannini; "Ah Love, But a Day", Protheroe, and "Earth is Enough", Warford. Inq. 12-19

38

Moves Up Step

Nelson Eddy Adds to Fame as Idol Baritone

Nelson Eddy, the idol baritone of local operatic circles, took another step toward fame when he sang the second of a series of recitals in the Warwick's ballroom last night. Once again he displayed his inimitable voice in a charming manner, proving that he can accomplish wonders on the concert platform in as big a way as he does before the opera footlights.

It was with Allen Jones, the Gotham tenor who had his beginning up Scranton way, that blond Eddy sang duets from the operas. Nelson's voice was advantageously heard in a rendition of a Boheme duet, that sent his listeners into tantrums of enthusiasm. His voice is rich and sonorous. Having watched it these past years grow in tone and volume, we predict even greater and more scintillating possibilities for this local songster.

Eddy has the knack of giving a zest to his notes. They seem liquid and yet they possess solidity that rarely is found in a baritone. He has pitch and range, together with all of the essentials One would think his voice is the most pleasing of its kind in these parts.

Jones sang several solo arias from the operatic writings, and a group of Italian and English compositions, portraying skill and versatility. Theodore Paxson's accompaniment was more than adequate.

News 12-19

BARITONE AND TENOR

Nelson Eddy and Allan Jones in Program of Solos and Duets

Continuing a series of six recitals, Nelson Eddy, baritone, appeared, last evening, in the ballroom of the Hotel Warwick, in second of the series, with Allan Jones, tenor, as the assisting artist.

Mr. Eddy opened the program with a group of Beethoven selections, including "In questa tomba oscura," "Adelaide" and Die Ehre Gottes aus der Natur," his well-controlled tone and excellent diction giving added significance to the numbers. Skill in modulation and beauty of expression were the outstanding characteristics of a group of Russian songs, including Rachmaninoff's "At Night," Tschaikowsky's "At the Cotillion" and "On the Steppe," by Gretchaninoff. A group of songs by Bantock, "Desolation," "Under the Moon," "The Celestial Weaver" and "The Return of Spring," were the baritone's only other offering.

Mr. Jones, a personable young man, with a pleasing lyric tenor voice, sang with ease and considerable artistry, although seeming to be a little nervous in the beginning. His selections included the popular "Questo o quella," from Verdi's "Rigoletto," and "O Paradis!" from Myerbeer's L'Africaine," the latter number being especially well-sung.

The two singers were at their best in the two operatic duets which competed their program, "O Mimi tu piu non torni," from Puccini's "La Boheme," and the beautiful "Solenne in quest'ora," from Verdi's "La Forza del Destino." Theodore Paxson was a capable and sympathetic accompanist. 12-19

Bulletin 12-19

An innovation of this season has been the series of six concerts by Nelson Eddy, young baritone of the Civic Opera Company, in the fine new ballroom of the Warwick Hotel. He is offering his third program this week with the coöperation of the Russian String Quartet. On Feb. 20 he will have the assistance of Alma Peterson, soprano. On March 12 the assisting artist will be Ronald O'Neil, pianist. Bianca Saroya, soprano, and Dimitri Onofrei, tenor, will be Mr. Eddy's associates in the final concert on April 10. MA 1-25

Musical America 1-25-30

from the operas. Nelson's voice was advantageously heard in a rendition of a **Boheme** duet that sent his listeners into tantrums of enthusiasm. His voice is rich and sonorous. Having watched it these past years grow in tone and volume, we predict even greater and more scintillating possibilities for this local songster…. Eddy has the knack of

GLEE CLUB CONCERT

University Male Chorus at Academy With Nelson Eddy Soloist

Offering a wide variety of folk songs, ballads and classical numbers, the University of Pennsylvania Glee Club, under the authoritative baton of Dr. Alexander Matthews, gave its annual Thanksgiving Eve concert at the Academy of Music last night. The 150 men, comprising the chorus, sang with good balance of parts and unity of purpose.

The club was at its best in the sacred "Seraphic Song," by Rubinstein, in which it was assisted by Nelson Eddy, guest soloist of the club, who was in exceptionally fine voice. His rich baritone, blended with the voices of the chorus, gave the large and enthusiastic audience the full beauty of the song.

The chorus opened the program with three rather slow love ballads, "Ride Out on Wings of Song," Berwald; "Come Again, Sweet Love," and "Tell All You Ladies Now on Land." In the second group, including "London Town" German, and "Lullaby," William S. Nagle (student conductor), the chorus did much better, partly because the numbers offered their voices a wider range and more power.

Mr. Eddy contributed largely to the success of the concert. He sang two group of songs, the first including "Non piu andrai," from "The Marriage of Figaro," and the "Song of the Flea," Moussorgsky. He seemed to enjoy the singing of these songs as much as the audience enjoyed hearing him. His second was made up of five little love songs, in as many languages. The best of these were "Niet, niet, is nie chotchou," Levinne, and "If God Left Only You," Densmore.

The chorus also sang the primitive pagan, "The Sacrifice of the Aryan Rose," Charles Cadman, in which it was again assisted by Mr. Eddy, and closed the program with "Long Ago in Alcala," arranged by Mr. Matthews.

Bulletin 11-27

FAUST AT ACADEMY

Civic Opera Sings Gounod's Work With Well Balanced Cast

The Civic Opera Company gave its best vocal performance this season last night, presenting "Faust," the melodious opera based on the Goethe tragedy.

Although dramatically some of the cast left much to be desired, the voices balanced against each other in the quartets and duets with true tonal quality, achieving excellent blendings and contrasts.

Anne Roselle sang the part of Marguerite, instead of Marie Sundelius, as originally announced. Miss Roselle possesses a voice of light texture, extremely true to pitch, and a clear, sweet tone which she used to great advantage in the love scenes. She also has sufficient flexibility to make of the "Jewel Song" something more than a mere exercise in scales.

Her volume, though not great, was yet forceful enough to be heard above the orchestra and the heavier voices matched against hers, and she did especially fine work in the final trio with Faust and Mephistopheles in the prison scene, as well as in the dramatic solo in the preceding cathedral scene.

For consistent dramatic presentation, as well as excellent execution of vocal requirements, the honors went to George Baklanoff, as Mephistopheles, and Nelson Eddy, in the role of Valentine, Marguerite's unfortunate brother. Baklanoff developed his role with a satirical humor that added zest to his burlesque solos, as well as singing with resonant, contrasting tones that lent richness and beauty to all of his vocal work.

As Valentine, Nelson Eddy took the role with ease and looked the part to perfection. He was in excellent voice last night, singing the "Farewell" in the second act with a tender simplicity and pathos not over-sentimentalized, and enacting the death scene in a convincing manner.

David Dorlini made a personable Faust, his lyric tenor being well suited to the melodious, tender flights of the role, although his acting was stiff and "stagy." He sang the "Salut Demeure" with fine feeling, bringing out the simple beauty of the melody, and achieved a notably fine effect in the duet with Marguerite at the close of the garden scene. Veronica Sweigart made an appealing Siebel, and Eric Belar sang the role of Wagner.

The quartet, "Eh Quoi, Toujours Seule," with Martha, well taken by Ruth Montague, Mephistopheles, Faust and Marguerite, was cleverly handled, while the male trio of Valentine and his antagonists in the duel scene, "Que-Voulez-Vous, Messieurs," was one of the best bits of the evening.

The weak spot was the chorus, which was woefully slim in tone, and whose tenors rasped badly, in the opening chorus of Act 2. The "Soldiers' Chorus" sounded better when the women's voices joined the ensemble. The off-stage choruses were well done.

Alexander Smallens conducted with his usual energy, giving the lilting ballet music a perfect rhythmic swing, and keeping the orchestra well in hand.

Bulletin 12-6

50

FAUST IS PRESENTED IN SPLENDID STYLE BY CIVIC COMPANY

Baklanoff and Anna Roselle in Stellar Roles Charm Large Audience.

SMALLENS AS CONDUCTOR

"Faust," as difficult an opera as it is popular, was presented by the Civic Company last night in the Academy of Music. With the splendid conducting of Alexander Smallens, whose interpretation of Gounod's beautiful score was superb, and the capable performance of George Baklanoff as Mephistopheles the opera was at once well acted and musically convincing.

The success of "Faust" depends largely upon its villainous trafficker in souls, and this baritone invested the role with the desired finesse, adding a rich and dramatic voice and a commanding presence. He sang the famous serenade and the song of the Golden Calf with sardonic humor. Without the exaggeration which very often transform this role into a caricature, Baklanoff portrayed the elegant Prince of Darkness with humor, intelligence and power.

Anne Roselle made a pictorial Marguerite, stately and graceful. Her voice has a clear, crystal quality and, although it lacks power, is extremely pleasant. Her low register is weak, but the role offers ample opportunity for a display of silvery tones, and the "Jewel Song" won for her the hearty approval of the large audience.

As Faust, David Dorlini proved himself a capable tenor. Nelson Eddy, looking very young and quite handsome as Valentine, gave, as usual, a splendid account of himself, especially in the aria of the first act. Veronica Sweigart rehabilitated the role of Siebel and sang the "Flower Song" with color and charm. Ruth Montague made a humorous Martha and sang her part with intelligence. Eric Belar was the Wagner.

The effect of the performance was augmented by a large and well-trained chorus in colorful costumes, which sang the "Soldiers' Chorus" with spirit as well as precision, and pretty sets and a ballet.

E. F.

51

Record 12-6

giving a zest to his notes. They seem liquid and yet they posses solidity that rarely is found in a baritone. He has pitch and range, together with all of the essentials. One would think his voice is the most pleasing of its kind in these parts.... Jones sang several solo arias from the operatic writings, and a group of Italian and English compositions, portraying skill and versatility. Theodore Paxson's accompaniment was more than adequate." *Bulletin,* "Mr. Jones, a personable young man with a pleasing lyric tenor voice, sang with ease and considerable artistry, although seeming to be a little nervous in the beginning.... The two singers were at their best in the two operatic duets which completed their program."

December 18, 1929, Nelson sang in a matinee performance of **Hansel and Gretl**. *Bulletin,* December 19, 1929: "Notably good, both vocally and in characterization, were Nelson Eddy and Ruth Montague, as Peter and Gertrude, parents of the mischievous pair of youngsters." [Note: Irene Williams was Gretl and Grace Leslie sang Hansel.] *Record:* "Nelson Eddy, who portrayed the father, happily demonstrated what good diction can accomplish in upholding English as an operatic language. Vocally he gave a delightful performance adorned with a crystalline clarity in handling our idiom." *Ledger:* "Nelson Eddy...confirmed a conviction that he is one of the most gifted baritones, histrionically and vocally, on Philadelphia's lyric stage." *Musical Courier,* January 11, 1930: "Nelson Eddy as Peter added another to his increasing list of successful roles--varied as they are in character--and confirmed the [conviction] that he is one of the best baritones on the Philadelphia lyric stage." *Inquirer:* "Nelson Eddy, as the erring, but amiable father, tottered, but did not tipple publicly in the presence of impressionable children." *Musical America,* January 10, 1930: "Nelson Eddy as the Father showed a gift for comedy equal to that already displayed in more serious roles." Nelson caused a furor, described in a letter to *Musical America:* "Nelson Eddy, as Peter the Broom-maker, came on the stage reeling drunk (I mean he acted reeling drunk, not that he himself actually was!) flourishing a hip flask. Now, as all the world knows, it's in the play. BUT the Executive Committee of the Whisky Can't Touch Us Society sent a letter of protest to about everybody remotely connected with the incident, stating that the scene was objectionable on account of the large number of children in the audience." Mrs. Elizabeth Ferguson, chairman of the committee, declared the scene was objectionable because of the number of children present. One copy was sent to Rev. Frederick W. Poole, chairman of the Philadelphia Board of Theater control. "I believe that no scene of drunken revelry should be performed before children, and that the opera could have been slightly altered if, as was charged, a drunken man was seen on the boards, in view of the ancient popular sanction of the fairy tale," Poole said. "However, in my opinion, it is ridiculous to become upset over it now." Karl T.F. Schroeder, stage manager of the opera company, reported that the performers drank only uncolored water. "If these good women object to the opera they should take up their objections with Humperdinck, the composer. Of course, we could censor the opera, but when we have to begin to censor fairy tales, it is time we awoke to our senses." [Note: Nelson apparently sang the role again on December 28th.]

January 2, 1930: Nelson sang in **Aida** at the Academy of Music. *Daily News,* January 3, 1930: "Nelson Eddy, as usual, was a high spot. Cast as the Ethiopian king, he proved his versatility in exceptional parts." *Inquirer:* "The superb soprano of Florence Austral dominated **Aida** when that Verdi perennial was presented by the Civic Opera Company in the Academy of Music last night.... After the opening scene, Mrs. Henry M. Tracy, president and general manager of the Civic Opera Company, came before the footlights and made an eloquent and appropriate plea for the early arrival of opera audiences. She quite pertinently pointed out that punctual attendance is obligatory at Philadelphia Orchestra concerts, since latecomers are barred from the auditorium until the intermission, and she asked the audience whether some such custom would find favor at opera offerings, for, as she remarked, to miss the overture often means missing 'the history of the opera' and some of the most beautiful music. Mentioning that **Siegfied** begins at 7:30 next Thursday, she requested all to arrive at 7:20 PM... Nelson Eddy infused force into both his acting and his singing as Amonasro, which is one of his best roles." *Ledger:* "Nelson Eddy... as usual, carried the role with ability and sang in unusually good voice." *Musical America,* January 25, 1930: "The Amonasro of Nelson Eddy was characterized with fierce intensity and he sang very finely." *Record:* "Nelson Eddy gave his usual excellent vocal and dramatic interpretation of the role of Amonasro." *Bulletin:* "Nelson Eddy again appeared as Amonasro, giving an interpretation which has been improved by a toning down of the acting, while he sings the part with more ease than formerly, with much of his well-known tonal beauty, although there is still some uncertainty in one or two of the higher tones and it is again evident that the popular young baritone is at his best in the lighter roles." *Musical Courier,* January 11, 1930: "Nelson Eddy was in fine voice, portraying the part of

JANUARY 17, 1930

CIVIC CO. PRESENTS 'TWILIGHT OF GODS'

Florence Austral and Hans Taenzler Lead in Fine Performance at Academy

LOCAL SINGERS EXCELLENT

By SAMUEL L. LACIAR

The amazing Civic Opera Company, which is always accomplishing the impossible, reached the summit of its achievements in this line last evening at the Academy of Music by giving a remarkable performance of Wagner's "Goetterdaemmerung," the closing opera of "The Nibelungen Ring," of which the Civic Company now has completed the first full performance by any local company.

The vocal honors of the opera were carried off by Florence Austral in the role of Brunnhilde. Miss Austral was in splendid voice, which was shown to its best advantage in the great Immolation Scene of the last act.

Hans Taenzler was an excellent Siegfried, both vocally and dramatically, doing the death scene with remarkable power and conviction and singing the difficult music very well.

Homecoming for Allen Hinckley

Allen Hinckley, formerly a resident of this city, made his first operatic appearance here in many years, taking the role of Hagen. His voice is deep and heavy and of the dark color required for this role, and his acting showed his thorough familiarity with the German tradition and with the Ring operas.

Nelson Eddy was the Gunther. He sang admirably as he always does, but even more striking was his delineation of the pathos and the inherent nobility of the character, while Hildegarde Bartz was an attractive and thoroughly acceptable Gutrune in every respect.

Ralph Jusko did the small but important role of Alberich convincingly and with unusually fine diction, a point in which he was excelled in the cast only by Mr. Taenzler, and Nevada van der Veer was effective in the beautiful Waltraute scene, one of the finest scenes in the entire Ring operas.

Local Singers Are Excellent

The roles of Norns and the Rhinemaidens were taken by local members of the company who distinguished themselves by excellent work.

The Rhine maidens were the same three who took these roles in "Das Rheingold," Elizabeth Wynkoop as Woglinder, Marie Buddy as Wellgunda and Mabel Marston as Flosshilde. The Norns were Olive Marshall, Veronica Sweigart and Ruth Montague.

Alexander Smallens conducted with that spirit and verve which he always exhibits and brought out the many beauties of the opera most successfully and Karl T. F. Schroeder accomplished wonders with the stage settings and scenery with material necessarily somewhat limited. The audience was both large and enthusiastic.

Philadelphia Civic Opera Company Reaches Peak of Perfection at Academy

Dr. Conwell's memorable Acres of Diamonds proved only too true once again, when the Philadelphia Civic Opera Co. presented one of the most splendid offerings of Wagnerian opera that has been seen and heard here for many a day. Despite the wide variety of Germanic song-stories that local opera-goers have been buying tickets for, the "Goetterdaemmerung," that was applauded so vociferously in the Academy of Music, last night, virtually reached the peak of perfection. And it set the goal for the same presentation that will be offered by the German Opera Co. tomorrow night.

Alexander Smallens, master wielder of the baton, was forced to split the major honors with golden-voiced Florence Austral, the warbler from the Antipodes. Although this fair lady has been heard here before, both in opera and concert, she never evinced the unusual powers and delightful qualities of her voice. Enthralling and charming, she delivered one of the most pleasurable and exacting renditions of Bruennhilde that these eyes and ears have witnessed. Even with cuts, "Goetterdaemmerung" ran for four hours. To be sure, interest in German opera is at the peak, but all enthusiasm is being reserved for the visiting troupe. But it is doubtful if any other company, no matter how skilled its singers might be, or how marvelous its sets, could have offered so matchless a presentation. The gods came down from their Valhalla to lend their aid and protection, so it seemed.

Florence Austral was dizzying in her spell. She seemed to trill so beautifully, so evenly. Her voice has a luster which was never before discerned. Her histrionics were never forced. She seemed to just fit a role that was created alone for her. Wagnerian opera is her true forte, and her contributions last night will go far in assisting her in this endeavor. Hans Taenzler, who, incidentally, was with Mr. Hurok's company last year, played Siegfried. Here is a capably voiced songster for "ring opera." He has power and range. His appearance adds indefinite charm. His work last night exceeded his accomplishments just seven nights before, when he was cast in the titular role of "Siegfried."

Allen Hinckley was the diabolic Hagen of the occasion, singing the deep role in a true style. Nelson Eddy, the ever-popular, was Gunther. His makeup was perfect, matching his vocal accomplishments. Hildegrade Bartz was Gutrune, exhibiting great charm and lovely voice. Ralph Jusko was the vile Alberich. And what gorgeous singing by the three Norns, Veronica Seigart, Ruth Montague and Okive Marshall!

Alex Smallens kept waving away in his same old vivacious manner, bringing the soul and depth of the Bareuthean music out so splendidly. Smallens completed his presentation of the story of the Niebelungen, a momentous and praiseworthy job. He was a bit foolhardy for attempting it, a thorough musician in doing it, and a hero for completing it!

Amonasro with excellent vocal interpretation and rather more of barbaric dignity than with the uncontrolled spirit of an injured king."

January 10, 1930, *Bulletin:* "The Germantown Choral Society, assisted by Henrietta Conrad, soprano, and Nelson Eddy, baritone, gave the first concert of its seventh season at the High School last night. An enlarged chorus, with a consequent welcome increase in volume, together with a sprightly program, made it probably the most enjoyable ever offered by the society.... Mr. Eddy added to his already large following in Germantown with solo numbers which showed him at his best, three dramatic numbers by Geoffrey O'Hara being especially well received. The duets by Conrad and Mr. Eddy also were much enjoyed."

January 14, 1930: Nelson sang at a women's luncheon at the Penn Athletic Club. As a closing number he did the drunken scene from **Hansel and Gretl**. An article in the *Ledger* commented: "Baritone Has His Joke," and elaborated: "Introducing the song, Mr. Eddy said he would sing it with fear and trembling. 'Under the instigation of the W.C.T.U,' he explained, 'I was nearly arrested the last time I sang it.' He referred to a resolution passed by the temperance society protesting against the scene, with special reference to it being offered before children."

January 16, 1930: Nelson sang in **Götterdämmerung**. [Although the complete Ring cycle was performed, he didn't sing in middle two operas.] *Bulletin,* November 17, 1930: "**Götterdämmerung** was given a finely wrought performance at the Academy of Music of Music last night by the Civic Opera Company, with Hans Taenzler in the tenor role of the heroic Siegfried and Florence Austral as Bruennhilde.... Some opera goers who are accustomed to consider Nelson Eddy as the possessor of a pleasant but light baritone, must have been surprised at his interpretation of Gunther, King of the Gibichungs... The wide tonal compass of this role was sung with richness and sonority with a genuine feeling for the spaciousness of the music and unusual beauty of tone. Histrionically Eddy was in keeping with tradition." *Record:* "Nelson Eddy was an effective Gunther." *Inquirer:* "Nelson Eddy competently carried the role of Gunther, so that none might have suspected it was his initial effort in this rigorous role." *Ledger:* "Nelson Eddy was the Gunther. He sang admirably as he always does, but even more striking was his delineation of the pathos and the inherent nobility of the character." *Daily News:* "Nelson Eddy, the ever-popular, was Gunther. His makeup was perfect, matching his vocal accomplishments." *Musical Courier,* February 1, 1930: "Nelson Eddy appeared to advantage in the rather ungrateful role of Gunther, which he invested with a tender pathos, and in which the beauty of his voice was always evident."

January 23, 1930: This week the Warwick Hotel concert co-starred the Russian String Quartet. *Record,* January 24, 1930: "Nelson Eddy...last night demonstrated a large degree of vocal technique during the musicale in the Warwick, almost wholly given to the famous compositions of Brahms. The capacity gathering... thrilled particularly to the singer's lush voice as Mr. Eddy obliged with a delightful encore. Accompanying him at the piano was his colleague and fellow artist, Theodore Paxson, who handled his part of the rendition well.... Mr. Eddy's ability to surmount the obstacles offered in Brahms' 'Minnelied' and 'Wie Melodien Ziehtes Mir' brought out the richest qualities of his ample voice." *Bulletin:* "Nelson Eddy, baritone, last evening added another notable performance to a long list of successful appearances before Philadelphia's audiences. With every available seat taken, there was evidence of the popularity of Mr. Eddy's recitals, while the prolonged applause which greeted his selections left no doubt of his audiences' appreciation of the mellow beauty of his voice and his skillful interpretation of the classic Brahms. His numbers [were] sung in German with excellent diction." *Camden Courier:* "Mr. Eddy's singing needs no commendation to those who have heard him.... Whether the occasion is a new appearance in opera or as a soloist, musical and artistic advance can always be noted. Mr. Eddy was in splendid voice last night and in just the mood for Brahms...One of the nice things about Mr. Eddy's singing is that you don't have to clap your hands off to get more. One of his encores, the charming serenade, 'The Disappointed Lover,' he was compelled to repeat.... Mr. Eddy is at his best in songs in which he can act and interpret varying moods as show in the encore serenade." *Daily News:* "His voice discloses improvement every time it is heard. And last night's program afforded him every opportunity to show the latest developments. Another thing that this Eddy has is poise. He can hold any group enraptured with his personality that virtually is encompassing. It is high time that Eddy starts off for broader fields. His repertoire of operas is large and varied." As for the Russian string Quartet, the *Camden Courier* noted, "The quartet's playing of the piano quintet was decidedly wobbly."

January 31, 1930, *Ledger:* "Julia Claussen, Paul Althouse and Nelson Eddy Carry Off Vocal Honors. ... The Civic Opera Company gave its tenth performance of the present season at the Academy of Music last evening with an excellent presentation of Saint-Saens' **Samson et Delilah** before an audience astonishingly large, when the bad weather is considered.... Mr. Eddy proved the role of High Priest is one of his finest. He was a commanding and authoritative figure in his acting and the music is ideally suited to the register and timbre of his voice." *Camden Record:* "Mr. Eddy can always be relied on to do his utmost with any part assigned to him. As the High Priest he proved a master of voice and dramatics. The music of the part is as if it was written for his voice and therefore the results throughout were most satisfactory. There is no guess-work about Mr. Eddy's work; he knows thoroughly ever role he essays." *Record:* "Nelson Eddy as the High Priest and Sigrid Nilssen as the old Hebrew sang with admiral tonal purity." *Inquirer:* "Nelson Eddy in masterful make-up gave his agreeable baritone to the part of the High Priest." *Musical Courier,* February 8, 1930: "Nelson Eddy proved the role to be one of his best, while his mellow baritone with a noticeable increase in power, exactly suited the music of the part. "

February 12, 1930, *Bulletin:* "The Matinee Musical Club Chorus...last night gave its annual mid-winter concert in the ballroom of the Bellevue-Stratford for the delectation of an audience so large that various uniformed satellites had to fetch extra chairs for the surplus.... Oddly enough, the Chorus did not start out last night's festivities. Nelson Eddy did that, his robust baritone booming out such offerings as 'Coates' Sea Rapture,' 'Water Boy,' by Robinson, and the perennial baritonic favorite, 'Give a Man a Horse He Can Ride,' by O'Hara. Vociferously encored, Mr. Eddy retaliated with a mellifluent aria from Meyerbeer's **L'Africaine**... The pièce de resistance, and last on the program, was Deems Taylor's 'The Highwayman,' a cantata for women's voice and a lone baritone... Mr. Eddy's dulcet vocalizing furnished the baritone solo with éclat. The work of the Chorus was exceptionally fine, although Mr. Taylor in the composition of this opus flung down notes and let the chips fall as they would. The Chorus began at a tempo that was a shade too rapid for the enunciation of the words, a thing deriving from their onomatopoetic character. Mr. Eddy's almost dispassionate calmness quieted things down somewhat so that the anti-climax, with the baritone singing against the Chorus, was carefully and accurately fitted together."

February 13, 1930: Nelson sang in **The Magic Flute** at the Academy of Music. *Inquirer,* February 14, 1930: "Undaunted by difficulties of staging, and the eleventh-hour inability of popular Irene Williams to appear in a prominent part, the Civic gave this 138-year-old 'sing-spiel' with eloquent emphasis upon those two elements of prime importance in any artistic undertaking--spirit and sincerity--again demonstrating the courageous resourcefulness of the organization, and putting the performance through with a brightness and buoyancy which gave little hint of the obstacles encountered, and overcome.... An especially engaging aspect of the occasion was the fact that Alexander Smallens alternated his able and sympathetic conduction by accompanying the singers upon a baby grand piano, placed squarely in the center of the musicians' pit, upon which as placed the conductor's score. Thus Mr. Smallens, approximating a performance upon the harpsichord, enhanced the atmospheric effectiveness of the occasion.... Nelson Eddy again exhibited his flair for comedy and sang with fine enunciation and rounded tones, the music of that curious creature, Papageno. His Papagena, originally scheduled for Miss Williams (who was still suffering from the effects of spraining an ankle in **Hansel and Gretl** Christmas week), was sung so agreeably and ably by Elizabeth Harrison in her single scene, as to arouse regrets that cuts were made." *Daily News:* "Last nights' offering established another record, for that blond baritone, Nelson Eddy, who achieved unlimited more applause than his usual receptive audience ever accorded him." *Musical Courier,* February 22: "Nelson Eddy, as Papageno, held the center of attention much of the time by his fine portrayal of this humorous role." [Other stars were Alma Peterson as Pamina, Made Cowden as the Queen, David Dorlini as Tamino and Herbert Gould as Sarastro.] *Bulletin:* "Nelson Eddy... in his feathery costume, as usual threw himself whole-heartedly into his part and was frolicsome and vocally alluring, with his supple baritone admirably used, scoring another success." *Record:* "Nelson Eddy, as Papageno, infused life into the very rudimentary comedy scenes." *Ledger:* "Nelson Eddy was an excellent Papageno, realizing to the full the comic aspects of the role, and singing as well as he acted."

February 20, 1930, the next Warwick Hotel concert co-starred Alma Peterson, soprano. *Record,* February 21, 1930: "An attractive recital... Mr. Eddy's admirable voice was heard effectively." *Ledger:* "Mr. Eddy sang, among others, 'Dweller in Dreams,' by Madeleine Walther. This was the first presentation of this number and it was given an

LE NOZZE DI FIGARO

Civic Company Presents Gay and Graceful Version of Mozart Opera

An exceptionally well balanced cast presented the further adventures of Figaro, the barber rogue of Seville, in the Mozart "Marriage of Figaro" at a sprightly pace and style which made this long and verbosely florid operatic comedy highly entertaining to the large audience in the Academy of Music last night.

With its many lengthy passages of recitatif, ornamental arias, and measured phrases, this four-act work of Mozart, involved as it is with plots, and counter-plots of Figaro and Susanna, betrothed servants of the Count and Countess Almaviva, and old-style discursive moments on the part of the protagonists, can be made unutterably dull by heavy handling, especially since the action proceeds far more slowly than that of "The Barber of Seville."

The Civic Opera cast, however, avoided the pitfalls of the piece, and gave the comedy with zest and sparkle, under the expert direction of Alexander Smallens, who kept orchestra and ensembles, in all the extremely difficult rapid chorus work, precisely in hand. The closing ensembles of the first, second and last acts were excellent examples of immediate attack, swift contrast and true "Mozart" tone and finish, having neither too much nor too little volume.

Each member of the cast acquitted his role deftly. Ivan Ivantzoff as Figaro, developed the self-assured but cleverly disguised arrogance of the cunning barber, and sang the several arias of the role with mellow tones and much flexibility. Irene Williams, as Susanna, played the part with flirtations grace and did beautiful vocal work, singing the exacting slow-tempo arias with clear sustained tone, and the lively airs with flexible ease and clever use of contrast.

Nelson Eddy, who during the past month has suffered from laryngitis, reappeared in the role of the Count, and displayed his customary stage presence and discriminating vocal talent; his voice, carefully used, showing no strain and but slightly below its usual resonance. Alma Peterson, as the Countess Rosina, made a striking blonde contrast to her little maid, and sang with finished phrasing and clarity most enjoyable. She won long applause after the "Dove Song" in Act 2, as did Miss Williams in the garden scene in the last act, after the "Deh Vieni, Non Tardar" (Why So Long Delay?), in which she attained an exquisitely clear and true high pianissimo.

Genia Zielinska, as the philandering Cherubino, played the role with a comic girlish simper and sang the "Voi Che Sapete" (What Is This Feeling?) with languishing appeal. The rest of the cast received frequent applause after their ensemble work. Marie Buddy, Sheldon Walker, Maybelle Marston, James Montgomery, Ralph Jusko and Louis Purdey complete the list.

The final garden scene, with its delicate foliage and blue lighting, produced lovely illusion of forgotten romance and adventure.

Bul. 3-28

CIVIC SINGERS GIVE 'MARRIAGE OF FIGARO' IN PLEASING MANNER

Mozart's Opera Presented With Fine Interpretation of Composer's Work.

SCORE FAIRLY SPARKLES

"THE MARRIAGE OF FIGARO," opera in four acts, music by Wolfgang A. Mozart, book by Lorenzo da Ponte, was presented last evening by the Civic Opera Company in the Academy of Music.

THE CAST.

Figaro	Ivan Ivantsoff
Count	Nelson Eddy
Countess	Alma Peterson
Susanna	Irene Williams
Cherubino	Genia Zielinska
Barbarina	Marie Buddy
Bartolo	Sheldon Walker
Marcellina	Maybelle Marston
Basilio	James Montgomery
Antonio	Ralph Jusko
Don Curzio	Louis Purdey

By H. T. CRAVEN

With the resourceful Alexander Smallens commanding the orchestral forces and keeping a vigilant eye on the singers, the Civic has acquired a comforting proficiency in the interpretation of Mozart. The assumption that vocalists of superlative caliber are indispensable in operas such as "The Magic Flute" or "The Marriage of Figaro" loses in this situation something of its traditional claim to respect. By good training, musical intelligence, excellent taste and artistic sincerity, the Civic's personnel has adapted itself to an exacting field.

There were no phenomenal voices in last night's production of "The Marriage of Figaro." But there was, on the other hand, a gratifying devotion to pitch, a flexible treatment of the Mozartian idiom and a very genuine appreciation, both in lyricism and acting of the Mozartian spirit.

Score Made to Sparkle.

The tempo of the proceedings had vivacity and fluency, especially after the second act, and in the midst of a complicated comedy intrigue, which only the hardiest of libretto fans are competent to follow, the spirit of eighteenth century gayety was engendered. The imperishable score sparkled and shimmered, and gems of pure song rightly held sway.

Nelson Eddy as the Count, Alma Peterson as the Countess, Irene Williams as Susanna and Ivan Ivantzoff as Figaro shouldered their responsibilities with a courageous gallantry that possessed an accent of authority. Positive brilliancy was scarcely ever present.

Eddy came nearest to being a stellar figure, with his virile baritone and winning personality. Miss Williams caught the piquancy and archness of Susanna. Genia Zielinska was a passable Cherubino, who rose to higher estate in the classic "Voi che sapete."

Smallens co-ordinated all the factors of value in the performance, fusing them with facility and grace. He made a difficult work seem easy and unstrained in interpretation. This is quite the effect that should be achieved in this blithe opera, whose musical subtleties and profundities lie beneath the surface.

Rec. 3-28

'LE NOZZE DI FIGARO' BY CIVIC COMPANY

Mozart's Sparkling Opera Is Sung Before Large Audience at the Academy

Philadelphia has been fortunate during the past season in hearing no less than four Mozart operas. That divine composer, "the master of us all," as Gounod said, has been too seldom given on the stage in recent years. Last evening that brisk and sparkling comedy, "Le Nozze di Figaro," was sung by the Civic Company at the Academy of Music before a large audience, whose applause revealed its appreciation. We have sometimes thought it would be interesting to hear "Le Nozze" and "Il Barbiere" in succession. Mozart takes up Almaviva and Rosina, of course, after they have passed the romantic age, though the Count is an incorrigible philanderer.

Never, surely, was more delightful music in this kind written than the Mozart work. Humor and beauty are nicely commingled in it. Though it runs trippingly along for the most part, there are sentimental interludes. The performance last evening owed much to Mr. Smallens, whose skill as a conductor overcame many difficulties. For the work of the orchestra there can be nothing but praise. The chorus was less efficient.

Mozart requires an elegance of which few singers of today are capable. The Susanna of Miss Irene Williams stood out from the other impersonations by reason of this quality. Her clear and true soprano is well adapted to the lighter measures; but in the beautiful aria of the last act, "Deh vieni," its exquisite quality was most fully disclosed. Her great personal charm completed the picture. Mr. Eddy was a highly competent Almaviva, and much the same thing may be said of Miss Peterson's Countess. Mr. Ivantzoff fell somewhat short of expectation as Figaro, and Miss Zielinska sang Cherubino's "Voi che sapete" rather badly. Still Mozart is Mozart.

Inq. 3-28

ovation. Miss Walther was present and was roundly applauded." *Bulletin:* "The interesting and admirably rendered program officially ended with a duet by Miss Peterson and Mr. Eddy, 'L'Oasis,' from **Thais**. However, responding to enthusiastic applause, they sang the duet from **The Magic Flute.** Theodore Paxson was the accompanist."

February 27, 1930: Nelson sang in **L'elisir d'amore** at the Academy of Music. *Record,* February 28, 1930: "A spirited presentation... Nelson Eddy donned the uniform and bristling mustachios of Belcore with a grand military gesture, and stalked with dignity through the part. His voice was adequate and he sang with pleasing assurance throughout.... Under the baton of Alexander Smallens, the score received a splendid reading." *Inquirer:* "Nelson Eddy's excellent baritone and comedy capabilities found expression as the military man, Belcore." *Bulletin:* "Mr. Eddy's baritone was sonorous and well controlled in the vocal flourishes that are required of him." *Ledger:* "Nelson Eddy is a baritone whose voice is not merely sonorous but musical, and he made a fine figure as Sergeant Belcore." *Musical Courier,* March 8, 1930: "Nelson Eddy, as Belcore, was highly satisfactory. His smooth, rich, baritone voice is a joy at all times and this performance was no exception. His acting as the dashing soldier was also good." [The cast included Genia Zielinska as Adina, David Dorlini as Nemorino, Giuseppe LaPuma as Dr. Dulcamara and Elizabeth Harrison as Gianetta.]

Undated clipping: "Nelson Eddy sang March 1 at March Musicales in Haddon Hall. Stars were Dusolina Giannin, soprano, Horace Britt, cellist, and Nelson Eddy. Nelson Eddy...found deserved favor with the audience. He possesses a baritone voice of most pleasing timbre and is imbued with a feeling for the textural as well as the musical significance of his romantic material. There was a nice sense of style in his delivery of Coates' 'Sea Rapture,' 'Robinson's Water Boy,' and Densmore's 'If God Left Only You.' More, he demonstrated how popular can be songs sung in English and made intelligible to an audience." *Atlantic City Union Ledger:* "Mr. Eddy sang with his usual perfect intonation and enunciation...Mr. Eddy was most cordially received and had to respond with encores after each appearance." *Bulletin:* "Mr. Eddy sang with the beauty of tone, artistic restraint and the musicianship that have won him great popularity. His diction, particularly in the English songs, was remarkably good. Early in the evening he seemed somewhat ill at ease in his upper register, but in his last group managed some high tones effectively." *Inquirer:* "Mr. Eddy was never in better form and his clear, voluminous and thrilling tones charmed as always."

March 12, 1930, the Warwick Hotel concert had guest pianists Ronald O'Neil and Theodore Paxson.

March 27, 1930: Nelson sang in **The Marriage of Figaro** at the Academy of Music. *Bulletin,* March, 28, 1930: "An exceptionally well balanced cast presented the further adventures of Figaro.... Nelson Eddy, who during the past month has suffered from laryngitis, reappeared in the role of the Count, and displayed his customary stage presence and discriminating vocal talent; his voice, carefully used, showing no strain and but slightly below its usual resonance." [The co-stars were Ivan Ivantzoff, Alma Peterson, Irene Williams and Genia Zielinska.] *Record:* "Eddy came nearest to being a stellar figure, with his virile baritone and wining personality." *Inquirer:* "Mr. Eddy was a highly competent Almaviva." *Ledger:* "Nelson Eddy, in the role of the Count, showed no apparent results of his recent illness and gave an exceptionally fine performance both vocally and dramatically, singing both his solo and ensemble numbers most artistically." *Daily News:* "His public was glad to welcome Nelson Eddy, blond baritone, back to the fold. Eddy, sick for a fortnight, rendered all of his notes with the clarity and personality that has made him the most popular of local songsters. He can be calculated on to fill every role well nigh perfectly." *Musical America:* "Nelson Eddy, recovered from his recent illness with voice unaffected, was superb as the philandering Count." Unnamed clipping: "Nelson Eddy, plucky as well as handsome and talented, made a capital Count Almaviva, both vocally and histrionically, which certainly gave his audience no intimation of his having left a sick-bed for the theatre and brought a bit of temperature with him."

April 3, 1930: Nelson sang in **Die Meistersinger** at the Academy of Music. *Record,* April 4, 1930: "When the great choruses and the stirring riot of trumpets resounded through the Academy of Music last night in the finale to **Die Meistersinger**, the Philadelphia Civic Opera Company closed its season and very possibly its career. Mrs. Henry M. Tracey explained the situation in a very frank address from the stage... A more satisfactory Kothner than Nelson Eddy's, in dry humorous appeal and tonal clarity, has not lately appeared here." *Ledger:* "Nelson Eddy used his fine voice and wonderfully clear enunciation to good advantage." *Bulletin:* "Herbert Gould and Nelson Eddy, as Pogner

'DIE MEISTERSINGER' SUNG BY CIVIC OPERA AS FAREWELL TREAT

Popular Wagner Production Admirably Presented by Selected Cast.

FINE WORK BY CHORUSES

"Die Meistersinger," opera in three acts by Richard Wagner, was presented last night by the Philadelphia Civic Opera Company in the Academy of Music. The cast:

Eva	Helen Stanley
Magdalena	Maybelle Marston
Walther von Stolzing	Hans Taenzler
Meistersingers—	
Hans Sachs	Fred Patton
Beckmesser	Ralph Jusko
Pogner	Herbert Gould
Kothner	Nelson Eddy
Vogelgesang	Ross Lockwood
Zorn	David Berkowitz
Moser	James Smith
Eisslinger	James Montgomery
Nachtigall	Peter Petraitis
Ortel	Sheldon Walker
Foltz	Paul D. Towner
Schwartz	Sydney Sutcliffe
David	Bernard Poland
A Night Watchman	Magnus Shillings

By H. T. CRAVEN

When the great choruses and the stirring riot of trumpets resounded through the Academy last night in the finale to "Die Meistersinger," the Philadelphia Civic Opera Company closed its season and very possibly its career. Mrs. Henry M. Tracey explained the situation in a very frank address from the stage. Alexander Smallens spoke through his orchestra, which he commanded with characteristic virility, and the audience conveyed its sentiments with a demonstration of applause and even cheers just before the second act.

"Die Meistersinger" may fitly serve to symbolize the swansong of any operatic organization of high spirit and artistic gallantry. These attributes distinguished last night's performance. This unique and incomparable non-tragic Wagnerian production had sturdy humor in its numerous comedy scenes, the right undercurrent of poetry in its passages of wholesome sentiment and musical resplendence and color in the magnificent ensembles.

Mr. Smallens' reading of the score illuminated its beauties. Occasionally the strings betrayed some insufficiency, but the authenticity of direction never flagged.

The cast, all-American, with one exception, and very largely Philadelphian, rose to its very considerable responsibilities in inspiring style.

Fred Patton's Sachs, mellowed dramatically and of admirable vocal quality, is beginning to rank among the best available. Ralph Jusko's venture in the exacting grotesque role of Beckmesser stands as a signal achievement of this highly promising young artist. Helen Stanley repeated her well-known and authoritative characterization of Eva, though with an occasional unwonted shrillness of tone. Hans Taenzler, the German member of the cast, brought his routine and seasoned competence in Wagnerian music drama to the part of Walther.

A more satisfactory Kothner than Nelson Eddy's, in dry humorous appeal and tonal clarity, has not lately appeared here. The splendidly trained choruses fairly outsang themselves in the "Glory to Hans Sachs" and the other pulse-quickening ensembles.

Even a fairly adequate performance of "Die Meistersinger" reflects balance, the right kind of artistic assurance and musical intelligence on the part of producers and interpreters. This Civic Troupe took its last bow with a great deal more than adequacy. For all the obstacles and in spite of a candidly recognized crisis there was an air of invigorating triumph in this final operatic gesture.

Rec. 4-4

MUSIC : By Samuel L. Laciar

"Meistersinger" Marks Exit

The Philadelphia Civic Opera Company concluded its seventh and probably last season, according to the statement by Mrs. Henry M. Tracy after the end of the first act, with an excellent performance of Wagner's "Die Meistersinger" in the Academy of Music, last evening.

In the performance it must be admitted the Philadelphians of the company considerably outclassed the imported members of the cast. This was especially the case with Ralph Jusko in the extremely difficult role of Beckmesser, Nelson Eddy as Kothner, Bernard Poland as David and Mabelle Marston as Magdalena.

Neither Hans Taensler nor Helen Stanley in the principal roles were in especially good voice, although both did their best work, as is apt to be the case under such circumstances, in the most difficult numbers.

Patton Excellent Hans Sachs

Fred Patton was an excellent Hans Sachs in every respect. His voice is well adapted to the role and he used it to good advantage, besides acting admirably.

Mr. Jusko's Beckmesser was very humorous without being overdone, as is so apt to be the case in this extraordinarily difficult role.

Mr. Poland gave an unusually good interpretation of David, both in voice and in action, and Nelson Eddy used his fine voice and wonderfully clear enunciation to good advantage in the role of Kothner, which next to Hans Sachs and Beckmesser is the most important of the Meistersinger roles.

Chorus Does Exceptional Work

The other members of the cast, all thoroughly adequate, were Herbert Gould, as Pogner; Ross Lockwood, as Vogelgesang; David Berkowitz, as Zorn; James Smith, as Moser; James Montgomery, as Eisslinger; Peter Petraitis, as Nachtigall; Sheldon Walker, as Ortel; Paul D. Towner, as Foltz; Sidney Sutcliffe, as Schwartz, and Magnus Shillings, as the Night Watchman.

The features of the performance, however, were the spirit in which the opera was given from beginning to end and the wonderful work of the chorus, especially in the very difficult number at the close of the second act and the superb chorale at the beginning of the last one.

Both of these were due to the splendid work of Alexander Smallens, the first in the masterly manner in which he conducted the opera and the second in the way he had trained the chorus. At the beginning of the second and third acts, especially, Mr. Smallens received the greatest ovation accorded any conductor in the Academy of Music within the memory of the present generation of opera or concert goers.

P.L. 4-4

Rings Down Curtain

MRS. HENRY M. TRACEY

President and general manager of the Civic Opera Company, who last night announced the dissolution of the company because of lack of backing.

Inq. 4-4

BEETHOVEN'S NINTH DELIGHTS STADIUM

Performance of Gigantic Work to Repeat Tonight.

With no rain to postpone it still another day, Beethoven's Ninth Symphony was given at the Lewisohn Stadium last night by the Philharmonic-Symphony Orchestra under Willem van Hoogstraten. The soloists were Jeannette Vreeland, soprano; Nevada Van der Veer, contralto; Arthur Hackett, tenor, and Nelson Eddy, baritone, and the chorus was made up of members of the Choral Symphony Society of New York. The performance will be repeated tonight.

The difficulties of performing the gigantic work at all are so proverbial (it is said that there was almost rebellion in the ranks of the singers on the occasion of its premiere more than a century ago), that Mr. Van Hoogstraten is to be congratulated for surmounting them annually. Thanks to his energy, industry and an unflagging devotion to his work, New York has come to regard the work as an outstanding feature of its summer festival, and whether it is due to a genuine love for it or merely to curiosity, the fact remains that twelve to fifteen thousand souls make an annual pilgrimage to the Stadium to hear it. And last night was no exception.

The performance, though it left much to be desired, came rather up to expectations. Too much time or preparation cannot be lavished on this Titan of symphonies. It is a known fact that even Toscanini approaches it with trepidation. With a concert on his hands every night, the care and time he might want to devote to it are not at Mr. Van Hoogstraten's command. Besides, the music of the chorus and soloists is none too merciful and yielding. To adapt a phrase of Philip Hale, the fault is not Mr. Van Hoogstraten's, or any other conductor's, that a performance of the work is not perfect, but Beethoven's! Curiously enough, Beethoven had no great love for his choral movement and, in fact, left behind a sketch for an instrumental one. Certainly, matters would at least have been easier had he worked it out.

The chorus of the Symphony Society is a well-trained one and abounds in fresh and vigorous voices. Under the baton of Mr. Van Hoogstraten last night it sang the sky-high measures of the "Hymn to Joy" with balance and infectious gusto. The effect of the many voices was an overwhelming one, although in matters of nuance, precision and perfect control much was wanting. Of the solo voices those of Miss Vreeland, Mr. Eddy and Mr. Hackett rang out with sufficient volume and conviction. The attack of the baritone's apostrophe, "O friends, no more these sounds continue!" was especially firm and distinct. At the finish there was long and lingering applause from the audience for all and sundry. The concert opened with the third "Leonore" overture.

L. L. B.

N. Y. Telegram 7-24

NELSON EDDY SINGS WITH SYMPHONY ORCHESTRA IN N.Y.

Philadelphia Baritone Well Received in Beethoven Work

New York, July 24.—In his first appearance as soloist with the Philharmonic-New York Symphony Orchestra, Nelson Eddy, twenty-nine-year-old Philadelphia baritone and one of the leading members of the Civic Grand Opera Company, was warmly received here last night.

The orchestra is playing the Ninth Symphony of Beethoven assisted by the Choral Symphony of New York and the following soloists: Jeanette Vreeland, soprano; Nevada Van der Veer, contralto; Arthur Hackett, tenor and Mr. Eddy. Curiously Mr. Eddy is away from his native city at a time when the Philadelphia Orchestra tonight gives a performance of the great Beethoven symphony at Robin Hood Dell.

Mr. Eddy achieved his debut with the Philharmonic-New York Symphony under trying circumstances in the Lewisohn Stadium, where the orchestra's summer concerts are given. He left Philadelphia with his evening clothes in a suit case. Upon his arrival in New York he learned that soloists and instrumentalists were to appear in blue coats and white flannel trousers, similar to those worn by the Philadelphia Orchestra in its outdoor concerts.

A special messenger was dispatched at once to Philadelphia to bring the required costume. By a series of fortuitous train and taxicab connections the messenger was able to get back to the Great Northern Hotel, New York, with the wardrobe in time for the performance.

The enthusiastic reception accorded Mr. Eddy by the good-sized audience in the amphitheatre last night presages his retirement shortly from the operatic stage in favor of the concert platform, his friends predicted today.

Mr. Eddy has appeared in some of the leading operatic roles in recent years with the Philadelphia Civic Grand Opera Company.

He started to work as an apprentice in the plumbing shop of his uncle at the age of fifteen, and his first musical exercises were beating the drum in a brass band. Later he became an advertising writer, but through the years he continued his vocal studies even after a severe strain to his voice necessitated a year's delay in his debut, nearly a decade ago. For a time he studied at Dresden with Vilonat. During the past winter he arranged for and appeared in a series of concerts at the Hotel Warwick, in Philadelphia.

bah!

Bulletin 7-24

and Kothner, brought depth and resonance to their renditions, each singing with flexibility and ease; Eddy performed the little by-play of the announcer with amusing tricks that completed the picture of the pompous assembly of good 'Masers.'" *Inquirer:* "Nelson Eddy...a Kothner who makes the most of the famous 'reading of the rules.'" [Note: The company, per Mrs. Tracy, must raise $100,00 during the summer months or shut down.] *Bulletin:* "Mrs. Tracy informed the huge house that the Civic had never incurred a cent of indebtedness, paying its bills as it went, and branding as untrue the rumor that the company was in debt $250,000. The company began seven years ago with fifteen dollars in the treasury and no subscription, and ends this season with a subscription of $50,000. Mrs. Tracey: 'My ideal when I formed the Civic Opera Company seven years ago was subsidized opera, and we were the first opera company in America to be subsidized. But one taxpayer took that away. If we are going to have one hundred per cent American opera, and not import artists, we must support it. I'm one hundred percent American, and I'm for opera in the vernacular. But we can't go on, so this is goodbye, and thank you for your loyal support.' Mrs. Tracey's speech elicited much applause, but applause became an ovation for Alexander Smallens when he made his appearance at the conductor's stand before both the second and third acts. The applause and even cheers continued while the conductor was forced to delay the performance in order to acknowledge."

April 4, 1930: The Philadelphia Civic Opera Company dissolved, becoming the Philadelphia Grand Opera Company. Nelson signed with the new company as one of their principal singers.

April 8, 1930: Nelson Eddy, baritone, and Albert Mahler, tenor, were soloists for Mendelssohn Club. Theodore Paxson accompanied them. *Inquirer:* "The Mendelssohn Club, under the admirable and artistic direction of Bruce Carey, gave one of the most ambitious and interesting performances of its history at its spring concert in the Academy of Music of Music last night... The audience that virtually taxed the capacity of the Academy received every number on the well-balanced and unusual programme with prolonged applause and the utmost enthusiasm.... The superb work accomplished by Mr. Carey in training these earnest and artistic singers was brilliantly exemplified in the two excerpts from the original version of Mussorgsky's **Boris Godunov**, which concluded the concert, with the support of the Philadelphia orchestra, and with Messrs. Eddy and Mahler in the baritone and solo parts of the presentation. ...The **Boris** excerpts followed a solo group of four numbers superbly sung by Mr. Eddy, all of which were well received." *Ledger:* "Mr. Eddy was in fine voice and sang with his usual beautiful intonation and enunciation. He was obliged to give an encore number, 'The Cloths of Heaven.'" *Bulletin:* "Mr. Eddy's voice was characterized by its usual finely sustained and resonant tone. In a solo group he sang Rachmaninov's 'No Prophet, I,' Dargomizhky's 'The Paladin,' Robinson's 'Water Boy,' and Carpenter's 'Young Man Chieftain.'" *Record:* "Nelson Eddy shocked the audience out of its conventional mood with a presentation of 'Young Man Chieftain,' a song after the modern manner, by Carpenter." *Musical America*, April 19, 1930: "This young baritone's voice is rich and resonant, his enunciation especially clear, and his stage presence highly pleasing."

April 10, 1930: The Warwick Hotel concert co-starred Bianca Saroya, soprano, and Dimitri Onofrei, tenor. This was the final concert in this series. *Warwick Longuette,* no date: "Nelson Eddy's six Musicales have attracted the attention of every dyed-in-the-wool music-lover. Blonde Eddy has created no less than a furor with his baritone singing. He has every facility for music-making, and the hundreds that flock to the ballroom of the Warwick always feel requited for their efforts. He has a good idea, too. Always another artist or group of musicians appear on the same program. Eddy is one of the prime recipients of our praise."

April 17, 1930: Last night Brahms Chorus of Philadelphia did **St. Matthew Passion**, by Bach, in the Church of the Holy Communion. Unnamed clipping: "Mr. Eddy revealed his usual fine enunciation and beautiful voice." *Musical Courier,* April 26: "Nelson Eddy in his singing of the part of the Voice of Christ, was superb--his smooth, rich voice conveying the beautiful words which were as clear as bells."

April 23, 1930: Nelson Eddy sang on WIP for the Newton Coal Hour. Songs were: "Serenade of Don Juan," and "Buy a Broom," an early German-American folk-song.

May 1, 1930: Nelson was soloist with Orpheus Club of 75 male voices at Shubert Playhouse. Wilmington, Delaware *Evening Journal,* May 2, 1930: "The success of last night's concert as augmented by the appearance of

Two of the Ninth Symphony Soloists

DOROTHEA FLEXER
Contralto

NELSON EDDY
Baritone

no!

Verdi's Requiem Presented At Stadium by Coates

Leads Philharmonic, Chorus and Soloists; Repeats Tonight

Verdi's Requiem, written to commemorate the death of his friend Allesandro Manzoni, was presented at the Lewisohn Stadium last night by Albert Coates, with the Philharmonic Symphony Orchestra, the chorus of the Choral Symphony Society of New York and Jeannette Vreeland, soprano; Kathryn Meisle, contralto; Arthur Hacket, tenor, and Nelson Eddy, barytone.

Mr. Coates is eminently well equipped to accentuate the theatrical elements of Verdi's Mass for the Dead. His is a strongly dramatic and forceful temperament, and one sympathetic to music of this type. He succeeded in transferring some of his enthusiasm and vitality to his forces. The chorus sang with energy, good intonation and, on the whole, voluminously. The dynamic values were admirably planned for the space to be filled.

Of the soloists, Miss Meisle was most consistently satisfactory. Her rich contralto voice is evenly produced, and, with the exception of a few high tones in the "Lux Aeterna" which were a trifle sharp, her adherence to the pitch was exemplary. Not so much can be said for Miss Vreeland. She flatted oftener than was agreeable, and her tones were often penetrating and unsteady. Mr. Hackett disclosed a fitting sense of style along with some throaty voice production. Mr. Eddy, who had recently effected a promising debut in Beethoven's Ninth Symphony, furthered the excellent impression then made to some extent. His voice is resonant and of considerable warmth, but he must guard against such unjudicious forcing as he was often led to last night if he does not wish to sacrifice the mellowness and evenness of his voice.

The audience was of good size and appreciative. The Requiem will be repeated tonight with the same forces.

J. D. B.

N.Y. Herald-Tribune
7-6-30

Music

Verdi's Requiem, a monument of grief to the memory of Alessandro Manzoni, Italian poet and dramatist, received its annual performance at the Lewisohn Stadium last night.

As on previous occasions of stadium fiesta, the voices of the Choral Symphony Society provided the requisite choral background and there were soloists: Jeanette Vreeland, soprano; Kathryn Meisle, contralto; Arthur Hackett, tenor, and Nelson Eddy, baritone. There were also two trumpeters perched on far ends of the amphitheater, a coatless Philharmonic-Symphony Orchestra and Albert Coates. The negligee was entirely Mr. Coates's idea and earned universal approval.

Mr. Coates conducted a finely chiseled and beautifully modulated performance. The score is full of operatic outbursts and stagey climaxes, although it contains many austere and awesome pages. Mr. Eddy, who made his debut recently in Beethoven's Ninth Symphony at the Stadium, seemed to me to be miscast, for the role is rather formidable for a purely lyric voice. And Mr. Eddy is a baritone, not a basso-profundo. In spite of these handicaps he acquitted himself with distinction. Mr. Hackett, I thought, has been in better voice, although he arose to the occasion nobly, especially in the tenor solo of the second section.

Miss Meisle, an able and experienced artist, occasionally wandered a bit from the key. Miss Vreeland did not force her high notes nearly as often as she is wont to do. The chorus sounded, from where I sat, rather thick and muffled, although the effect may have been entirely satisfactory farther back.

Following are the programs of the Philharmonic - Symphony Orchestra and the Goldman Concert Band tonight:

Lewisohn Stadium

(In case of rain the Requiem will be postponed until the following day and a substitute orchestral program will be played in the great hall.)

Requiem .... Verdi

Soloists: Jeanette Vreeland, soprano; Arthur Hackett, tenor; Kathryn Meisle, contralto; Nelson Eddy, baritone, assisted by the chorus of the Choral Symphony Society of New York.

N.Y. World
7-6-30

NELSON EDDY STAR AT N. Y. CONCERT

Former Plumber's Apprentice Wins Acclaim as Symphony Soloist

By a Staff Correspondent

New York, July 24.—Nelson Eddy, Philadelphia baritone, who learned opera arias from a phonograph and did his practicing between writing newspaper stories, appeared here last night at Lewisohn Stadium as the soloist in Beethoven's Ninth Symphony with the Philharmonic-Symphony Orchestra.

Eddy, who had overcome obstacles that would have turned back many another singer from the path of fame, and although only 29 years old, enthralled New York music-lovers by his finished rendition of the difficult Beethoven symphony. He proved that the time he spent in his uncle's plumbing shop in Philadelphia, as a drummer in a band at $12 a week; as a reporter and as an advertising-copy writer, had not been wasted, for it was during the time served in those vocations and from the money earned in them, that Eddy had prepared his voice.

Eddy started to work as an apprentice plumber at the age of 15, but his goal always was the concert stage, and when money did not come fast enough to pay for his singing lessons he laid aside his wrenches to become a reporter.

As a newspaperman Eddy made good, and through the gauntlet of obituary writer to the copy desk he worked, and between times he sang, and eventually the news room tired of his singing and Eddy became an advertising man.

The money earned in writing advertising copy gave him singing lessons but just as it appeared he was ready for his stage appearance, he strained his voice and the debut was deferred for another year.

At the end of the year he was given a small part with the Philadelphia Civic Opera company and in a short time was winning attention as a concert singer, with his ambition partly realized.

His parts became more important and in January of this year, he had one of the leading roles when the Civic Opera company presented "Hansel and Gretel."

Eddy studied in Dresden under Vilonat and returned for his New York debut—and even then he was faced with last-minute obstacles.

Instead of the dress suit he had brought to New York from his Philadelphia home, he received belated instructions to appear in a blue coat and white flannels. He had none with him so while a boy was despatched to Philadelphia for the blue coat a tailor was set to work on the flannels and another boy scurried for white shoes.

Although he had but little time the costume was assembled before time for the curtain to rise and Eddy sang with the symphony orchestra.

Blah!

lies!

Ledger 7-24

not.

As soloist in Beethoven's "Ninth" and Verdi's Requiem, Nelson Eddy will sing baritone with the Philharmonic-Symphony at the Stadium

Musical Digest Aug. '30

Nelson Eddy, Philadelphia baritone, who was a member of the Philadelphia Civic Opera Company before its disbandonment several weeks ago. Mr. Eddy is only 29, and he is handsome, and posses a remarkably fine singing voice. What impressed the audience last night was the apparent ease with which he rendered his selections. This was Mr. Eddy's third appearance in Wilmington as a soloist, and if popular demand means anything it won't be the last." *Wilmington Morning News:* "The tenth spring concert of the Orpheus Club, given last night in the Shubert Playhouse, scored another triumph.... The feeling among the audience was that this was the best concert in the history of the club.... Many of those who were unable to be present at the Shubert Playhouse last night heard the concert as it was broadcast over WDEL."

May 16, 1930: Nelson and Dorothy Fox, soprano, were soloists at the May Festival of Music at Baptist Temple. *Evening Bulletin:* "The soloists were received with much enthusiasm, the applause, in fact, being more enthusiastic than discriminating.... Mr. Eddy's popularity was again evidenced by his enthusiastic reception and the applause which greeted the effective use of his much-admired baritone in two groups of songs, followed by well-chosen encore selections. Soprano, tenor and baritone also were heard with the chorus in the trio, 'Heavenly Angels' from Gounod's opera **Faust**.... Theodore Paxson at the piano for Mr. Eddy." [The tenor was Daniel L. Healy.] *Ledger:* "Mr. Eddy easily took first honors for his two groups of solos, each of which brought forth demands for encore numbers. He was in excellent voice and his accustomed poise, technical mastery and sincerity of expression won ready appreciation."

July 20, 1930: *New York Times* (with photo): "Nelson Eddy makes his New York debut on this occasion." Nelson sang in Beethoven's Ninth Symphony at Lewisohn Stadium on Tuesday, July 19 and Wednesday, July 20. The Tuesday performance was broadcast live on WOR at 8:30.

July 24, 1930, *New York Times:* " The presentation of Beethoven's third 'Leonore' overture and Ninth Symphony, which was postponed because of rain Tuesday night, was heard last night at the Lewisohn Stadium.... Of the solo quartet, Nelson Eddy was the newcomer. He sang with clarity of enunciation, good diction, excellent resonance and feeling for phrase. The extreme lower register was a bit weaker than the rest of his range, and the music from his throat would have gained had it been more vibrant and emotional. It was a more than promising debut under difficult circumstances." The symphony repeats tonight. There were 18,000 people in the audience. *Evening World:* "The only newcomer in the quartet was Nelson Eddy, who made a good impression." *Herald-Tribune:* "Mr. Eddy, after some nervousness in his opening measures, gave evidence of having a well schooled voice of warm timbre, and of considerable power. He lent vitality and mood to his lines." Other soloists were: Jeanette Vreeland, soprano, Nevada Van der Veer, contralto, Arthur Hacket, tenor. *Telegram:* "Mr. Eddy and Mr. Hackett rang out with sufficient volume and voncition. The attack of the baritone's apostrophe, 'O friends, no more these sounds continue!' was especially firm and distinct. At the finish there was long and lingering applause." [For this performance, Nelson left Philadelphia with his evening clothes in a suitcase. Upon his arrival in New York he learned that soloists and orchestra were to appear in blue coats and white flannel trouser. A special messenger was dispatched at one to Philadelphia to bring the required clothes. His clothes arrived just in time for the concert.] *Bulletin:* "The enthusiastic reception accorded Mr. Eddy by the good-sized audience in the amphitheater last night presages his retirement shortly from the operatic stage in favor of the concert platform, his friends predicted today."

July 25, 1930: Nelson sang in Verdi's **Requiem**. Soloists were Jeanette Vreeland, soprano, Kathryn Meisle, contralto, Arthur Hackett, tenor, and Nelson Eddy, baritone. *New York World,* July 26, 1930: "Mr. Eddy, who made his debut recently in Beethoven's Ninth Symphony at the Stadium, seemed to me to be miscast, for the role is rather formidable for a purely lyric voice. And Mr. Eddy is a baritone, not a basso-profundo. In spite of these handicaps he acquitted himself with distinction." *Herald-Tribune:* "Mr. Eddy, who had recently effected a promising debut in Beethoven's Ninth Symphony, furthered the excellent impression then made to some extent. His voice is resonant and of considerable warmth, but he must guard against such injudicious forcing as he was often led to last night if he does not wish to sacrifice the mellowness and evenness of his voice."

[Note: these first New York concerts are his very first "bad" reviews. Nelson wrote "Bah!" in the margin of the review that mentions that "He started to work as an apprentice in the plumbing shop of his uncle at the age of fifteen, and his first musical exercises were beating the drum in a brass band."]

August 8, 1930, *Bulletin*: "'Death of Samson' Brings the Police." Nelson was rehearsing on the fifteenth floor of the Lenox apartments at 13th and Spruce. [Note: He lived there thanks to one of his mentors, Mrs. Gertrude Evans.] By the time the Delilah (unnamed in article) left the apartment, there was a large crowd gathered outside, looking upward. Nelson was accompanying them at the piano, "although he does not claim to be a Hoffman or Paderewski." After the singer left, a police sergeant arrived and went to the elevator operator. "Where's the corpse?" "That wasn't no murder," replied the young man. "That was a young woman singing in Mr. Eddy's studio." By now the entire fourteen-floor apartment house was covered. Nelson explained what had happened. "Well, it didn't sound like singing to me," said a regular patrolman who had called in for backup.

Verdi's **Requiem** was sung August 5 and 6, and Beethoven's Ninth Symphony on July 23 and 24, both with Nelson. On August 30, *Musical America* (re: the Ninth Symphony) noted that all singers "acquitted themselves well." As for the **Requiem**, "All acquitted themselves with credit, Mr. Eddy, a newcomer, revealing a voice of unusual beauty."

September 1, 1930, *Bulletin:* "Some very fine singing by Nelson Eddy added a note of distingue to the atmosphere of light gaiety that prevailed throughout last night's concert in Robin Hood Dell.... Close to 7,500 persons gathered inside and outside the Dell to hear the popular baritone; and no soloist the season of summer concerts has been so uproariously received as was Mr. Eddy. Both his offerings, the aria, 'An Jenen Tag,' from Marschner's opera, **Hans Heilig**, and 'Adamastor, Roi des Vagues,' from Meyerbeer's **L'Africaine** had to be repeated. So much as already been written about Nelson Eddy, and he is so well known here that further appraisal of his work would be superfluous. Suffice it to say that he sang with the restraint and beauty of tone that have become characteristic of his work. His enthusiastic reception was fully merited." *Ledger*: "Nelson Eddy Wins Triumph At Dell. One of the largest crowds yet attended last evening's concert.... Mr. Eddy, who is exceedingly well known in Philadelphia...scored the most emphatic success of any of the soloists of the season, being obliged to repeat each of the two numbers he sang. He was in splendid voice and exhibited great artistry and that clear enunciation which always features his work.... Owing to the crowd, 600 extra chairs were placed in the auditorium."

September 27, 1930, *Bulletin:* "Under the auspices of the Girl Scouts of Philadelphia and Chester County and for the benefit of the Girl Scout Camp Fund, the Newton Coal Orchestra presented an interesting program last evening, in the ballroom of the Penn Athletic Club.... Assisting the orchestra were Lisa Lisona, soprano, and Nelson Eddy, baritone.... Mr. Eddy's rendition of the 'Largo al Factotum,' from Rossini's **Barber of Seville**, was excellent, as were his other numbers, 'Give a Man a Horse He Can Ride,' and numerous encores. The spontaneous applause which greeted the baritone at all times gave evidence of his continued popularity."

October 26, 1930, unnamed clipping: "Nelson Eddy will continue Warwick concerts. Guests to be Helen Oehlehim, contralto, November 12, Ted Paxton and Madeleine Clark Walther, composer, December 10, Christine Murdoch Kendrick, soprano, in her recital debut, January 7, Phillips Jenkins Quartet, February 11, Marjorie Fulton, violinist, March 4, Geoffrey O'Hara, composer and pianist, April 8."

October 26, 1930: Nelson Eddy and Kathryn Meisle, contralto are soloists for this season's **St. Matthew Passion** of Bach. Nelson is also to sing at the Penn Athletic Club on November 23.

[Note: Around this time Nelson seemed to be having more press releases coming out about his coming concerts.]

Nelson started his new Warwick concert series on November 12, 1930. *Bulletin,* November 13, 1930: Nelson was "greeted with enthusiasm" by audience. "Beauty of tone, ease of manner and finished style, together with his ability to lose his identity in the ever-changing moods of his songs, make Mr. Eddy's singing a source of real pleasure to his listeners.... Mr. Eddy and Miss Oelheim completed the recital with an excellent rendition of a duet from **Samson and Delilah**. " *Inquirer*: "An absorbing and artistic programme.... While the offerings of this pleasing pair were more or less low in range of register, they were admirably altitudinous in art, and excellent in interpretation....

Rotogravure Picture Section
Bronx—Harlem—Washington Heights

The New York Times

Sunday
August 17, 1930

GREETING A DISTINGUISHED CONDUCTOR FROM ABROAD: ALBERT COATES

of England, Who Assumed the Leadership of the Philharmonic-Symphony Orchestra for the Three Weeks' Absence of Willem van Hoogstraten, With Soloists and Members of the Chorus of the Choir Symphony Society of New York Who Participated in the Opening Concert of the Guest Conductor in Lewisohn Stadium, on the Heights.
(Brown.)

both were in excellent voice, and were most cordially received." *Daily News:* "Eddy's voice seems to improve on each succeeding season. A group of Spanish songs displayed his ambidexterity. Here he seemed light and gay. The English ballad group on his program provided every chance to show his tunefulness. He was at his best, perhaps, when he sang with Miss Oelheim. The famous duet from **Samson and Delilah** brought the greatest ovation of the evening from the listeners." *Record:* "The duet from **Samson and Delilah** brought the artists together with fine blending of voices." *Ledger:* "Mr. Eddy was in exceptional voice, and sang with that beautifully clear enunciation which always distinguishes his work in addition to a superb quality of tone and high artistry in interpretation." *Musical America*, November 25: "Mr. Eddy's art has ripened in the last few years. He encompassed with ease the varying emotional and musical demands."

November 16, 1930, clipping: Nelson Eddy and Josef Hoffman, pianist, were guest artists on Atwater Kent Hour, over WEAF.

November 19, 1930, clipping: Rehearsals are going on three days a week for the Charity Ball at Pennsylvania Athletic Club. Nelson Eddy has the leading role.

November 22, 1930, *Evening Bulletin:* "It's too bad when one who has yearned to be a trap drummer fails to realize his ambition and becomes instead an outstanding baritone." The article explained that Nelson once worked as a telephone operator, to which he sometimes refers as his early "vocal training." Then he worked with a plumbing fixture firm. One night, Nelson had an invitation to substitute for a sick trap drummer at a Jenkintown dancing academy, but last-minute changes intervened, and he couldn't play. Then Nelson decided to be a banker, but then decided, "Every consultation with a banker ended the same way. They all seemed impervious to the possibilities of adding a future Morgan to their staffs." More quotes from this article: "I was fired from two jobs for singing. They didn't tell me as much at the time, but I know now what a nuisance I must have been and I apologize." Regarding his voice: "I was pretty rotten for along while and quite discouraged. One day Edward Lippe, a well-known Philadelphia singer, told me right out I didn't know how to sing. That might have made me mad, but the truth was I knew it as well as he. So I just asked him what to do. He came over to my home every day and gave me lessons. Then he sent me to William W. Vilonat, who had been his teacher. I studied with Vilonat in New York, Paris and Dresden. Vilonat taught me how to sing.... Of course, there's that old line about 'hard work,' but no matter how old it is it's true. I worked, worked, and worked. And it's a constant grind even today. I don't believe anyone realizes how hard I work because I try to make it all look easy. It might detract from their enjoyment of the songs if they knew that I stayed awake nights, pulling at my hair and chewing my fingernails trying to learn them... You've got to keep the people interested. You can't keep on singing the same old things time after time. I'm always hunting for new things to do for my home audiences. I try to make good use of the element of suspense. The people never quite know what I'm going to do next--and they stay interested." [Note: This was his first extensive newspaper interview.]

November 24, 1930, *Ledger,* "Kathryn Meisle, contralto of the Chicago Opera Company, and Nelson Eddy, baritone of this city, gave a joint recital last evening in the series of the Penn Athletic Club Musical Association. The usual large audience attended and gave the singers an enthusiastic reception. Each recitalist sang an operatic aria and appeared in two groups of songs, then appeared together in a duet from **The Barber of Seville** as a closing number.... Mr. Eddy opened the program with the aria 'Viravviso,' from Bellini's **La Sonnambula**, a number of extreme brilliance and requiring great execution. It was finely sung and well received.... Throughout, Mr. Eddy showed ... the distinctively beautiful tone quality which he always possesses. His German group was finely sung..." *Inquirer:* "It was one of the most enjoyable concerts of the present season and well deserved the 'standing room only' audience which was attracted... Mr. Eddy proved that he was in exceptionally fine voice and this with his ever present artistry was all that was necessary for his hearers' enjoyment." *Record:* "Nelson Eddy sang with his usual charm and full-throated eloquence... It was 'Water Boy,' probably the most popular composition in the baritone's repertoire, that brought prolonged salvos of appreciation from his auditors.... An amusing expression of artistic temperament was provided by the changing of lighting effects for each of the soloists. Eddy likes his music hall lighted, while Miss Meisle prefers hers darkened, so the lights alternated to suit their individual tastes." *Bulletin:* "Mr. Eddy maintained his traditional poise and eloquence, displaying a marvelous capacity to spin his tones with

In Joint Recital

HELEN OELHEIM
NELSON EDDY
Who will appear in joint recital in the first of a series of Mr. Eddy's recitals at the Warwick, Seventeenth and Locust streets, Philadelphia, Nov. 13.

Camden Cour.-Post 10-31

Camden, N.J., Courier-Post Nov. 13

MUSIC

By HENRY C. BECK

NELSON EDDY'S RECITAL KEEPS STANDARDS HIGH

With a program as distinctive as it was musical, Nelson Eddy, baritone, opened his series of musicales last night at the Warwick Hotel, Philadelphia. Mr. Eddy's concerts last year opened up a field all their own and from last night's beginning it is apparent that this unusual Philadelphia singer intends to keep the soil well-tilled.

Under ordinary circumstances it would be all right to say that Mr. Eddy was assisted by a soloist and his accompanist. But Miss Helen Oelheim proved more than an assisting artist and Mr. Theodore Paxon much more than the young man at the piano. Miss Oelheim is a contralto who, like Mr. Eddy, combines an unusual personality with a delight in singing. Mr. Paxon, to my mind, is one of the best, or even the best accompanist now in the Philadelphia area.

Of course, the program itself had a lot to do with it. Mr. Eddy's programs are never those one can hear anywhere. They combine all kinds of music in which the singer can display his ability to portray many moods, as in the famous Figaro aria from "The Barber of Seville." And when the song needs more explanation than its music or text can convey, you can trust Mr. Eddy to give a short delightful description.

Mr. Eddy began with "Vi Ravviso" from La Sonnambula of Bellini and was duly encored. Then Miss Oelheim sang Verborgenheit of Wolf, two songs of Brahms and Der Seiger of Kaun. The young singer's voice has a remarkable freshness and an ease which completes its charm. The audience was quick to recognize these things and in return Miss Oelheim sang as an extra the Brahms Cradle Song.

Mr. Eddy came right along with a group of eight short songs, "Songs of the Pyrenees." All were unusual. Of the group, "Dodo," arranged by Mr. Paxon, and "Me Gustan Todas" were the most beautiful, at least to this reviewer. Of course, one could go on and on listing these compositions, saying "beautiful" here and "glorious" there, but that was unnecessary. The remainder of the program included compositions of Rachmaninoff, Carpenter, Shaw, Golde—sung by Miss Oelheim, and songs of Aylward, Quilter and Reddick, sung by Mr. Eddy.

There were encores all along the route, Miss Oelheim being superb in "Love Is in My Heart," and Mr. Eddy particularly robust in "The Song of the Bow." His encores included "My Native Land" of Gretchaninoff and Dvorak's "Going Home." After the finale, "Il Faut pour assouvir ma haine" sung by the two vocalists, a new wind-up was demanded and the artists complied with the ever popular "Still wie die Nacht."

The only thing wrong with the concert was a few empty chairs. Music lovers don't know what they're missing.

effortless ease and a keen musical intelligence in presenting the atmosphere and feeling of his songs with clarity and insight. Something of the operatic manner remains with him in the gestures with which he seeks to stress some vital phrase."

November 25, 1930: Nelson sang with the Milwaukee Musical Society and Arion Musical Club. *Milwaukee Journal,* November 26, 1930: "With Nelson Eddy, baritone, as soloist, the choruses presented a big and interesting program. The audience was not so large as it should have been, but the people listening were friendly and most appreciative. They liked Mr. Eddy.... Mr. Eddy was immediately a favorite with the audience. He demonstrated at once that he owns a voice of power and quality, a capital voice for singing big songs with flourish. His share of the program was devoted to sturdy and popular airs, wisely chosen in the way of variety. His success, in this first Milwaukee hearing, was all but complete.... The baritone is a singer who can afford to be generous with tone. He loses something in effective contrast by his uniformly ample flow of rich sonority, but the listener's ear is never cheated or abused. Occasionally the tone is not pointed to the best focus, but it is always firm. The baritone makes some sacrifices in interpretation because of his laudable interest in voice production, but he is always saved from becoming uninteresting by the verve with which he sings. He has a personality that wins an audience and holds it." *Chicago Tribune:* " Nelson Eddy, the assisting soloist, has a most ingratiating manner, and a beautiful baritone voice. Although he is young, his voice has the volume and range of maturity. The future should hold much for this young man. Mr. Eddy's first number was an aria from **Tannhäuser**, in which he was so successful that he was obliged to add 'The Evening Star' from the same opera. Two songs by Brahms followed and then two arias from Jonn Spielt Auf, which brought down the house." *Milwaukee Leader:* "It was Mr. Eddy... who roused the audience to greatest enthusiasm. In choosing songs well adapted to the mood of the occasion, this pleasing young blond won smiles and nods and pounding palms.... Besides a fine voice, with large possibilities, Mr. Eddy possesses that rare ability to obliterate the music-box aspect of his physical presence. His frame, due either to complete self-command or complete unselfconsciousness, becomes an almost fluid part of his voice instead of its casing. The result is a free flow of magnetism, which captivated last night's audience and will undoubtedly weigh heavily in his future triumphs.... Milwaukee will be glad to have that young man come back." [Note: This review was written by Harriet Pettibone Clinton.] *Wisconsin News:* "A stunning young baritone...still under 30, with a superb singing physique... won a marked success. Blond, with hair like burnished copper, he has a taking personality, puzzling but winning the audience completely. In several groups of most interesting songs, he revealed a voice of glorious beauty, even and true. Though he vocalized rather than sang, he did it with pleasure for the auditors... From an interpretive angle some executions were close to musical murder of songs, yet he greatly impressed and was recalled many times, and added several encore numbers." *Milwaukee Sentinel:* "Mr. Eddy offered one of the most diversified lists of songs that we have head in some time. He appears to be at home in several languages and knows his music so well that even the usual little book was not in use.... Mr. Eddy's voice is a ringing baritone of unusual range and under splendid control. He knows the why and wherefore of how to sing, and is fortunate in possessing an attractive stage presence that immediately wins his audience. His enunciation and diction are well nigh impeccable, and it may be said at once that he captured his audience both on the stage and in the hall. If there is any lack--and in justice to Mr. Eddy, it was not apparent that the majority of listeners discovered it -- it is in a tendency to stress the method of singing rather than the content of the song. One almost wished that he would sacrifice the beauty of the tone at times to the meaning of the words.... He has no lack of vitality, but rather that Anglo-Saxon tendency to repress feeling where a Latin or a Teuton or a Russian would throw caution to the winds. Aside from this, he is a thoroughly delightful singer." *Musical America,* December 10, 1930: "Mr. Eddy established himself at once as a prime favorite."

December 2, 1930: Nelson was soloist at the Church of Holy Communion, when the Brahms Chorus of Philadelphia gave its first concert of fifth season, performing the **Christmas Oratorio** of Bach.. There were 120 singers. *Inquirer,* December 3, 1930: "Nelson Eddy's breadth of quality proved tremendously effective in the recitative passage. Mr. Eddy has a voice that is splendidly attuned to the simple grandeur contained in such a great religious epic of music as this oratorio." *Record:* "Nelson Eddy once more sang the bass parts in his resounding and maturing tones." *Bulletin:* "Mr. Eddy sang with his accustomed beauty of tone."

Undated clipping: Nelson sings regularly at two Philadelphia churches, will do the annual Charity Ball pageant at the New England Society annual meeting. He is also booked to sing in New York, Boston, Detroit, Milwaukee,

A 67

As soloist in Beethoven's "Ninth" and Verdi's Requiem, Nelson Eddy will sing baritone with the Philharmonic-Symphony at the Stadium

Musical Digest

Warwick Lorgnette Nov.

NELSON EDDY

Nelson Eddy, Baritone, whose series of concerts at the Warwick will begin this month.

NELSON EDDY TO RESUME MUSICALES AT WARWICK

Nelson Eddy, baritone, will continue his series of six musicales on Wednesday evenings in the ball-room of The Warwick, Seventeenth and Locust streets, Philadelphia, this season.

Others who will sing or play on his program are: Helen Oelheim, contralto, of New York, who will make her Philadelphia debut on November 12; Theodore Paxson, pianist, and Madeleine Clark Walther, composer, on December 10; Christine Murdock Kendrick, Philadelphia soprano, in her recital debut, on January 7; The Phillips Jenkins Quartet, consisting of Mary Schwartz lyric soprano, Charlotte Bentley, dramatic soprano, Natalie Ruth, mezzo-contralto, and Albertine Hundertmark, contralto, with Virginia Snyder accompanying, on February 11; Marjorie Fulton, violinist, artist-pupil of the Curtis Institute of Music, on March 4; and Geoffrey O'Hara, composer, pianist, singer and speaker, on April 8. C.C. 10-24

Camden Courier-Post

10-24

The Penn Athletic Club recently presented, in the Sunday evening series, Kathryn Meisle, contralto, formerly of the Chicago Civic Opera Company, and Nelson Eddy, popular operatic and concert baritone, one of the leading artists of the Philadelphia Civic Opera Company during the life of that organization. Miss Meisle sang arias from Rossini's Barber of Seville and Donizetti's Favorita and songs by Schubert. She is equally at home in the dramatic and lyric style of singing, and in the Rossini aria (which she sang as originally written for coloratura contralto) she displayed enviable technical ease. Mr. Eddy's offerings included an aria from La Sonnambula, two German songs by Wolff and an English group. He sang with richness of tone, excellence of diction and that indefinable quality of sympathy which makes him so beloved by his audiences wherever he appears. Miss Meisle and Mr. Eddy joined in a duet from the Barber of Seville. Both artists granted numerous encores to the warmly applauding audience. M. M. C.

MC 12-30

Courier 12-30

Haddonfield, New Jersey; Carlisle, Reading and Ridley Park, Pennsylvania; Wilmington, Delaware; Overlea, Maryland and Nashville, Tennessee.

One Philadelphia critic told Nelson Eddy, "We're for you, kid, as long as you don't get a swelled head from all your big jobs. But the minute you do, we'll pan the ears off you!" Nelson replied: "That's a bet! If you see my feet getting off the ground, give me the works, I know it will be good for me."

An *Evening Bulletin* reporter asked Nelson what his secret of success was. His answer: "First of all, I guess it's being just natural. A fellow's friends quickly detect artificial mannerisms and are the first to be annoyed by them. Then, you've got to keep them interested. I'm always hunting for new things to do for my home audiences. I like to sing the latest songs of Philadelphia composers. I try to make good use of the element of suspense. The people never quite know what I'm going to do next--and they stay interested.... Vilonat taught me to sing. Please make a point of that. He has a wonderful method."

December 5, 1930, *Bulletin:* "The fifty-first annual Charity Ball, preceded by a concert and pageant, 'Under the Greenwood Tree,' was held last night in the ballroom of the Penn Athletic Club. The boxes were draped with strands of southern smilax and large clusters of yellow chrysanthemums.... The stage also presented a colorful picture with a background representing a woodland scene. Palms and ferns were on each side of the stage on the ballroom floor. 'Charity,' in electric lights, was above the stage....'Under the Greenwood Tree,' opened with a prologue by Nelson Eddy, baritone, after which he sang 'Oh Promise Me.' Groups of young girls, including a number of debutantes, danced in the various sets in colorful costumes. Each group represented one of the beneficiaries for which the ball was given. Groups of costumed girls represented the Saxon folk from the great forest, from Nottingham, Derby, York and Barnsdale. As each group appeared, Nelson Eddy sang the solos, 'The Tailor's Song,' 'The Vagabond Song,' 'Brown October Ale,' and 'The Tinker's Song.' At the sound of Robin Hood's horn, the Robin Hood bandsmen in hunters green appeared. They were the chorus from the Mask and Wig Club of the University of Pennsylvania. The finale consisted of a grand march by the entire ensemble. General dancing followed." *Ledger:* "Nelson Eddy as Robin Hood was perfectly splendid.... Needless to say, the affair was a tremendous success, and a goodly sum was realized for the hospitals that will benefit by the affair." *Inquirer:* "The sophistication of modern days was joyously laid aside for a few brief hours last night by Philadelphia society folk when they turned out to enjoy the simplicity and the subtle charm that lurked 'Under the Greenwood Tree,' a pageant that featured the fifty-first annual Charity Ball. Robin Hood and 200 of the merriest maids possible, all vying for the honors of the famed Marion, made the throngs of men and women present believe for awhile that the ballroom of the Penn Athletic Club was actually Sherwood Forest. Nelson Eddy, Philadelphia's famed baritone, in the role of Robin Hood left nothing to be desired in the matter of personableness for the vagabond hero of medieval times.... Mr. Eddy gave 'The Song of the Bow.' Mr. Eddy was exceptionally well accompanied by Theodore Paxson, whose temperament admirably blends with that of the baritone."

December 10, 1930: Nelson sang at the Warwick Hotel with Ted Paxson and Madeline Clark Walther, composer. *Camden Courier-Post,* December 11, 1930: "Mr. Eddy's concerts...are more than mere recitals of singing. Music lovers fortunate enough to attend them always leave more informed, musically, than they were when they came. Mr. Eddy, when his restless hearers give him a chance, always explains what he sings and the explanations are usually as characteristic as the songs. Mr. Eddy's program last night got off on the right foot with a group of German songs by Erich Wolff. These were delightfully sung as well as delightfully explained. The singer has the knack of picking songs that are especially suited to his voice and that is an artistic feat by itself... The concert, in mood, was much different from the last. There was less sparkle, perhaps, and more to think about." *Ledger:* "An unusually fine concert. Mr. Eddy, in excellent voice, sang with that perfection of diction and rich, clear tone he always exhibits in concert or opera. His interpretation was also exceedingly good."

January 16, 1931, *Wilmington Morning News:* "Mildred Dilling, one of America's premiere harpists, and Nelson Eddy, recognized as one of the most promising of the younger baritones in this country...were heard last night at The Playhouse by a small but thoroughly appreciative audience. Probably the inclement weather was responsible for the fact that The Playhouse was little more than half-filled." [Note: This concert was given under the auspices of the Delaware Musical Association.] "Both Miss Dilling and Mr. Eddy were generous in their response to the delighted audience and gave a large number of encores. Mr. Eddy, accompanied on the harp by Miss Dilling, rendered the old favorite, 'Drink To Me Only with Thine Eyes' as the final encore. Mr. Eddy was entirely taken to the corporate heart of the audience when at the conclusion of one encore after a group of songs, he came out to the center of the stage smiling broadly and remarked, 'All right, I'm in no hurry to go home; it's raining,' and then launched into a second encore. Probably the 'hit' among the encores given by Mr. Eddy was 'Route Marching,' composition of George Chadwick Stark... Mr. Eddy explained that Mr. Chadwick, who lives in New England, heard him sing a radio program one evening, and wrote saying, 'You ought to sing one of my songs, 'Route Marching.' Mr. Eddy said, 'Here it is, for the first time.'" *Willington Evening Journal:* "A singer who enunciates his words so clearly that they are understood without any sacrifice of tonal quality was the rare treat provided the large audience that braved the inclement weather to hear Nelson Eddy.... A genial, handsome entrepreneur of the vocal arts, Mr. Eddy more than repaid the small but discriminating audience with a variety of songs that exhibited to a marked degree a wide range of voice and a magnetic personality." *Every Evening:* "A program of high merit... well received throughout, the audience calling and demanding encores following each group of selections by the respective artists... by far the best part of the program was the concluding number, 'Drink To Me Only with Thine Eyes' when both the harpist and singer came nearer approaching forgetfulness of themselves in their rendition than at any other time. This too was accomplished during the harp selection 'Song of the Volga Boatman,' when Mr. Eddy softly sang from back stage. Otherwise it might be said that the stage presence of the artists was a bit too studied. They knew they were there and so did the audience." *New York Evening World,* January 8, 1931: "There is also a baritone who has suffered. He is Nelson Eddy, who failed to reserve a rehearsal studio before his recent broadcast over WABC. Arriving there, he found them all in use. Being a regular fellow, without the usual affectations of temperament, he simply stepped into a phone booth and rehearsed by himself without piano accompaniment. The difficulties of getting a piano into the booth were found too great." *Bulletin:* "Christine Murdoch Kendrick, known to Philadelphia audiences from her former appearance with the Savoy Opera Company, made her debut in a joint recital with Nelson Eddy last night at the Hotel Warwick.... Mr. Eddy, who is giving the series of musicales, opened the program with the aria from **L'Enfant Prodigue**, the 'Faites Silence,' by Debussy, which he gave with his most resonant tones and full dramatic swing. This was the only operatic number he offered during the evening. His second group consisted of brief Italian love songs. Both the baritone and audience seemed to enjoy the explanations of the joys, sorrows and humors of love, with which Mr. Eddy prefaced each number. His singing of them, however, seemed to lack much of the color and musical feeling of which the former member of the Civic Opera Company is capable. In fact, one or two seemed somewhat carelessly presented.... The duet from **The Magic Flute**, 'La Dove Prende,' was sung by Miss Kendrick and Mr. Eddy as the closing number, which received enthusiastic applause." *Ledger:* "Mr. Eddy...was his usual urbane, vocally gifted self." *Record:* "Eddy, with his usual good taste... presented a fresh and interesting program of songs." *Camden Courier Post:* "I know quite well that many roses have been hurled in this column in comment on the series of concerts being presented at the Warwick this year by Nelson Eddy, playboy baritone of Philadelphia. Now, Mr. Eddy may not like that title at all, but it just about fits the delightful informality, the superb musical charm and the inimitable atmosphere of his recitals. Last night's program...was the best yet.... Let's say right off that Miss Kendrick's singing was ass tasteful and as charming as her appearance, that Mr. Eddy got as much fun out of singing as his audience got in listening, and that if you missed the whole of it, today is not Thursday at all, but Blue Monday.... The songs have ceased to be the motivating interest of these programs. The chief distinctions are the moods of the artists, their encores, their personalities and the jovial spirit of everybody, clashing with evening gowns and formal attire.... The final peak of the evening, which included as many encores as the audience tumultuously demanded, came when Mr. Eddy, to satisfy his customers, sang a cycle of nine songs, 'Vaudeville,' in which he played the overture, did an animal act, became a jazz singer... put on black face, soared to the rocky steppes with the prima donna and even performed on a trapeze (vocal, of course). Not until then was the audience content to call it an evening." [Henry C. Beck authored this review.]

THE SUN, BALTIMORE, SUNDAY MORNING, FEBRUARY 15, 1931

Music—Another

Nelson Eddy Will Make Local Debut

Barytone Will Appear In Concert This Afternoon At Overlea — Compinsky Trio Here Tomorrow

Final Concert Of Season By The Philadelphia Orchestra To Be Given On Wednesday

By HELEN S. TAYLOR

WITH scarcely room for breath in between, one must go from a busy week into another which is almost as full musically. Beginning this afternoon with the second of the series of concerts at the Maryland School for the Blind, at Overlea, Nelson Eddy, American barytone, will make his local debut.

NELSON EDDY

Eddy, barytone, will be heard in recital at the Maryland School for the Blind, at Overlea, this afternoon

FROM RHODE ISLAND

Nelson Eddy, the barytone, who will sing this afternoon at Overlea, comes from Providence, R. I. He has had European as well as American training.

His operatic debut was made in New York with the Philadelphia Grand Opera Company in 1924, though he has just within the past two years entered the recital field. He has sung extensively in oratorios. Mr. Eddy will sing the following:

Aria, Largo al factotum, from the Barber of Seville..............Rossini
At Night..................Rachmaninoff
The Paladin..............Dargomnashky
Amid the Cotillon........Tschaikowsky
Mephisto's Song of the Flea, Moussorgsky

Piano Solos

Rhapsody in G minor...........Brahms
Chorale, Jesu, Joy of Man's Desiring, Bach-Hess
Perpetual Motion.................Weber

Mr. Paxson

Minnelied ....Brahms
Vergebliches Standchen.........Brahms
Friede.......................Eric Wolff
Es ist ein Schnitter........Eric Wolff
Will the Red Sun Never Set? Woodforde-Finder
Route Marchin'...................Stock
Red Bombay.....................Reddick

Nelson Eddy, baritone, recently made his Baltimore recital debut. Mr. Eddy scored an instantaneous success with both audience and critics, receiving the cordial applause of the former and the printed commendation of the latter.

N.C. 3-7

Clipping, *New York Sun:* Nelson Eddy to sing at Carnegie Hall on January 29, 1931 with Schola Cantorum. *New York Sun,* January 30, 1931: "Nelson Eddy, barytone, acquitted himself with credit." They did five pieces, including **Stabat Mater** of Karol Szymanowski, who was at that tie one of the more popular composers of the modernist movement. *New York American:* "Nelson Eddy was propulsively effective in the Sibelius opus [**Ukko**]. *Musical Courier*, February 21, 1931: "When Nelson Eddy, baritone, appeared with the Schola Cantorum in Carnegie Hall, New York, January 29, few people in the audience realized that he was suffering from an attack of influenza, which had caused him to cancel several engagements." *Evening Post:* "Mr. Eddy's youthful voice was vital and strong." *Evening World:* "He disclosed an exceptional voice." *New York Times:* "Mr. Eddy summoned sufficient dramatic force, resonance and accent to project his part successfully against heavy choral effects and orchestration." *New York Evening Post:* "Mr. Eddy sang the Sibelius solo well, and realized to the full the somber effect of the monotone which precedes the first entrance of the chorus. His diction was particularly clean-cut." *New York Telegram:* "The soloists – Ethel Hayden, soprano, Eleanor Reynolds, contralto, Nelson Eddy, baritone, and Colin McPhee -- all did well.... The audience received the program with unusual enthusiasm." *New York Evening World:* "Miss Reynolds and Mr. Eddy both disclosed exceptional voices in their many solos." *Musical Courier*, February 7. 1931: "The notable redeeming feature of the performance was the beautiful singing of Nelson Eddy, whose rich and resonant baritone gave forth a great wealth of noble tones, and whose musicianly and spirited delivery and lucid diction compelled genuine admiration. Mr. Eddy is an artist whose solo services should be most arduously sought by oratorio and choral societies." *Musical America*, February 10, 1931: "Mr. Eddy's sonorous voice rang out thrillingly in certain of his solo passages."

February 11, 1931: Nelson sang his fourth recital at the Warwick. *Ledger*, February 12, 1931: "Mr. Eddy has never been in better voice than he was last evening, singing with a superb quality, artistic interpretation and that remarkable clearness of diction which he always shows in any language.... The recital was one of the most successful that Mr. Eddy has yet given." *Bulletin:* "By far his finest offering was the opening number, 'An jenem Tag'.... Other numbers on Mr. Eddy's program were interpreting and entertaining, not very exacting as to the singer's ability, but given in a artistic and appealing manner that pleased his hearers." *Record:* "Nelson Eddy sang his program with his usual grace." *Camden Courier-Press:* "Mr. Eddy seems to reserve his best voice for these recitals, if such a thing can be done, and as a result his singing was exceptional as usual. His program was slightly different in character from those which have preceded it and in its new mood the artist showed his charm of personality, his remarkable diction and his delight in singing.... I hope before the season is out Mr. Eddy will put on some of those costumes his managers photographed him in last summer, permitting his audience to come along for a sort of Bohemian soiree in attire in which they can become as enthusiastic as they want. The decorum of starched dress cries for release at one recital, anyway." *Musical America*, February 25, 1931: "His customary fine artistry was displayed in a varied program."

February 15, 1931, *Baltimore Sun:* Photo of Nelson announcing his singing this afternoon at the Maryland School for the Blind, at Overlea.

February 16, 1931, *Baltimore Sun:* "A thoroughly normal, typical young blond American, radiating health and vitality, is Nelson Eddy, barytone, who appeared in recital yesterday afternoon at the Maryland School for the Blind at Overlea. His is a fresh, vigorous voice, almost boyish, the kind that has an especial appeal for a masculine audience… There is no special art about his singing. He sings as naturally as he talks, with an ingeniousness that is quite delightful, and which naturally finds its best medium in character songs and those popularly described as songs of the he-man sort.... 'Largo Al Factotum' from the **Barber of Seville** was very entertaining although it lacked many of the subtle touches a more sophisticated artist would have given it. The singer's tone production is excellent and his mezzo-voce is exceptionally beautiful and has a bright cast of tone even in its softness. His German enunciation is good." *Baltimore Times:* "This was Mr. Eddy's first appearance in Baltimore, and the impression he made was decidedly favorable, being a fine, upstanding young man, with an agreeable personality pervading everything he does, and a pleasing sense of humor...I don't know if the soloist had a cold, but I do know that his voice, a powerful organ, was very uneven in quality, extremely fine in the upper registers, while manifesting rough spots throughout the lower tones." [Carlisle, Pennsylvania] *Evening Sentinel:* "Mr. Eddy, who is well known in Carlisle by reason of his previous appearance here was...

enthusiastically received... His varied array of songs demanded that versatile interpretive and technical facility that Carlisle audience have learned he possess in a marked degree. Mr. Eddy sang in rich, vibrant tone and with clear enunciation and understanding of each number."

February 22, 1931: Nelson sang on Dutch Masters Program. This was the first show in a new series, and Nelson's co-star was Lillian Tiaz.

February 27, 1931: Nelson sang on the Congress Cigar Program, details unknown.

February 28, 1931, clipping: Nelson sang recently before the Art Alliance, Philadelphia.

Clipping, undated: Nelson is singing with the Philadelphia Orchestra in Bach St. Matthew Passion on March 13, 14 and 16th. He sings with the Detroit Symphony Orchestra on April 1 and 2nd; and on April 5 he sings with the Handel and Haydn Society of Boston in Parker's **Hora Novissima**. Nelson is singing nine times in Philadelphia alone this season.

March 2, 1931: Nelson sang for the Mendelssohn Club of Sunbury. *Sunbury Daily*, March 3, 1931: "Mr. Nelson Eddy, the guest soloist, held his audience spellbound with his rendition of the baritone solos, possessing a beautiful voice as well as a radiant personality. It seemed to be the unanimous opinion of the audience that they heard far too little of his glorious voice. The chorus was so well pleased with Mr. Eddy's work, that they have engaged him as soloist for their Hospital Concert which will be given in May." *Sunbury Item:* "Eighty singers took part in the big choral numbers. Solo parts were taken by Nelson Eddy, distinguished New York (sic) baritone.... It was announced that Mr. Eddy will return to Sunbury for the May festival of the club.... The sensational success of Mr. Eddy last night will assure a large audience for this big event."

March 5, 1931, *Public Ledger,* review of Nelson's fifth Warwick concert: "Mr. Eddy was again in excellent voice and sang with his customary artistry and marvelous diction." [Note: Marjorie Fulton was the guest violinist.] *Bulletin:* "An excellent presentation of a well-chosen and interesting program." *Camden Courier-Press:* "Last night Mr. Eddy was not in his usual playboy mood. Last night he was Heinrich Sclusnus and I mean that literally, not because his program was mostly German but because of the ease, the pleasure and the tireless joy of singing. Composers, if you ask me, should be scurrying to have Mr. Eddy sing their songs. When he sings them, songwriters will hear things they never meant to be there, things that stamp the songs above the average.... Mr. Eddy's encore best illustrates what I have been trying to tell you for ever so long. He obtained the song 'The Bellman' only the day before. He liked it, he said, and he hoped the audience would. From now on, those who heard the song will be requesting its inclusion on the next and final program. It is a moody bit in which Mr. Eddy becomes not a baritone but the Bellman himself." [Note: this reviewer was Henry C. Beck, who became a champion of Nelson's and never passed up an opportunity to announce to his readers that Nelson should be a major star!] *Musical Courier,* March 7, 1931: "Nelson Eddy, baritone, recently made his Baltimore recital debut. Mr. Eddy scored an instantaneous success with both audience and critics, receiving the cordial applause of the former and the printed commendation of the latter. Mr. Eddy's voice is of such a beautiful quality, his use of it so skillful, his enunciation so clear and his stage presence so pleasing and easy, that it would be difficult to improve on the combination. He carried his audience with him from beginning to end."

March 13, 1931: Nelson sang in Bach's **St. Matthew Passion** at the Met. It was a matinee given by the Philadelphia Opera, Mendelssohn Club, Boys Choir of Girard College and five soloists, Richard Crooks, Jeanette Vreeland, Nelson, Kathryn Meisle and Fred Patton. It was performed at the Met due to needing a larger stage and seating capacity than the Academy of Music. *Inquirer,* March 14, 1931: "Mr. Eddy sang with the fine phrasing and excellent intonation that are qualities of his splendid baritone." *Record:* "Mr. Eddy, voicing the passages assigned to Jesus, was at his eminently satisfying best." *Ledger:* "Very fine work of the soloists, especially Mr. Crooks, Mr. Eddy and Mr. Patton.... The soloists were very good in every respect.... the conductor has three vocalists who are all remarkable in this respect [enunciation] as well as being singers of the highest order.... Mr. Eddy sang very finely the music allotted to the baritone." *Bulletin:* "Nelson Eddy, in the thoughtful and appreciative use of his rich, well-rounded baritone, indicated that he may find in oratorio an advantageous field for the use of his ample vocal resources." *Musical Courier*, March 21, 1931: "Mr. Eddy, in the part for the voice of Christ, sang with a richness, sympathy and pathos, which, added to his equally fine diction, were extremely impressive."

March 23, 1931, evening edition of *Nashville Tennesseean:* "The Ward-Belmont girls were given a treat for the eye and the ear last night when Nelson Eddy sang, and their reception of him was a wildly enthusiastic one. Mr. Eddy, who is a baritone and an artist to his fingers' tips, is a young man in his late twenties, whose singing, fine as it is, is only one of his many assets, as he looks like an athletic blonde Viking, a movie star, and a pictured ad for men's' full dress, all rolled into one. He has a voice of great power...." *Nashville Banner,* March 19, 1931, evening edition: "Nelson sang in Ward-Belmont schools' auditorium under the auspices of that group. His voice is one of rare purity, power and vibrance. And it has a quality that reminds one of the cello at its best and in its best range. His control of tone is at all times complete and he exerts that control without a particle of evidence that he is doing anything out of the ordinary, so natural is his finished art. And as for his speech; if his Spanish and his Russian were as perfectly sung as were his English, German and Italian, then there was nothing left to be desired. The intelligence of the man was always to the fore. He put into each offering just that thought and emotion that was appropriate. And as to his personality, he had a large dose of artistic 'it.' An American Adonis. How could his predominately feminine audience have remained cool!"

March 23, 1931: Nelson sang in **The Crucifixion** at the North Baptist Church with the choral Club of the Musical Art Society. *Camden Courier Post,* March 24, 1931: "Mr. Eddy was in splendid voice. His ease of singing, something achieved through ours of careful work, was again in evidence and particularly suited to the occasion."

April 2, 1931, *Detroit Evening Times:* Nelson sang with the Detroit Symphony Orchestra: "Not before has a Detroit performance had the services of so fine a baritone as Nelson Eddy turned out to be..." *Detroit News:* "A singer new to this city, who made a very deep impression indeed. He is Nelson Eddy, baritone -- or, if you ask me, basso cantante -- who sang the role of Jesus. Mr. Eddy's singing is not over-dramatic but a lovelier legato is not to be found among voices of his quality. If vocal students wish to study the matter of head-resonance, he is an excellent man for them to listen to. When his voice is fluently expended on a note, the overtones chime in one's ear almost as clearly as the fundamental. Not in years, in the field of oratorio, have we heard anyone as promising as Mr. Eddy." *Detroit Free Press:* "The baritone, new here, created a fine impression. Mr. Eddy has a voice of great range and sonority, warm and appealing in quality and handled with intelligence. He showed himself an artist of distinguished musicanly feeling."

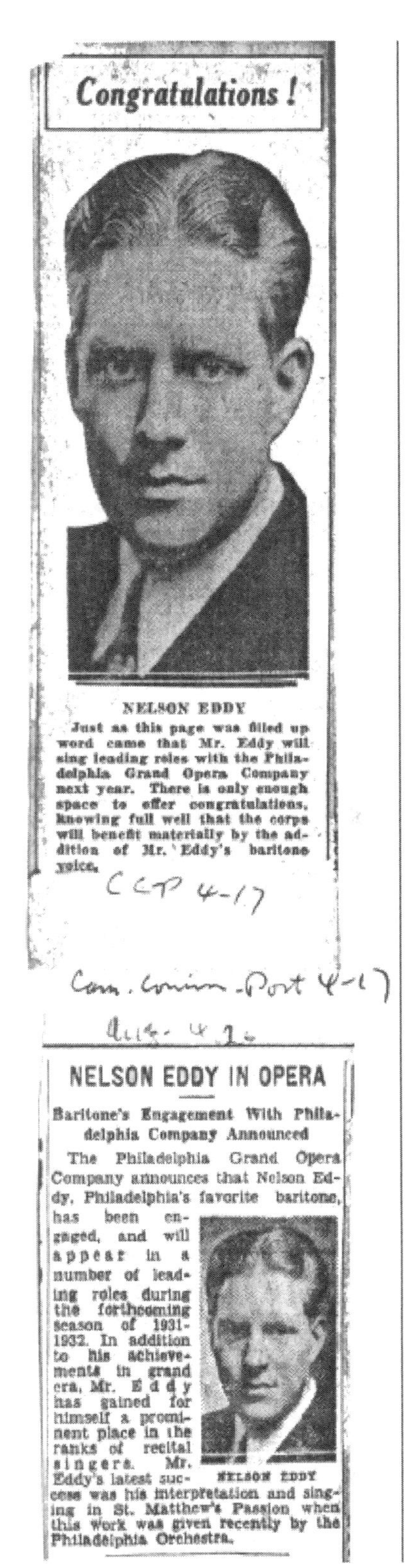

Congratulations!

NELSON EDDY

Just as this page was filled up word came that Mr. Eddy will sing leading roles with the Philadelphia Grand Opera Company next year. There is only enough space to offer congratulations, knowing full well that the corps will benefit materially by the addition of Mr. Eddy's baritone voice.

CCP 4-17

Cam. Courier-Post 4-17

NELSON EDDY IN OPERA

Baritone's Engagement With Philadelphia Company Announced

The Philadelphia Grand Opera Company announces that Nelson Eddy, Philadelphia's favorite baritone, has been engaged, and will appear in a number of leading roles during the forthcoming season of 1931-1932. In addition to his achievements in grand era, Mr. Eddy has gained for himself a prominent place in the ranks of recital singers. Mr. Eddy's latest success was his interpretation and singing in St. Matthew's Passion when this work was given recently by the Philadelphia Orchestra.

NELSON EDDY

ANN ARBOR LISTS FESTIVAL PROGRAMS

Paderewski and Lily Pons Among Soloists to Be Heard

ANN ARBOR, April 5.—The complete list of soloists for the Ann Arbor May Festival, which will be given here from May 13 to 16, has recently been announced. Six concerts will be given during four days. As in previous seasons, the University Choral Union, under Earl V. Moore, will be assisted by the Chicago Symphony, under Frederick Stock and Eric De Lamarter.

Lily Pons, coloratura soprano of the Metropolitan Opera, will be the soloist with the Chicago Symphony, under Mr. Stock, on the evening of May 13.

Pierné's "St. Francis of Assisi" will be sung by the chorus and orchestra on the evening of May 14, under Mr. Moore, with the following soloists: Hilda Burke, soprano; Eleanor Reynolds contralto; Frederick Jagel, tenor; Nelson Eddy, baritone, and Fred Patton, bass.

The festival chorus of children, under Juva Higbee, will participate in the afternoon program on May 15, with Miss Burke, Mme. Reynolds, and Palmer Christian, organist, as soloists. Harvey Gaul's "Johnny Appleseed" will be one of the works sung.

Ignace Jan Paderewski will be the distinguished soloist with the Symphony, under Mr. Stock, on the evening of May 15. Ruth Breton, violinist, will be the soloist with the orchestra on the afternoon of May 16.

The final concert, on the evening of May 16, will be devoted to a concert performance in English of Moussorgsky's opera "Boris Godounoff."

The soloists will include Chase Baromeo, bass of the Chicago Opera, as Boris; Cyrena Van Gordon, contralto of the Chicago Opera, as Marina; Walter Widdop, British tenor, as Dmitri and Shuisky, and Mr. Eddy and Mr. Patton, in other roles.

Mu. Am. 4-10

Musical America

4-11 PUBLIC LEDGER

Joins Phila. Grand

NELSON EDDY

NOTED BARITONE SIGNS

Nelson Eddy Has Been Engaged by Opera Company for Next Season

Nelson Eddy, popular Philadelphia baritone, has been engaged by the Philadelphia Grand Opera Company for the 1931-32 season, it was announced yesterday.

Mr. Eddy, regarded as one of the finest young singers of the day, has gained a prominent place on the concert stage. His latest success was gained in Bach's "St. Matthew Passion," with the Philadelphia Orchestra.

4-26

Bulletin 4-26

ENGAGED FOR OPERA

Nelson Eddy to Appear In Leading Roles with Phila. Company

B

Nelson Eddy, Philadelphia baritone, has been engaged to appear with the Philadelphia Grand Opera Company in several leading roles during the coming season of 1931-32, it was announced today by Mrs. William C. Hammer, director.

Mr. Eddy, who is well known to Philadelphia audiences, was heard here recently in St. Matthew's Passion, when this work was given by the Philadelphia Orchestra.

Nelson Eddy
(Photo by Bacrach)

April 5, 1931, *Boston Traveler:* "The Handel and Haydn Society in its 116th season gave its 852nd concert in the afternoon before a large and enthusiastic audience in Symphony Hall. The two oratorios were **Exultate Deo**, by Mabel Daniels, for the 50th anniversary of the founding of Radcliff college, and **Hora Novissima,** by Horatio William Parker. Certainly Jeanette Vreeland, soprano, Kathryn Meisle, alto, Dan Gridley, tenor, and Nelson Eddy, bass, gave a thrilling performance of this great oratorio." *Boston Herald,* April 6, 1931: "There is dramatic force to the bass solo, 'Spe modo Vivitur,' impressively sung by Mr. Eddy." *Boston American:* "It was a pleasure to hear them." *Boston Post:* "To say that of the four solo signers, Kathryn Meisle, the contralto, and Nelson Eddy, the bass, made the strongest impression, is not to say that the others, Jeanette Vreeland, soprano, and Dan Gridley, tenor, failed to give pleasure." *Boston Globe:* "Mr. Eddy's solo, 'Spe modo vivitur,' had appropriate style and emotional intensity, but the singer seemed not to be in good voice." *Boston Transcript:* "The four singers of the solo quartet did their tasks of uneven demand... In no case did they appear to fall short... often raising to high effectiveness."

April 8, 1931: Nelson sang at the Treble Clef Concert at Bellevue-Stratford Ballroom. Treble Clef was an organization made up entirely of women singers, and was the oldest women's chorus in Philadelphia, having been around for 46 years. *Bulletin:* "Nelson Eddy...sang with the chorus and also provided two solo groups, one in French and German, and the other in English. His voice was resonant and full-toned, although at times his high tones seemed pinched." *Musical Courier*, April 18, 1931: "There is no doubt that Mr. Eddy is artistic in whatever he does, and his voice is always pleasing, as he uses it with much skill and intelligence... At each appearance he was applauded vociferously for his fine work."

April 9, 1931: Nelson sang the last in this Warwick series, with Geoffrey O'Hara. *Bulletin:* "A delightful program." *Daily News:* "Eddy's voice has been increasing in power and beauty since he was first introduced publicly, several years ago. He has a vibrant, resonant baritone that has a wide range and a well-trained intonation. When he sang an aria from **Boris** his voice indicated the high quality that has given him a reputation of note." *Camden Courier-Post:* "I won't make any bones about it and I don't care who feels offended, I have enjoyed this concert series of Mr. Eddy's more than any other music of the year. That I have a lot of people on my side is indicated by the large and enthusiastic audiences that have made their regular appearance since the first crusaders found out what Mr. Eddy was up to. The artists that Mr. Eddy has introduced have been decidedly worth hearing. They themselves have had the unquestionable advantage of being presented on a program of a singer whose youth, whose love and ease of singing and general sterling artistry stamps him not only a vocalist outstanding in Philadelphia but one of far-reaching importance. If you knew how much I mean that you would never again doubt my sincerity.... There was an added memory in last night's finale. Somebody brought forward a big basket of fruit. Remembering Mr. Valee's fruity experience, Mr. Eddy remarked that ordinarily singers do not receive such delicacies in so orderly a fashion. Then he made a boyish speech about the most enthusiastic rooter he has had for the concerts, one who had done more, he said, to make them a success than anyone else. And he walked down through the audience to give his mother the basket. It was a real tribute.... If there is no Eddy series next season, I'll take up plumbing."

April 17, 1931, *Camden Courier Post:* In a non-review column, they ran a picture of Nelson with heading "Congratulations! Just as this page was filled up word came that Mr. Eddy will sing leading roles with the Philadelphia Grand Opera Company next year. There is only enough space to offer congratulations, knowing full well that the corps will benefit materially by the addition of Mr. Eddy's baritone voice."

April 22, 1931: Nelson sang with Penn Athletic Glee club last night, with 50 male chorus. Nelson "was enthusiastically received an called upon for a number of encores. He was in unusually good voice." *Inquirer:* "All the humor of old glee club songs was brought out last night by the Penn Athletic Glee Club when it gave an invitation concert at the clubhouse, Eighteenth and Locust streets. The ballroom was literally packed and people were standing to hear the songs by the club and also by Philadelphia's best known baritone, Nelson Eddy.... Mr. Eddy's fine voice rang out clearly in sea songs and other numbers that had a martial air." *Record:* "Mr. Eddy...tuned his program to match the gay mood of the evening." *Ledger:* "Mr. Eddy was in his customary excellent voice and sang with beautiful quality of tone and perfect intonation and enunciation. He appeared in two groups of solos and was obliged to respond with encore numbers each time."

April 26, 1931: Nelson Eddy signed with the Philadelphia Grand Opera Company for the 1931-32 season.

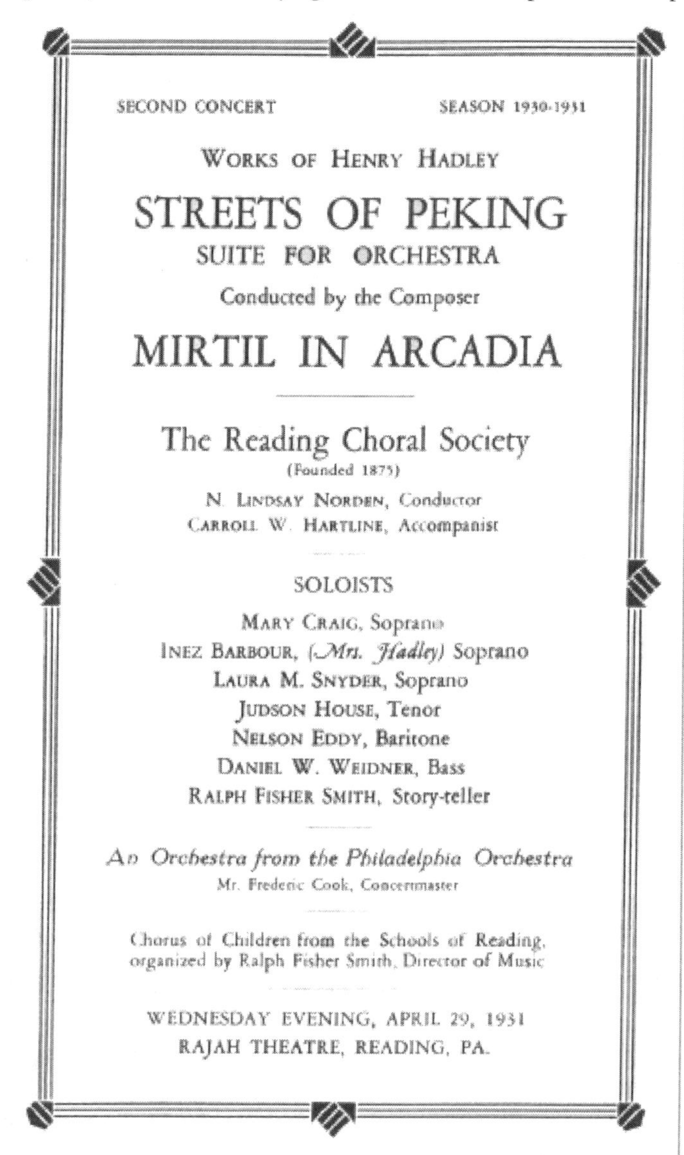
SECOND CONCERT SEASON 1930-1931

WORKS OF HENRY HADLEY

STREETS OF PEKING

SUITE FOR ORCHESTRA

Conducted by the Composer

MIRTIL IN ARCADIA

The Reading Choral Society

(Founded 1875)

N. LINDSAY NORDEN, Conductor

CARROLL W. HARTLINE, Accompanist

SOLOISTS

MARY CRAIG, Soprano

INEZ BARBOUR, (Mrs. Hadley) Soprano

LAURA M. SNYDER, Soprano

JUDSON HOUSE, Tenor

NELSON EDDY, Baritone

DANIEL W. WEIDNER, Bass

RALPH FISHER SMITH, Story-teller

An Orchestra from the Philadelphia Orchestra

Mr. Frederic Cook, Concertmaster

Chorus of Children from the Schools of Reading, organized by Ralph Fisher Smith, Director of Music

WEDNESDAY EVENING, APRIL 29, 1931

RAJAH THEATRE, READING, PA.

April 29, 1931: Reading, Pennsylvania, at the Rajah Theater, Reading Choral Society did a concert devoted to Dr. Henry Hadley, a contemporary composer. He was present along with 6 soloists, a large chorus and a chorus of children. *Ledger:* "The soloists were all in excellent voice... Mr. Eddy was especially impressive in the tragic 'The Winds of Doom.'"

May 7, 1931: Nelson sang with Mendelssohn Club, and than 80 voices last night at the Sunbury High School auditorium. *Sunbury Item:* "Mr. Eddy's numbers were well chosen, for the most part being descriptive, the effects heightened by the capable assistance of Theodore Paxson, his accompanist." *Sunbury Daily News:* "It was the outstanding event of Sunbury's observance of Music Week and was declared by those who attended to have been the greatest concert even given in Sunbury.... Nelson Eddy, baritone soloist, of the Philadelphia Grand Opera Company, who featured in the concert, won the hearts of his audience. Not only does he have a voice of unusual tonal quality but at the same time is possessed of a personality that finds its way over the footlights in a captivating manner.... Mr. Eddy will be the soloist Friday afternoon and evening at the annual Mozart festival in Harrisburg, and will sing May 11 at the University of Michigan Music Festival in Ann Arbor.... His readings last evening were entirely of his own interpretation and were given with unusual technical ability. Mr. Eddy was very generous with his encores and expressed himself as well pleased with the work of the chorus of eighty voices that supported him."

May 7-9, 1931: Nelson was part of the Harrisburg Mozart festival; other soloists included Rose Bampton. Nelson sang in **Hora Novissima**. *Harrisburg Patriot:* "Nelson Eddy, baritone soloist, whose marvelous power and clear tones delighted his audience..." [Note: they also sang Mozart chorus' new choral work, performed in William Penn High School auditorium, with a chorus of 150.] "The afternoon concert yesterday presented three of last night's soloists in a charming song recital...[others two were Lillian Gustafsen and Nevada

Vanderveer] Mr. Eddy, of commanding personality and of stage appearance like a Leyendecker pastor, sang so well that three encores were demanded." More on **Hora Novissima,** *Harrisburg Evening News:* "The rendition of the number was a fine bit of work, the rich tonal quality of the voices being in conspicuous evidence." *Musical Courier*, May 16, 1931: "Nelson Eddy, a newcomer to Harrisburg, offered 'Ode from Ossian's Poems' by Hopkinson and 'Serenade' by Carpenter. Mr. Eddy has a voice of great beauty and a fine stage presence. His diction is clear... The audience showed their delight in his singing by demanding numerous encores." [This review was of Nelson's second concert, on May 8th. Earlier that day he had sung in the Mozart "C Minor Mass."]

May 14, 1931: Nelson sang Pierne's **St. Francis of Assisi** at Ann Arbor May Festival, with the Chicago Symphony. Soloists are Hilda Burke, soprano, Eleanor Reynolds, contralto, Frederick Jagel, tenor, Nelson Eddy, baritone, Fred Patton, bass.

May 15, 1931, *Detroit News:* "Thursday night May Festival was University Choral Union, they did Pierne's **St. Francis of Assisi.** Frederick Jagel got a rave review and most prominent among the other soloists were Hilda Burke, soprano of the Chicago Opera Company, and Nelson Eddy.... Detroit has discovered Mr. Eddy's quality. He gave an admirable demonstration of it here." *Detroit Evening Times:* "Nelson Eddy, whom Detroit learned to admire in the baritone part of the Bach **St. Matthew Passion** a few weeks ago, sang Friar Leon splendidly." *Detroit Free-Press:* "Nelson Eddy's baritone voice was well adapted though the more dramatic part of Friar Leon, the artist bringing a profound sincerity and unerring beauty and power of his voice being displayed to a fine degree." *Michigan Daily,* May 17, 1931: "The production was considerably aided by the splendid singing of Nelson Eddy, Fred Patton, and Walter Widdop in their several parts." *Musical Courier*, May 23, 1931: "Nelson Eddy's vibrant and beautiful baritone was a notable feature of the performance."

May 16, 1931: Nelson sang in Ann Arbor, a concert version of **Boris Godunov** in English. Chase Baromeo, bass of the Chicago Opera and Fred Patton were the other stars. *Detroit Free Press:* "Nelson Eddy, the popular baritone, sprained his ankle Saturday morning but appeared despite the injury. He did major service in the roles of Andrea and the ribald Varlaam besides singing several of the lesser baritone parts." *Musical Digest,* June, 1931: "Some fine work was done by Chase Baromeo in **Boris Godunov**, and Nelson Eddy's singing in the same opera showed that this young man has made definite advance in his art."

More reviews on later performances of **Boris** and **St. Francis**: "The singing of Nelson Eddy and Fred Patton in the varied and numerous parts allotted them was extraordinarily fine. Mr. Nelson's (sic) resonant baritone was particularly effective in the bold folk song 'By the Walls of Kazan' in the first act." [Note: Paderewski and Lily Pons were also soloists in the May Festival] *Musical America*, May 25, 1931, re: **St. Francis:** "Nelson Eddy made a deep impression." Re: **Boris:** "Nelson Eddy confirmed the very favorable impression of his earlier appearance."

May 23, 1931, *Musical Courier:* "Nelson Eddy has been forced to cancel his annual trip to Europe because of his numerous summer engagements in this country. Among these are four appearances with the Philharmonic Symphony at the New York Stadium concerts, one with the Philadelphia Orchestra in Robin Hood Dell, and July 16 Atwater Kent Broadcast. All of these are re-engagements. Mr. Eddy's bookings for next year have almost doubled. He'll also sing six leading roles with the Philadelphia Grand Opera Company."

May 28, 1931: Last night Nelson made Albany debut with the Mendelssohn Club. *Knickerbocker Press,* Albany: "No audience had ever responded more spontaneously, more hungrily in its desire for more, or left the hall with a greater satisfaction.... Nelson Eddy was new to Albany last night, but, with his strong, resonant, evenly scaled voice and his friendly manner, he walked right into its friendship. In enunciation, phrasing, tone control he is a fine artist; one of the best the club has ever presented... As encore, he sang Mussorgsky's 'Song of the Flea,' and even with memories of the great Chaliapin and Tibbett and others in this song, one knows he sings it as it should be sung.... There will always be a great welcome for Nelson Eddy." *Musical Courier*, June 13, 1931: "Nelson Eddy scored his usual success in his Albany debut last month." *Albany Evening News,* May 28, 1931:

"Nelson Eddy, baritone, made his Albany debut last night and just rushed into the good favor of the audience. His voice is so rich, so well controlled and so finely timbered that, in a series of songs by such masters as Beethoven, Massenet and Brahms, he satisfied everyone at once that here was a man who lived for song and its interpretation. Perhaps you felt the artistry he put in such a song as 'Si Tu Veux, Mignonne,' by Massenet, and accepted him right there. Later he sang a group of English songs and slyly advised his audience that 'The Bell Man,' by Forsythe should be sung in some phrases off the tone (which fact was not evident to one music critic, he said, and which should have been, because of Eddy's previous numbers). As an encore he sang 'The Song of the Flea,' by Mussorgsky, and here you paid deep respect to his powers of interpretation. He sang 'Water Boy' superbly and ended with a rousing chantey by Deems Taylor, 'Cap'n Stratton's Fancy.' He is an artist and a rare personality and you may like to know that the Troy Chromatic Society has engaged him for a concert next season with the Barrere Ensemble.

June 6, 1931: Nelson sang at a Robin Hood Dell concert. *Daily News:* "A triple celebration was staged when the Philadelphia Orchestra played at Robin Hood Dell last night. Of major importance was the appearance of the popular Nelson Eddy, baritone, as soloist. Then came the first American rendition of a part of the 'Taming of the Shrew,' a musical suite by Albert Coates, the guest conductor. And finally was the marking of the 24th anniversary of Louis Mattson as the assistant manager of the orchestra. More than 4000 persons flocked to the outdoor stadium to hear this concert, with assurances of a popular program under the direction of a batonierre who has assumed mighty importance. But it undoubtedly was the appearance of the blond Eddy as the soloist of the event that acted as a magnet for the greater portion of the ticket buyers. Eddy's voice is as delightful as it has ever been. He seems to have acquired a more distinctive charm than the operatic stage ever afforded him. He rendered a Mozartean air with all of the charm imaginable. For an encore he sang the 'Route Marching,' by Starr. Here he exceeded himself, with the uncanny singing of this Kiplin-worded song. An aria from **Boris Godunov** was repeated after the insistence demands of his listeners." *Evening Public Ledger:* "Mr. Eddy, whose popularity in Philadelphia undoubtedly had something to do with the size of attendance, sang two numbers, one in each half of the concert. He was in superb voice and his ringing tones carried to the extreme ends of the Dell." [Note: His other number was "Non Piu Andrai" from **Marriage of Figaro**.] *Inquirer:* "The singer was in excellent voice." *Bulletin:* "Nelson Eddy's ability to sing Mozart was demonstrated.... The lyric quality of his voice, the smooth, even scale, his fine sense of phrase, and a natural turn for comedy make his handling of Mozart's vocal style a thing to remember with pleasure. The Mozart was better suited to his talents than the aria 'The Siege of Kazan' from Mussorgsky's **Boris Godunov** which he sang later. **Boris** is big music with a broad declamatory vocal line and an orchestration that suggests girth, rather than quality of voice. Mr. Eddy sang the aria with dramatic sweep." *Record:* "The vocal contributions of Nelson Eddy, as soloist... expanded the holiday spirit."

June 19, 1931, *Doylestown Intelligencer:* "Doylestown had the good fortune to hear again, last evening, Nelson Eddy.... The great variety of Mr. Eddy's program provided a wide scope for the superb quality of his beautiful voice."

July 5, 1931: *New York Herald-Tribune:* Eighth annual series of Artistic Mornings at the Hotel Plaza will consist of eight concerts.

July 11, 1931, Nelson sang a concert. *Stroudsburg Record,* July 16, 1931: "Nelson Eddy, who used to be a newspaper reporter in Philadelphia, gave a recital at the Auditorium at Buck Hill Falls Saturday evening with the Ensemble Art Trio. Mr. Eddy is a splendid baritone singer and has been so successful that he has given up newspaper work for the concert stage.... It has been my pleasure to have heard a number of America's foremost artists during the past two seasons at Buck Hill, but none of them has ever been given a greater reception than was accorded Mr. Eddy Saturday night.... There were ten songs on his program, and he gave eight encores, and there was genuine enthusiasm shown by the audience over his success. I had a little chat with him after the concert, and he told me how he had started as a reporter on the old Philadelphia Press. And, strange enough, Secretary of the Commonwealth Beamish, who was in the audience, was directing editor of the *Press* when Mr. Eddy began his newspaper career there. He later worked on the *Public Ledger* and *Bulletin.*" *Buck*

Hill Breeze, July 17, 1931: "It is hard to speak of Nelson Eddy and his recital last Saturday without resorting to superlatives…. From this first note until the last one of the evening, the audience thrilled to the purity and resonance of his voice, marveled at the clarity of his enunciation, and his mastery of languages. He sang with such understanding that no matter whether the selection was in Latin, French, Spanish, German or Russian, the audience listened with rapt attention and sensed the spirit and mood."

July 15, 1931, Nelson sang at Robin Hood Dell. *Ledger:* "The jinx which seems to lie in wait for choral numbers at the Robin Hood Dell concerts of the Philadelphia Orchestra was present last evening and at a few minutes before nine o'clock one of the hardest rainstorms that has visited Philadelphia broke over the auditorium.... Dr. Tily had conducted the opening chorus of Elgar's **King Olaf** and Nelson Eddy, baritone soloist, had just called upon Thor 'the god of thunder,' to appear when there was a tremendous rash accompanied by a terrific rain. Mr. Smallens then announced the program would be postponed until this evening, when the same tickets would be honored, and the audience fled. The chorus remained in the shell and gave an impromptu concert for themselves until the worst of the rain was over." *Daily News:* "Then came the chorus, with Nelson Eddy singing the baritone solo parts with his usual sonorous beauty." [Note: The second night, Stokowski conducted for first time at Robin Hood Dell. Chorus was the Strawbridge & Clothier Chorus directed by Dr. Herbert Tily.]

July 16, 1931, *Record:* "In the cantata two soloists have parts, which they sang very effectively, Miss Hitner contributing a fine soprano and Mr. Eddy a rich baritone." *Ledger:* "All of the soloists were in good voice and sang artistically." *Bulletin:* "Mr. Eddy did his usual artistic work."

July 19, 1931, *New York Tribune:* Photo of Nelson, Vreeland, Gridley and van der Veer for an upcoming Beethoven's Ninth Symphony soloists Thursday and Fri evening, at Lewisohn Stadium.

July 24, 1931: *Herald Tribune:* "Mr. Eddy again exhibited a voice of very pleasing quality for his first recitative, if not entirely sure of himself in the opening notes... The performance of the Ninth Symphony was of the usual Stadium standard for this work." *Musical Courier,* August 1, 1931: "Nelson Eddy, in the baritone music, intoned the recitative with fine enunciation, and sang throughout his part with the ease and noble tone which distinguish him."

July 1931: Photos of Nelson on vacation in York Harbor, Maine appeared in *Musical Courier.* One was a candid of him sunbathing, lying on some rocks. The caption read: "Busily preparing new scores" and the article read: "If Mr. Eddy's method of cultivating his noted baritone voice is truly pictured above, there is no doubt that sun-bathing will immediately be taken up by other singers in the hope of attaining similar success."

August 16, 1931, *New York Tribune:* Large photo of Nelson. On August 19th, that paper covered the Verdi's **Requiem** at Lewisohn Stadium yesterday evening, with Philadelphia Symphony Orchestra and Schola Cantorum. "Mr. Eddy... maintained a good quality of tone and vocal style with notable consistency." *New York World-Telegram:* "Though Nelson Eddy's baritone may not have quite the depth and character for the bass music, it is a voice of rare beauty, used with intelligence, musicianship and technical skill." *New York Times:* "The large audience followed the interpretation with keen interest and appreciation." *Musical Courier,* August 29, 1931: "Mr. Eddy's beautiful tones were heard to advantage.... The soloists were Jeanette Vreeland, Dorothea Flexer, Arthur Hacket, and Nelson Eddy, each completely competent. Some excellent singing was done by them individually."

August 20, 1931: Nelson sang on a New York radio show entitled "Lewisohn Stadium Concert," details unknown.

September 17, 1931: Nelson sang in Philadelphia. *Evening Bulletin,* September 18, 1931: "Philadelphia's new Convention Hall, ablaze with the brilliancy of multi-colored lights and vibrating with melodies produced by the foremost musicians of the city, was formally dedicated by Mayor Mackey last night before 10,000 persons.... Nelson Eddy, Philadelphia's popular baritone, gave a generous and varied selection of songs."

[Note: Until the summer of 1931, Nelson labeled all the clippings himself. After this time, it's more difficult to ascertain some dates of the reviews, plus it's uncertain as to how complete the reviews are in regards to his very busy career at this time. He still identified the source of each review and some of them are still dated.]

September 28 or 29, 1931: Nelson sang in **Elektra** with the Philadelphia Grand Opera Company at the Academy of Music. "Nelson Eddy gave emphasis to the comparatively brief part of Orestes." Other singers were Rose Bampton and Helen Jepson. *Morning Ledger:* "Nelson Eddy, having his debut with the Philadelphia Grand Opera Company, was a splendid Orestes, making the most of a very difficult and none too grateful role." *Daily News:* "His is a voice that will remain shining the constellation of stars." *Record:* "Nelson Eddy, whose progress I have traced with unflagging interest, made his debut with the company in the role of Orestes. It is a difficult assignment for a debut, but Eddy, always the equal of any occasion, made his work memorable." This review was by Henry C. Beck, now with the *Record*, and still routing for his success. *New York Times,* review of September 29 by Olin Downes: "Strauss' **Elektra** is Superbly Given... That of Orestes needed more authority and dramatic life; it gave the impression of a young singer who has still to find himself on the stage." *Musical Courier*, November 7, 1931: "Nelson Eddy, a stately figure, did Orestes with dignity, feeling, and a sonorous voice well used." *Musical America*: November 8, 1931: "Nelson Eddy, making his debut as a member of the company, was a stately and rich-toned Orestes, with a valid conception of the character of a sane avenger. His scene with Elektra was one of the supreme moments of the presentation." *Evening Bulletin,* September 29, 1931: "Nelson Eddy had little to do as the avenging Orestes, but was dignified and made good use, in warm, rich tones, of his limited vocal opportunities, undoubtedly welcome being his presence as a member of the Philadelphia Company." *New York Times,* September 30, 1931: "Nelson Eddy 'filled with ability' his role." *New York Herald:* "Mr. Eddy, announcing himself in full, sustained dark-hued tones, deserved high praise for his singing as Orestes." [Note: this was the first playing of **Elektra** in America in nearly 22 years, and the first ever given in original German.]

October 25, 1931: Nelson sang on Congress Cigars radio program. [Note: it is believed that he had been appearing numerous times on this show since the end of February.]

November 5, 1931: **Madama Butterfly** was done at Academy by the Philadelphia Grand Opera Company. Stars were the Japanese prima donna, Hitzi Koyke, tenor Dimitri Onofrei and Nelson. "Nelson Eddy, who has been added to the baritones of the company this year, offered the best Sharpless seen here for many seasons, presenting a truly American consul. Despite indisposition, Mr. Eddy sang very well, giving no indication of his discomfort." [Note: Helen Jepson had a small part in this production.]

November 11, 1931: Nelson sang in Fort Dodge, Iowa. *Messenger and Chronicle:* "Nelson Eddy, young American baritone, was given an unprecedented ovation by a Fort Dodge audience when he appeared in concert at the high school auditorium Tuesday evening. The program of songs was the first number on the Community Concerts Association course in Fort Dodge and his reception launched the course on what promises to be the most successful musical season Fort Dodge has had... The Philadelphia singer has been taking the east by storm, according to the eastern critics, and after hearing him Fort Dodge agrees with the east and goes a step further by adding the middle west to the sentence... Nelson Eddy has everything a singer should have. A beautifully rich voice, clear and resonant; wonderful diction, a charming personality, expression and interpretation, breath control and an easy stage presence. It may sound exaggerated but it isn't and when one considers that the audience last night called him back time and again for encores, it is proof positive that the artist is fulfilling all that he should.... For those who sat far enough front to watch his facial expression, it was a rare treat, for the singer interpreted his numbers largely by the expression on his face and in his eyes... Mr. Eddy's home is in Philadelphia and he explained to his audience that he usually sings 'The Trumpeter' on Armistice Day when he is home. 'You haven't asked me to sing it tonight,' he said, 'but I am going to sing it anyway,' and he surely did. His second encore was a number that is popular on Broadway, 'That's Why Darkies Were born.'"

November 12, 1931: Nelson sang again in **Madama Butterfly**. "Nelson Eddy was excellent as Sharpless." *Morning Ledger:* "Mr. Eddy gave a remarkable performance considering that he appeared against his physician's orders. At 6 PM he was suffering a temperature of 103 degrees, but declined to forego his first appearance with the company in the role of Sharpless." *Record:* "I am wondering, too, if young Mr. Eddy wasn't a bit miscast in a part that demands a man of 45. I am not criticizing Mr. Eddy's work -- I think sometimes that this versatile Philadelphia baritone could do a singing version of Ed Wynn and make an opera of it. He was surely vocally beyond assignment, but as a chap the same age as Pinkerton he lacked a convincing quality, and seemed to know it. Perhaps the company is sacrificing something in pushing Mr. Eddy into every cast for the benefit of his admiring hosts. I do not consider that Mr. Eddy has yet made his debut with the company, despite his taking part in two operas.... Mr. Eddy's charming mother and Chief Caupolican, who was last year's Sharpless, both of whom I could see from my point of vantage, must have some ideas on these fleeting considerations. I should like to know what they are." The *Record* review was by Henry C. Beck. *Inquirer:* "Nelson Eddy gave his usual sympathetic performance as Consul Sharpless, but was curiously under-keyed vocally and at times hardly audible in the first act." *Evening Bulletin:* "Nelson Eddy was quite at ease as Sharpless.... commendable in his acting and the evidence that he gave of taking interest in what the others were doing even when he hadn't much to do himself. While he has little opportunity for vocal display in this role, Mr. Eddy sang suavely and with smooth richness of tone." *Musical Courier*, November 14, 1931: "Nelson Eddy, in the role of Sharpless, made his second appearance with the company at this time. Although suffering from a heavy cold and disregarding his physician's orders by singing, he made a personable Consul, singing and acting artistically." *Musical America:* "Nelson Eddy, as Sharpless, had his first opportunity of the season in what approximates at all a major role. He very sensibly refrained from an effort towards power of tone until the warm air of the theater had dissipated the effects of a late cold, after which he sang as lusciously as usual; and he has made quite noticeable strides in ease of stage movement."

November 24, 1931: Stokowski conducts **Wozzeck** at the Met, with the Philadelphia Orchestra and Philadelphia Grand Opera Company. Stars were Anna Roselle, Ivan Ivantzoff and Nelson. **Wozzeck** had been first done in America eight months before; this was only the second presentation in the country. *Evening Bulletin:* "Last night's performance enlisted the same cast which enacted the opera last spring, with the exception of Nelson Eddy who replaced Gabriel Leonoff as the 'lady-killing' drum major." *Inquirer:* "Mr. Eddy portrayed his part with excellent art, and sang as well as the music permitted." *Record:* "Mr. Eddy did more, vocally, with the part than the artists of the premiere lineup -- and any vocal accomplishment in **Wozzeck** is worth a headline." *Ledger:* "In the lesser roles, Nelson Eddy made an imposing drum major, resplendent in shako and with a fearsome red beard." *Daily News:* "**Wozzeck** Still Dull.... Nelson Eddy, the only addition to the principals of the cast, was a welcome one. He added just the touch to make this role appealing." *New York Herald Tribune:* "The substitution of Mr. Nelson Eddy for Mr. Leonoff as the Drum-Major, which was advantageous; though this role is not yet satisfactorily realized." *New York American:* "Nelson Eddy as the romantic Drum Major deserved commendation. Where or not any of these artists sang in tune or sharp or flat, it is not safe to say. The music disarmed the listener on that score." *New York World Telegram:* "Nelson Eddy had replaced Gabriel Leonov as the Drum Major to the benefit of the performance." *New York Evening Post:* "The new Drum Major, Nelson Eddy, possessed the vocal and physical requirements." *Musical Courier*, November 28, 1931: "Mr. Eddy's powers, both as singer and actor, were outstanding in this role.... The Drum Major, interpreted by Nelson Eddy, had appropriate pompousness and was sung with unusual spirit and musical understanding." *Musical America*, December 10, 1931: "A great improvement as the Drum Major was Nelson Eddy, vocally and dramatically."

December 2, 1931: Nelson sang the title role in **Gianni Schicchi**; it was performed in English as a double bill with **Cavalleria Rusticana**. Stokowski conducted. *Ledger:* "Nelson Eddy was admirable in the title role. His diction, always one of his principal assets both in opera and in concert, was clear from beginning to end, and his dramatic talent in humorous roles had ample scope, which he improved to the utmost." *Record:* "Any singer who can step from a part in **Electra** and do a lively, humorous and completely artistic Schicchi must wear a special badge." *Record:* "Nelson Eddy sang the title role and revealed for the first time this season some of the qualifications that are going to make him indispensable." *Bulletin:* "Nelson Eddy again showed his marked talent for comedy.... The music does not give much opportunity for vocal display, but Mr. Eddy made much of his one sustained passage, 'Farwell, Dear Florence,' which was beautifully sung." *Inquirer:* "The vocal and mimetic gifts of Nelson Eddy were well employed in the titular role." *Daily News:* "It afforded Nelson Eddy, most promising member of this company's songsters, the grandest opportunity to prove that he excels in every line of singing. Here was comedy, low comedy, sung in a beautiful style." *Musical Courier*, December 12, 1931: "Nelson Eddy gave a fine interpretation of the title role, bringing out the humor, but no over-emphasizing it. With the exception of Mr. Eddy, all of the cast were from the Curtis Institute of Music, and worked together in perfect accord, having evidently had the advantage of many rehearsals." *Musical America*, December 25, 1931: "Nelson Eddy had the title role, which he characterized in brilliant fashion."

December 3, 1931: Nelson started another series at the Warwick Hotel. First guest artist was Helen Oelrich, contralto. Clipping: "He sang with tonal beauty and ripe musicianship, and was enthusiastically applauded."

December 10, 1931: Nelson at Warwick again, with Theodore Paxson as guest pianist. Madeleine Walther, pianist, also guested, and accompanied Nelson in her songs. Clipping: "Nelson Eddy opened the program with a group by Erich Wolff, to whose works, he announced, he intends to devote more attention in subsequent recitals. Mr. Eddy's is a most commendable gesture to an unjustly neglected composer.... Mr. Eddy did his best work of the evening in these songs, particularly in the soft passages, where his voice took on an almost velvet quality.... Mr. Eddy sang [Walther's songs] with his familiar qualities of rich, vibrant tone, excellent diction and interpretation."

December 12, 1931: Nelson starred in **Hansel and Gretl**, sung in English, with the Philadelphia Grand Opera Company, at a matinee performance. Paceli Diamon was Hansel and Natalie Bodanskaya was Gretl. *Bulletin:* "Nelson Eddy sang the role of Peter with his familiar skill and acted the part in a manner which accentuated the naive and simple characteristics of the children's father more than is usually the custom. This variation was much to the benefit of the performance."

Hansel and Gretl was repeated the following week. *Record:* December 20, 1931: "For once in its long career of formal proprieties, the Academy of Music had a good time yesterday afternoon... Nelson Eddy, as Peter, was the best father we have had in the children's opera here. I have remarked somewhere that Mr. Eddy is a playboy at heart. More recently it appeared to me from casual observation that he was working too hard -- he looked tired. But he looked and sang and acted in his own fine fettle yesterday." *Inquirer:* "Nelson Eddy was the tipsy father who never heard of prohibition. He was quite nice, with surprisingly smooth singing voice and quite a cultivated vocabulary, too, for a woodchopper. Probably he was a tree surgeon!" *Ledger:* "Nelson Eddy gave a splendid interpretation of the role of the Father both vocally and dramatically." *Musical Courier*, January, 1932: "Nelson Eddy as Peter did fine singing and enunciated clearly adding greatly to the enjoyment of the hearers."

No date, Cedar Rapids, Michigan, *Gazette-Republican*: "A newcomer for the Cedar Rapids concert-going public, Nelson Eddy, American baritone, who appeared last night at Coe Chapel in the first of the Community Concert Course series has shown himself to be a singer of exceptional caliber. His fame is of comparatively recent date and extends to the field of operatic music as well as concert performance.... To begin with, Mr. Eddy possess a most winsome personality, the kind that an audience will sense and recognize very quickly; for which -- if he has it -- a singer may be forgiven many a slip, but without it the atmosphere remains cool. But Mr. Eddy also has the fundamental requirement of an outstanding voice. Its resonance is deep and rich. Sympathetic it always remains. The singer's technic (sic) is undoubtedly of a high perfection and from it results an excellent flexibility.... As most impressive among technical achievements stood out the artist's perfect diction: every word being enunciated with surprising clarity and unfailing regard for verbal accent and rhythm.... The audience received him very enthusiastically, recalling him many times."

Ledger, no date: Brahms Chorus of Philadelphia gave its first concert of the season last evening in Temple R. Shalom, did Mendelssohn's oratorio **Elijah**. "Nelson Eddy, whose fine voice had splendid enunciation made his work notable all through, but especially in the number 'It is Enough,' with its effective violoncello obbligato." *Bulletin:* "It was to Nelson Eddy, basso, that a large part of the solo work fell, beginning with the introductory recitative preceding the overture. His rich, resonant voice, aided by the superb acoustics of the Temple, soared over the huge audience impressively. Especially fine was Mr. Eddy's solo 'Lord God of Abraham.'"

December 20, 1931: Nelson sang at a Charity Ball. *Record:* "'A Knight of Opera,' as the pageant was called, was most successfully portrayed by Nelson Eddy... The evening proved to be amusingly novel and was well received by an enthusiastic audience.... Mr. Eddy's fine vocal work in ['The Toreador Song'] and his excellent histrionics... made the effect of this episode one of the most pleasing of the evening."

December 22, 1931: Nelson sang in a Pittsburgh production of **The Messiah,** with Nevada Van Der Veer, Harold Hough and Martha Roberts. *Pittsburgh Press*, December 23, 1931: "Handels' magnificent oratorio, **The Messiah**, a work that has been featured for years in the yuletide observance by the Mendelssohn Choir, was given a compelling performance last night in the Carnegie Music Hall with Ernest Lunt directing 200 men and women singers.... Nelson Eddy sang the bass solos in faultless style. He has everything that a voice of his type should possess: color, quality and volume, which with a superior order of musicianship, and an intelligence utilization of his vocal equipment, gave great enjoyment. It is not often that one hears such fine passage singing handled with such finesse as Eddy revealed in his several solos." *Pittsburgh Post-Gazette:* "Nelson Eddy was a most impressionable basso-cantante." *Pittsburgh Sun-Telegram:* "Among the soloists, Nelson Eddy was the most impressive, both because of his fine singing and his comprehensive approach to the text."

January 1, 1932, clipping: Nelson sent autographed books of Christmas carols as holiday greetings.

January 5, 1932, *Johnstown Tribune:* "Presenting a repertoire of songs that were notable for their variety, beauty and possibility of expression, Nelson Eddy, outstanding young American baritone, sung his way into the hearts of Johnstown music lovers last night as the second artist on the current Community Concert Series." *Johnstown Democrat:* "A voice of excellent quality, smooth, flexible and highly trained, his perfect intonations and elocutionary powers were ably displayed as he sang with clear diction songs in Italian, French, Spanish, Russian and German... Both Nelson Eddy and his accompanist [Theodore Paxson] are true artists and their work pleased immensely."

January 9, 1932, *Johnstown Democrat* interview with Nelson: "During the opera season I sang eight roles although I have thirty-three roles in my repertoire. I am now on concert tour, and I sing once a week over radio station WOR."

January 23, 1932: Nelson Eddy heard in joint recital with Ethel Bartlett and Rae Robertson, two pianists, at the Penn Athletic Club tonight. *Daily News,* January 24, 1932: "The blond baritone, Nelson Eddy, stole the show when he was only supposed to supply a musical interlude for the piano playing duet of Bartlett and Robinson.... It was perfectly natural that the hall full of listeners enthused over the warbling of this songster who sang lieder songs, Scotch pipe songs, flossy patter and Negro spirituals. He actually warmed them into believing that a vocal attraction could be interesting. They called him time and again for encores which he graciously and facetiously offered." *Inquirer:* "Mr. Eddy was in his almost invariable excellent voice, and sang with fine poise and command of style. Especially appealing were his German songs." *Bulletin:* "Although the songs in the first group, comprising four songs in German, were well sung they did not serve to bring out the best qualities of Mr. Eddy's vibrant baritone. In the second group, however, was justification of all the [praise] heaped upon the young singer in the past, and reason for expectation of greater accomplishments by him in the future." *Ledger:* "Mr. Eddy was in fine voice and sang with his usual clear diction and artistic interpretation, being received with thunderous applause after each number."

I obtained an interview with Nelson Eddy, the Philadelphia baritone, and found him a very delightful and a very frank young man. Mr. Eddy did not arrrive in town until 6 o'clock and so the only possible time that I had to interview him was while he and his accompanist, Theodore Paxson, had their dinner at the Fort Stanwix hotel.

Nelson Eddy.

After Mr. Eddy had given his order for a very hearty meal, I looked at him horrified and said:

"But aren't you supposed to adhere to a very strict diet before your concerts? I remember Martinelli was allowed only stewed celery."

Mr. Eddy laughed as he answered: "Yes, I started out by observing all that nonsense and found out that when I was half through singing an operatic role, that I was nearly starved to death, and as a result was fatigued. I've discovered that if I eat an ample dinner a reasonable time before singing, that it does not affect my voice in the least."

"Tell me something about yourself?" I questioned.

"Well," and he hesitated, then continued with a twinkle in his eye. "I'm kind to my mother, don't beat my father and received this gorgeous yellow tie for Christmas." And he indicated the one he was wearing, then he continued seriously: "I've also been a reporter, as I was four years with the Philadelphia Evening Bulletin. Now, I suppose your next question will be —'how did I happen then, to become a singer?' I sang at entertainments, in choirs and in drawing rooms. Finally I was paid for such appearances, more than I was earning as a reporter, so I decided to leave my job and become a singer. Little did I realize at the time how much one had to work at this job of being a singer. I studied in Philadelphia, New York, Dresden and Paris. I made my operatic debut with the Philadelphia Civic Opera Co., but am now with the Philadelphia Grand Opera. I sang operatic roles very early in my career—you know—local boy makes good."

"Do you think that these organized concerts make it difficult for the young artist who has not as yet established a reputation," I asked.

"Yes, it does make it harder, but then if a person possesses real talent and is courageous, he can build up a reputation little by little by his drawing room and church appearances. As for a singer, it is quite easy to obtain an audition with any opera company in the country. Your knees might knock together in your fright and you might sing like a crow, but you can get an audition. If you are good you have your opportunity, for opera companies are as anxious for good singers as the singers are anxious for the job."

"What have you done this season?" was my next question.

"During the opera season I sang eight roles, although I have 33 roles in my repertoire. I am now on concert tour and I sing once a week over station W. O. R. Really you see my career has not been flaming or spectacular. I might sing kingly roles on the stage, but when the curtain rings down I'm just a regular fellow. During my interviewing days as a reporter I found that the real artist was just himself, and what a pleasant fellow he usually was. But the man who was a poseur was rather pitiful. No poseur is so accomplished that you cannot penetrate the sham. It is difficult enough to play a role on the stage, but to try to carry it over to every day life —good heavens—how horrible!" I finished laughing.

And indeed Mr. Eddy had adhered to his belief, for this young baritone is certainly an unaffected and charming man.

"How do you select a program for your concert appearances?" I questioned.

"That is really a very delicate as well as difficult matter, for if you sing too heavy a program the audience thinks that you are 'high hatting' them, while if your selections are too light they might think you are patronizing them."

"But, then how do you judge the musical status of a community?" I interrupted.

"That is easily done, by considering the number of years that the community has had a series of concerts. Therefore Johnstown rates fairly high.

After Mr. Eddy had finished a dinner that put to shame the thoughts of stewed celery, he announced: "The zero hour has arrived. You know I have a phobia —I always fear that something will happen to my dress shirt, because so many awful and embarassing accidents have occurred. One time I discovered that I had not brought a single shirt stud with me, and so I sewed the holes together and linked-in two beautiful realistic studs." And so with the telling of this amusing incident, Mr. Eddy terminated a most delightful interview.

Johnstown Democrat — Jan. 9, 1932

Eddy Gives Recital in Johnstown, Pa.

Nelson Eddy recently appeared in recital in Johnstown, Pa., on the local Community Concert Course. The Johnstown Tribune said: "Nelson Eddy, outstanding young American baritone, sang his way into the hearts of Johnstown music lovers." The Johnstown Democrat: "Possessing a voice of excellent quality; smooth, flexible and highly trained; his perfect intonation and elocutionary powers were ably displayed."

M.C. 1-23-32

February 1, 1932, Wilmington, North Carolina, Nelson gave a concert. *Morning Star,* February 2, 1932: "When the last gossamer-like pianissimo of the final note of the 'Volga Boatman's' Song died away into silence, Nelson Eddy, in the Issac Bear School auditorium, had completely captured and captivated his Community Concerts audience last night. As a matter of actual fact, the conquest of the audience was made at the beginning of his program, was intensified as the evening wore along, and was made absolute and complete by the end. This sterling young baritone has a gorgeous voice coupled with an intelligence that makes full use of its loveliness and power.... Nelson Eddy has everything a singer should have, personality plus, appearance (he's a very decided blond), voice, intelligence in using it, repertoire, and anything else you can think that a most successful concert and opera singer should have. The audience liked him, and showed it in enthusiastic greeting."

February 2, 1932, Charlotte, North Carolina, Nelson gave a concert at Charlotte's Central High School Auditorium. *Charlotte Observer,* February 3, 1932: "Mr. Eddy is not only young, but handsome as well. Tall, blonde, with nice shoulders and hefty physique, he missed a grand opportunity if he did not halfback somewhere during his undergraduate days. It was refreshing, no doubt, to many of the ladies in the audience to discover that a man can be so good looking and yet sing so well." *Charlotte News:* "Mr. Eddy is a singer of no mean accomplishment. He possess a baritone voice of pleasing quality and personality which charmed his audience, who caught the spark and what might have been an impersonal concert immediately became an intimate recital, enjoyed by singer and audience."

February 6, 1932, clipping: Nelson stars on Hoffman Hour on WOR at 9 pm Fridays.

February 8, 1932, "Letters to the Editor" in the *Public Ledger:* "Sir -- In the February 2 edition a certain Giuseppe Boghetti gives as his opinion that John Charles Thomas has the most beautiful male voice in America... We have right here in Philadelphia a baritone that has a fully equal voice, possessing all the fine qualities of voice and as an actor far surpassing Mr. Thomas. In the opera of **Aida**, Mr. Nelson Eddy plays the part of the African King the finest of any one I have heard in an operatic experience of fifty years. I have followed the career of Mr. Thomas from the time he was playing in **Maytime.** He has a carefully trained voice and has been a student, but there are others!" C.L. Dexter, letter dated Feb 3, 1932.

February 8, 1932, Nelson gave a concert at Passaic High School, New Jersey. *Daily Herald,* February 9, 1932: "Mr. Eddy, whose rise in the musical world has been unusually rapid for one so young, offered a light but highly pleasing program and left an excellent impression. The artist was detained a half hour following his performance by both young men a and women clamoring for his autograph. He seemed to enjoy his popularity and graciously acceded to the wishes of his admirers.... He has a delightful stage poise and pleasant manner. He sings with no apparent effort; has excellent control and perfect diction." *Passaic Daily News:* "Undoubtedly the finest of the concerts given in this city during the current year.... Mr. Eddy, baritone soloist is blessed with everything that makes for fame -- a magnificent voice, a gracious stage presence, a handsome face and an appealing personality. He also has that all too rare attribute, a sense of humor.... Last evening's audience greeted his every number with applause sincerely expressing true appreciation of his artistry.... One of the most pleasing features of Mr. Eddy's performance was the restrain which characterized his singing.... Mr. Eddy's popularity was not limited to the older members of the audience, for following the program he was surrounded by a group of admiring youngsters, eager for a glimpse of the stalwart young baritone who had pleased them so greatly."

February 15, 1932, Nelson gave a concert at the Burlington, Vermont City Hall. *Daily News*, February 16, 1932: "Apart from his art and gift, a rare, true voice, Mr. Eddy had something more for his audience, a histrionic adaptability and a most pleasing personality that captivated his audience.... The singer was fascinating.... The blond, handsome, youthful baritone is a New Englander by birth, and in the thirty years of his life has crowded in unlimited study and training of a glorious voice and his voice in turn, has brought him to a leading position among American baritones." *Burlington Free-Press:* "A big, blonde youth named Nelson Eddy, who has sung his way into the high places of the world of music, sang and acted and smiled his way into the hearts of an audience of Burlington music lovers.... Music critics may differ as to how high a place Nelson Eddy has achieved among the vocalists of the present day, but we believe the average lover of music who goes to concerts to enjoy music and not to criticize it will come away from one of Eddy's concerts with the feeling that this young man is one of the leading American baritones and that he will go far in his chosen career. For Eddy is only 30 years of age and he has already achieved what few men achieve in a lifetime of effort.... Nelson Eddy not only has an exceedingly pleasing voice of wide range and sterling quality, but he sings with authority, with fine modulations which indicate the true artists and with a virility which is the expression of his abundant vitality and winning personality. With the figure and face of an athlete, he is the type which draws the audience from the moment he steps on to the stage. And he sings with an ease and power which is both delightful and exhilarating.... Eddy is an actor as well as a singer."

February 18, 1932: Nelson sang in **Lohengrin** given by Philadelphia Grand Opera Company at the Academy of Music. *Ledger,* February 19, 1932: "One of the most impressive that the company has staged this season. The opera was well sung and acted... and superbly directed by Fritz Reiner.... The music of the Herald was finely adapted to the voice of Nelson Eddy, who sang it superbly." *Inquirer:* "Nelson Eddy sang robustly the music of the Herald." *Record:* "Eddy's name in the principal list is always a welcome one. This time his part was closer to his caliber of artistry, although the peculiar demands of the part are not exactly what this Philadelphia baritone needs for a real success." *Bulletin:* "Mr. Eddy made good use of limited opportunities in his authoritative delivery of the Herald's calls and announcements."

February 22, 1932, clipping in the Newark, New Jersey *News:* Nelson Eddy will sing "Largo al Factotum" in his March 4 WOR broadcast. "Several readers have asked us lately why we don't comment on WOR's 9 o'clock program Sunday evenings. Because we think it is terrible. The cheap and inconsequential chatter about movie stars and Broadway characters, the music and the general tone of the whole program seem to be quick lacking in any material worthy of space in a radio column. We tuned in last night to find our earlier impressions revived. When you can broadcast a program like the Nelson Eddy Hour Friday over the same station and draw one of the largest fan mails in radio history why bother with such ordinary humorless stuff as the aforementioned Sunday show?"

February 23, 1932: Nelson sang in Buffalo at the Elmwood Music Hall. *Buffalo Evening News,* February 24, 1932: "Mr. Eddy offered a program of pleasing quality.... Mr. Eddy is an upstanding young man of gracious manner, who is able readily to establish himself on cordial terms with his audience. He has much to offer, and what he does is estimable. The vocal organ is a rich one, of liquid, flowing quality and brilliance, and the singer's use of the voice is admirable. Listening to his interpretations the auditor finds it in his heart freely to commend the baritone's accomplishments in the way of finished style, beauty of vocal utterance, excellence of diction and fine enunciation in the various languages he essays. Not forgetting this goodly array of singing virtues one hopes sincerely for Mr. Eddy's further artistic growth to the stature that will permit freedom and spontaneity in measure sufficient to replace the studied methods now apparent in his singing. Indication that Eddy may be capable of greater artistic achievement came with his convincing singing of Forsyth's 'The Bell-Man,' the Deems Taylor 'Capt. Stratton's Fancy' (in this he was quite inimitable) and the encore 'Glory Road,' these the last three offerings of the evening.... The baritone pleased his audience greatly and generously granted about nine encores." *Buffalo Courier-Express:* "Mr. Eddy is a splendidly equipped artist, with a fine stage presence and a baritone voice of beautiful quality, even register and a breath control that never lessened throughout a long and taxing program. " *Buffalo Times:* "A rising star, already high above the horizon.... This handsome blond, who looks 25 and is, in reality, not much older, has apparently all the gifts the gods can bestow. Personality in large measure, an excellent voice, admirably produced and controlled, and glowing dramatic temperament, are all his. To these native endowments, he has added unquestionably the talent of industry, for he has many virtues acquired only through hard work. Among them are an exceptional clarity of enunciation, fine diction in the different languages utilized in last night's program, ability to color the tone as he wills, and power to project over the footlights the mood of whatever song he sings. The artist has a virile voice of agreeable quality, full and brilliant.... Eddy might almost be styled a singing actor, so pronounced is his interpretive genius... His success with his audience was immediate and complete."

February 24, 1932, Nelson sang with the Mendelssohn Club at Chancellors Hall in Albany, New York concert. *Knickerbocker-Press,* February 25, 1932: "Nelson Eddy, who stands with Lawrence Tibbett and John Charles Thomas as one of the three best baritones in America, came into the house of his friends. They recalled from last season a voice of abundant tone, of glowing resonance, of perfect control in phrasing and in building up a crescendo; of dramatic power and genial humor. They heard it again last night; a rare, gratifying, inspiring voice..." *Albany Evening News:* "One of the best liked soloists who ever appeared in Albany…. Mendelssohn patrons were waiting to give Nelson Eddy a rousing reception, for he scored one of those electric hits last season that insured his return. He came back, a finer artist than before. A man who has a platform presence that would carry a smaller voice to success. But he has both the personality and the voice, and last night the audience heard superb control, flawless phrasing and diction and tone that was rich and radiant. And an ability to characterize the pathos or drama or humor of a song that is a gift entirely aside from a fine voice.... It should be a law of the club to bring Eddy back every year."

Negro Spiritual Songs Furnish Background Of American Music—Eddy

American music, whether jazz or modern, may be analyzed and traced back to the old Negro spiritual themes in the opinion of Nelson Eddy, baritone, who has sung his way into the high places of the world of music.

The primitive Negroes of the South, Nelson Eddy believes, have furnished the basis for what might have been or what may be the greatest American music. Artists have taken these themes and transcribed them into some of the most popular music of today. American music has developed from the Indian and Negro music, with growth of Southern folk songs constituting a big stride in the development of American music. Not only have American artists taken the Southern folk song themes for the basis of their work, but European artists have done the same, he says.

Nelson Eddy believes that the audiences of noted artists, whether the community be a large one or small, accept the artist with about the same intelligence and reactions. He saw little difference in the audience which heard him in his concert in the high school auditorium last evening from the audience of 4,000 which heard him in Buffalo, N. Y., a few days ago, or from other audiences.

"Through experience I have come to knew when they will laugh and what groups will bring encores. Almost all audiences react the same. The same program is given in every community where a concert is held. The size of the town does not change the type or length of program given."

Southern hospitality has made a particular impression on this artist, who says he admires and loves the Southern people. He has appeared in numerous concerts throughout the South.

With the figure and face of an athlete, Nelson Eddy is a "regular fellow." He is not in sympathy with the artist who dotes on being "abnormal," who cannot eat or do anything on the day of a concert. Eddy has an unusually winning personality.

"Singers are the most childish, the most primitive, with their long hair and unusual dress, and the most conceited people of any people in the world. My prayer has been that I might remain normal and be myself."

Music critics differ as to how high a place Nelson Eddy has achieved among the vocalists of the present day. Though Eddy is only 30 years of age, he has already achieved what few men accomplish in a lifetime of effort.

Nelson Eddy believes Lawrence Tibbett to be one of the greatest singers of the day and prizes his friendship. Some critics say that Eddy ranks close to Tibbett.

Asked if he would enter motion pictures, he said he might if an interesting opportunity afforded itself, though his heart and soul was in art and art alone. He does not believe that opera and classical music will ever enter into motion pictures.

From here Mr. Eddy will go north to fill several operatic engagements.

Times - Herald
Newport News, Va. 3-8-32

March 3, 1932: Nelson sang again in **Elektra** at the Academy of Music. *Record,* March 4, 1932: "A record in music was achieved here last night when the Philadelphia Grand Opera Company presented an opera for the second time in a single season. The work was **Elektra**.... Nelson Eddy, the Orestes, while limited in the demands of the assignment, was impressive." *Bulletin*: "It would be hard to imagine a better cast than was recruited last night. The beautifully modulated and dramatic baritone of Nelson Eddy as Orestes was used with fine effect." *Inquirer:* "The minor roles were taken with the same praiseworthy competence that marked them last fall." *Daily News:* "Nelson Eddy, always assured of offering a superb performance, was in good form. Too little of his voice is heard in these parts."

March 8, 1932: Nelson in Newport News, Virginia, for a concert at Newport News High School. Interview with Nelson from the *Times-Herald,* Nelson on himself: "Through experience I have come to know when they will laugh and what groups will bring encores. Almost all audiences react the same. The same program is given in every community where a concert is held. The size of the town does not change the type or length of program given…. Singers are the most childish, the most primitive, with their long hair and unusual dress, and the most conceited people of any people in the world. My prayer has been that I might remain normal and be myself." The reporter: "Nelson Eddy believes Lawrence Tibbett to be one of the greatest singers of the day and prizes his friendship. Some critics say that Eddy ranks close to Tibbett…. Asked if he would enter motion pictures, he said he might if an interesting opportunity afforded itself, though his heart and soul was in art and art alone. He does not believe that opera and classical music will ever enter into motion pictures." Concert reviews: *Time-Herald:* "Not in many years has an audience of Newport News music lovers been as thoroughly rewarded as with the Community Concert Association presentation of Nelson Eddy last evening.... A gifted artist.... An ecstatic audience called Mr. Eddy back for three encores." *Virginia Post,* Norfolk: "Mr. Eddy is a lover of good music and imbued with a real musicianship and technique.... Mr. Eddy immediately won his audience... Mr. Eddy sang with a clear rhythmic tone and good diction."

March 10, 1932: Nelson sang in **Secret of Suzanne** with the Philadelphia Grand Opera Company at the Academy of Music. It was a double bill with **I Pagliacci**, and John Charles Thomas was Tonio in **I Pagliacci**. In **Secret of Suzanne**, Nelson and Helen Jepson starred, singing in English. *Bulletin:* "The vocal parts, compared with the acting, do not bulk large in the total effects, but they were finely rendered by Miss Jepson and Mr. Eddy…. Mr. Eddy's aptitude in comedy parts is no longer news. Again he gauged the pace and character of the comedy perfectly, making the most of slim material and never allowing the performance to slip into the other world of burlesque." *Inquirer:* "Mr. Eddy and Miss Jepson gave the vocal parts just the right emphasis. They also looked refreshingly believable as young newlyweds, and were at the opposite pole from the frayed and frazzled veterans too often found." *Record:* "Eddy and Miss Jepson sang with splendid articulation.... If the contracts of these artists had run all year, just for last night's work they would have been decidedly worthwhile." *Daily News:* "He can always be counted on for a splendid performance."

March 16, 17 and 18 at Carnegie Hall, New York City, was the American premiere by the New York Philharmonic of Respighi's **Maria Egiziaca.** Nelson sang the roles of Abbot Zosimo and the Pilgram. *New York Sun,* March 17, 1932: "The program was one of exceptional importance.... Nelson Eddy as the Pilgrim and the Abbott did some good singing.... Mr. Respighi conducted skillfully." *World-Telegram:* "At the conclusion of the performance Mr. Respighi was recalled several times. Many members of the audience rose to their feet and shouted 'Bravo' and 'Bravi' as the composer-conductor and the singers came forth holding hands in a long chain." *Musical Courier*, March 19, 1932: "Nelson Eddy posses a baritone organ of singular fullness, strength, and euphonious [pleasant in sound] appeal. He put into his measures a compelling degree of earnestness, warmth and musical weight. His enactment of the Pilgrim's forceful strictures had exceptional authority." *Musical America,* March 25, 1932: " As the Pilgrim and Zosimo, Nelson Eddy sang glowingly and proved himself a highly gifted actor as well. He is one of the best baritones of the day." [Note: Nelson's photo appeared in most of the New York City newspapers for this occasion.]

March 19, 1932, *Philadelphia Evening News* article about Nelson as a singer and radio star: "He has no tricks of manner, no affectations, none of the facial contortions which mar a singer. His voice flows effortlessly and as you watch him you are conscious that he is not concerned with Nelson Eddy, or the effect he is having on his listeners. Everything he has, all his imagination, all his intelligence, his strength, is poured into the music, he is absorbed in the role he portrays. The English cockney stands before radio station WOR's microphone, talking about the death of his friend. The singer's shoulders droop forward, he seems suddenly to grow small and frightened. 'They are hanging Danny Deever, you can hear the dead march play.' Danny marches again across the silence of the studio, the thud of feet, the anguish of the friend who watches him tramping along the road from which there is no return. There is no sound in the crowded control room in which we sat. People seem hardly to breathe. The singer straightens, his head snaps back, his fingers double, and the muscles of his arm flex…. 'And he'll hang in 'alf a minute,' the gorgeous voice rings out in the agonized protests of a helpless buddy. The music ended. Mr. Pasternack dropped his arm and the control room listeners did a thing which we never heard in such a place and never expect to hear again. They broke into cheers. The singer could not hear them. He did not even glance at them to see whether they had liked his song. It was an irresistible expres-sion of emotion.... Mr. Eddy had gone over to a corner of the room and sat leaning forward in his chair, the spell of the song still on him. No one spoke to him. It was obvious that his fellow artists felt that a trivial compli-ment would be in-adequate. They waited for him to come back from that land where Danny marched into the endless halls of time."

STAGE SETTING AND PRINCIPALS OF RESPIGHI'S MARIA EGIZIACA, to be given its world première by the New York Philharmonic, March 16, at Carnegie Hall. New York, for the benefit of the Orchestra Pension Fund. Repeat performances will be part of the March 17 and 18 concerts. Charlotte Boerner, Nelson Eddy, Myrtle Leonard, Alfredo Tedesco and Helen Gleason comprise the cast. Armando Agnini is stage manager; Joseph Urban, in charge of scenic background; and Giulio Setti, director of the chorus. The composer will conduct.

MUSICAL AMERICA ***for March 25, 1932***

Respighi Triptych Has New York World-Premiere

(*Continued from page* 3)

age, offering herself in payment. A pilgrim, about to embark, warns the sailor, but the scarlet woman succeeds in having her way. In the second scene, she is repulsed as she attempts to enter the sacred portals, and in the final episode, appearing as an old woman, she receives the blessing of the Abbot Zosimo as she dies.

A Setting of Emotional Beauty

Signor Guastalla's libretto has a decided appeal and is written in beautiful Italian. Respighi has set it with remarkable skill, revealing not only his extraordinary technical resource, but, more important, a definitely emotional beauty, ever in keeping with the ecclesiastical tone of his subject.

Whereas in his operas "Belfagor" and "La Campana Sommersa" he has at many points written music that is more symphonic than operatic, here he gives us page upon page that are musical dramatic writing of a high order. To a musical speech that is often dramatic recitative in the present-day manner, he adds some sustained vocal writing that is certain in its melodic appeal. In short, he is here revealed as a music-dramatist, far more so than in those of his stage works with which we are acquainted.

Maria's music in the first episode is unusually fine, as are the offstage choruses, the final duet between Maria and Zosimo and the orchestral interludes. Spare in his use of instruments —the score is for flute, oboe, bassoon, trumpet, two clarinets, two horns, two trombones, strings and a clavicembalo part played on the piano—the composer obtains, through his mastery of his orchestra, unusually sonorous effects in his climaxes. Of Respighi's new works, "Maria Egiziaca" is undoubtedly one of the most worthy, recalling that fine gift first revealed to us in his "Fountains of Rome."

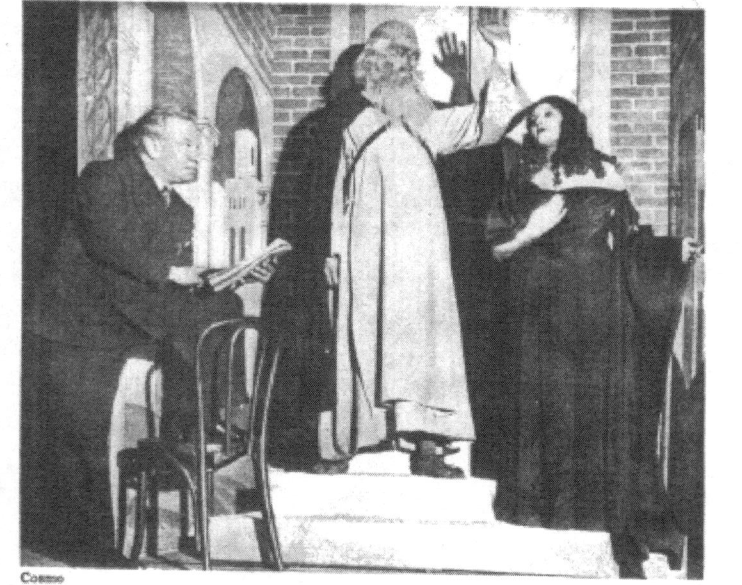

Cosmo

Leading Figures Active in the World-Premiere of Ottorino Respighi's Triptych, "Maria Egiziaca," Given by the New York Philharmonic Symphony and Soloists under the Composer's Baton: Left to Right, Mr. Respighi; Nelson Eddy, Baritone, Who Sang the Roles of the Pilgrim and the Abbot Zosimo; and Charlotte Boerner, Soprano, Who Was Heard in the Title Role

Charlotte Boerner, soprano, who has sung with the Philadelphia Grand Opera Company this season, sang the title part with brilliance and acted with distinction. She has a dramatic voice of singularly vibrant quality, and a thrilling upper range. As the pilgrim and Zosimo, Nelson Eddy sang glowingly and proved himself a highly gifted actor as well. He is one of the best baritones of the day. Alfio Tedesco (not Alfredo, as the program had it) was excellent as the sailor and the leper. The smaller parts were well sung by Helen Gleason, soprano, and Mrytle Leonard, contralto.

Giulio Setti trained the chorus admirably; the stage director was Armando Agnini, the scenic production that of Lillian Gaertner Palmedo, "under the supervision of Joseph Urban," whatever that may mean. The scenes and costumes, of genuine beauty, were by Nicola Benois.

Signor Respighi and his interpreters were applauded to the echo at the close of the work by an audience that seemed to enjoy every moment of it.

Orchestral Works Given

Prior to the presentation of the new triptych, the composer led the orchestra in his suite "The Birds," based on harpsichord and clavichord pieces of old French, Italian and English composers, and his "Trittico Botticelliano," similarly for small orchestra. These charmingly conceived pieces had an unqualified success. In them there is real wizardry of instrumentation rather than a definite musical message.

A. WALTER KRAMER

March 20, 1932: The Buffalo Orpheus gave its second concert. *Musical America,*March 25, 1932: "Nelson Eddy showed himself to be an interpreter of remarkable ability, with a vocal organ which responded well to all demands made upon it. His success with the Buffalo audience was instant and complete."

March 25, 1932, *Musical America:* "Nel-son Eddy to be soloist in Ann Arbor for 39th May Festival of 6 concerts, May 18, 19,20,21… It is easy to explain why Nelson Eddy is fast becoming one of America's most popular artists. In only 24 months he has the record of 64 concerts, 16 major orchestra appear-ances, 27 oratorios, 11 operas, 3 festivals, 24 guest church appear-ances and 57 radio evenings. His large number of re-engage-ments proves the solidity of this young singer's career."

March 31, 1932: *Columbia Missourian:* "Eddy Captivates Large Audience, Crowd Holds Baritone an Extra Hour at Concert…. Nelson Eddy, celebrated baritone, completely captivated a large audience at the last concert of the College of Fine Arts Series in the auditorium last night. An excellent voice coupled with a pleasing personality held the audience an hour longer than the previous concerts and brought forth nine encores and numerous curtain calls...Quite a number in the audience came form nearby towns to hear the concert, some from more than sixty miles away. All were enthusiastic in their applause for the youthful singer."

April 1, 1932: Nelson sang at Cincinnati's Mozart Festival, which ran from March 31-April 2. *Cincinnati Times-Star,* April 2, 1932: "On Friday morning [April 1] the Matinee Musicale presented Nelson Eddy…. As for Nelson Eddy, whose success has from time to time floated westward from his native Philadelphia to this Midwest oasis of musical predilections, he created a furor…. It is possible to predict that, equipped as Mr. Eddy, with every gift the kindly gods can present to a mere mortal, he will become one of the greatest, most justly famed of American singers. The handsome head of this fortunate youth will not be turned by success. He has the saving grace of American humor…. Mr. Eddy has a full, softly toned voice, so well managed that he sings with equal artistry some illusive Massenet music, the robust 'Ballare' of **Figaro**, and Papageno's pipings to which he smartly added the quaint off-key tootings of a small flute. Mr. Eddy has, beside voice, training and that sense of artistic values which imposes restraint and forbids exaggerations." *Cincinnati Post:* "Gifted with a splendid, resonant barytone voice, excellently placed, he is also an interpreter with style and eminently correct taste…. Nelson said he liked to play the little pipes in Papageno number.... He was enormously well received, and graciously shared the applause with his splendid accompanist, Theodore Paxson." *Cincinnati Inquirer:* "His fine, virile, voluminous tenor is one of reserved, controlled exuberance. He achieves emotional effects without apparent strain or loss of evenness. He is accurate in diction both musically and verbally. To this he adds a pleasing, dignified, youthful personality. [Nelson's aria] was the vocal triumph of the evening." *Musical Courier,* April 16, 1932: "Nelson Eddy created a furor. His personality, musicianship, interpretation, and above all, his voice -- were faultless. His program was chosen to give pleasure in arias and songs from Mozart, and he graciously responded to the tremendous applause with encores."

April 2, 1932: Nelson sang in Klamath Falls, Oregon. *Evening Herald:* "Nelson Eddy... thrilled his audience of Klamath Falls music lovers with his artistry, his superb tone quality and his charming personality in his concert presented at the auditorium of Klamath Union High School Monday night. He was in splendid voice, and his program, from the first to last number was perfectly balanced, and contrasted to a nice degree.... Unwilling to allow the good-looking young singer with the lovely voice to conclude his concert, his audience called him back again and again."

April 4, 1932: Nelson sang in Little Rock, Arkansas: *Arkansas Democrat:* "Perhaps no artist has ever received more enthusiastic or appreciative applause than greeted this young singer following each song. His art was displayed with a natural ease and beauty that exacted encore after encores, so graciously given by the singer who is conceded one of the most outstanding appearing under the management of Arthur Judson, Inc., a division of the Columbia Concerts Corporation. Mr. Eddy possesses a splendid state presence and captivated his audience from the first number." *Arkansas Gazette:* "Possibly not since Tito Schipa has a singer received such enthusiastic and wholehearted applause from a Little Rock audience as was given Nelson Eddy, young American baritone, last night at Parnell Hall…. This young singer seems destined to have a noticeable career...

EVENING NEWS, SATURDAY, MARCH 19, 1932

"Let's get to it," said Nelson Eddy, easing down into a corner of a comfortable couch in the reception room of WOR. "I live on an island and I never had any parents."

In the laugh that followed the icy depths of the usual interview were broken. It would be impossible to be stilted when talking with Mr. Eddy. He doesn't wait to be cross-questioned; he talks easily and naturally about the things you want discussed with a delightful sense of fun from which the vernacular of Broadway is entirely lacking.

But at the same time, in a medium in which the superlative is frowned upon, it's not going to be easy to write of him. His is an extraordinary personality, blessed with uncommon good looks, tremendous vitality, a keen ambition coupled with a modesty about his attainments and an intelligence which does not allow him to take his art lightly or himself too seriously. How are you going to write temperately of such a person? It would take the pen of a fellow barytone scoured with jealousy to do it.

Eddy was born on the 29th of June, 1901, in Providence. As a boy he sang in the church choir, but he gave no further attention to music until he had tried various jobs and finally ended in a newspaper office. He then began to study singing in the evenings and the late David Bispham heard him, took him on as a pupil and prophesied great things. Mr. Bispham died and Eddy studied with various teachers who encouraged him to the extent that he gave up any thought of another career. In 1924 he made his operatic debut with the Philadelphia Civic Opera Company as Tonio in "Pagliacci" and is now a member of that company and commutes to New York for his WOR broadcasts.

His radio work is quite new. He made his first New York broadcast with the Atwater Kent program some months ago, but he professes a serious interest in radio and a great enjoyment in his present series.

"Some of my friends turn on the radio in the morning and let it go all day," he said, "and that is frightful. I enjoy it very much, I think you can learn a great deal from it but it must be used with discrimination. I read my newspaper schedule and pick my programs with great care. In that way it is always interesting. I like jazz for example and I think you can learn a great deal about diction from the crooners, they are masters of it."

Mr. Eddy has a profound admiration for the work of Lawrence Tibbett but he resents the publicity which couples their names. "To be perfectly honest, I think it is very bad taste," he said. "I don't belong there, Tibbett is a superlative artist."

Eddy makes no effort to learn any special technique of the microphone. "I am studying for concert work and opera," he said. "If my voice as I use it there is adaptable to radio, well and good, if not then radio is not for me."

When he went into the studio for his broadcast we sat in the control room together with about fifteen other guests of the sponsors and the station. And it was there that the conviction came to us that we were listening to a great artist. There is a quality about his work which lifts him head and shoulders above the pleasant singers we hear so often and who will remain pleasant singers and nothing more. Watch him with us, as he stands before the microphone singing "Danny Deever." He is a big man, six feet tall at least, with broad shoulders and the muscular look of an athlete in training. Josef Pasternack, small, fiery, with wild gray locks, stands on his dais to Eddy's left; the large orchestra which fills the room is at his back. Opposite, seated against the wall, are Veronica Wiggins and Mary McCoy, both in white satin and long white gloves. Beside them are the members of the male quartet. Mr. Pasternack raises his baton, Mr. Eddy slips one hand into his pocket and the other he puts over his left ear to deaden the sound of the orchestra which is so close to him.

He has no tricks of manner, no affectations, none of the facial contortions which mar a singer; his voice flows effortlessly and as you watch him you are conscious that he is not concerned with Nelson Eddy or the effect he is having on his listeners. Everything he has, all his imagination, his intelligence, his strength, is poured into the music—he is absorbed in the role he portrays. The English cockney stands before WOR's microphone, talking about the death of his friend. The singer's shoulders droop forward, he seems suddenly to grow small and frightened. "They are hanging Danny Deever, you can hear the dead march play." Danny marches again across the silence of the studio, the thud of feet, the anguish of the friend who watches him tramping along the road from which there is no return. There is not a sound in the crowded control room in which we sat; people seem hardly to breathe. The singer straight-

Nelson Eddy

He is most engaging, and gave an individual touch to his songs. His voice control is excellent, and his tones are full and free."

April 5, 1932, Nelson sang in Jackson, Tennessee. *Jackson Sun,* April 6, 1932: "Audience Refuses to Leave at End of Concert, Demanding More Songs. The last song had been sung, there was a burst of deafening applause as Nelson Eddy and Theodore Paxson walked from the stage and into their dressing room.... Those who have attended concerts in Jackson for the past seven years know just how unusual this is. Jackson audiences for years have been noted for 'walking out' as the last number was sung, but not with Nelson Eddy as the singer.... Never before has a Jackson audience been so complimentary to a visiting artist... Nelson Eddy has a powerful voice and a youthful freshness, his interpretations in the concert last night were magnificent, and his command of his audience is indescribable. His amazing variations of tone added refinement to his natural dramatic intensity. As a concert singer it may be said that he 'has everything.'.... [Nelson and Ted Paxson] played the entire concert without notes. In fact not one sheet of music was carried to the auditorium."

April 13, 1932: Nelson sang in Ogden, Utah. *Standard Examiner,* April 14, 1932: "Mr. Eddy is considered one of the leading American baritones. His style of singing is smooth and easy. He sings with restraint and yet his tones are beautifully rich and full. The delightful informality of his personality charmed the audience and put everyone in good humor. His clear enunciation was noted throughout the program whether he sang in English or in a foreign tongue."

April 15, 1932: Nelson sang in Helena, Montana. *Montana Record-Herald:* "Nelson Eddy does not talk in public about his singing, therefore the only way to get acquainted with the voice of the American baritone is to attend one of his concerts." Concert reviews, April 16, 1932: *Helena Daily Independent:* "Seldom does an artist appearing in Helena receive the enthusiastic reception as that accorded Nelson Eddy when he delighted a fine audience last night at the Consistory Shrine auditorium as the third and concluding number of the Community Concert Association series for 1931-32... It is little wonder that he has risen to the rank of not only leading American baritone but one of the favorite artists appearing in concert today. His marvelous voice and winning personality form a rare combination and it is without mental reservation that we accord him the palm as the most delightful entertainer appearing on a Helena concert stage.... From his first number Mr. Eddy was called back with outbursts of spontaneous applause to offer repeated encores to his difficult and highly entertaining program which offered a wide range and proved conclusively that he is an artist Helena might well be considered fortunate in securing. He was a generous young man and gave several numbers at the conclusion of his regular program as well as offering many encores during the evening.... Mr. Eddy said last night that it was a pleasure to sing to the audience that greeted him at the Consistory Auditorium. He remarked that this was the first time he had ever given two encores as early as his first selection but added that it was a pleasure to do so as the audience made both he and Mr. Paxson believe their efforts were appreciated." *Montana Record-Herald:* "Encores mingled in the young artist's program freely."

April 26, 1932: Nelson sang in Hartford, Connecticut, in Verdi's **Manzoni Requiem**. *Daily Courant,* April 27, 1932: "The rendition of the splendid **Requiem** of Verdi was a triumph for the Oratorio Society and its directory, Tuesday evening, and all concerned are to be congratulated on the concert. There was a large audience but there should have been a larger -- for singing of music like Verdi's, done in the way that it was done by the large and well-balanced chorus and the excellent soloists of the evening, should have been heard by a crowd limited only by the size of Bushnell Memorial Hall. As it was it is greatly to be hoped that the large expenses of the production was covered. If they were the Oratorio Society will be well satisfied -- for no one expects to make money out of a big choral concert with Boston Symphony players assisting, anyway.... Mr. Eddy came a stranger to most of those present and made a fine impression in every way. His voice has power and sweetness, is admirably controlled; his diction is unusually good and his sense of drama is sure not only in solo work but in his passages in concerted numbers as well." *Hartford Daily Times:* "Musical honors among the soloists must be given to Mr. Eddy, who came to Hartford last evening a total stranger, but who left with the plaudits of his hearers ringing in his ears. No more capable male soloist than Mr. Eddy has ever appeared with

THE JACKSON SUN

JACKSON TENNESSEE

WEDNESDAY, APRIL 6, 1932.

EDDY ENTHRALLS WITH PURE BEAUTY OF SINGING TONE

Audience Refuses to Leave at End of Concert, Demanding More Songs.

(By Guy Windrom)

The last song had been sung, there was a burst of deafening applause as Nelson Eddy and Theodore Paxon walked from the stage and into their dressing room. "I have enjoyed singing in Jackson; you have an intelligent audience and a splendid concert hall," said the artist. As the words were spoken all those "back stage" realized that something unusual was happening—the audience was not leaving, they were not even putting on their coats in preparation to leaving, they were just sitting, waiting for more songs.

Those who have attended concerts in Jackson for the past seven or eight years know just how unusual this is. Jackson audiences for years have been noted for "walking out" as the last number was sung, but not with Nelson Eddy as the singer.

He returned, sang the rollicking "Tallyho" by Leoni and still they wouldn't leave, so back he came to sing the descriptive "Glory Road," in which he put all the feeling, pathos and spiritual exultation of the Southern negro and then answered three curtain calls before the concert could be over.

Never before has a Jackson audience been so complimentary to a visiting artist.

The Eddy concert was the third and last of the series sponsored by the Jackson Community Concert Association, which is composed of some three hundred members. A campaign for another season will be staged in Jackson in the fall, according to present plans, and it is believed that at least 500 will compose the next association group.

Nelson Eddy has a powerful voice and a youthful freshness, his interpretations in the concert last night were magnificent, and his command of his audience is indescribable. His amazing variations of tone added refinement to his natural dramatic intensity. As a concert singer it may be said that he "has everything."

Since we are living in sensational times and times especially of musical wonders, we must not pass unnoticed the performance of Theodore Paxon, who came here last night as accompanist to Mr. Eddy. He completely submerged himself during the Eddy portion of the program, but in his group he gave a demonstration of intelligence, musical instinct, feeling for tonal beauty and warmth of expression that set him apart. In Chopin's three etudes, his delivery showed much poetry. His encore was the ever lovely Strauss "Fleidermaus Waltz."

Both artists played the entire concert without notes. In fact not one sheet of music was carried to the auditorium.

Mr. Eddy opened his program with the Ode from Ossian's poems, a selection from the most important work of Francis Hopkins. This story of the Irish king is in five parts, ending with "I Will Not Return," a dramatic and stirring war cry. Mr. Eddy's encore was Handel's Largo. This was followed by a group of six sprightly love songs, in Italian, French, Spanish, German and American respectively, which took the fancy of the audience and were enthusiastically encored. Mr. Eddy sang four encores for this group including the Brahms Serenade and the amusing little "Flea," always a baritone favorite.

The two arias, "Avant de Quitter Ces Lieux" (Gounod) and "O, Thou Sublime Sweet Evening Etar" also were beautifully sung. The program closed with a group of typical English songs, "Come to the Fair" (Martin); "Route Marchin," a particularly fine war song; the "Bell Man," with its lingering cadence, and "Captain Stratton's Fancy," Deems Taylor's ballad of the bottle. As the audience was in no mind to let Mr. Eddy go, he obligingly and charmingly came back for two encores, "Glory Road" and "Tally Ho."

The Jacksonville Daily Journal
Ill. May 17

PAGE TWELVE

NELSON EDDY, BARITONE, WINS LOCAL AUDIENCE

Gives Closing Program in This Year's Association Series

A magnificent singer, whose human touch, sense of the dramatic and refreshing humor make him doubly fascinating to his audience, appeared last evening before Jacksonville Community Concert Association members and their guests in the person of Nelson Eddy, one of the foremost baritones of this country. In this closing number of the Association year given at the Jacksonville high school auditorium, Mr. Eddy won his listeners completely as with an intriguing and varied program he displayed a rich, powerful voice coupled with superior artistry and interpretation.

Sharing honors with Mr. Eddy and winning throughout, the enthusiastic applause of the good sized audience, was his accompanist, Theodore Paxson. Mr. Paxson in his accompaniments and in his own solo numbers showed a faultless technique and beautiful delicacy.

Mrs. John R. Robertson, opened the program at eight-fifteen with a few welcoming words, reminding the members that application for new memberships will be received next fall.

Perhaps the first quality to be noticed in Mr. Eddy's work last evening was the smoothness and utter ease with which he sings. In his opening number, "Ode from Ossian's Poems" by Francis Hopkinson, America's earliest composer, his voice flowed rich and full and with a sustained power which denoted perfect control. From the deep, thrilling notes of the true baritone he can change to the soft, sweet voice of the appealing singer who brings a significant hush over his audience.

The charm which is such a vital part of Mr. Eddy's music was particularly manifest in his second group, Love Songs from Six Lands. The Italian, French, Spanish, German, Russian and American were each taken in turn and were in choice and presentation, captivating. Gay or tender he carried his listeners from one land to another, giving an encore of a particular nationality when the applause denoted a preference. His explanations of the story added much to the color of th[e pro]gram. As an enco[re he] decided, as he to[ld,] sing about a flea, hilarious and mer[ry] concert audience

Gives Concert

NELSON EDDY

Superior Musicianship

The superb quality of Mr. Eddy's tone and his superior musicianship were brought to the fore in his beautiful Aria from Gounod's "Faust" — "Avant de quitter ces lieux." Based on the famous story of Goethe, Mr. Eddy created the scene where the soldier Valentine prays for the divine protection of his sister, Marquerite, before going off to war, and did it in exceptional voice and complete understahding of the beauty of the song. An encore at the close of this number was "Johnson's Water Boy" in which the rich, lazy tones of the negro were perfectly caught.

Mr. Eddy's last group contained four highly interesting pieces ranging from the jolly swing of Martin's "Come to the Fair;" to the quaint song of the Seventeenth century Bellman and the rollicking ballad entitled "Captain Stratton's Fancy" by Deems Taylor. In no one of these did Mr. Eddy merely sing—he acted and created vivid personages as well as haunting music. The singer's final encores were enthusiastically received. He gave the stirring "Glory Road", a negro song, and closed with "Believe Me If All Those Endearing Young Charms" and "The Volga Boatman."

Whispers of admiration for the young accompanist of Mr. Eddy, Theodore Paxson, swept the audience at the close of the first number. His touch is sure yet delicate and conveys an entire new meaning to his audience. Three etudes by Chopin comprised his solo group and here his talents had full opportunity for demonstration. Each one utterly different in type, he handled them all with the deft and sympathetic skill of the real musician. His title as one of the foremost young American interpreters of Chopin was fully understood as he completed his trio. His audience demanded two encores and he gave one of Strauss' a beautiful waltz by Strauss and the poignant, appealing "Traumeri."

Musical America 5-10

Keystone-Underwood

At Right, Clad in Shaggy Brown Coats, Nelson Eddy, Baritone (Left), and His Accompanist, Theodore Paxson, Are Seen on a Cross-Country Hike While on a Recent Concert Visit to Newport News, Va.

the Society. His voice is lovely in its tone quality, and he sang with evident sincerity as well as evident desire to and modern, 'sacred and profane.' Encore after encore was given, even after 10 o'clock.... Something many never saw before was an entire long program given without anything which even looked like a scrap of paper, before either the singer or the accompanist. This is especially remarkable, as the accompanist had all sorts of complicated scores to play from memory, but he did it so easily that his only thought was to keep his eye on his soloist." *Newport Herald:* May 4, 1932: "Mr. Eddy's reputation had anticipated his arrival here, but the realization of his perfect rendition of his magnificent program, established him in the hearts of his hearers far beyond the expectations of the most sanguine. The beautiful natural quality of his voice, his wonderful technical ability, his superlative command and training have combined to produce an artist of the highest order. He carried his audience far out of themselves, and each song was tumultuously applauded."

May 5, 1932: Nelson sang in Jackson, Tennessee. *Jackson Sun,* May 6, 1932: "The last song had been sung, there was a burst of deafening applause as Nelson Eddy and Theodore Paxson walked from the stage and into their dressing room. 'I have enjoyed singing in Jackson; you have an intelligent audience and a splendid concert hall,' said the artist. As the words were spoken all those 'back stage' realized that something unusual was happening -- the audience was not leaving, they were not even putting on their coats in preparation to leaving, they were just sitting, waiting for more songs.... Those who have attended concerts in Jackson for the past seven or eight years know just how unusual this is."

May 7, 1932, *Courier* clipping: "Nelson Eddy returned form a concert tour which took him through 23 states within 3 weeks." *Times-Star,* Cincinnati, "He created a furor." He was immediately re-engaged for next season. Little Rock *Democrat:* "Perhaps no artist has ever received more enthusiastic or appreciative applause than greeted this young singer." Jackson, Tennessee *Evening Herald:* "Never before has a Jackson audience been so complimentary to a visiting artist." *Evening Herald,* Klamath Falls, "Nelson Eddy, young American baritone, thrilled..." *Standard Examiner,* Ogden, Utah, "The delightful informality of his personality charmed the audience and put everyone in a good humor."

May 10, 1932: Nelson sang in for a Mendelssohn Club benefit in Sunbury, Pennsylvania. *Ashland Daily News,* May 11, 1932: "That the audience was thrilled with the dozen or more numbers given by Mr. Eddy, is probably the best way to express their enthusiasm. Undoubtedly he is the most gifted vocal artist the Ashland people ever had the pleasure of hearing in person, and there appeared to be no limit to the possibilities of his vocal accomplishments." *Sunbury Item:* "Such talent and ability as he displayed are rarely heard outside the larger musical centers. He is thoroughly representative of the modern idea of singing. The words were understood as well as though they were spoken. He sang with ease, without that physical distortion which characterized operatic stars of a former generation, and with rich resonant tone quality which in itself was most pleasant." *Sunbury Daily:* "A brilliant success was scored by the Mendelssohn Club... Nelson Eddy, the guest soloist of the evening, held his audience spellbound in each and every number and his generosity in answering to encore after encore proved the love of his artistry, moving his audience to laughter and the next minute to tears. His great talent as an actor and his beautiful voice thrilled his audience because of its perfect concert, clear, resonant tone and the exceptional quality, together with an unusual personality.... The only regret is that the auditorium was not filled to capacity which would have aided the hospital, a local institution, which in times of distress and depression, meets the need of all, in a more substantial way."

May 15, 1932: Nelson sang in Jackson, Illinois. May 17, 1932, *Jacksonville Daily Journal:* "A magnificent singer, whose human touch, sense of the dramatic and refreshing humor make him doubly fascinating to his audience, appeared last evening before Jacksonville Community Concert Association members and their guests in the person of Nelson Eddy... one of the foremost baritones of this country.... Mr. Eddy won his listeners completely as with an intriguing and varied program he displayed a rich, powerful voice coupled with superior artistry and interpretation."

May 21, 1932: Nelson sang at the May Festival in Detroit, appearing in **The Legend of the Invisible City of Kitesh and the Maiden Fevronia**, by Rimsky-Korsakov (sung in English), which was given its American premiere. "Nelson Eddy handled a minor part quite competently." *Musical Courier,* June 4, 1932: "The work is typically Russian, somewhat after the style of **Boris Godunov** with solo parts for soprano, contralto, tenor, baritone, bass and numerous minor roles.... Eddy brought his resonant tones and forceful picturization to the characters of Feodor Poyarok and a Tartar chief, Burundai."

May 26, 1932: Nelson sang in Philadelphia last night at the Penn Athletic Glee Club annual spring concert. *Ledger,* May 27, 1932: "In spite of a severe cold which threatened the completion of his program, Mr. Eddy delighted his audience in two groups of light songs. He also appeared as soloist in two of the best-sung numbers by the chorus -- 'The Skipper of St. Ives,' by Roeckel, and 'The River and Me,' by Warren." *Bulletin:* "Despite a severe cold, Mr. Eddy's contributions to the program were well done and enthusiastically received. Throughout his two solo groups his singing was marked by a confident caution."

June 5, 1932: *New York Times* article states: "Nelson Eddy will appear in a benefit of **I Pagliacci** at Robin Hood Dell in Philadelphia on June 21. Nelson Eddy tells a funny story that happened one evening when he was riding home from the Dell concerts on a bus top. He heard four young men doing some barbershop harmonizing. Without thinking, Nelson started to chime in, according to him, 'providing about $100 worth of free singing. Suddenly, one of the boys looked around with a scowl and said, 'Say, somebody's awful lousy! I decided I wasn't so good after that, and so I kept quiet.'"

June 21, 1932: First opera ever presented in the Robin Hood Dell was **I Pagliacci**, followed by solo and ensemble dances. *Ledger,* June 22, 1932: "The cast was excellent and, despite necessarily few rehearsals, worked exceedingly well together. Nelson Eddy as Tonio sang and acted admirably. He introduced some new things in stage 'business' and while most of them were justifiable, some were not entirely convincing. His singing of the prologue gave him a splendid opportunity for the display of his remarkably smooth and even voice and throughout he made the most of the role's possibilities. At the close he received a great ovation upon taking, as did all the other principals, a solo curtain call." [Note: co-star was Irene Williams.] *Record:* "Nelson Eddy lent a special bit of color in the role of Tonio. The blond idol of all local music lovers cast aside tradition and turned the conventional villain into an almost unrecognizable character. His Tonio was more of the gentle halfwit than the familiar vindictive one. Eddy even introduced the novelty (as far as local audiences are concerned) of donning the cap and bells of his role-within-a-role during his singing of the prologue. He also accentuated the comedy in the act-within-an-act by a silly wig, which jumped up and down at his command. Many conventional opera-goers might object to the liberty Eddy took with the role. But it was fresh, it was intelligent, and his voice, as always, was good to hear." *Bulletin:* "Nelson Eddy, as Tonio, brought craftsmanship to the role in which he is familiar to audiences here. His Prologue was done with sustained even resonance that surmounted with high range of the closing passage with no loss of tone, while his subsequent work was consistently in character." *News:* "The popular Nelson Eddy, as the clowning Tonio, added new flares to this well-grooved role. His first innovation came with the rendering of the prolog. (sic) Eddy appeared with his makeup box and costume, and proceeded to don costume as he sang those dramatic notes. Even through the opera he spared no opportunity of revealing new modes and methods of interpretation, which evinced his originality and statecraft." *Inquirer:* "Mr. Eddy sang as ably as he acted, and it was he who provided the innovations that ranged from the startling to one that was literally hair-raising, for after his effective stunt in 'making up' before the audience in singing the prologue, he astounded the audience in tense moments of the second act by making his red wig literally rise from the roots and stand on end." *Musical America,* July, 1932: "Nelson Eddy... sang superbly."

July 8, 1932: Nelson started a weekly radio program, the "Hoffman Variety Hour" which ran through December 30, 1932. It was broadcast at 9:00 pm on Fridays from WOR studios in New York City. On the first program there was no co-star. [Note: From this point on, only Hoffman Hours with interesting guests, or unusual programs will be listed here.]

July 15, 1932: On the Hoffman Variety Hour, the highlight was Nelson singing the **Faust** trio with Margaret Speaks and Harold Hansen.

Broadcasts Winnowed

BY THE DIALIST

* * *

Impressions of WOR Friday Night at 9

The long, long trail which winds from the WOR reception room to the studio where William Daly's men were tuning up, and along the trail, casualties! The featured singers surreptitiously dropping cold medicine up their noble noses, WOR artists being in the throes of the fashionable snuffles and sniffles.

The control room finally attained, occupied only by a blond-haired engineer, feverishly manipulating the valve on the radiator instead of the dials on the radio board. The outside temperature had gone up and the steam heat had followed suit.

An easy chair, an ash receiver and a wide window through which to stare at the big studio filled with musicians; Daly on the conductor's stand in baggy trousers and a blue shirt with one sleeve rolled up to the elbow, the other dangling at his wrist.

The doors at the rear of the room opened by a page who shows in the small group of men and women who can be seated in the studio. They are gathered in the rear of the room, behind the bass viols and the drums—small chance of hearing the singers who stand with their back to the room. One feels sorry for their eagerness, so often to be disappointed. A few more fortunate persons are seated on the side quite close to the mikes—they will be able to hear.

Westbrook Van Voorhis, a tall and thin young man, looking rather fagged after a day of recording, takes a survey of the room, mikes, props, piano and music racks for the soloists. Everything apparently satisfactory, he disappears and the row of chairs reserved for the singers stands empty. People in the audience begin craning their necks watching for the entrance of the celebrities.

A little stir among the spectators; a tall slender girl with smooth yellow hair, uncurled and knotted at one side of her head, slips up the aisle. Margaret Speaks, looking like the sweet young debutante daughter of a conservative family; color that comes and goes, soft young lips and blue eyes full of wistfulness, but twinkling with humor from time to time and a voice like the lark at heaven's gate.

Next Veronica Wiggins, in black velvet, her thick black hair waving about her fine head; eyes full of fun and hidden under long lashes; a poise and dignity that become her well and a companionship with old man mike which few sopranos, and almost no contraltos, possess.

A small, sedate looking young man hurrying up the aisle and joining the two girls. Harald Hansen, an immaculate looking person, a bit phlegmatic in type, but a remarkably easy and accomplished performer behind the mike.

Nelson Eddy Enters And the Program Is on

A stir at the door, a big blond man in a brown suit and a pink collar stopping to beat the drums and nudging the drummer in the ribs before he bursts into the quiet group along the wall—Nelson Eddy. Daly mounts the stand and raps the musicians to attention; the announcer addresses the mike anent the virtues of his product. The air's most popular semiclassical program is under way.

One after another the singers go over to the mike for their solos and William Daly leads his men by a series of graceful, vigorous and arresting gymnastics. His blue shirt becomes soaked with honest sweat and between numbers he pulls a gray brown sweater, elongated with age, from a corner and puts it on, buttoning it all the way up. His fringe of black curly hair is glistening with moisture; his forehead and cheeks are bathed in water and he waves a dripping handkerchief at the control booth and in dumb show, pleads for a fresh one.

Waves of suppressed laughter come from the spectators in the control room at the antics of radio's bad boy, Nelson Eddy. Prefacing each of his numbers with some typical Eddy clowning which may be boyish high spirts but has the effect of poor showmanship—a false note in a seriously beautiful concert. Veronica sings a lullaby exquisitely but Eddy steals the spotlight as far as the visible audience is concerned by flinging himself down and yawning prodigiously, not in boredom but to illustrate the song. Before his magnificent rendering of the "Song of the Shirt" he makes a rueful face at his coat and stripping it off throws it across the room to his chair. "He certainly doesn't take himself seriously," says the woman beside us, laughing, but there is a note of chagrin in her voice. Our musical royalty should not wear the motley when we of the open spaces have so regally decked them in the purple.

The quartet of soloists group around the mike; the orchestra breaks into a swinging measure; Mr. Daly raises his baton for his men and turns his face toward the waiting group of singers: "To you and to you, our friends ever true." The perfectly blended voices ring out in the brilliant toast, the gorgeous barytone of Nelson Eddy dominating them all. Van Voorhis is at the mike; the blond engineer turns a dial; the concert is over. The singers hurry through the room and disappear; the spectators draw a breath of relief after the enforced silence—to be unable to applaud such music is an actual physical hardship. The musicians pack their instruments into the velvet lined cases; the page returns and straightens the chairs. The song is ended but the melody lingers on.

* * *

July 19-20, 1932: Nelson sang in Beethoven's Ninth Symphony again at Lewisohn Stadium in New York, for an audience of somewhere between 9,900 and 14,000, depending on the source. Other soloists included Sophie Braslau, contralto, Nina Morgana, soprano and Paul Althouse, tenor. "The solo singing varied and perhaps was best in the opening phrases by Mr. Eddy." *Musical Courier*, July 20, 1932: "Nelson Eddy intoned the baritone recitative flawlessly, exemplifying the beautiful natural quality of his voice and his excellent technic." (sic) *New York World-Telegram:* "Last evening Nelson Eddy deserved more cordial praise for his masterly treatment of the baritone part, and it was always a pleasure to listen to his fresh, resonant voice."

August 1, 1932: Nelson sings with his current voice coach, Dr. Douglas Stanley, during "how to sing correctly" voice lesson that was taped in the Irvine Auditorium at the University of Pennsylvania. [Note: The complete lesson was released on Mac/Eddy Record Series #JN110. Nelson also sang Schubert's "Serenade" after the lesson.]

August 4, 1932: Nelson sang again at the Robin Hood Dell. [Note: the performance had been scheduled for August 3 but was cancelled due to rain.] *Evening Ledger:* "The soloist received an immense reception upon his first appearance, and this was repeated at the close of both his scheduled numbers. Mr. Eddy was in splendid voice, and his tone seems to have gained in resonance and quality since his last appearance here, while his remarkable diction and admirable interpretations deserved all the enthusiasm accorded him." *Record:* "For his programmed offerings, Mr. Eddy sang two famous arias from the operatic repertoire, 'Largo al Factotum'... and the 'Vision Fugitive' ...He was enthusiasti-cally acclaimed by a large audience and was called upon for three encores. Mr. Eddy got away with the difficult piece (Largo) very successfully, but it seemed nevertheless an ill-advised choice. It is an aria which lies more naturally in a larger and more robust voice than Mr. Eddy's, and it calls for size as well as for the excellent comedy touches which he gave it. 'The Herodiade' aria was well suited to Mr. Eddy's excellent legato singing and his evenly produced tones. He gave a distinctive artistic touch to his performance of the famous piece and was enthusiastically applauded by the musicians and the audience." *Record:* "Eddy's popularly disproves all the theories that local talent is never credited at home. This handsome young native's entire career has progressed in this city. And music lovers have watched and encouraged him with the faithful devotion of a patron." *Inquirer:* "Nelson Eddy earned emphatic success in the numbers he was scheduled to sing the previous evening, when the heavy rain necessitated cancellation of the concert. The Philadelphia baritone was in excellent voice and his vigorous and artistic singing... carried clearly throughout the Dell." *Daily News:* "This outdoor singing is tricky business, even for the best of voices. There is that doubtful acoustical problem to be bothered with. But it didn't faze Nelson. Right into it he warbled his best, achieving the plaudits of the 4500 or so who visited the outdoor arena of music.... No matter how you look at it, Nelson is a songster of exceptional qualities." *Musical Courier:* "He was in particularly fine voice."

August 12, 1932: Another Hoffman Hour, with no guest. Nelson sang his own song, "The Rainbow Trail."

September 2, 1932: The highlight of this Hoffman Hour was Nelson dueting "Si pei ciel" from **Otello** with Harold Hansen.

October 14, 1932: At this Hoffman Hour Oscar Levant is first noted as the pianist for the show. He remained the pianist until the end of the show.

October 19, 1932: *Newark Evening News* description of Nelson arriving for his radio show: "A stir at the door, a big blond man in a brown suit and a pink collar stopping to beat the drums and nudging the drummer in the ribs before he bursts into the quiet group along the wall -- Nelson Eddy....Waves of suppressed laughter come from the spectators in the control room at the antics of radio's bad boy, Nelson Eddy. Prefacing each of his numbers with some typical Eddy clowning which may be boyish high spirits but has the effect of poor showmanship – a false note in a seriously musical concert. Veronica (Wiggins) sings a lullaby exquisitely but Eddy steals the spotlight as far as the visible audience is concerned by flinging himself down and yawning prodigiously, not in boredom but to illustrate the song. Before his magnificent rendering of the 'Song of the Shirt' he makes a rueful face at his coat and stripping it off throws it across the room to his chair. 'He certainly doesn't take himself seriously,' says the woman beside us, laughing, but there is a note of chagrin in her voice. Our musical royalty should not wear the motley when we of the open spaces have so regally decked them in the purple."

October 25, 1932: Nelson sang in Buffalo. *Buffalo Courier Express:* "Nelson Eddy, that brilliant young artist with the beautiful baritone voice and persuasive personality, opened the Van De Mark series of concerts for this season in the ballroom of Hotel Statler last evening. Mr. Eddy repeated his success of a year ago when he was heard here for the first time. His program was one of balance and thoughtful selection, calculated to display his vocal resources and the scope of his cultivation. Few young singers are able to sing in five languages and project such varied moods as Mr. Eddy negotiated last evening with such inimitable style.... Mr. Eddy was compelled to sing extra numbers after every group of songs." *Buffalo Times:* "Eddy's singing is a model of vocal control. He knows exactly how he is going to produce each tone, and there is no uncertainty in results. He is a singer who does not have to be 'warmed up' to his task. From start to finish, his voice is resonant, flexible, and beautiful in quality. By reason of his fine diction and distinct enunciation, as well as the meaning he gives to his art, he is intelligible in all languages. In the matter of interpretation, Eddy gives each song its own mood, quite as well defined as a painting to the eye. And it is in this respect that he is truly remarkable, and thus able to rivet attention and hold the keen interest of the listeners throughout his program.... Seldom have we heard a more individual interpretation of the first number ['Non piu andrai'] than that given by Mr. Eddy. It was as artistic as it was compelling. There was beautiful serenity in the second and delightful comedy in the third." *Buffalo Evening*

Oct. 26

FFALO COURIER-EXPRESS,

EDDY, BRILLIANT BARITONE, OPENS CONCERT SERIES

Young artist repeats success he scored on first Buffalo appearance

Nelson Eddy, that brilliant young artist with the beautiful baritone voice and persuasive personality, opened the Van De Mark series of concerts for this season in the ballroom of Hotel Statler last evening. Mr. Eddy repeated his success of a year ago when he was heard here for the first time. His program was one of balance and thoughtful selection, calculated to display his vocal resources and the scope of his cultivation. Few young singers are able to sing in five languages and project such varied moods as Mr. Eddy negotiated last evening with such inimitable style.

His opening number, the recitative and aria, Non Piu Andrai, from The Marriage of Figaro by Mozart, was delivered with the authority of a veteran singer. His singing of German lieder as presented in three numbers, Who Is Sylvia by Schubert, Du Bist So Jung by Wolff and Der Rattenfaenger by Hugo Wolf, in such contrasting moods were eloquent presentations.

Seldom have we heard a more individual interpretation of the first number than that given by Mr. Eddy. It was as artistic as it was compelling. there was beautiful serenity in the second and delightful comedy in the third.

In the recitative and aria, Vision Fugitive, from Herodiade by Massanet, the singer's operatic equipment was brilliantly revealed. Hopak by Moussorgsky was given with moving force and a sensing of the comic spirit. Mr. Eddy's great number of the evening was The Prophet by Rimsky-Korsakoff, which he presented with a superb sweep of long sustained phrases and a kindling of temperamental warmth that left a profound impression. Of three songs in English, My Sword for the King by Head was tremendously dramatic, and the simple melody, Sailor Men by Wolfe, won its own special tribute.

Mr. Eddy was compelled to sing extra numbers after every group of songs and scored in The Last Hour by Kramer, Vergebliches Standchen by Brahms, The Flea by Moussorgsky, Sea Fever by Ireland, Captain Stratton's Fancy by Deems Taylor, and The Home on the Range.

Theodore Paxson was accompanist and also contributed three piano solos with such success that he was recalled for an encore.

M. B. S.

---

watch and see.

Buffalo Times Oct. 26

MUSIC

Nelson Eddy Proves Right to Place Among Notables

By MARY M. HOWARD

Nelson Eddy, American baritone, gave his second recital in Buffalo last evening in the Hotel Statler ballroom, and again proved his right to be classed among the most brilliant young artists now on the concert stage. It was an auspicious opening of the Van De Mark series of five concerts, and was attended by an audience that waxed more enthusiastic with each number of the program.

Eddy's singing is a model of vocal control. He knows exactly how he is going to produce each tone, and there is no uncertainty in results. He is a singer who does not have to be "warmed up" to his task. From start to finish, his voice is resonant, flexible, and beautiful in quality. By reason of his fine diction and distinct enunciation, as well as the meaning he gives to his art, he is intelligible in all languages. In the matter of interpretation, Eddy gives each song its own mood, quite as well defined as a painting to the eye. And it is in this respect that he is truly remarkable, and thus able to rivet attention and hold the keen interest of the listeners throughout his program.

He opened his list last evening with Figaro's aria, Non Piu Andrai, from The Marriage of Figaro, and included later the recitative and aria, Vision Fugitive, from Massenet's Herodiade, displaying in both his familiarity with operatic tradition and style. Songs in German, Russian and English followed, with encores almost too many to count. Among the songs notable both for intrinsic beauty and their manner of delivery were Du Bist So Jung, by the late Erich Wolff, and Der Rattenfaenger, by Hugo Wolf. Eddy sang the poignantly tender Wolff song in a way that pulled at the heartstrings, and the second song very amusingly, with a notable exhibition of breath control at its close.

His command of the heroic mood was shown in Head's My Sword for the King, and Ireland's Sea Fever was finely stirring. Moussorkskys Hopak was given with wild delirium and The Prophet by Rimsky-Korsakoff, with great dramatic fervor. Double encores after each group were the order of the evening, and the audience gave him up very reluctantly even at the end of his generous list.

Theodore Paxson was again Eddy's accompanist, and a splendid one, infallible in balance and sympathy, and gifted with a lovely touch. He also played a solo group by Handel, Mendelssohn and Chopin, with the last composer's E minor waltz as encore. The Handel Chaconne in G major was a delightful number, played with admirable technical mastery and very beautiful coloring.

Buffalo Times 10-26

Buffalo Even. News 10-26

Nelson Eddy Gives Enjoyable Recital

American Baritone Opens Van De Mark Series in Hotel Statler Ballroom.

By EDWARD DURNEY

Nelson Eddy, young American baritone, who made his local recital debut last season in the Van De Mark concert series, returned to open this season's Van De Mark course Tuesday evening, in Hotel Statler ballroom. Eddy's one appearance here was sufficient to establish him in popular favor, and this second occasion witnessed his cordial welcome by a good-sized audience.

Mr. Eddy departs little from convention in his choice of program and in his manner of presentation. Perhaps he comes nearest to individual performance in songs which call for character portrayal. He is an engaging, fine-appearing young chap, generous with his gift of song, and he enjoys goodly measure of success in catching popular fancy.

The baritone's crowning virtue is his glorious voice, an organ of rich timbre and even scale, which he employs in exemplary fashion. Sheer vocal beauty delights the ear from the beginning to the end of his program. * * *

Interpretatively, Eddy has acquired well recognized essentials of good style and taste. His singing is a disclosure of general finish, to which admirable diction and polished phrasing contribute significantly. His deeds are excellent and his faults are not sins of commission. This second hearing of the baritone but confirmed a first impression. Convincing qualities are lacking.

Among his admirable deliveries were the Mozart air, "Non piu andrai," from "The Marriage of Figaro," the "Vision fugitive," from Massenet's "Herodiade" and the lovely song "Du bist so jung," Wolff. We are still wondering who advised the singer to adopt that funereal tempo for the Schubert "Who is Sylvia."

He did well with Russian songs of Moussorgsky and Rimsky-Korsakoff, offered a group of Head, Wolfe and Kountz with English text, and he sang about eight encores, for the most part sure-fire favorites. Of course there was "The Flea," Moussorgsky, and, after the last song group, the Deems Taylor "Captain Stratton's Fancy," in the presentation of which Eddy quite excels.

Again the baritone was fortunate in his associate, Theodore Paxson, whose accompaniments were of artistic quality wholly satisfying. Mr. Paxson offered solo numbers of Handel, Mendelssohn and Chopin, and he responded to applause with the inevitable E Minor Waltz, Chopin.

News: "The baritone's crowning virtue is his glorious voice, an organ of rich timbre and even scale, which he employs in exemplary fashion. Sheer vocal beauty delights the ear from the beginning to the end of his program." *Musical Courier.* "A fine voice, dramatic instinct, ingratiating personality, a charming informality in the presentation of an excellent program, combined with beauty of presentation, won his hearers completely. The enjoyment of the capacity audience was evidenced in prolonged applause, and triple encores were the rule of the evening." *Musical America*: "Mr. Eddy's beautiful baritone voice is under perfect control, and his art was well revealed."

November 1, 1932: Nelson sang in York, Pennsylvania. "He scored a decided success. The applause from the audience was deafening at times.... It was his deciding informality as well as his nearly perfect voice technique which created for himself a warm spot in the hearts of his York listeners. In a charming manner he described the encores he was to sing in addition to merely presenting the titles and the composers."

November 8, 1932: Nelson sang in East Orange, New Jersey, at the Hotel Suburban. It was a joint concert with Alice Mary Anderson. *Evening Newark News,* November 9, 1932: "The effects of Mr. Eddy's personality, voice and singing in the concert room are more compelling than they are when he broadcasts over the radio and the impression he left on his first appearance in this neighborhood was so gratifying that all who heard him must wish for a return engagement at no distant date. He has an ingratiating stage presence and a voice so fresh, resonant and skillfully controlled, so expressive as a medium for conveying widely differing moods and sentiments, that, combined with his other qualifications for the tasks he sets himself, delighted the audience.... Besides his bright, flexible tones, to which he imparts a variety of musical coloring, he brings to his undertakings an intelligence, an emotional resource and an instinct for just phrasing that enable him to get to the heart of the matter in the lyric." *Musical America*: "Nelson Eddy was justly applauded."

November 9, 1932: Nelson sang in a condensed version of Richard Strauss's **Salome,** with Maria Jeritza and the Musicians' Symphony Orchestra at the New York Metropolitan Opera. Fritz Reiner conducted. *New York Times:* "Eddy sang his few measures of Jochanahan's music intelligently and with excellent quality of tone." *New York Sun:* "Nelson Eddy sang the Jochanahan music admirably." *World Telegram:* "Nelson Eddy sang bravely as the much beset prophet, but his fine, fresh baritone is still a trifle light for the arduous duties of Strauss' Jochanahan." *Musical Courier:* "Eddy, portraying the ill-fated John rang out above the tremendous orchestra, in the seduction scene. The richness and perfect evenness of his voice, as well as the intelligence he displays in his singing, have made him within a period of only a few seasons one of the outstanding and yet most promising of the American list of singers." *New Yorker Magazine:* "The words of Jochanahan in the seduction scene were sung admirably by Nelson Eddy, who doubled efficiently as announcer of election returns." [The performance took place during the Presidential election, and apparently Nelson announced that FDR had won.] *Musical America*: "The volume of sound from 200 players was frequently overpowering and caused Mme. Jeritza to force her voice, otherwise she sang with unusual beauty of tone. Nelson Eddy wisely did not attempt to drown the overwhelming accompaniment and the result was most happy. Both artist were accorded an ovation that threatened to hold up the performance." *Musical Courier,* November 19, 1932: "Eddy portraying the ill-fated John, rang out above the tremendous orchestra in the seduction scene. The richness and perfect evenness of his voice, as well as the intelligence he displays in his singing, have made him within a period of only a few seasons one of the outstanding and most promising of the American list of singers." [Note: This was a benefit, and they did a condensed concert version of the opera. Jeritza always wanted to sing it at the Met but they wouldn't let her. They'd just let her go this season in cutbacks.]

November 14, 1932: Nelson sang in Cincinnati. *Cincinnati Times-Star,* November 15, 1932: "Last season, when Nelson Eddy sang at the Matinee Musicale, he created such a furor that a brisk bidding for his local reappearance immediately ensured. With becoming enterprise the Matinee Musical instantly re-engaged Mr. Eddy, who thus opened the season of their concert series at the Hotel Bigson on Monday morning. Mr. Eddy is endowed with tall the gifts which are happily bestowed upon great artists and several ordinarily denied to any but those upon whose cradle the gods have smiled.... His voice is a rich, deep barytone, sympathetically responsive to every thought suggested by his music. It seems a voice perfectly trained, artistically employed. For the encouragement of the discouraged, who study voice methods, it is possible to quote Mr. Eddy on the matter of voice training. He has had twelve teachers, two of whom so completely injured his voice that for months he was almost speechless. The intelligence of the singer remedied these unhappy situations.... Of all the songs Mr. Eddy sang, Massenet's 'Quand reviendra l'Hiver,' chanted in half voice with rhapsodic effect, was perhaps the most thrilling, and it was an encore." *Cincinnati Inquirer:* "Yesterday's musicale tended to support the excellent impression he made at his previous recital and to strengthen convictions of his artistry and musicianship." *Cincinnati Post:* "He is one of the most interesting singers before the public today. In our opinion, Mr. Eddy has more bass than barytone quality, but has the necessary range to encompass anything he cares to sing."

November 15, 1932: Nelson sang as soloist in Pittsburgh in Brahms's **Requiem**. *Sun-Telegraph,* November 16, 1932: "Nelson Eddy confirmed our former impressions of this fine baritone and sang his difficult solo with much repose and real command of music." *Pittsburgh Press:* "Nelson Eddy again proved his right to be among the greatest baritones of this country. Vocally, musically and artistically he ranks with the best we have heard in concert. His superb voice has a compelling beauty throughout its wide range for whether he employs top, middle or low tones purity of tone is always in evidence. To each of his solos he imparted breadth and dignity." *Post-Gazette:* "Nelson Eddy, baritone, has been heard here before and his resonated voice much admired. He was decent in the 'Lord, Make Me to Know' and stretching and stressful in the 'On This Earth.' He is not the best baritone in oratorio captivity, but he is fair enough."

November 26, 1932: Nelson sang in **Salome** with Helen Jepson.

December 6, 1932: Nelson sang in the city of London, in Ontario, Canada. *Ontario Free Press,* December 7, 1932: "Mr. Eddy has most excellent vocal equipment, but were his warmly melodious vice much less pleasing he could yet hold an audience by his sheer ability, dramatic as well as vocal. He sings with the utmost intelligence, with a keen and vital appreciation of every phrase of every number, with a complete absence of mannerism and with a pure and lovely diction -- all of which go to make up a most satisfying performance.... Mastery of that flexible instrument, his voice is Mr. Eddy's possession, either by divine right or hard work, probably both. That he has worked hard is no secret.... His histrionic ability is remarkable. He can and does throw himself with a relish into every role and has a freshness and a vitality in rendition that bring new life to time-honored numbers without being in any way radical. So impressed is one by Mr. Eddy's ability to sing that one turns to his voice almost as a secondary consideration. Yet it is a fine voice, warm and rich in texture, lucid in quality, powerful yet truly melodious in all its registers. Here is a personable young man who should by his charm, intelligence and talent carve a really important place for himself in the operatic and concert world." *London Advertiser:* "The audience was so enthusiastic in its reception of Mr. Eddy that they prolonged the evening's entertainment by half its scheduled length with encores after every group, graciously complied with by the personable young singer. Nelson Eddy has had a remarkable rise to fame since his debut in 1924... Now only 31, and looking at times five or six years younger, he is a singer with an assured and enviable reputation ranking with Bonelli and other outstanding men of the day.... Unlike so many singers, Mr. Eddy is not afraid that his artistic dignity will be lost if he gives, not only his delightful flow of song, but some of his personality to his audience in its interpretation. He compels the audience to his song's mood, and gains the desired response instantly. Apart from the fact that Mr. Eddy has one of the most liquid and satisfying of tones, which he manipulates in high and low register with equal facility, his showmanship is also commendable."

December 12, 1932, *Trenton State Gazette:* "Mr. Eddy, in fact, was so well received, that before the evening was over, he had sung what practically amounted to two programs, one which was printed and another which the audience demanded as a gratuity. Before his final bow, Mr. Eddy's encores (he is an exceedingly obliging performer) had accumulated to program length, and he was neither weary nor vexed." *Trenton Evening Times:* "Mr. Eddy captured his audience with his very first number.... Together with his rich beautiful baritone, Mr. Eddy has exceptionally fine enunciation, and with it all a discriminating sense of interpretation, which caught and held his audience from the beginning though the end of his very generous program. He set a fine standard for this season's concerts."

December 24, 1932, *Musical America*: "A letter was sent to Nelson Eddy's managers about his radio performances by Batten, Barton, Durstine & Osborn read as follows: 'It is, of course, hardly necessary for us to tell you the unlimited enthusiasm which Mr. Eddy's performances in this hour have inspired in both our client and this agency. He has proven himself not only an artist of the very first rank and a singer second to none (which we knew), but an extraordinarily adaptable performer in the many and diversified parts he was called upon to play during the series. It is a real and unforgettable pleasure to work with such a person and I hope and am sure that our association with him will last for a long, long time. – Edgar Shelton.'"

January 2, 1933: Nelson on the Socony-Vacuum Radio Show, details unknown. [Note: Nelson was thought to have become a "regular" on this show, with his last appearance being June 9, 1933.]

January 5, 1933, *Hollywood Citizen News:* "Nelson Eddy... will be presented for the first time on 'Captain Henry's Show Boat' tonight at 6 over KFI. The baritone is scheduled to sing 'My Message' and 'Stouthearted Men.' The Show Boat Four and the Show Boat Singers, a double quartet, are two other new features of this program."

January 10, 1933: Nelson sang in Ft. Wayne. *Journal Gazette,* January 11, 1933: "Mr. Eddy possesses a full, rich voice which he uses in an artistic manner, although at times his numbers were overacted." *News-Sentinel:* "Nelson Eddy, baritone, showed that he is able to use his strong-fibered, virile and resonant voice with admirable effectiveness. His winning personality and the evident gusto with which he sang captured the audience at once. Encore after encore was asked for and cheerfully given... There are times when one would welcome a little more restraint in this artist's singing. The infectious joy and exuberance with which he puts every fiber of his being into his readings induces him occasionally to endeavor to reinforce them too strongly with his excellent abilities as an actor. But the art of a man who is filled with such an abounding love of music and with such an unmistakable capacity for hard work will continue to grow in force and richness."

January 11, 1933, Nelson sang in Kalamazoo. *Kalamazoo Gazette,* January 12, 1932: "A slightly skeptical audience, or at least one in a somewhat 'Missouri' mood, gathered at the Civic Auditorium Wednesday evening to hear Nelson Eddy, baritone, in the second program of the Community Concert Association course. What that audience thought after two hours of listening to a glorious voice was aptly expressed by one member in the lobby -- 'He had everything, didn't he?' Eddy captured his audience with his first number, and as was amply demonstrated by the prolonged applause. From then on through a long program in which he was generous with his encores he displayed a versatility and command of every mood that thoroughly justified his reception.... Smooth, round and resonant, his voice gives the impression of unlimited reserve. His singing is effortless, yet there is a wealth of color and a 'cello-like timbre that leaves a feeling of satisfaction with every tone. His dramatic passages are handled in an operatic manner marked by perfect poise and dignity. The impression is that he is for the moment the character he is portraying, and he is always in character."

NEWSPAPERS OF 1933 ANALYZE SUCCESS OF

NELSON EDDY

Sixth Sense

"An artist must possess a sixth sense—a sense which transcends but never does violence to the demands of technical proficiency. Nelson Eddy is endowed with this qualification to a high degree."
—*Fort Wayne News Sentinel.*

Unlimited Reserve

"Smooth, round, and resonant, his voice gives the impression of unlimited reserve. His singing is effortless yet there is a wealth of color and a 'cello-like timbre that leaves a feeling of satisfaction with every tone.—*Kalamazoo Gazette.*

Big Voice

"He captivated his audience with his mimicry, his rollicking good-humor and his impersonations of a dozen characters in as many parts of a carefree, happy world. A big man with a big voice."
—*Saginaw Daily News.*

Gift of Song

"Nelson Eddy came to Portland a stranger. He is no longer that. Rarely has a new singer found such immediate favor with Portland audiences and before the evening was over he had won his place among favorite artists. It is difficult to say whether his spontaneity of manner or his generosity with his gift of song contributed most to his popularity."
—*Lewiston Evening Journal.*

Mastery of Control

"His is a baritone voice rich, round, and amply powerful, as magnificent in its mastery of control as it is skilled and discriminating in its subtlety."
—*Troy Record.*

Refreshing Sincerity

"Perhaps no more satisfying singer has appeared in Scranton than Nelson Eddy; contacting easily with his audience, delivering his songs with refreshing sincerity, filled with good humor, sufficient vocal power for all concert purposes, an appealing personality and a glorious voice; these are the assets that make his appearance in any city a noteworthy event."—*Scranton Republican.*

Accuracy of Pitch

"Nelson Eddy has a warm and glowing voice which he handles with ease and fine skill. There was an accuracy of pitch, and, as the occasion demanded, an infectious humor, dramatic appeal, or tender wistfulness."—*Syracuse Herald.*

Rare Talent

"Nelson Eddy is a concert artist of the highest order. He has that rare talent, and one that is not always given to the great artist, of being able to capture his audience and carry it with him through every emotion."—*Columbus Ledger-Enquirer.*

Graciousness

"Nelson Eddy was given the biggest ovation of any artist heard in Chattanooga for several seasons, his fine singing and his graciousness more than meriting his reception."
—*Chattanooga News.*

Sense of Humor

"He is a singer with rare gifts, being a tall, good-looking blond, with a powerful voice of fine quality, great intelligence, and artistry, a keen sense of humor, a pleasing personality, fine musicianship, and a gift for languages."—*Nashville Tennessean.*

Histrionic Ability

"Nelson Eddy brought to his audience a rich mellow voice that has been exceedingly well trained, breath control that is something to marvel at, enunciation that gets every word clearly across the footlights to his hearers, and histrionic ability of the first rank."—*San Angelo Morning Times.*

Artist of Mood

"From the land of musical Utopia came a stranger to rekindle and warm the memories of graciousness, sincerity, artistic endeavor, and youthful freshness, qualities possessed so rarely in the virtuoso of today. An artist of mood and a master of vocal technic, a king of rags, and yokel in satins—such are the impressions carried away from the Nelson Eddy concert."
—*San Diego Aztec.*

Romantic Presence

"Nelson Eddy, a youth of romantic presence and endowed with the golden gifts of a divine singer, stood forth last night at the Philharmonic Auditorium and literally swept the audience off its equilibrium to the extent of demanding encores after every number of the regular program."—*Los Angeles Evening Herald.*

Extraordinary Personality

"For the fact is that Eddy's success was nothing less than a sensation. He combines a good voice, well trained and in perfect control, with a most extraordinary personality."—*Fresno Bee-Republican.*

"Puts it on Ice"

"It is impossible to be cold and calculating when judging Nelson Eddy's art—his personality is so much a part of his interpretation, and when he sings a song one might say that he 'puts it on ice'."
—*Norwalk Hour.*

Laugh and Weep

"Eddy achieved more than a merely successful recital. He prodded a conservative audience out of its apathetic interest, made it laugh, even weep a little—and won the most enthusiastic and sincere applause that any artist has been accorded here."
—*Lancaster Intelligence-Journal.*

Eating from His Hand

"It is safe to say that this will not be Nelson Eddy's last visit because, from the moment he burst on the stage, he had the audience eating from his hand."—*Cleveland Plain Dealer.*

Sings for Joy of It

"Eddy possesses one of the finest stage personalities I ever saw. A giant of a fellow, who beams a smile across the footlights, and, although it may sound like a bromide, has every appearance of singing for the joy of it. He sang and sang and sang, when he wasn't bowing, bowing, and bowing, because it was what might be termed a sensationally successful local debut."
—*Cleveland News.*

Dignity and Force

"Nelson Eddy sang the part of Gurnemanz. He gave a splendid performance, admirable in its dignity and force. It was one of the finest, if not the finest, thing he has done locally in his successful career."—*Philadelphia Record.*

Beautiful Wagner

"Eddy did some of the most beautiful and convincing vocal work that could be heard in Wagner."—*Philadelphia Evening Ledger.*

Orchid to Eddy

"An orchid to Nelson Eddy, one of the most popular singers this city has contributed to music."—*Philadelphia Daily News.*

Fifth Appearance

"Making his fifth appearance in this city, Nelson Eddy as usual captivated the audience with his singing and personality."
—*Sunbury Daily.*

Magnificent Baritone

"Nelson Eddy has been heard in Newport before and never was more pleasing than in last night's concert. His magnificent baritone voice is a delight to listen to."—*Newport Herald.*

Hypnotized Audience

"Eddy won his audience as soon as he crossed the stage in his virile, business-like way. And from that point on he held his listeners under the charm of his rich baritone voice. To say that he electrified his audience is to put it mildly. To be frank, he fairly hypnotized them, causing them to smile as he smiled and frown as he frowned."—*Lowell Sun.*

Masculine and Vital

"He has youth, a personality second to none, and a voice as masculine and vital as any we have heard. He can convey the true mood of a song by the movement of a single finger or a shrug of the shoulders in just the right place."—*Springfield Union.*

Perfect Tone

"The voice is young and fresh and the singer produces his tone apparently without effort. With arms at his sides, the youth stood perfectly still and emitted round and perfect tone in perfect pitch and with extraordinary ease."
—*The San Francisco Call-Bulletin.*

Exciting Person

"The first impressions of Nelson Eddy lasted throughout the evening. An exciting person, he exudes fire and feeling. His voice is rich, resonant, and full-toned, always under command. I would have willingly listened to him the rest of the night."—*Albany Evening News.*

Combination of All

"The reasons for the singer's astounding success have been perfectly patent to every hearer. It was his combination of about all that makes for success—voice, diction, intelligence, and personality."
—*Nashville Banner.*

Golden Voice

"Song swayed a large audience into continuous applause for Nelson Eddy, the singer with the golden baritone voice." —*Los Angeles Evening Herald.*

Magnetism

"They clapped and they clapped and he sang and he sang! He has a rare magnetism for an audience."—*Los Angeles Times.*

January 12, 1933: Nelson sang in Saginaw, Michigan. *Saginaw Daily News:* "Nelson Eddy stepped out of the conventional role of a concert artist Thursday night to captivate a Saginaw audience with his mimicry, his rollicking good humor and his impersonation of a dozen characters in as many parts of a carefree, happy world. A big man with a big voice, perfectly controlled and used effectively. His offerings for the evening were nearly doubled in number by long periods of applause accorded each of Mr. Eddy's appearances."

January 17, 1933: Nelson sang in Ft. Wayne, Indiana.

January 18, 1933: Nelson sang in Columbia, Missouri. *Columbia Missourian*: "Waging a gallant and successful fight against a severe cold which robbed his top tones of much of their accustomed brilliance and shadowed the clarity of his mezzo-voce, Nelson Eddy... last night built even more firmly upon the foundation of popularity he laid here last year. The large audience in the University Auditorium was his from start to finish. Mr. Eddy overshadowed his handicap by his artistry, his personality and sheer perfection of technique. His program, itself hardy fare for an evenings' singing, was augmented by nine encores and could perhaps have included as many more, for the listeners were loath to let him go. The singer's voice, a baritone of lyric texture, smooth, rather light, is greatly reminiscent of that of John Charles Thomas -- far more so than of the heavier baritones and bass-baritones. His singing is authoritative and his interpretations consistently unhackneyed and fresh -- particularly in lighter numbers, the singing of which seem to afford Mr. Eddy as much pleasure as his hearers received by listening." *Columbian Daily Tribune:* "With a barrage of curtain calls, request numbers and encores which, as Eddy himself put it, gave his audience not only his 1933 program, but most of his 1932 numbers as well, the singer delivered a big money's worth to his appreciative audience."

January 23, 1933: Nelson sang in Portland, Maine again, replacing Paul Robeson. *Levitan Evening Journal,* January 25: "Nelson Eddy, American baritone, came to Portland City Hall Monday evening a stranger. He is no longer that. Rarely a new singer finds such immediate favor with Portland audiences and before the evening was over he had won his praise among favorite vocal artists. Every number received hearty applause from an audience which included a goodly number of music-lovers from Lewiston and Auburn and surrounding towns.... He is a tall, well set-up young man with wavy blonde hair and merry blue eyes and he has a certain magnetism in his personality and style of singing that should place him at the top among recitalists -- and he has humor. It is plain that Mr. Eddy prefers the vigorous to the romantic type of song but he is capable of much tenderness, when he makes use of a beautiful pianissimo, and he seems to have a special fondness for folksongs, which he sings with art and in a diversity of languages. Monday evening he sang in French, Italian, Spanish, Russian, German, English and American Negro dialect, and in all his accent and diction were a delight.... Mr. Eddy says, however, that he is a real Yankee, altho (sic) for the last few years he has been more in the South. It is his ambition to spend an entire summer vacationing in Maine." *Portland Press Herald:* "Throughout the evening the artist kept his audience in constant rapport. Mr. Eddy displayed a voice of exceptional quality, even throughout its wide range and well handled at all times. He brought many a lesson in diction, breath control and effortless production." *Portland Evening News:* "A large and enthusiastic audience of music lovers greeted the performers warmly and with every evidence of deep appreciation applauded each selection, demanding and securing generous encores." *Portland Evening Express:* "Mr. Eddy... was secured by the Portland Music Commission to replace Paul Robeson, the Negro vocalist, who has been forced to abandon his American tour this season." Nelson's voice quality was said to be "superb."

January 26, 1933; Troy, New York. *Troy Record,* January 27, 1933: "Troy had been promised a concert by Mr. Eddy during the last Chromatic subscription season. But Mr. Eddy, because of an unfortunate and unpreventable circumstance, was unable to fulfill that engagement. The cancellation of that appearance was rather a disappointment, but it served the more to heighten anticipation, for Chromatic immediately promised to engage him for this season. On every side that anticipation was readily apparent as Mr. Eddy made his first quick-stepped entry.... His is a barytone voice rich, round and amply powerful, as magnificent in its mastery of control as it is skilled and discriminating in its subtlety. Particularly delightful were those semi-comic renditions that he effected in a light opera mood." *North Adams Evening Transcript:* "Mr. Eddy made a distinctly favorable impression in a program calculated to appeal to a wide variety of musical tastes.... Mr. Eddy was at his best in

Eddy Delights Audience With Vocal Powers

Baritone Displays Finished Technical Excellence in Recital Before Thursday Morning Musicales—Has Direct, Simple Appeal

By Carolyn Ruth Doran

Nelson Eddy, baritone, with Theodore Paxson as piano-accompanist, was presented in a memorable concert by the Thursday Morning Musicales in the lecture room of The Park Church last night. Intelligent, versatile, possessed of extraordinary dramatic force and, above all, recipient of a gift of beautiful vocal powers which he uses with authority and with that apparent ease which is the result of finished technical excellence and the accomplishment of true art, Nelson Eddy in his charm of youth and his challenge to the finest in musical appeal is a vocalist to arrest favorable attention of the most critical mind.

So direct and so apparently simple is his appeal, so richly rounded his whole technique both in manner of presentation and in the musical content of his extraordinarily interesting program, his audience last night was immediately captivated and its attention held throughout an unusually long program. The listed offerings left the audience clamoring for more; and encore after encore followed each group as the recitalist generously acceded to the demands of his enthusiastic audience.

Appears With Jeritza

In approaching any direct comment on the style and vocal abilities of Mr. Eddy, one is forcibly reminded of the fact that he made a memorable appearance last autumn in New York with the famed operatic star, Jeritza, wherein a revival of part of the sometimes offensive indelicacies of "Salome" brought to him praise and enthusiasm from critics of metropolitan dailies. While the greater praise was naturally accorded the one who sang the title role much against the misgivings of many supporters of opera of another color and odor, Nelson Eddy, who essayed the part of Jochanaan, participated in the tremendous triumph that was accorded the two singing artists in the Metropolitan Opera House, filled to capacity, if you please, even on election night.

This event is noted by way of revealing to the uninformed that the dramatic verve of Mr. Eddy's style of interpretation has had larger scope than that permitted on a concert stage. Opera is his accustomed medium, as this event discloses, as well as his fine rendering last night of Massenet's Recitative and Aria, the "Vision Figitive," from "Herodias," which incidentally treats from a different point of view the same theme as that of "Salome." The Massenet number became a vibrant and moving episode in the tragic tale of King Herod as the vocalist dramatically enunciated in precise recitative the prelude to the area itself; and the lovely phrasing of Massenet's musical score fell with exceeding charm upon the ear and artistic consciousness of listeners.

Dynamic Appeal

Mozart's opera, "The Marriage of Figaro," also had place in the operatic excerpts offered last night. Even his less pretentious selections, the vocalist charged with the same dynamic appeal, bringing to each full complement of its dramatic accompaniment of spirit as well as satisfying vocal ability.

Encompassing all sorts of moods and manners in his interesting collection of songs, listeners will probably remember with special note the recitalist for the Russian spirit exemplified by him in the Moussorgsky and Rimsky-Korsakoff selections. A group of simpler songs at the close of the program, sung in English, and a German group, including the lovely Scubert number, "Who Is Sylvia?" completed the vocalist's listed numbers.

Mr. Eddy is especially fortunate in his accompanist, for Theodore Paxson bring to his pianiste ability the essential quality of complete sympathy with the moods and singing style of the vocalist. In addition, Mr. Paxson offered three piano numbers, all giving further evidence of the technical excellence and deep feeling for admirable tonal quality manifest in his previous role of accompanist. He played Chopin especially well, the composer's Scherzo in C-sharp minor bringing spontaneous and deserved applause at the close of his part of the program.

The Program

The entire program was as follows:

I

Recitative and Aria: "Non piu andrai" .... Mozart
(from the Opera "The Marriage of Figaro")

II

Who Is Sylvia? .... Schubert
Du bist so jung! ...... Erich Wolff
Der Rattenfaenger ..... Hugo Wolf

III

Recitative and Aria: "Vision fugitive" .... Massenet
(from the Opera "Herodiade")

IV

Piano Solos:
Chaconne .... Handel
Spinning Song ....Mendelssohn
Scherzo in C-sharp minor ..Chopin
Mr. Paxson

V

Hopak .... Mourssorgsky
Prorok .... Rimsky-Korsakoff

VI

Sailor Men .... Jacques Wolfe
Home on the Range ..Arr. by Guion
The Sleigh .... Kountz

Elmira, N.Y. Star-Gazette 2-10

the lyric numbers which he gave and in those which spoke in a light and amusing idiom and presented the opportunity for the artfulness of interpretation that is an essential part of a concert singer's equipment." *Albany Evening News:* "What began as a very stiff and formal even, drawing only polite and perfunctory ripples of applause (a piano concert by Frances Bartlett and Rae Robertson), developed into a genuinely entertaining performance last night in Troy's Music Hall. [The audience] waited patiently for him."

January 27, 1933: Nelson was noted as being on the Socony-Vacuum Show.

February 7, 1933, Kingston, New York *Daily Newsman:* "Mr. Eddy has a delightfully satisfying baritone voice and he is master of his voice. He has the rare dramatic sense that comes of a vivid imagination. What is more he makes his audiences see what he sees and hear what he hears as he sings. He is very versatile, and he has and makes use of a perfect sense of pulsing vibration which we call rhythm.... This young man has the ability to convulse his audience with laughter at the humor of some of his songs while they resent their own laughter lest they lose one note of the fine voice and splendid musical performance." *Daily Leader:* "A brilliant song recital. Eddy's rich, sympathetic voice brought to the audience distinctive interpretations of several of the better known arias in his vast repertoire."

February 7, 1933: Nelson sang in Elmira, New York. *Advertiser:* "Once again the Thursday Morning Musicales did a great service to musical Elmira, when they presented Nelson Eddy, barytone, in a recital Thursday evening in the Park Church lecture room. Their efforts were rewarded by the enthusiastic applause of an audience that should have been three times as large. It goes without saying that Mr. Eddy gave a beautiful and delightful program. His choice of songs and arias ranged from the classicism of Mozart to the more modern composers and even to the folk songs of the prairie. In all of them he captured the mood and meaning of each and presented each song as a perfect gem of interpretation. He has a beautiful voice of great richness and purity which he has always under perfect control. Added to this he has great histrionic ability and the combination of the two to make him an artist to be reckoned with." *Star-Gazette:* "Nelson Eddy, in his charm of youth and his challenge to the finest in musical appeal is a vocalist to arrest favorable attention of the most critical mind. So direct and so apparently simple is his appeal, so richly rounded his whole technique both in manner of presentation and in the musical content of his extraordinarily interesting program, his audience last night was immediately captivated and its attention held throughout an unusually long program. The listed offerings left the audience clamoring for more; and encore after encore followed each group as the recitalist generously acceded to the demands of his enthusiastic audience."

February 8, 1933, *Scranton Times:* "The concert will long be remembered as one of special delight with a warm bond of sympathy between audience and artists. Having heard Mr. Eddy it is not difficult to understand why he has risen with remarkable rapidity to a leading position among American baritones. Mr. Eddy is a young man with a rich, sympathetic voice which is especially sweet in its upper ranges. He sings as though he enjoys it and puts dramatic gestures into his singing which are in no way overdone. His response to the enthusiastic encores of the audience last night was generous and cordial. There seemed to be no inclination of either artists [Nelson or Ted Paxson] to leave the auditorium. Mr. Eddy's personality is contagious and altogether pleasing." *Scranton Republican:* "Perhaps no more satisfying singer has appeared in Scranton than Mr. Eddy; contacting easily with his audience, delivering his songs with refreshing sincerity, filled with good humor, sufficient vocal power for all concert purposes, an appealing personality and a glorious voice; these are the assets that make his appearance in any city a noteworthy event."

February 12, 1933, Columbus, Georgia *Ledger Enquirer:* "Never before in the life of this reviewer has a Columbia [concert series] audience given as enthusiastic a reception to any artist as was accorded Nelson Eddy Friday evening when he was presented in concert by the Three Arts League. As he stepped out on the stage, vibrant with life and the joy of lifting his voice in song, the audience sat up, realizing that this was to be no ordinary concert. At the conclusion of the first number, Mozart's dramatic recitative and aria, 'Non pieu andrai' from **The Marriage of Figaro**, the house rang with the thunderous applause that was to continue through the entire program and be given with the same spontaneity to the last encore.... Mr. Eddy is a concert artist of the highest order. He has that rare gift, and one that is not always given to the great artist, of being able to capture his audience and carry it with him through every emotion. He leaves you alert and gay in response to the sparkling humor of Figaro; he stirs you with the rare beauty of Schubert, with the pathos and tenderness of 'Du bist so jung,' with the majesty of the arias 'Vision Fugitive' and 'The Prophet,' only to throw you into gales of laughter with his interpretation of the rollicking boastful 'Rat Catcher.' He is at his best in the intensely dramatic numbers where the audience is given the benefit of his great interpretative powers and his delicious sense of humor. So strong is his personality and so vibrant his dramatic temperament, that it is impossible to think of the quality of his voice alone.... A large portion of the audience went behind the scenes to meet him. A very real person he proved to be then as he autographed programs for the young girls and responded to the enthusiasm by sitting at the piano, entirely surrounded, and singing informally with Mrs. Wm. S. Eley, whose dramatic soprano was exquisitely lovely in the bits of opera she sang."

February 14, 1933, Syracuse *Evening Journal:* "Decisive acclaim demanded encore after encore... until he was reluctantly let go well beyond his program schedule." *Herald:* "Mr. Eddy has a warm and glowing voice which he handles with ease and fine skill. There was an accuracy of pitch and, as the occasion demanded, an infectious humor, dramatic appeal or tender wistfulness. His poise and a certain restraint of manner won instant favor with his listeners." *Post-Standard:* "Last night there were more encores than programmed numbers... Mr. Eddy has a voice of good timbre and range and an engaging personality. There is that vibrant ring to his upper tones which is so essential to many of the operatic arias for baritone, and there is a roundness and freedom to his lower tones that is quite bass-like in quality. He can produce a lovely pianissimo and has an ample supply of power at instant command."

February 15, 1933: Nelson sang in Newport News, Virginia. *Daily Press,* February 16, 1933: "The popularity of Nelson Eddy as a concert baritone was given additional evidence last night when the largest audience yet to attend a Williamsburg Community Concert Association recital heard him sing.... The audience received him with unusual warmth and demanded encore after encore, which he willingly gave -- singing almost as many encores as scheduled numbers."

February 21, 1933: Nelson sang in Chattanooga. "Mr. Eddy was given the biggest ovation of any artist heard in Chattanooga for several seasons, his fine singing and his graciousness more than merited his reception.... Mr. Eddy, who has a beautiful voice of wide range and great power, sings with the lack of self-consciousness and naiveté of a child, but with the artistry of the matured musician. He has absolutely no mannerisms of any kind and has a breath control nothing short of marvelous." *Chattanooga Times:* "With a rich and even tone which he maintained throughout a varied program, Nelson Eddy, American baritone, pleased a large audience last evening." *Nashville Tennesseean:.* "He is a singer with rare gifts, being a tall, good looking blond in his late twenties, with a powerful voice of fine quality, great intelligence and artistry, a keen sense of humor, a pleasing personality, fine musicianship, and a gift for languages." *Banner:* "When one hears an artist of the caliber of Nelson Eddy one's regrets for the passing of singers of the older generation is unmixed with fears that there will be none among the younger aspirants to fill their places. Here is a fine type of American manhood, young, virile and richly endowed, who is inevitably pushing his way toward the front rank of our vocalists.... Mr. Eddy, indeed, has a rare combination of gifts. His personality is compelling and winning; his voice is smooth and of lovely texture, controlled through a remarkably efficient vocal technique, and with his pronounced interpretative ability he combines the expressive understanding of the actor. In short, he has everything that goes into the making of a first-rate singer... In order to keep the record straight, it must be noted that Mr. Eddy does not possess one of the largest or loudest voices, nor does he attempt to excite superficial emotionalism through exaggerated effects of vocalism or gesture. He is temperamentally averse to these cheaper effects."

February 24, 1933, San Antonio *Evening Standard:* "Nelson Eddy of a rich baritone voice set a new standard of generous entertainment here Thursday night when he responded to 11 encore numbers, one more selection than was listed on his formal program. The audience at the Municipal Auditorium marveled at the endurance of human voice and cheered him liberally.... Mr. Eddy brought to his audience a rich mellow voice that has been exceedingly well trained, breath control that is something to marvel at, enunciation that gets every word clearly across the footlights to his hearers, histrionic ability of the first rank and a delightful naiveté that takes the edge off any formality that might have been inherent in the proceedings. He sang in German, French and Russian as well as English with selections from the leading classical, romantic, French and Russian as well as modern composers, with Negro spirituals thrown in for good measure. He was so thoroughly at home in all schools that it is difficult to select those he excelled in."

February 26, 1933: clipping notes that Nelson now has more than 30 operas in his repertoire and that he has sung with the following: "Philadelphia, Detroit and New York Philharmonic Symphony Orchestras, Philadelphia Grand Opera Company, Philadelphia Choral Society, Troy Chromatic Society, Boston Handel and Haydn Society, New York Stadium concerts, Schola Cantorum of New York, the Harrisburg and Ann Arbor festivals and others."

February 27, 1933: Nelson sang at the Savoy Theater in San Diego. *San Diego Tribune,* February 28, 1933: "There was no fuss or feathers about Nelson Eddy, the baritone who graced the Amphion concert series last night. He stood squarely on his feet, made no gestures. He has a fine voice and never spared it, although he never forced or strained it. He announced his songs in an informal, boyish manner, and always included his accompanist, saying: 'We shall give you--' as he presented them. His songs were not merely a part of a well chosen group of great or interesting airs. Each was an entity in itself. Each had a personality all its own, and each was thoroughly alive." *San Diego Sun:* "Nelson Eddy, the baritone who is better than his publicity... His concert Monday night at the Savoy Theater was the sort of triumph young singers dream of. All of Eddy's advance notices said that he was 'tall, blonde, and young,' but no one mentioned that he looks like Adonis, Rupert Brooke, the poet, and the more attractive younger knights of King Arthur's court. And he has the most generous and friendly attitude to his audience, began singing encores after the first number and sang fourteen in all, besides a program of songs and arias in six languages that would have exhausted both the vocal organs and mentality of the average concert artist.... Although Eddy's voice is beautiful enough to be kept under glass, he doesn't hoard it. He sings so easily that at the end of two hours singing, his voice was as fresh and rich as when he began. Eddy can take a climax without calling all the blood vessels into play, as in apoplexy. He just sings. And he is kind to his accompanist. He doesn't wait until the end of the evening to appreciate Theodore Paxson, who plays excellent accompaniments, all from memory including encores, and a very worthy group of piano solos with two encores midway the program." *San Diego Union:* "The charm, freshness of his youth, plus a seemingly intelligent personality, made Eddy the favorite of his listeners from the moment he first hustled on the stage. His ability to lose his identity in the varying moods of his songs gave the audience real pleasure, and its enjoyment was heightened when it saw that Eddy derived real pleasure from singing.... Samples from his operatic repertoire indicated what an asset his handsomeness and youth must be in costume to opera, and also showed what a sharp dramatic sense he possesses. The beauty of tone he achieved in tender songs displayed his fine control." *State College Aztec:* "An artist of mood and a master of vocal technic (sic)...such are the impressions carried away from the Nelson Eddy concert.... Nelson Eddy can sing...From the very first aria to the last folk song, Mr. Eddy held his voice in control, as one would a carefully constructed and manipulated machine. Now letting it out, now restraining, here quietness, and there pulsations as from infinite power." [Note: another clipping states that Nelson sang 19 encores!]

February 28, 1933: Los Angeles debut concert. Reviews were dated March 1, 1933: *Los Angeles Evening Herald:* "Nelson Eddy, a youth of romantic presence and endowed with the golden gifts of a divine singer, stood forth last night at the Philharmonic Auditorium and literally swept a good sized audience off its equilibrium to the extent of demanding encores after every number of the regular program. The singer's willingness to give was as unreserved and candid as youth sometimes is, and his repertoire, though limitless, never called for notes or memoranda... It was a very perceptible fact that the audience had been taken entirely by surprise in the qualifications of this newcomer and was not quite ready to be so completely captivated, but the encores began and continued until after bout 40 songs in all had been sung with a lavish expression that knew no bounds." *Los Angeles Examiner:* "With a voice of exceptional range, and magnificent breath control, Nelson Eddy

Coming in Amphion Concert

Nelson Eddy, young baritone with 10 years of busy career as singer in operas, oratorios, concerts and recitals behind him, will be presented at the Savoy theatre tomorrow night by the Amphion club.

EDDY TO APPEAR IN SONG RECITAL ON SAVOY STAGE

Eagerly awaited by lovers of the male voice as the only widely-known male vocal artist to appear in San Diego in recital this season, Nelson Eddy, baritone, will appear at the Savoy theatre tomorrow night in the fifth Amphion club event of the season.

Nelson Eddy is 32 years old, tall, blond and handsome. Before 1922 he was a newspaper writer and advertising man. Singing was his hobby. A fortunate accident caused him to display his well-trained voice to a critical audience as a substitute recitalist. His fame grew immediately.

His experience in 10 years has been busy and has taken him through a roster of engagements that could well attract the envy of artists much older than he. He has sung with the Philadelphia, Detroit and New York Philharmonic Symphony orchestras, the Philadelphia Grand Opera company, the Philadelphia Choral society, the Troy Chromatic society, the Boston Handel and Haydn society, the New York Stadium concerts, the Schola Cantorum of New York, the Harrisburg and Ann Arbor festivals and other organizations.

His recital, as are other Amphion events this season, is open to the public, which is invited to avail itself of tickets for the single event.

POPULAR WITH COLLEGIANS

Fredric March is the most popular screen actor with students of the Henderson State college at Arkadelphia, Ark., the Paramount star was notified in a letter from that institution.

THE SAN DIEGO UNION: SUNDAY MORNING, FEB. 26,

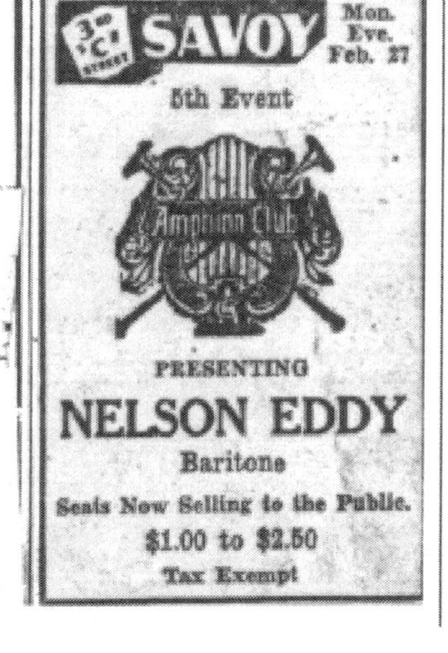

NEW SINGER PLEASES AT AUDITORIUM

Powerful Voice Revealed by American Baritone in Interesting Concert

BY ISABEL MORSE JONES

The singing of Nelson Eddy, a baritone new to Los Angeles and heard in the Behymer series at the Philharmonic Auditorium, was second in attention-getting to his extraordinary good looks and the splendid power of his voice. He has natural equipment for success and has acquired a large repertoire by study, but he has shading, dramatic fire, subtle nuance and the finer poetic meanings to add to his store of musical knowledge before he can take his place on the top rung of the ladder.

Eddy is an American, a young man from Rhode Island, who has had the benefit of popularity in Philadelphia. He looks decidedly Nordic and verifies this by singing Russian songs in that language with a strong flavor of the same soil Chaliapin has his musical roots in. At other times he suggests Lawrence Tibbett and it is good suggesting, too, but Eddy sings too well not to develop his own style more completely and put himself over.

The audience last night was not much help. It clapped incessantly until the idea of the presence of a claque could not be kept out. Even the raising and lowering of the piano lid caught applause. Encore after encore was allowed to destroy whatever continuity there was to the program and the indiscriminate noise which climaxed every song became a little absurd. Mr. Eddy is too good for that sort of thing to be necessary. He has tone beauty, resonance, exact intonation, rhythm and knows the value of many a singer's stratagem. For instance, he can hold a note in full power for an unbelievably long time, but on the other hand, he has still to learn the value of a pause. European finesse would be an advantage to this promising singer.

Mr. Eddy brought with him an unusually good pianist, Theodore Paxson. Mr. Paxson's accompaniments were unobtrusive and musically intelligent. His solos: Handel's Chaconne, the Spinning Song by Mendelssohn, a Scarlatti delicacy and a Bach chorale arranged by Myra Hess were grateful to the ear.

Los Angeles Times

NELSON EDDY'S SONGS HAILED AT AUDITORIUM

By RAYMOND E. MITCHELL

A most unusual spectacle was that afforded by the concert of Nelson Eddy, American baritone of the Philadelphia Grand Opera Company, which took place at Philharmonic Auditorium last night. It was an extraordinary experience to witness an American youth in his early thirties triumph to such a degree before an audience of distinction and under his own native skies. There was praise for his superb voice, his dignified, unaffected bearing, the subtle blending of tone and text, and for a temperament that comprehends all that is human and much that is spiritual.

The program began with Recitative and Aria, "Non piu andrai," from Mozart's "The Marriage of Figaro." It was sung with a purity of style and beauty of tone almost past belief. Back of this voice is an artist and a personality, a fine, big, virile nature, strong with all the strength of a real man, yet tender, poetic and sane in sentiment.

In the group that followed, "Who Is Sylvia," Schubert; "Du bist so jung," Erich Wolff, and "Der Rattenfaenger," Hugo Wolf, not a nuance, not a shade of expression escaped the fascinated listener. The second of the group brought to realization the unfailing technical skill of the singer. Recitative and Aria, "Vision Fugitive," from Massenet's "Herodiade," sung by Eddy, preceded a group of piano solos played by Theodore Paxson, the accompanist of the evening. They, too, were aristocratically finished renditions. The group contained "Chaconne," Handel; "Spinning Song," Mendelssohn, and "Scherzo," C-sharp minor, Chopin.

Two show pieces, "Hopak," Moussorgsky, and "Prorok," Rimsky-Korsakoff, were dashed off with a spirit and brilliance which made them positive and alive. They were especially applauded. The English group brought Wolfe's "Sailor Men," Guion's setting of "Home on the Range," and "The Sleigh," Kountz.

A feature of note was Mr. Eddy's generosity in the matter of encore songs. He had many walks to the footlights after each group, most of them ending with extra numbers coaxed by the eager listeners.

Hollywood Citizen-News

delighted and amazed his audience last night at Philharmonic auditorium. The singer, new to the Western concert stage, is youthful in appearance, with a frank smile and an eager manner. He's never bored with applause and responds with encores lavishly. Mr. Eddy's repertoire includes German lieder and 'Mandalay.' He sings each with ease and assurance. His operatic numbers show finesse, but over and above all else is his triumphant voice of a quality which recognizes no barrier of phrasing volume or tempo." *Los Angeles Times:* "The audience... clapped incessantly until the idea of the presence of a claque could not be kept out. Even the raising and lowering of the piano lid caught applause. Encore after encore was allowed to destroy whatever continuity there was to the program and the indiscriminate noise which climaxed every song became a little absurd. Mr. Eddy is too good for that sort of thing to be necessary. He has tone beauty, resonance, exact intonation, rhythm and knows the value of many a singer's stratagem. For instance, he can hold a note in full power for an unbelievably long time, but on the other hand, he has still to learn the value of a pause. European finesse would be an advantage to this promising singer." *Hollywood Citizen-News:* "A most unusual spectacle.... It was an extraordinary experience to witness an American youth in his early thirties triumph to such a degree before an audience of distinction… There was praise for his superb voice, his dignified, unaffecting bearing, the subtle blending of tone and text, and for a temperament that comprehends all that is human and much that is spiritual." *Daily News:* "That the time-worn phrase, 'a prophet is not without honor save in his own country,' has no longer the forcefulness it once obtained, was evidenced when Nelson Eddy, the young American baritone, received a welcome which is rarely accorded to the most distinguished foreign artist of the same quality of voice by Philharmonic Auditorium audiences…. Nor has this welcome been undeserved, since in addition to consummate artistry, Mr. Eddy was, as regards the display of his vocal ability at a concert this week, the most generous of all artists presented this season. Evidently, to him, singing is as much a pleasure as it is a profession.... With handsome features, the physique of a college athlete and gifted by nature with an exceptionally fine voice, the outstanding things on his program were a freshness and vitality that is all too rare on the concert platform, a robustness and ability to sustain musical passages almost indefinitely, clarity of diction and, withal, a depth of feeling and remarkable dramatic expression that designates the true artist…. Originally engaged to fill a gap created by the forced cancellation early in the season of Lotte Lehmann's engagement, Nelson Eddy's versatility and personality are such that his re-engagement in future seasons may be regarded as a matter of course." [Note: The *Courier du Pacifique,* a French newspaper, noted that Nelson's "Vision Fugitive" was interpreted in impeccable French. Also a German paper reviewed the concert.]

[Note: After signing with RKO on Saturday, March 4, and canceling the rest of his tour, Nelson found himself a free man again on Monday the 6th. He figured he was through with Hollywood, and continued with his previously scheduled singing engagements.]

March 8, 1933: Nelson sang in Fresno, California. *Fresno Bee Republican:* "Eddy's success was nothing less than a sensation. From the moment he rushed on the stage for his first number until two hours later, he rushed off after his last encore, there was not a wasted minute. In addition to a long and heavy program he must have sung a dozen encores, and always in response to a persistent demand for more. It looked for a while as though the lights would have to be turned out on the crowd to get them to go home. The empty seats consisted a real tragedy, for the ticket holders who stayed at home missed one of the most enjoyable concert programs in many years…. Eddy combines a good voice, well trained and in perfect control, with a most extraordinary personality. His success is due quite as much to the one as to the other. He is an absolute dynamo of activity, and he simply radiates good nature and good health. He startles his audience first with his breathtaking appearance, and then he captivates them with his really fine singing and acting and generosity. His voice is a baritone of excellent range and flexibility, not particularly rich or colorful, but very true and usable. His diction is natural and unstudied and his breath-control is phenomenal, amounting to little less than sheer exhibitionism at times."

March 10, 1933: Nelson sang in Boise, Idaho. A MGM representative tried to intercept him as he got off the train, but Nelson wasn't interested. *Idaho Free Press,* March 11, 1933, quoted Nelson: "Opera will come back. Our little company folded up so out we went. Singers must be made to sing in English so that audiences can understand. Radio singing is definitely harmful to the voice if radio station instructions are obeyed. They want the singer to sing softly – to hold his voice back. I refuse to do that." *Idaho Statesman,* March 11, 1933: "A tall, golden-haired lad with a big golden voice is Nelson Eddy, who held Boiseans enthralled for two hours Friday night by the magic of his song.... For one quality alone, if for no other, Eddy is deserving of the highest praise. Every word stood out distinct, gemlike. The enunciation was so perfect that his French and German were more understandable to the indifferent student of those tongues than the English of most singers." *Boise Capital News:* "He sang at least 10 encores, four of them after his program was completed. There was not a vestige of doubt in the minds of his audience that he is the rival of Lawrence Tibbett. His personality is striking and he is a comedian as well as a singer. He had no greatest hit, for his songs were all hits." *Boise Free Press* interviews him as to his ideal woman: "Don't I wish I knew," he responded with a trace of sadness in his voice. "I might make up my mind about her and then an entirely opposite type would come along and bang would go my theory... In general, she is so gorgeous, so beautiful, so wise, so gentle and understanding, so cultured, so full of life, that when I did find her she wouldn't' have me. This woman must also be educated and much smarter than I -- so she will make me do things and I won't know that she is making me do them. You know what I want--just a pal. And now let's talk about something else." [re: his mother] "She spends most of her time trying to keep me out of trouble. She has lots of attention paid to her and lots of beaux--many more than I have girls. I am quite jealous of her." Nelson reveals he has a New York and Philadelphia home. He's asked if his mother is a good cook. "Mr. Eddy looked hard pressed for a truthful answer. 'Well, when friends ask me if I want apple pie, I ask them if it is the kind my mother used to make and they always say 'yes.' Then I tell them I don't want it because my mother makes awfully punk apple pie.' They tried to sign him for a picture, but it didn't work out. 'It was a very nice musical picture.' He's asked about his diet. 'What do I eat? Am I careful about my diet? Goodness no, we aren't prima donnas. We're just a couple of young fellows out for a good time. I eat anything I want... I love children. I play tennis, ride horseback and sail boats. Those are my recreations.'"

March 13, 1933: Nelson gave an interview in Grand Island, Nebraska: "After this tour I may go to Europe. I don't know just what I will do. I have been abroad three times and have studied there." That evening he sang a concert at the senior high school. *Independent:* "Possessing a voice of remarkable beauty, Mr. Eddy has much more than this gift of nature to add to his singing. There is great satisfaction in the purity and resonance of his tone and as the program progressed the perfection of his technical equipment, his ability as an actor and his rare musicianship were increasingly evident while his direct and simple manner and engaging personality were extraordinarily pleasing."

[Note: In March 1933, Nelson sang in Decatur, Illinois and Lancaster, Pennsylvania.]

March 29, 1933: Nelson sang in Cleveland, Ohio. *Cleveland News:* "Eddy possesses one of the finest stage personalities I ever saw. A giant of a fellow, who beams a smile across the footlights, takes up the task in hand, and although it may sound like a bromide, he has every appearance of singing for the joy of it. His range is wholly adequate, being particularly notable in the booming lower tones, his diction is faultless, and he sang and sang and sang, when he wasn't bowing, bowing and bowing, because it was what might be termed a sensationally successful local debut." *Plain Dealer:* "Eddy is a young singer whom America may be proud to call its own."

March 31, April 1 and April 3, 1933: Nelson sang Gurnemanz (a bass role) in **Parsifal**, with Stokowski conducting at the Academy of Music. The cast included Rose Bampton, Robert Steel, Dudley Marwick, Alexis Tcherkassky and Leonard Treash. A group of 12 singers from the Curtiss Institute of Music were flower maidens and the ensemble numbers were sung by the Brahms Chorus, Philadelphia Grand Opera chorus, and the glee clubs of Princeton University, Mt. St. Joseph's College and Bryn Mawr College. This was a concert version, with no cuts, over three days, and marked the American premiere radio broadcast of this opera. The first act was sung on the afternoon of March 31, second act on April 1st and the last act on April 3rd. *Philadelphia Record,* April 1, 1933: "Nelson Eddy, well known local singer, sang the part of Gurnemanz, a role which carries the greatest part of the vocal score of the first act. He gave a splendid performance, admirable in its dignity and force... The part is a trying one, containing long passages made necessary in the opera. It was one of the finest, if not the finest, thing he had done locally in his successful career." *Evening Bulletin:* "Mr.

PUBLIC LEDGER—PHILADELPHIA, SUNDAY MORNING, MARCH 26, 1933

·ERAS, RECITALS FEATURE M

Principals in "Parsifal" Performance

NELSON EDDY
"Gurnemanz"

ROSE BAMPTON
"Kundry"

ROBERT STEEL
"Parsifal"

Orchestra Will Present 'Parsifal'

One Act Will Be Given at Each of Three Concerts

WAGNER .... "PARSIFAL"
Leopold Stokowski conducting.

FRIDAY AFTERNOON
Act I

Prelude.
Scene 1. In the domain of the Holy Grail.
Intermission
Scene 2. In the hall of the castle of the Holy Grail.

SATURDAY EVENING
Act II

Prelude.
In the keep of Klingsor's magic castle.
In the garden of the Flowermaidens.
Intermission
Act III
Interlude.
Finale. In the hall of the Holy Grail.

MONDAY EVENING
Act III

Prelude.
Scene 1. Landscape in the domain of the Holy Grail.
Intermission
Scene 2. In the hall of the Holy Grail.

The first presentation of the complete score of Richard Wagner's "Parsifal" will be given, with the three acts presented consecutively at three separate performances, by the Philadelphia Orchestra, with Leopold Stokowski conducting at the next concerts. At those, next Friday afternoon and Saturday evening, will be given the first and second acts of the opera complete, with the addition to the Saturday night's program of the finale from the third act in the hall of the Holy Grail. At the Monday evening concert, on April 3, the third act of the opera will be given in its entirety.

Assisting the orchestra will be six well-known soloists, eighteen artist-students from the Curtis Institute of Music, who will fill minor roles; and a chorus of 350 voices. These singers, all volunteers, have been recruited from the ranks of eleven organizations in Philadelphia and vicinity, making a chorus of approximately 200 men's voices, thirty boy's voices and 115 women singers.

The feature of the three-day presentation, according to Mr. Stokowski, is the use of Wagner's original "Parsifal" score, which for the first time will be given by the orchestra here without cuts or omissions.

The assisting soloists will be Robert Steel, in the role of "Parsifal"; Rose Bampton, as "Kundry," Nelson Eddy, as "Gurnemanz"; Alexis Tcherkassky as "Amfortas," Dudley Marwick, as "Klingsor," and Leonard Treash, as "Titurel." The roles of the First and Second Knights will be sung respectively by Eugene Ramey and Benjamin de Loache. The four esquires will be Agnes Davis, Edwina Eustis, Daniel Healy and Eugene Lowenthal. The Flowermaidens will be sung by Marie Buddy, Irra Petina, Paceli Diamond, Henrietta Horle, Irene Beamer, Ruth Gordon, Irene Wallington, Ruth Carhart, Irene Singer, Cecelia Thompson, Agnes Davis and Edwina Eustis.

At the Friday afternoon performance will be given the prelude and Scene 1 in the domain of the Holy Grail. After the intermission will be the second scene in the hall of the castle of the Holy Grail. The men's voices will be supplied by singers from the following organizations: Brahms Chorus, N. Lindsay Norden, conductor; Fortnightly Club, Henry Gordon Thunder, conductor; Bach Society of Delaware County, James Allan Dash, conductor; Princeton University Glee Club, Alexander Russell, conductor; Haverford College, William P. Bentz, conductor; and the Reading Choral Society, N. Lindsay Norden, director. The boys' voices will be supplied by St. Mark's Choir.

On Saturday evening, there will be the prelude to the second act, followed by the scene in the keep of Klingsor's magic castle and the scene in the garden of the Flowermaidens. After the intermission there will follow an orchestral interlude and the final scene from the third act of the opera in the hall of the Holy Grail.

In addition to the mens' organizations used on Friday, there will be utilized for the Flowermaiden scene women singers from the following organizations: Bryn Mawr College, F. H. Ernest Willoughby, conductor; the Curtis Institute of Music, Sylvan Levin, conductor; Mt. St. Joseph's College, Sister Regina Dolores, director, and the Philadelphia Grand Opera Chorus, Sylvan Levin, conductor.

The Monday evening performance will open with the prelude to the third act, which will be followed by the scene laid in the landscape in the domain of the Holy Grail. Following the intermission will be the second and final scene of the opera in the hall of the Holy Grail.

Eddy… truly a worthy successor to Michael Bohnen, who was an ideal Gurnemanz."[Note: About ten minutes excerpt of this opera can be heard – only in fair sound – on the Mac/Eddy Series #123, "Operatic Recital #3." It is the only known existing recording of Nelson Eddy singing in an actual opera.]

April 10, 1933: Nelson sang in Pawtucket. Unnamed paper: "Mr. Eddy was in rare good voice, and brought a spirit of joviality to his home city which increased with each number. His power of endurance in being able to render his full program and also to add eight 'encore' pieces in equally strong voice, was a remarkable achievement." *Newport News:* "The critic heartily agreed with everybody else that this concert was in a class by itself, and the ordinary sort of criticism was just forgotten."

April 18, 1933: Nelson sang in Lowell, Massachusetts.

[Note: On April 22, according to newspaper reports, Nelson signed an MGM contract.]

April 23, 1933: Nelson sang in Norwalk, Connecticut. *Norwalk Hour,* April 24, 1933: "It is impossible to be cold and calculating when judging Nelson Eddy's art…. There were many phases of artistry to be admired yesterday – first of all his tone, of gorgeous quality, beautiful sonority, of a warmth and liquidity rarely found in the baritone vocal range; next, a maturity and depth of interpretation almost belieing (sic) his youth; then, diction which was well-night perfect; the, marvelous breath control, a felicity of phrasing; a flair for the dramatic which made every song more of a little drama than the written word could possibly ever do; plus a much-heralded but completely realized manly pulchritude to delight the eye – plus – but words are poor things, after all, in describing that which is ne plus ultra."

April 27, 1933: Nelson sang in Schenectady. *Union-Star,* April 28, 1933: "Eddy possesses a fine voice of exceptionally even development, a power of sensitive interpretation and a fascinating personality. He received an ovation on his appearance last night, and kept his audience completely with him throughout the program."

May 16, 1933: Nelson sang in Sunbury.

May 24, 1933: Nelson sang in Albany. Review: "Singing in splendid voice, he succeeded in projecting into each interpretation much of his own exciting personality, much of the spirit of the several composers. Confident, dynamic, he acted as well as sang each number, as though already he was facing cameras, as though he were living in that exotic world toward which he is destined."

June 1933: Nelson reported to MGM. He unsuccessfully tested for a small role in Greta Garbo's **Queen Christina**. Then the trades started announcing a number of musical films he might make, all with Jeanette MacDonald. Jeanette had also just signed with the studio but was in Europe and wouldn't report to the studio until the end of July.

June 9, 1933: Nelson mentioned again as being on the Socony-Vacuum Radio Show, details unknown.

[Note: Nelson's voice teacher around this time was Dr. Lazar Samoiloff, a Russian baritone who had sung in the Moscow and Odessa Operas. Samoiloff's daughter Zepha was also hired as a companion for Nelson's mother Isabel while Nelson left again on tour in 1934. Nelson studied with Samoiloff until late 1934 when he returned to Eduoard Lippe. This was while **Naughty Marietta** was being filmed and Lippe also had a small role in the film.]

Summer, 1933: Nelson filmed his single scenes for **Dancing Lady** and **Broadway to Hollywood**. Both films had gone into production in June, but **Dancing Lady** was an "A" picture and took longer to complete. [Note: After seeing how plump Nelson photographed, studio head Louis B. Mayer put Nelson on his "chicken soup" diet. By the time Nelson filmed his spot for **Broadway to Hollywood** he was his thinnest ever.]

THE PHILADELPHIA INQUIRER, WEDNESDAY MORN[ING]

Nelson Eddy to Sing on Screen Opposite Jeanette MacDonald; Random Shots of Hollywood Folk

By LOUELLA O. PARSONS
(Copyright 1933)

LOS ANGELES, April 25.

EIGHTEEN encores for one solo at the Philharmonic brought Nelson Eddy, operatic and concert singer, to the attention of Louis B. Mayer. Plenty of singers loose in the world, but not many of them with this Lawrence Tibbett personality. Eddy has it, and now it is to be circulated through the medium of the screen by Metro-Goldwyn-Mayer. He was signed by Mayer.

Jeanette MacDonald

Nelson Eddy

The new screen discovery reaches here August 1 and his first picture will be "I Married an Angel" opposite Jeanette MacDonald. Interesting history attached to Eddy, whose home is in Philadelphia, who started in life as a choir boy. He made his debut in "Pagliacci" in 1924.

* * *

Beverly Wilshire. She was with Laddie Sanford; Colleen Moore and Al Scott. The

job as news editor of the student publication after a two-day spree in which he employed his temporary power as editor-in-chief to launch

"The purpose of m[y] been accomplished," took dynamite to a[n] and dynamite was

APRIL 26, 1933

Nelson Eddy Signed to Act In Pictures

Nelson Eddy, who sang in the Schenectady concert of the Thursday Musical Club last night, has been signed for a motion picture contract by Louis B. Mayer, president of Metro-Goldwyn-Mayer. The contract, it was learned yesterday, followed the call for 18 encores after Eddy sang one song with the Los Angeles Philharmonic Society recently.

Mr. Eddy will go to Hollywood June 7 to begin production of "I Married an Angel," in which he will be co-starred with Jeanette MacDonald. He will sing with the Mendelssohn Club of Albany on May 24.

The newest star of the concert stage and talkies made his debut in "Pagliacci" in 1924. He began as a choir boy in Rhode Island.

EDDY GOING TO HOLLYWOOD

Singer Will Play Opposite Jeanette MacDonald

Nelson Eddy, operatic singer, is going to Hollywood.

He has signed a contract with Metro-Goldwyn-Mayer and will start a picture in August, playing opposite Jeanette MacDonald, a Philadelphia girl. "I Married an Angel" is to be the title of the production.

Nelson Eddy

Eddy, who is 31 and lives at 13th and Spruce sts., came to the attention of the picture company when he was given 18 encores after a solo at the Philharmonic in Los Angeles.

He was employed as a reporter on The Bulletin, and with an advertising company. He sang with the Philadelphia Grand Opera Company, and two weeks ago he was soloist at the Philadelphia Orchestra presentation of "Parsifal."

September 15, 1933: **Broadway to Hollywood** released to lukewarm success. Nelson is heard singing one short song as a vaudevillian named "John Sylvester" but is only pictured onscreen for a few seconds; the rest of the time the camera is elsewhere, featuring a loud argument going on backstage. Nelson's brief appearance was only noted in one newspaper, the ever-loyal *Philadelphia Inquirer*: "Nelson Eddy makes an unfortunate debut as a 'ham' vaudeville singer."

Eddy Making M-G-M Film

Nelson Eddy, baritone, now in Hollywood under contract to Metro-Goldwyn-Mayer by arrangement with his managers, Columbia Concerts Corporation, is to make his screen début in The Prisoner of Zenda opposite Jeanette MacDonald. Mr. Eddy is of the opinion that experience in the films does a great deal to improve the acting of the opera singer. He cites Lawrence Tibbett as an example of such development.

Although Mr. Eddy is under contract to Metro-Goldwyn-Mayer until Christmas time, the company has given him permission to sing five engagements on the Pacific Coast during that period. On October 23 Mr. Eddy gives a recital in Fresno and during November appears in San Diego, Claremont, Los Angeles, and San Francisco.

When his first picture is finished he will start his concert activities. During January and February he is booked for a tour opening in Canada with engagements in St. John, N. B., Charlottetown, Prince Edward's Island, Halifax, N. S., and Kitchener, Ont. His next engagements are for recitals in Great Neck, N. Y., Norfolk, Va., Harrisburg, Pa., Syracuse, and Troy, N. Y., Scranton, and Pittsburgh, Pa., Columbus, O., St. Paul, Minn., Appleton, Wis., Louisville, Ky., Wheeling, W. Va., Roanoke, Va., Peoria, Ill., Hattiesburg, Miss., Birmingham, Ala., and Cleveland, O.

MC 7-29-33

October 23, 1933: Nelson sang in Fresno.

November 9, 1933, Nelson and Jeanette sang (separately) at Marie Dressler's birthday party, which was broadcast.

November 10, 1933: Nelson sang in San Diego.

November 21, 1933: Nelson sang with the Los Angeles Philharmonic. (This is the concert at which Jeanette walked in fifteen minutes late to audience recognition and buzz, and Nelson called out "It's a good thing you're pretty!"). *Hollywood Citizen News*: "Many movie folk were in evidence in the audience and they evinced sincere enthusiasm. Eddy… sang with beautiful ease and assurance, in a voice of lovely baritone quality, resonant and of fine timbre. While his extreme high and low tones might be somewhat improved to compare with the even timbre of his normal range, his singing was virtually perfect vocal production, given with admirable style and an inimitable quality of characterization."

November 22, 1933: Nelson sang in San Francisco (Jeanette MacDonald attended).

November 24, 1933: **Dancing Lady** released. Nelson sang a full number and was billed as himself. *Philadelphia Inquirer*: "Nelson Eddy, Philadelphia baritone who made good in opera and concert, and turned a willing ear to Hollywood's siren song, is to be seen and heard in one musical number as a typical revue singer."

December 22 and 23, 1933: Nelson was guest soloist with the San Francisco symphony concerts. *Musical West*, January 1934: "Mr. Eddy has an unusual vocal equipment, breadth of tone and a free production, plenty of power and a beautiful quality. It appears highly probable that America will have reason to be proud of this native son in the years to come."

[Note: By the end of 1933, Nelson's manager Arthur Judson reported that Nelson has performed in the past two seasons: 59 song recitals, 30 concert, orchestra and oratorio performances, 65 radio appearances, 8 opera performances, 28 special church services and 3 film appearances. The films were **Dancing Lady**, **Broadway to Hollywood** (which was released before **Dancing Lady** and so is officially considered Nelson's "first" film, and **Student Tour** (which was released in 1934: Nelson played himself and had grown a rather hopeless mustache).]

January 3, 1934: Nelson sang again in San Francisco. [Note: He flew from Los Angeles and got so airsick that he debated canceling; in the end, he went on because he didn't want to lose the night's pay.]

January 4, 1934: The trades announce that Nelson will co-star with Jeanette MacDonald in **Naughty Marietta**. [Note: Nelson's contract would have lapsed at the end of 1933, but due to his sudden good fortune, on January 5th it was announced in the trades that he had signed a new, long-term contract.]

January 8, 1934: Nelson sang in Santa Barbara (Jeanette MacDonald attended).

[Note: On January 12, 1934: Nelson sang in Claremont, California, then headed north for a January 13 concert in San Francisco and an Oakland concert on January 16. From there he headed East.]

January 26, 1933: Nelson sang in Halifax, Nova Scotia. *Mail,* January 27: "There is in [Nelson's] baritone voice which has won him such fame a singularly haunting resonant timbre that individualizes it and instantly arrests... He is as distinguished a comedian as he is a singer. The evening abounded in proof of it... [He] is on an exacting tour with three concerts a week until the end of May, when Mr. Eddy is to be back in California to go on with his moving picture work."

[Note: Nelson's concert dates included January 29: Portland, Maine, February 8: Harrisburg and February 15: Scranton, Pennsylvania.]

February 18, 1934: Nelson gave a Town Hall recital in New York City. (Jeanette MacDonald most likely attended, as she had taken the train to New York several days earlier and newspapers on the 19th commented that she had just arrived.) *New York American:* "Mr. Eddy's fine voice and excellent interpretations are well known to N.Y. audiences, but none of them ever heard him in more complete command of his tonal and musical resources than at this recital. He employed exquisite 'half-voice', chiseled his phrases faultlessly and featured a breathing technic of remarkable control and repose. Mr. Eddy made an overwhelming hit with his atmospheric and feeling presentation of this delightful set of pieces (in the last one of which he trilled like a coloratura)." *New York Sun:* "In a number of ways the singing that Mr. Eddy accomplished was a quality to invite enthusiasm; he commands a scale to beautiful evenness; the placement of his voice is admirable; its texture is firm; its lyric richness has not been corrupted by misuse." *Musical America,* February 251, 1934: "Nelson Eddy, in his first song-program here, formally joined the ranks of America's foremost baritones after having established himself elsewhere.... His beautiful voice, mellow in quality and rich in color, has smooth and resourceful technique in

'Joy to Sing'

NELSON EDDY, baritone, enthusiastic yesterday over his rehearsal for concerts with San Francisco Symphony tonight.

THE SAN FRANCISCO EXAMINER: FRIDAY, DECEMBER 22, 1933

Curran Th...

S. F. CONCERT THRILLS SINGER

Nelson Eddy, noted baritone, came to San Francisco yesterday to attain the fulfillment of a long desired experience—that of singing Wagner's "Wotan's Farewell," with a fine orchestra under an able leader and in a fitting environment.

Eddy explained the desire after he had rehearsed yesterday with the San Francisco Symphony Orchestra in the War Memorial Opera House. As guest artist he will appear in concerts with the Symphony tonight and Saturday night at the Opera House.

"I am thrilled beyond words," he said. "It is a joy to sing here."

Members of the Symphony enthusiastically applauded Eddy at the conclusion of the rehearsal, and Issay Dobrowen, conductor, shook Eddy's hand with the praise:

"You are the finest of the young artists of this generation that I have heard."

all that pertained to voice production and word clarity, the variety and expressiveness of his interpretations and the winning quality of his personality united to make this first Manhattan song program a success such as ordinarily is won only by those artists on the high road to an enduring fame."

[Note: During February and March, Nelson continued touring in the Eastern U.S.]

March 23, 1934: Nelson and Rose Bampton gave a concert in Pittsburgh. *Press:* "Mr. Eddy's voice is of uncommonly fine texture throughout its enviable range, and whether he essays top, middle or low notes his production is as effortless as it is easy to listen to."

March 29, 1934: Nelson sang on radio for the "Ford Sunday Evening Hour." [He would appear on this show periodically well into the 1940s.]

[Note: During April 1934, Nelson was still touring on the East Coast.]

May 28, 1934: Nelson sang on NBC radio on a program called "Ship of Joy," details unknown.

June 25, 1934: Nelson and Jeanette sang together at the Marion Davies Foundation benefit at the Biltmore Bowl.

August 2, 1934: Nelson sang at the Hollywood Bowl in an all-Wagner concert. *Los Angeles Examiner,* August 3, 1934: "Nelson Eddy, with his beautiful baritone voice and fine stage presence, was the outstanding figure in last night's Bowl concert. The singer gave the poignant 'Wahn Wahn' from **Die Meistersinger** as his first number, and when the audience thundered continuous plaudits, returned to the stage and added the aria 'To the Evening Star' from **Tannhäuser**." *Hollywood Citizen News:* "Nelson Eddy won his audience at once, and was recalled many times after each number by vehement and prolonged applause. He sang with fine musicianship and a voice of exceptionally beautiful quality. His resonant tones came cleanly through the full orchestra mass, in true pitch and ringing overtones. He appeared to have gained somewhat in resonance since his last concert appearance here, and if he continues as he undoubtedly will, he should become one the great baritones of musical history.... Every word, both in German and English, was clearly enunciated and distinctly understandable. In 'Wahn, Wahn' from **The Meistersingers** he obviously deeply felt the role of Sachs, and expressed the famous cobbler's philosophy with ardent sincerity. He chose to give the 'Song to the Evening Star' from **Tannhäuser** in English, a finely poetic version which lost nothing in the translation and added much to the enjoyment of the auditors. He gave a memorable reading of the tremendous 'Farewell' of Wotan from **The Valkyries**.... The airplane nuisance was renewed again with no less than three planes audible in the sky within a period of ten minutes. Such stupid pilots may yet manage to run into each other if they continue to fly close to the Bowl merely to annoy the music lovers."

August 24, 1934: Nelson sang again at the Hollywood Bowl in a concert version of **Carmen**. Co-stars were Nina Koshetz and tenor Tandy Mackenzie.

October 5, 1934: **Student Tour** was released into theaters. *Los Angeles Times:* "It is disappointing not to see more of Mr. Eddy, who radiated vitality plus a suave acting style." *Variety:* "Nelson Eddy is worked into the final scene at the Monte Carlo party, effectively doing a baritone solo." [Note: In some ads, Nelson is the only person pictured, with this title: "You'll thrill to see Nelson Eddy singing The Carlo."]

October 6, 1934, *Hollywood Citizen News:* "Nelson Eddy and the Los Angeles Philharmonic Orchestra, conducted by Nathaniel Finston, will be heard at from KHJ. Mr. Eddy will sing 'The Dusty Road,' 'Journey's End,' 'The Carlo,' and an aria from **Manna** (sic) **Vanna."**

November 1934: Nelson began singing once or twice monthly on the "Voice of Firestone" radio show.

November 6, 1934: Nelson sang **The Secret of Suzanne** at the Los Angeles Shrine Auditorium. His co-star was silent film star Doris Kenyon. [Kenyon apparently introduced Nelson to her close friend and his future wife, Ann Franklin.] Nelson's then-voice coach, Edouard Lippe, sang the role of Sante. *Musical Courier*, November 17, 1934: "Doris Kenyon, soprano, a familiar film figure, and Nelson Eddy, baritone, made their operatic debuts and were gladly welcomed. They gave a vocally lively reading of this comedy of errors. Attendance and interest ran uncommonly high because of the Doris Kenyon and Nelson Eddy operatic first appearance. They sang with assurance of veterans, adhering to vocal standard of fine taste." [Note: In general the Los Angeles press thought the opera "mediocre and banal" but found the singers excellent. Much ado was made over the fact that Jeanette MacDonald was in the audience, and the critics described in detail what she was wearing.] *Los Angeles Examiner*: "Nelson Eddy is possessed of as beautiful a baritone voice as mere mortals have the right of expecting to hear... One wonders why he should be languishing in motion pictures when the opera stage needs him so."

Monday Night, November 26, at 7:45
Saturday Night, December 8, at 7:45

TANNHAUSER

Opera in three acts and four scenes. Music and text (in German)
by Richard Wagner

THE CAST

Elizabeth, *niece of Hermann*	ELISABETH RETHBERG
Tannhauser, *a minstrel knight*	*LAURITZ MELCHIOR
Venus	QUERITA EYBEL
Herman, *landgrave of Thuringia*	EZIO PINZA
Wolfram (*Minstrel knights*)	NELSON EDDY
Walther (*Minstrel knights*)	MAREK WINDHEIM
Biterolf (*Minstrel knights*)	ALFREDO GANDOLFI
Heinrich (*Minstrel knights*)	RAYMOND MARLOWE
Reinmar (*Minstrel knights*)	LOUIS D'ANGELO
A Young Shepherd	LILLIAN CLARK

*San Francisco début.

Chorus of Thuringian Nobles and Knights, Ladies, Elder and Younger Pilgrims, Sirens, Naiads, Nymphs, Bacchantes

Incidental Dances Arranged by ADOLPH BOLM
Irene Isham, principal dancer, with Carla Bradley, Irene Flyzik, Nicholas Visilieff; and Corps de Ballet
Three Graces: Clare Lauché, Iris de Luse, Victoria Albertson

Conductor: ALFRED HERTZ
Stage Director: ARMANDO AGNINI
Chorus Master: ANTONIO DELL'OREFICE

TIME AND PLACE: Beginning of the Thirteenth Century; Vicinity of Eisenach

ACT I	Scene 1	Within the Hill of Venus
	Scene 2	A Valley near the Castle of Wartburg
ACT II		The Great Hall of Song, Castle of Wartburg
ACT III		The Valley of the Wartburg

Bell rings three minutes before curtain rises
Encores not permitted

November 12, 1934: Nelson sang on "The Voice of Firestone" with Richard Crooks and Gladys Swarthout. His numbers were "Sylvia" and "Di Provenza" from **La Traviata**.

November 12, 1934, *Hollywood Citizen News:* "Jeanette MacDonald and Nelson Eddy are scheduled to start today on the musical, **Naughty Marietta** which W.S. Van Dyke will direct."

November 17, 1934: Nelson again on "Voice of Firestone".

November 20, 1934: Nelson sang in Claremont, California.

November 23, 1934: Nelson sang in Fresno.

November 26, 1934: Nelson sang with the San Francisco Opera in **Tannhäuser;** co-stars were Lauritz Melchior. Ezio Pinza and Elisabeth Rethburg..

November 27, 1934: Nelson sang in Los Angeles. *Hollywood Citizen News:* "It will be a different Nelson Eddy who appears tonight in a song recital at Philharmonic Auditorium. For weeks he has lived in retirement, devoting all his time to studying – and to growing whiskers. The crop has turned out to be a good one, and it will be an interesting spectacle to watch the crowd's reactions when he steps on the stage. Eddy has broken with the stereotyped concert program. He sings groups of Italian, French and English songs in addition to a series of baritone solos from **Die Meistersinger**." *Los Angeles Examiner,* November 28, 1934: "A colorful program provided magnificent opportunity for Nelson Eddy in his recital last night.... Few singers have presented a more varied and interesting list of vocal numbers than Mr. Eddy selected, and his songs in Italian and French were cordially received. To further enhance his standing as an artist of ambition and musicianship, the soloist included many numbers from **The Meistersinger** in the second part of his program. This was an innovation on the local concert stage and delighted his listeners…. 'L'Incontro,' by Santoliquide proved one of the highlights from the first group with the singer's beautiful legato well emphasized in the limpid phrases of the song. Comedy was evidenced in 'Au Pays' by Augusta Holmes, with a lightly staccato movement and the simulation of soldiers marching. The two encores following this were in light but eminently musicianly mood. Theodore Paxson provided excellent accompaniments and offered Chopin solos in an interesting style." *Hollywood Citizen News:* "Eddy unquestionably has all the qualifications for one of the outstanding vocal talents of the present generation. His baritone voice is of exceptional beauty in its fresh, virile timbre, it is even from top to bottom, and he handles it with artistic style and finesse, while his enunciation is a continual joy to the ear. A fine stage presence, good looks and histrionic ability contribute to make one of the most enjoyable musical personalities now before the public…. The highlight of the evening was his selection of songs from Wagner's **Meistersingers**, arranged in a continuity of his own devising…. 'Smilin' Through' was an unfortunately banal final encore, and of course all the ballads suffered by comparison with the finer work preceding them."

No date, *Chicago Tribune* clipping: "I did four days work in **Dancing Lady**, in a bit that ran one-half minute on the screen. In **Student Tour** I appear for three minutes in 'The Carlo' number. Yet I am amazed to see the results that I am getting from these in my fan mail. There is no doubt that going in the films does an opera singer an amazing amount of good with the public."

December 8, 1934: Nelson sang **Tannhäuser** again at the San Francisco Opera House, with the same co-stars. *San Francisco News,* December 9, 1934: "Nelson Eddy made a tremendously fine impression. His voice was rich and resonant… He belongs in that fine group of baritones which includes Lawrence Tibbett, Richard Bonelli and John Charles Thomas." *Musical Courier,* December 22, 1934: "Eddy replaced Bonelli in the part of Wolfram and sang admirably."

December 18, 1934, *Hollywood Citizen News:* "Nelson Eddy will be appearing at 8:30 over KFI. The baritone will interpret 'Brindisi' from Thomas' **Hamlet**, 'Kashmiri Song,' 'Water Boy,' and 'La Paloma.' At least, those are the numbers he is scheduled to sing."

December 27, 1934: Nelson sang with the Los Angeles Philharmonic.

[Note: In March 1935, **Naughty Marietta** was released and became a smash hit. On March 11, Nelson recorded the hit songs from the film for RCA. He then left on his concert tour, to find he was now a super-star and his life was changed forever. The following are some of his comments.]

April 13, 1935, *New York Telegram:* "A great many singers think that strenuous exercise is bad on their voices. Personally I've never found that to be so. I've never done anything or refrained from doing anything because of my voice. I eat what and when I like, smoke frequently, take a drink occasionally, and in general do just about anything I like…. Singers are the most childish, the most conceited people of any on earth. My prayer has been that I might remain normal and be myself."

April 23, 1935, *Richmond News Leader:* "I always thought it was silly for these movie stars to have bodyguards and personal representatives and secretaries and what not. But now I've got to do all that. And I don't like it."

April 20, 1935, *Newark Evening News:* "Movies are only secondary. I haven't changed my personal ambitions in the least. I have always known what I wanted to do and Hollywood isn't going to thwart me…. When a thing like this happens to you the people you used to go to for counsel are no help, they all turn into 'yes men'. This business of the future is a one-man proposition. I've got to work it out myself. I don't know all the answers yet but I know what I want to do, what I am determined to try to achieve."

May 30, 1935: Nelson sang the Second Puritan in the world premiere of Howard Hanson's **The Merry Mount**, in Ann Arbor, Michigan. His costars were Rose Bampton and John Charles Thomas.

Programme

AIDA

Monday Night, November 11, at 8:00

Opera in four acts and seven scenes. Music by Giuseppe Verdi
Text (in Italian) by Antonio Ghislanzoni

Aida, *an Ethiopian slave* . . . . ELISABETH RETHBERG
Amneris, *daughter of the Egyptian King* . . . KATHRYN MEISLE
Rhadames, *captain of the Egyptian guard* . GIOVANNI MARTINELLI
Amonasro, *King of Ethiopia (Aïda's father)* . . . NELSON EDDY
Ramfis, *High Priest of Isis* . . . . EZIO PINZA
The King of Egypt . . . . DOUGLAS BEATTIE
Messenger . . . . MAREK WINDHEIM
Priestess . . . . GERALDINE WATT

Priests, Priestesses, Ministers, Captains, Soldiers, Officials, Ethiopian Slaves and Prisoners, Egyptians, etc.

Incidental Dances arranged by ADOLPH BOLM
Frances Giugni, Evelyn Wenger, Eccleston Moran, Elva Dimpfel, Principal Dancers; and Corps de Ballet

Conductor: GAETANO MEROLA
Stage Director: ARMANDO AGNINI
Chorus Master: ANTONIO DELL'OREFICE

TIME AND PLACE: In Pharaoh's Time; Memphis and Thebes

Act 1	Scene 1	Hall in King's Palace at Memphis
	Scene 2	Temple of Isis
Act II	Scene 1	A Hall in Amneris' Apartment
	Scene 2	The Gate of Thebes
Act III		Shores of Nile, near Temple of Isis
Act IV	Scene 1	Outside the Judgment Hall
	Scene 2	Above—In Temple of Vulcan
		Below—Vault beneath the Temple

Bell rings three minutes before curtain rises
Encores not permitted

[Over]

[Note: Nelson's opera career had ended, except for one final **Aida**. He would continue a yearly concert tour and a weekly radio show, but his life had been trans-planted to Los Angeles and his interests and career decisions would largely be centered around the movies and his constant co-star in that medium, Jeanette MacDonald. The difference in Nelson was evident by reviews such as the following, from late 1935.]

Los Angeles Times: "To most of the auditors, Eddy's musical peak was attained with his rendition of 'Ah, Sweet Mystery of Life.' When he de-clared, 'I don't sing it without Jeanette MacDonald,' the audience applauded vociferously, in the obvious hope that she would emerge from the audience in approved vaudeville style and make it a duo. But she went only so far as to bow, and exchange salutations."

Screenplay Magazine, Lee Temple: "In Hollywood these days the name Jeanette MacDonald is the best romantic copy. Every day one sees her name coupled with either that of her manager, Bob Ritchie, or Gene Raymond. Each one has had it said about him that he will be the lucky one to lead Miss MacDonald to the altar, and maybe one of them will, but some can't help but discount it. There seems to be something stronger behind all this. Many can't help but feel that in **Naughty Marietta** and in Jeanette MacDonald, Nelson Eddy has found the antidote for loneliness. They can't help but feel that if it wasn't for Eddy's sanely and sensibly looking at the situation, long before this the newspapers and magazines would have been running stories of their romance. Just recently something happened to confirm these feelings…. Eddy was appearing in a concert in Los Angeles. Jeanette MacDonald was there in the audience; Eddy didn't know this. It came time for him to sing. He did. The applause demanded an encore. Nelson began, and the aria was 'Love's Old Sweet Song.' Suddenly he stopped, waved to his accompanist to stop. He took a step toward his audience and in a voice that seemed to quake a little, he said, 'This piece – this 'Love's Old Sweet Song,' without Jeanette MacDonald at my side, I doubt my ability to give it its proper interpretation. So please bear with me as I try to sing this lovely old favorite…. Out in the audience a woman rose from her seat – it was Miss MacDonald. For a few hurried moments they looked at one another. Then the song, and Nelson Eddy gave it a deep, soft interpretation that will last in the memory of every one who heard."

November 11, 1935: Nelson's opera career ended as it had begun, with **Aida**, sung at the San Francisco Opera. Co-stars were Elisabeth Rethberg, Kathryn Meisle, Giovanni Martinelli and Ezio Pinza. *San Francisco Examiner,* November 12, 1935: "Beautifully, nobly sung was the Amonasro of Nelson Eddy." *Oakland Tribune:* "Just for the sake of the record, let it be noted that, according to the management of the opera house, the crowd last night was the largest ever to witness an opera there – surpassing even the throngs which attended the opening in 1932." *Call-Bulletin:* "As Amonasro he burned with hatred and plotted with malevolence. His voice was produced with ease and rang with tremendous vitality. Hollywood has done much histrionically for the young baritone." Unknown clipping: "Nelson Eddy's Amonasro was something new – a vocally suave, handsome and royal Ethiopian King. His characterization made the relationship to Aida credible." More reviews: "We have never heard such a magnificent sextet at the close of the triumphal scene as Rethberg, Martinelli, Meisle, Eddy, Beattie and Pinza gave us last night." *San Francisco Chronicle:* "He is one of the great voices of the century, suave, aristocratic, yet as forceful as the music demands. He is one of the major reasons for believing that, at least so far as baritones are concerned, America need not import its future opera stars from abroad."

Jeanette MacDonald's Opera Career

While Nelson Eddy came from opera into films, Jeanette MacDonald did exactly the opposite. Her film career was virtually over and she was one month shy of forty before she finally stepped onto the opera stage. For a gal who'd wanted to be an opera singer since childhood, she certainly took her time getting around to it!

Lotte Lehman coached Jeanette in the mid 1940s and had this to say about her: "When Jeanette MacDonald approached me for some coaching lessons I was really curious how a glamorous movie star, certainly spoiled by the adoration of a limitless world, would be able to devote herself to another, a higher, level of art. I had the surprise of my life; there couldn't have been a more diligent, a more serious, a more pliable person than Jeanette. The lessons, which I started with a kind of suspicious curiosity, turned out to be sheer delight for me. She studied Marguerite with me – and Lieder. These were the ones which astounded me the most. I am quite sure that Jeanette would have developed into a serious and successful Lieder singer if time would have allowed it."[34]

With her voice teacher, Grace Newell.

There are those who feel Jeanette's voice was not operatic, or that the studio "manufactured" it, but this was untrue. She was a light, lyric soprano so perhaps it was a smaller voice. But to really hear what she was capable of, one should listen to her 1948 Hollywood Bowl Recital, which was broadcast on the air and is available to enjoy. There were no studio sound men to "tamper" with or "fix" the notes -- just Jeanette singing live with Nelson's accompanist Theodore Paxson and the orchestra. She sang arias, classical songs and her movie favorites. Even the toughest critic would be amazed at the power in her voice, as well as the length of time she held the high note in "Italian Street Song "— which drove the audience wild, by the way.

Ezio Pinza, who co-starred with her in both **Romeo et Juliette** and **Faust**, became irate when Jeanette's voice was maligned. "I loved singing with Jeanette," he asserted. "Those damn fools expected a grand diva rendition of Juliette. Jeanette sang her role as though she were fourteen years old entranced by love! As to her voice being thin and small I say bunk! It was beauty to the ear and to the eye an enchanting performance."

Playing Isolde in **Oh, For A Man.** *Her manager is a pre-* **Dracula** *Bela Lugosi.*

It's not really a matter of whether or not Jeanette was capable of having an opera career, because she was. The fact is that she just started it too late in life.

Jeanette Anna MacDonald was born in Philadelphia on June 18, 1903 into a middle class family. Her father wasn't particularly successful and died before Jeanette achieved real success. Stage mother Anna MacDonald steered her three talented daughters into show biz. Elsie, the oldest, played the piano; Blossom, the middle daughter, was a dancer, and Jeanette sang. But when Elsie eloped and Blossom started a vaudeville act with her husband, Anna pinned her hopes on her youngest and prettiest daughter.

Jeanette first sang before an audience at age three, and there was no stopping her from that point on. Throughout her early years she sang in kiddie vaudeville reviews and even cut a record. She had a fierce ambition, certainly as strong as Nelson's. Her goal was to "be a grand opera star and buy a gold bed and a pink limousine for mother."

When Blossom moved to New York to dance on Broadway, Jeanette followed her, happily dropping out of high school. From chorus girl she graduated to singing ingénue roles, receiving good reviews in plays that flopped. Throughout the 1920s she was on the stage until movie director Ernst Lubitsch "discovered" her and brought her to Hollywood in 1929.

In 1925, Jeanette auditioned for European conductor Ferdinand Torriani, one of the finest voice teachers in New York. (Torriani's father had trained Adelina Patti.) Torriani took Jeanette on as a student but when he died in 1926, Jeanette began studying with his associate, Grace Adele Newell.

Jeanette's first movie, **The Love Parade**, teamed her with Maurice Chevalier. The Paramount film was a smash hit, nominated for Best Picture and Actor, and made Jeanette an overnight movie star. Between 1929 and 1931 she made a total of nine films. After **The Love Parade**, none were particularly outstanding with the exception of **Monte Carlo** (1930), in which she introduced "Beyond the Blue Horizon." She looked gorgeous and sang prettily in an early Technicolor production of **The Vagabond King** (1930), but in a little-known Fox film, **Oh, For a Man** (1930), she played a temperamental opera singer similar to her **Rose Marie** character. The film's highlight was her singing 'Liebestod" in a staged scene from **Tristan and Isolde**.

Nineteen thirty-one found Jeanette burnt out with Hollywood. She felt her career was stagnating, so she took off to Europe for an extended concert tour. It was a triumph, especially in France, plus she was offered an opera contract. She turned it down, preferring like Nelson to sing at home. She returned to Paramount for two more films with Chevalier, then in 1933 sailed to Europe again for another tour. Similar again to Nelson, she repeatedly avoided MGM's persistent attempts to sign her up. But while in Europe she met up with Irving Thalberg and his wife Norma Shearer, and Thalberg convinced her to join the MGM family.

During her heyday, Jeanette sang many arias on film. She served as an inspiration to countless young girls wanting to sing opera, including future stars such as Joan Sutherland and Beverly Sills.

Nelson always gave Jeanette credit for teaching him how to act for the camera. What is lesser known is that he coached her on her singing and breath control. A careful listener will notice the difference in strength of her voice from **The Merry Widow** (1934), her last movie with Chevalier, and **Naughty Marietta** (1935).

As a team, Nelson and Jeanette were unbeatable. Nelson may have been the more seasoned singer, but Jeanette was a fine actress. Each brought different strengths to the union. Together they made onscreen opera and operetta a magical experience for audiences in a way that no other singers have ever done.

The strength of their chemistry as a team can be measured by the disappointing audience response to their solo MGM films. Live audiences who followed Nelson's radio career over the years were also quick to notice how they were "that way" in real life. Whenever Jeanette was his guest star, he demonstrated an unusual excitement and pride, and sang with more fervor and tenderness than normal.[35]

Jeanette never gave up her dream to sing live opera, even if Nelson had lost interest. When he walked out of MGM, she followed shortly after. Nelson looked to Universal Studios as possibly a new home for them, rushing right into **Phantom of the Opera** (1943), but Jeanette stepped up the voice lessons and prepared to start a new career.

With her good friend, Lily Pons.

In February 1943, a newspaper blurb announced that she would make her debut at the Metropolitan Opera in the fall in Gounod's **Romeo et Juliette**. This seems to have been a press plant, since the Met's manager, Edward Johnson, denied signing her or knowing anything about her plans. One of Jeanette's friends claimed that the Met wouldn't even consider Jeanette without an audition, that her friend Lily Pons arranged one, but Jeanette declined, realizing the Met didn't want her. The Metropolitan's archives do not indicate that an audition was ever held.

But she was determined to sing Juliet. Perhaps she chose Montreal for her debut because in the movie **Rose Marie**, she played an opera singer who sang Juliet in Montreal! Whatever the provocation, it was a shrewd choice. Jeanette landed a stellar cast, Ezio Pinza as Friar Lawrence and Armand Tokatyan as Romeo. Wilfred Pelletier -- Rose Bampton's husband -- conducted. To prepare for the role Jeanette coached with Pelletier and the Met's French bass Leon Rothier.

Rose Bampton told this author that her husband, Wilfred Pelletier ("Pelle"), was surprised and impressed with Jeanette. After all the years of unkind rumors that Jeanette's voice was manufactured for films, was inaudible, thin, and not suited for opera, Pelletier didn't know quite what to expect. "Pelle said she came so well prepared that she knew that role perfectly when she got here for the rehearsals," said Bampton. "Pelle had never worked with anyone like that before. He said she was absolutely marvelous, he never worked with an artist so eager to get things right. And he said she would stop and say, 'Oh, maestro, that wasn't quite right, could we try it again?' I never heard her performances because I was busy at the time, but if Pelle said she was great, she was great. I would believe him over the critics. He was very honest."[36]

Jeanette didn't begin yearly concert tours until 1939. Like Nelson, she sang operatic selections in all her concerts. And – as with Nelson, her fans patiently sat through all the "long hair" stuff, waiting for the movie songs.

Left: Jeanette portrayed Tosca in the final scene of the opera, from Rose Marie.

In San Francisco, *Jeanette played Violetta in* La Traviata. *One newspaper reviewer commented on the film: "Jeanette MacDonald is superb. Looking more attractive and appearing in better voice than ever before, she plays the part with uncommon charm, forbearance and emotional depth. Not onlyh does she give the finest performance oj her screen career, but she has never sung more thrillingly than she does here."*

This page: more of Jeanette's operatic scenes in films. Left: As Juliet in Rose Marie. *Bottom left: Singing "Un Bel Di" in* Broadway Serenade. *She repeated the aria in her last movie,* The Sun Comes Up, *which was released in 1949. Below: the Page Boy scene from* Les Hugeunots, *from* Maytime. *Bottom right: Snippets from* Carmen *and* Faust *were sung in* I Married An Angel. *Jeanette is pictured here as Marguerite.*

The Faust *trio as sung in* San Francisco.

One reviewer wrote of a Jeanette concert: "Such beauty is in her that she could have just stood there and recited the alphabet."

"She was a beautiful and sensitive Juliet, poetic in the balcony scene and passionate in the last two scenes," Pelletier later wrote. "Her success as an operatic singer was genuine, and as a colleague she was admired and beloved by her companions, the orchestra and the chorus."[37]

Jeanette overworked herself preparing, fell ill and had to delay final rehearsals in Montreal. She claimed she had pneumonia and was still unwell on opening night, although the cast and audience were unaware of her discomfort. Her debut on May 8, 1943 was "a triumph for Miss MacDonald and an honor to Montreal," according to the *Montreal Gazette.* "The voice is sweet in quality. It has in person that sureness and cleanness which has always been noted in the soprano's screen work and has made her one of the most accomplished singers Hollywood ever had.... Her personal beauty, softer and more fragile than when seen through the eye of the camera, was admirably suited to the part."

"She telephoned me from Montreal on Mother's Day, the morning after the opera," wrote Jeanette's mother Anna MacDonald. "I had been worried because of her illness and wondered if she would be able to stand the ordeal of opening in a brand new role in a new field with a bad cold. The succeeding performances at Quebec and Ottawa have been just as sensational and much easier for her, I am very thankful to say."[38]

In Toronto Jeanette also received raves. "Not a quiver spoiled the limpid steadiness of her light floating voice," noted the *Toronto Telegram.* "Her tones were sweet, serene and comforting to the very last." "Most of Juliet's music is for middle voice and the sincerity of her phrasing and tender beauty of her production carried conviction at all times," added the *Globe and Mail.* "Her middle and lower tones are singularly warm and beautiful." At the end of the performance when Jeanette took a solo bow, the audience rose to their feet, stamped, cheered and whistled. One reviewer noted, "It was, in fact, the most deafening demonstration of approval I have ever heard in my life."

Over the next year, Jeanette was wrapped up with concertizing and raising money for the war effort. She also pushed herself traveling in the States until she collapsed with a breakdown.[39] By the fall of 1944 she had recuperated and was ready for her American debut as Juliet, at the Chicago Lyric Opera on November 4. (The other cast members included Captain Michael Bartlett, USMC and Nicola Moscona.)

Most of the reviews were gratifying after all the months of preparation (which Jeanette termed "the grimmest time of my life"). "Jeanette MacDonald set her Juliet cap at opera and to judge by the uproar, opera capitulated," wrote *Chicago Tribune* critic Claudia Cassidy. "Her Juliet is breathtakingly beautiful to the eye and dulcet to the ear… an exquisite performance within her vocal limitations, and considering the way she looks, not many are going to quibble about a few notes here and there." "A personal triumph," praised the *Herald-Tribune*, nicknaming her the "Princess of Opera." *The Sun* noted: "The singer has the small, almost adolescent voice, which gave her vocalism the girlish timbre at least, which some other Juliets of operatic history – most of them fair, fat and forty – generally have lacked."

With Ezio Pinza.

On November 15, Jeanette sang her first **Faust** with the Chicago Lyric; her co-stars were Ezio Pinza and Raoul Jobin. Claudia Cassidy, usually hard to please, again raved. "**Faust** is superbly sung. From where I sit at the opera, Jeanette MacDonald has turned out to be one of the welcome surprises of the season...and her Marguerite was better than her Juliet.... beautifully sung with purity of line and tone, a good trill, and a Gallic inflection that understood Gounod's phrasing. She had something more than mere stage presence – a kind of intuition that makes an actor do the right thing at the right time. Lotte Lehmann's coaching did this quality no harm, but all the coaching in the world cannot create it where it does not instinctively exist…" The *Daily News* added, "Jeanette...deserved the gale of applause she got last night at the Civic Opera House for the Jewel Song. In the scene in the church, however, between Mephistopheles and Marguerite, Miss MacDonald acquitted herself vocally and dramatically with the highest operatic power she has shown in her whole 'career' in her new medium... The emotion she and Pinza together stirred here was as authentic as it was gripping."

A newspaper interview at this time reported that Jeanette planned to debut one new opera a year. "Last year it was **Romeo et Juliette**. This year is the **Faust** year. **La Boheme** is set for next year. And from overhearing a conversation with Oscar Hild (the Opera Association manager), there's a bet on about **Traviata**."

But it was not to be. In 1945 Jeanette returned to the Chicago Lyric for repeats of **Romeo et Juliet** and **Faust.** Claudia Cassidy praised her Marguerite as "a singing actress of such beauty you felt if Faust must sell his soul to the devil, at least this time he got his money's worth." Jeanette then sang both operas for the Cincinnati Opera, in an outdoor pavilion in the heat of summer. John Brownlee co-starred with her in **Romeo et Juliette**. After the July 25th performance, Brownlee's secretary was puzzled by Jeanette's behavior. "Jeanette kept herself together for the rehearsals, but was devastated afterwards. After the performance she took only three curtain calls, without a smile on her face, and didn't return to the stage even though the applause continued for several minutes." The secretary went backstage to see if there was a problem; Brownlee told her Jeanette had collapsed and the doctor thought it might be the heat. He added: "But of course I know better."

Noted Film Star In Opera Debut

Jeanette MacDonald Makes New Venture in Gounod's 'Romeo and Juliet'

By THOMAS ARCHER.

Instances are comparatively rare in the history of music to match Jeanette MacDonald's courageous venture into opera which occurred on Saturday night at His Majesty's Theatre when the screen and musical comedy star appeared for the first time in Gounod's Romeo And Juliet. And, it may be said at once, it was in more ways than one an auspicious debut, a triumph for Miss MacDonald and an honor to Montreal.

The singer, who is familiar to everyone for her many appearances in motion pictures, undertook the role of Juliet with a determination and a vocal ability that called for more and more admiration as the evening's proceedings went on. Romeo And Juliet, stylistically, is one of the most difficult operas in the French repertory, and the French repertory admittedly makes more demands upon the artistry of the performers than either the Italian or the German.

Miss MacDonald was fortunate in that she was supported by an experienced cast, most of the members thereof, including the chorus and ballet, having been drawn from the forces of the Metropolitan Opera Company. She had Armand Tokatyan as her Romeo. Mr. Tokatyan may not be necessarily a specialist in French opera, but he is obviously a past master of the routine of the operatic stage.

Also Miss MacDonald had Ezio Pinza in her cast. Mr. Pinza, one becomes more convinced every time one is fortunate enough to hear and see him, is one of the finest singing actors on the lyric stage today. Last September his Father in Louise was, to say the least, memorable. His Friar Lawrence in Romeo And Juliet is even more so. That magnificent voice, superb and dignified presence, faultless style alone would have set this Romeo And Juliet apart.

Nevertheless the main responsibility rested upon Miss MacDonald. It was to hear and see her that every seat was occupied and people crowded into the limited space available for standing. They must have felt she was justified in choosing the role for her debut. Her personal beauty, softer and more fragile than when seen through the eye of the camera, was admirably suited to the part. She was obviously nervous in the first act and inclined to make her gestures too stereotyped and emphatic. But once that hurdle was taken she fell into the requisite pattern and gave during the rest of the performance an interpretation which had charm, was unforced and thoroughly ingratiating.

The voice is sweet in quality. It has in person that sureness and cleanness which has always been noted in the soprano's screen work and has made her one of the most accomplished straight singers Hollywood ever had. The music of Romeo And Juliet is far from easy. Like the acting, it requires an ability to execute the text with exactly that balance between word and music values which is the secret of French operatic style. Miss MacDonald obviously had that style in mind and more often than not she attained it.

Next to Miss MacDonald, and Messrs. Pinza and Tokatyan, Lionel Daunais' Mercutio calls for special mention. More perhaps than anyone on the stage, Mr. Daunais knew and was able to translate into terms of gesture and voice what his role demanded. This was a beautifully styled performance, one that was in a class by itself. Mr. Daunais never made a move that did not reflect the intention of the composer and his librettists. In its way this Mercutio was a classic.

The lesser roles were all well taken. Alessio de Paolis put plenty of fire and energy into the part of Tybalt. He, Mr. Daunais and Mr. Tokatyan made an impressive thing of the quarrel scene. John Gurney was a capable Capulet and Gerard Gelinas made his mark in the small role of Gregorio. Alice Howland was a pretty Stephano and Jeanne Desjardins deserves special tribute for her neat, unobtrusive appearances as the Nurse. George Cehanovsky and Mr. Tortolero were well cast as the Duke of Verona and Paris respectively.

Wilfred Pelletier was a tower of strength as conductor. Much of the success of the production is due to his masterly direction. The chorus sang acceptably throughout and the ballet bits were well handled. The stage direction was carried out by Desire Defrere with his usual forethought.

The opera will be repeated tonight with a substitute for Mr. Pinza in the role of Friar Lawrence.

MacDonald As Juliet

Pinza and Pelletier Shone in Gounod Opera

WITH much of the circumstance of a great event; with every possible seat and standing place in His Majesty's Theatre filled by her admirers, Miss Jeanette MacDonald made her entry into grand opera on Saturday evening; and she could probably have chosen nothing which fitted herself or the occasion better than the melodious and brightly colored music of Gounod's "Romeo and Juliet."

* * *

MISS MacDONALD was, inevitably, a most charming Juliet, full of vitality, though with a certain self-consciousness quite appropriate to a first appearance. She gave the part a new and rather modernized character, and brought out, very properly, the striking difference between Gounod's Juliet and Shakespeare's. She sang tunefully and with confidence; her voice, if somewhat light for some of the music was cleverly managed, and went best with the gentler and simpler passages of the balcony scene. Armand Tokatyan remembered that Romeo was not so young as Juliet and behaved with becoming gravity. He put some warmth of feeling into his arias and made his voice agree well with Miss MacDonald's in their duets.

* * *

IN MANY performances of this opera Friar Laurence is something of a bore, but on Saturday, with Pinza in the part, one wanted more of him. Mr. Pinza sang splendidly and, in the few minutes that are given to the Friar, made the part more important than anything else in the opera. The other supporting parts were well filled, some of them by Montreal singers who appeared in them under Beecham last year. Alessio de Paolis swashbuckled finely as Tybalt; Lionel Daunais again sang and acted with much spirit as Mercutio; Jeanne Desjardins again showed how well the part of Gertrude, Juliet's nurse, fits her; Alice Howland as the page, John Gurney as old Capulet, Tortolero and George Cehanovsky as Paris and the Duke all did their work well.

* * *

THE production was well put together. The scenery was of the old convention, but the chorus sang well and had been thoroughly drilled in its business by Desire Defrere. The orchestra was excellent and its playing, under Wilfred Pelletier's direction, was a chief factor in the general success of the performance.

"Faust" Easy on the Eye; Ear Rewarded, Too

BY CLAUDIA CASSIDY

[Reprinted from yesterday's late Tribune]

The eye rejoiced and the ear had no cause to cringe at Saturday's "Faust," which marked the half-way point of the six week season of Chicago Opera at the Civic Opera house. With Jeanette MacDonald, Nino Martini, Richard Bonelli and the up and coming Nicola Moscona in leading roles, and with the seemingly tireless Fausto Cleva in the orchestra pit, Gounod's opera sustained its stature as one of the masterpieces of the repertory.

Countless performances have been more richly sung, but this one had compensations. It was fluent music drama, almost invariably believable, often beautiful. The focus was not on stars, but on Gounod and Goethe.

This might have been surprising had we not glimpsed last season the extraordinary development of Miss MacDonald under the clairvoyant tutelage of Lotte Lehmann. Saturday she was Jeanette MacDonald, the movie star, up to the point that without her wide popularity her slight but sweet and skilfully used soprano might not have entered the portals of grand opera.

But from there on she was no visiting celebrity on the wrong stage. She was Marguerite, a singing actress of such beauty you felt if Faust must sell his soul to the devil, at least this time he got his money's worth.

But that beauty, no matter how shrewdly costumed in blue that turns violet with dusk, no matter how enhanced by jewels that glitter like the real thing [they are the best Parisian paste], that beauty is only the sheath of what is to me a fascinating performance. Her voice has found dramatic focus and it holds up in its slender fashion thru the closing trio. The Jewel Song was much better than last year's, with greater freedom and sparkle.

And while you would expect her to do the garden scene curtain with more than ordinary grace, there is a distinct shock of pleased surprise in the fey delicacy with which she follows that masterly score to madness.

Mr. Martini's Faust was a gentle knight in the poetic mood of medieval legend, and he sang well in a tenor more noted for charm than brilliance. There were several vocal gearshifts in the Cavatina, but it ended in high, with an expert violin obbligato.

Mr. Bonelli sang beautifully in the melancholy vein of Valentin, and Mr. Moscona had a resounding success as a Mephisto with a coal black basso rich in range, individual in quality. He needs more sardonic brimstone in later scenes to match his brilliant "Calf of Gold" and his spine-tingling way with the scene of swords.

Doris Doe was a deft nurse, and Rosalind Nadell could be an attractive Siebel if she would discipline her fresh mezzo-soprano. The stage pictures were good despite indications of animation at any cost, and the chorus did some admirable work, notably in Valentin's death scene, tho it lacks the seasoned strength for singing massed against brass.

The quartets were better balanced than last season because amplification had withdrawn its ugly head. Mr. Cleva's orchestra was a major asset, save in Mephisto's serenade, where the whole performance missed the taunt of curled lip mockery.

Miss M'Donald Stars; 'Faust' Is Superbly Sung

"FAUST."

Opera by Charles Gounod, book by Barbier and Carre after Goethe. Presented in French by the Chicago Opera company at the Civic Opera house Wednesday evening, Nov. 15, 1944.

THE CAST.

Faust....................Raoul Jobin
Mephistopheles....................Ezio Pinza
Marguerite....................Jeanette MacDonald
Valentin....................Francesco Valentino
Siebel....................Lucielle Browning
Martha....................Doris Doe
Wagner....................Wilfred Engelman
Conductor....................Fausto Cleva

BY CLAUDIA CASSIDY.

[Reprinted from yesterday's late Tribune.]

From where I sit at the opera, Jeanette MacDonald has turned out to be one of the welcome surprises of the season. Her Juliet was decorative, intelligent, and well sung within her vocal scope, and Wednesday night her Marguerite was better than her Juliet. It was a stagewise performance as French as Yvonne Gall's, beautifully sung with purity of line and tone, a good trill, and a Gallic inflection that understood Gounod's phrasing. Exquisitely dressed in blue that turned violet with lights to set off her golden hair, she was a Marguerite to give point to a love scene, and she had something more than mere stage presence—a kind of intuition that makes an actor do the right thing at the right time. Lotte Lehmann's coaching did this quality no harm, but all the coaching in the world cannot create it where it does not instinctively exist. Because of it, Miss MacDonald is lovely to the eye. She has dramatic rhythm.

In general, this second "Faust" was so improved as to make the season's first performance look like a bad dress rehearsal, but it had one major flaw. At the right of the stage some one had set a nest of microphones lurking like cobras to strike at any hapless voice that turned their way. No doubt this was kindly meant as aid to Miss MacDonald, who didn't need it. She sounded far better when her voice was normally projected. And you should have heard what this amplification did to the garden scene quartet when Ezio Pinza happened to be standing by those microphones. It's the first time I ever heard it as a bass solo.

However, Mr. Pinza was in splendid voice and coöperative mood, inclined this time to sing the score as written and to limit his clowning to certain sardonic humors popular with Mephistos ever since Chaliapin. The scene of the swords still lacked the prescient malevolence he can give it when he likes, but the "Calf of Gold" was back in scintillant style, sung with a voice unique in its kind today. Mr. Jobin was in happier voice for the title role, achieving a line that made his beautiful tenor all more of a piece, less inclined to explode on a high note. Mr. Valentino again sang Valentin admirably, and Miss Browning's Siebel was considerably more convincing than at her first try.

But now for the staging. Remember how Lothar Wallerstein got the discredit for the first "Faust"? He swears he never touched it, and the opera says he is right. It should have been Gustaf Bergman's name in the program. So Mr. Bergman staged the first "Faust," which was poor. Now Mr. Bergman's name was in the program this time as having staged the second "Faust," which was improved. But Mr. Bergman has left town. Anyway, whoever staged Wednesday night's performance deserves at least a small bow.

Ironically, the only "real" opera they sang together on film – except for short excerpts, was the Act II scene from Tosca *for the "lost"* Maytime. *In the mid 1950s, Nelson stated that he'd recently been at MGM where they were screening that footage, so it was still in existence at that time. Whether the first* Maytime *has truly survived is unknown.*

"She has everything in the world that any woman could want, except happiness.," he continued. "She's the most unhappy person I have ever known—" His wife cut him off, warning him he'd said enough.[40]

And that was it.

There were a variety of factors in Jeanette's deciding to call it quits. It was very hard work and too demanding on her health. She was also under a lot of personal stress that her public knew nothing about. Too, she had proved to herself and the opera world that she could do it – and do it well, so that goal had been reached. But she wanted to sing at the Met. Other opera houses offered her virtually any role she wanted; but nothing was as prestigious as the Met. And despite a lot of back and forth, Edward Johnson was not inclined to hire her. Jeanette seemed to think it was because she was a movie star, and Johnson had his nose in the air about that.[41] In those days, an opera star was still thought to be "slumming" if he/she went to Hollywood. Just a few years later Robert Merrill experienced being told by Johnson that if he signed a movie contract, he was out of the Met.[42]

Her only opera sung in her home town of Philadelphia was a single performance of Faust *in 1951.*

But Jeanette had been off the screen since 1942. And she had so many friends in the opera world – some under contract to the Met – who would have surely spoken up for her. So, maybe there's more to it than meets the eye… and maybe not. The point is, Jeanette resumed the tried and true concert circuit, where her fans could hear her singing the movie songs they preferred anyway.

In the late 1940s, Jeanette alienated some of her fans – and Nelson -- by returning to MGM to play two mother roles. She was hoping for a third film that they could make together (and even optioned a book), but it fell through, as finally did their shaky personal relationship at this time.

In 1950, Jeanette attempted a stage comeback with her husband in **The Guardsman**. They'd hoped to take it to Broadway but the show didn't make it– even when Jeanette added a mini-concert to please her fans.

On December 12, 1951, Jeanette sang a single performance of **Faust** with the Philadelphia Grand Opera at the Academy of Music. The following year she was back concertizing. During the 1950s she would do TV, summer stock productions of **The King and I** and **Bittersweet** and a record with Nelson. She tried Vegas but it was too strenuous for her. She and Nelson appeared on variety shows together and there was talk of their hosting a TV show of their own. There were also aborted attempts to get a film off the ground with Nelson.

By the 1960s, her bad heart forced her into retirement. Her last years were filled with trying to write an autobiography and making personal appearances when her films were re-released theatrically to a new generation of fans.

She died on January 14, 1965 at age 61, much mourned by her loyal fans, the film industry and a certain baritone.

Their Opera in Film

Jeanette MacDonald had been in movies for only one year before she sang her first on-screen aria. In **Oh, For a Man** (1930) she played a temperamental opera singer similar to her character in the more famous **Rose Marie**. The movie opened with her character singing "Liebestod," smiling graciously at her adoring audience and then stomping off the stage with scathing anger.

Later in the same film she came offstage dressed as Juliet, though she didn't sing.

Rose Marie (1936) found Jeanette singing Juliet's Waltz Song, as well as a quick montage of the entire Gounod **Romeo et Juliette**, and the final scene from **Tosca**. In both sequences her co-star was tenor Allan Jones.

Jeanette played an opera singer again in **San Francisco** (1936), singing the "Jewel Song" plus a montaged medley from **Faust** culminating in the famous trio. Later she sang "Sempre Libera" from **La Traviata**.

The movie **Maytime** began as an Irving Thalberg production in the fall of 1936. The plot and supporting cast were completely different from the version that we know. When Thalberg died suddenly, the near-completed production was scrapped. A new screenplay was written and production began anew.

From the extensive photographs remaining from the "lost" **Maytime**, we learn that the big production number was the second act of *Tosca.* There's also a photo of Nelson in costume as Escamillo for another sequence.

The "second" **Maytime** (1937) was an opera-lover's delight. It featured an operatic medley, "Ham and Eggs," sung by Nelson on the streets of Paris. In this number were snatches from **Rigoletto, The Barber of Seville, Tannhäuser, Faust, Il Trovatore,** and the **William Tell** overture. Later, Jeanette sang "Nobles Seigneurs, Salut" and "Une Dame Noble et Sage" from **Les Huguenots**.

A brilliant **Maytime** montage featured Jeanette singing a medley from several operas, serving to show the passage of years in the plot. Selections from the following were utilized: **Il Trovatore, Faust, Tristan and Isolde, La Traviata, Le Prophete, Bohemian Girl, Martha** and **Lucia de Lammermoor**. Added to this, posters and musical scores flashing across the screen announced that Jeanette's character had also starred in **Tannhäuser, Maritana, Lohengrin, Norma, Don Giovanni** and **The Barber of Seville**. While musically and cinematically a masterful scene, opera purists snickered at this unrealistic "repertoire," which ranged from coloratura to dramatic soprano.

The climax of **Maytime** was the "shadow" opera **Czaritza,** which utilized Tschaikovsky's Fifth Symphony. Sung as a duet between Nelson and Jeanette, it was an electrifying sequence that has been called of the greatest dramatic scenes in movie history.

In **Rosalie** (1937), Nelson sang "M'Appari" from **Martha**.

The team split up (temporarily) in 1939. That year, Nelson sang a **Carmen** medley including the Toreador Song and "Si Tu M'Aime" in **Balalaika**, with co-star Ilona Massey. Jeanette sang a fully staged "Un Bel Di" in one of the only redeeming moments of **Broadway Serenade**.

A brief operatic medley was sung by Jeanette and Nelson in their last film together, **I Married An Angel** (1942). They sang "Chanson Boheme" from **Carmen** and the **Faust** trio.

In **Cairo** (1942), Jeanette and Ethel Waters sang a comic duet version of the **Lucia** sextet.

Nelson played an opera singer in **Phantom of the Opera** (1943). He sang a fully staged "Porter Song" from **Martha** and the lead role in another "shadow" opera, **Le Prince de Caucasie**. This was adapted from Tchaikovsky's Fourth Symphony. Nelson sang magnificently (though fans cringed at seeing him in a black wig and mustache). Universal's sound director, Bernard Brown, had built a special sound booth and Nelson was never recorded better on film. Unfortunately, the "opera" ends prematurely when that pesky chandelier falls from the ceiling.

In Disney's **Make Mine Music** (1946), Nelson sang and spoke every voice for the "Willie, The Operatic Whale" segment. He sang "Largo al Factotum," all the voices of the **Lucia** sextet, some tenor excerpts from **I Pagliacci**, both Tristan and Isolde, Boito's **Mephistophele** (bass role), and tenor and baritone roles in **Martha**. This movie is considered a lesser Disney effort, but Nelson's segment was and still is considered the best part of the film.

In Jeanette's last film, **The Sun Comes Up** (1949), she reprised "Un Bel Di" at a recital. Production stills indicate that she and Armand Tokatyan also sang a duet from **La Traviata**, though this was cut from the film. But a recording of the duet has survived and was released on the Mac/Eddy Series #23 album: "Operatic Recital #3."

Nelson and Jeanette were the first operatic-style singers to really "make it" in movies. They triumphed in a medium where Grace Moore, Lawrence Tibbett, Lily Pons, Gladys Swarthout and other opera greats failed. Obvious-ly, a superb voice alone doesn't guarantee success on the screen.

For many Depression-era audiences, Nelson and Jeanette represented the best in opera. No singers since have duplicated their magic.

Nelson's Operatic Roles

The following list is a compilation of operas in Nelson's repertoire. A few roles, such as Escamillo, Rigoletto and Boris Godunov were sung in excerpted, concert format. Scarpia was only sung – as far as we know – in the "lost" ***Maytime***..

Aida (Amonasro)

Ariadne auf Naxos (Wigmaker, Harlequin)

La Boheme (Marcello)

Boris Godunov (Various baritone roles, and Boris)

Carmen (Escamillo)

Elektra (Orestes)

Faust (Valentine)

Feuersnot (Hämmerlein)

Gianni Schicchi (Gianni Schicci)

Götterdämmerung (Gunther)

Hänsel and Gretel (Peter)

Iolanthe (Strephon)

L'elisir d'amore (Sergeant Belcore)

Legend of the Invisible City of Kitesh and the Maiden Fevronia (Feodor Poyarok)

Lohengrin (Telramund and the Herald)

The Love of Three Kings (Manfredo)

Madame Butterfly (Sharpless)

The Magic Flute (Papageno)

Manon Lescaut (Lescaut)

Maria Egiziaca (Abbot Zosimo and Pilgrim)

Martha (Plunkett)

The Marriage Tax (King of Greece)

The Marriage of Figaro (Count Almaviva)

Die Meistersinger (Kother)

Merry Mount (Second Puritan)

La Navarraise (Bustamente)

I Pagliacci (Tonio and Sylvio)

Parsifal (Gurnemanz)

Pirates of Penzance (Major General)

Das Rheingold (Donner)

Rigoletto (Rigoletto)

Romeo et Juliette (Mercutio)

Salome (Jochanahan)

Samson et Delilah (Abimélech, High Priest Satrap)

Secret of Suzanne (Count Gil)

Tannhäuser (Wolfram)

Tosca (Scarpia)

Wozzeck (Drum Major)

Nelson's Oratorios

Bethlehem (Maunder)

The Creation *(*Haydn)

Elijah (Mendelssohn)

L'Enfant Prodigue (Debussy)

The Fall of Babylon (Spohr)

The Messiah (Handel)

Olivet to Calvary (Maunder)

The Passion According to St. John (Bach)

The Passion According to St. Matthew (by Bach)

Redemption (Gounod)

Requiem (Brahms)

Requiem (Verdi)

St. Cecilia's Mass (Gounod)

St. Paul (Mendelssohn)

Nelson's Chaliapin Screenplay

In the early 1940s, Nelson was looking for better movie scripts. He finally wrote one for himself, a biopic of his idol, Feodor Chaliapin. It was titled *Song of the Giant.* Nelson authored it under a thinly-disguised pseudonym: "A musical by Isaac Ackerman, from an original treatment by Feodor Chaliapin, Jr." Issac was the first name of his paternal grandfather, Ackerman the last name of his paternal grandfather (and Nelson's middle name). In case one didn't see through the disguise, the title page of the script advised the reader to "Please return to: Nelson Eddy, c/o Famous Artists Corp., California Bank Building, in Beverly Hills, California."

Nelson was to play both Chaliapin and himself in the screenplay.

Obviously the film was never made. In the original version, the scene opened with a studio general conference, where a couple of guys are talking to none other than -- Nelson Eddy.

(In consideration of space, the dialogue below has been taken out of standard screenplay format.)

HEAD MAN: Nelson, we'd like to use you in a picture, but we haven't been able to decide on a subject for you.
ASSISTANT HEAD: Yeah, no story.
PRODUCER: Is there some famous character you would like to play -- George Washington, maybe?
MUSIC HEAD: No, he couldn't carry a tune. Eddy's got to sing.
DIRECTOR: Who's your favorite singer of all time?
EDDY: That's easy. Chaliapin.
UNIT MANAGER: Chali...Who's he?
WRITER: A big Russian guy.
ASSISTANT PRODUCER: Never heard of him.
HEAD MAN: I've heard of him, but don't know much about him. Any romance?
ASSISTANT HEAD: Yeah, any love life?
WRITER: Sure, dames all over the place.
DIRECTOR: Drank hard, didn't he?
WRITER: Oh, he took a slug of vodka now and then.
STORY DEPARTMENT HEAD: Should we make a Russian picture? It may be touchy.
EDDY: It happened in Russia, but it could have happened anywhere. Chaliapin might have been an American. His heart beat the same as ours. Americans were crazy about him.
HEAD MAN (to Eddy): Are you familiar with his whole story?
ASSISTANT HEAD: Yeah, ever meet him?
EDDY: I sure did, right here in Hollywood.
HEAD MAN: Maybe there's a story here. Tell us about him, briefly.
ASSISTANT HEAD: Yeah, shoot.
EEDY: Briefly?
HEAD MAN: well, go ahead. If it's got a punch, we'll keep listening.
ASSISTANT HEAD: Yeah, we'll stick with you.
EDDY: Okay, you asked for it. Chaliapin was born in the little town of Kazan.
DIRECTOR: Skip the baby stuff. When did things start to happen?

EDDY: All right...Nine years later...a kid friend of his, Kolka, gave him a ticket to his first show -- the opera, *Faust.* He was enchanted by it. For the first time in his life he saw there was something in the world besides dirt, drunkenness and hunger....

And we flashback to the story.
The original ending was as follows:

The camera has dollied in to Eddy's face. There is a trick dissolve to his face at the present time and, as it pulls back again, we see that it is Eddy finishing his narration to the executives. We see the group again in the executive office.

HEAD MAN (thinking): I don't know.
ASSISTANT HEAD: Yeah, maybe not so good.
MUSIC DEPT HEAD: It's got some swell tunes.
UNIT MANAGER: It wouldn't make a nickel at the box office.
HEAD MAN: But--we have an obligation to the public.
ASSISTANT HEAD: Yeah, if they'd take it, we gotta give it to 'em.
PRODUCER: Boss, I like it. I'll take a chance. You put up the money and I'll make the picture.
HEAD MAN: All right. It's in your lap. Get busy.
ASSISTANT HEAD: Yeah. Get going, men. We've got a great idea here!
PRODUCER: Thanks for thinking of it.
ASSISTANT HEAD: Oh shucks--all in a day's work.

The meeting breaks up with a bustle. Eddy stands around, being ignored.

ASSISTANT HEAD (to Eddy): Scram, pal, we gotta work this out.

□

In the revised version, Nelson changed the ending this way:

233. The film ends with a fade in: insert, newspaper headline, Chaliapin to tour America! Then a montage, which includes, Chaliapin arriving on a liner, walks on a street, sings in concert, in *Faust, Don Quixote, Barber of Seville, Boris Godunov.* Audience applauds, rushing train, stock, sign HOLLYWOOD and ends with him watching the shooting of a picture in a film studio. End montage. Dissolve to

234. Drawing room, medium-day, home of Hollywood hostess (Doris Kenyon. Could use.)

Chaliapin is being lionized by a smart Hollywood group. A tall, blond young man, his back always to the camera, is introduced to him by the hostess.

235. Drawing room -- medium close

HOSTESS: ...He is an ambitious singer. One of your greatest admirers.

The men shake hands.

YOUNG MAN: This is a great moment in my life.
CHALIAPIN: Thank you. Do you sing some of my songs?
YOUNG MAN: Many of them. I am working on one of them right now--but I'm having a little difficulty with the Russian.

Chaliapin is glad to have the chance of doing something besides being lionized.

CHALIAPIN: Maybe I can help you. Come over here.

236 Corner of drawing room -- close -- Chaliapin, young man.

They sit in a corner of the room and Chaliapin politely waves other guests away.

CHALIAPIN (interested): Now, you recite the Russian. I will correct you.
YOUNG MAN: Thanks. It is your great aria, the Prophet...Prorok..."Doo chov noi zhazhdoyoo tomim"...

Drawing Room – group of guests -- medium

They eye the two men and are sweetly annoyed.

237.
FIRST GUEST: Looks like a private party.
SECOND GUEST: Rather rude of them to go off by themselves.
THIRD GUEST (to hostess): Better do something.
HOSTESS: I'll give them another minute, then I shall.

238. Drawing Room -- close

YOUNG MAN (reciting the last line): ...Glagolom zhgi serdtsya lioodye!
CHALIAPIN: Good. You see, God says to the prophet, "Go forth and preach my word on land and sea!"

He puts his hand on the young man's shoulder.

Chaliapin: Now you do the same! Take what I have given you and give it to your people as I did to mine. I am sure you can do it. Good luck!

They rise and shake hands.

239. Drawing room -- medium close -- then dolly in

HOSTESS: Mr. Chaliapin, I hate to disturb you, but I want you to meet some more of our guests.
CHALIAPIN: Thank you.

He bows, goes off with the hostess, leaving the young man alone. He turns around and faces us for the first time. We DOLLY IN close to his face. There are tears in his eyes.

YOUNG MAN (Nelson Eddy): What a man! FADE OUT. (Music-reprise of [*Boris Godunov*] Coronation scene, chorus, bells, etc.) The End

Source Notes

[1] Nearly all endnotes can be referenced to the book *Sweethearts, the Timeless Love Affair – on screen and off – between Jeanette MacDonald and Nelson Eddy,* © 1994 and 2001 by Sharon Rich. This book and any of the Mac/Eddy Series mentioned below can be ordered from www.maceddy.com or write for catalog: Mac/Eddy Club, PO Box 1077, New York, NY 10002. The quote about Nelson's birth came from a newspaper clipping.
[2] Details of their marriage came from the divorce court transcripts of Isabel vs. William Eddy.
[3] The recordings of Nelson's grandmother and mother mentioned here are available on Mac/Eddy Series #JN121, "Nelson and his mother." Nelson duets with his mother on *Mikado* excerpts and "Love's Old Sweet Song."
[4] Newspaper interview.
[5] Newspaper interview.
[6] Newspaper interview.
[7] This recording can be heard on Mac/Eddy Series #JN110, "The Early Years."
[8] Newspaper interview.
[9] Nelson wrote a movie script for himself to star in about the life of Chaliapin, but never sold it.
[10] Newspaper interview.
[11] Malcolm Poindexter quotes came from Jean Warren interview, 1990, plus author's taped phone interviews and meeting with him that same year.
[12] Various newspaper reports and interviews.
[13] Nelson later made derogatory statements about Mayer to various press, such as Charles Higham, and to two lady friends who were interviewed for *Sweethearts.*
[14] Per newspaper clippings and interviews, the date that they first met would be around November, 1933. There are photos of them together in mid 1934. *Naughty Marietta* began shooting in late 1934.
[15] TV interview for the news the day Jeanette died.
[16] Details of this are in Isabel Eddy's unpublished memoirs.
[17] Sybil Thomas to Diane Goodrich. Verified by Marie Collick, a friend of Nelson's.
[18] A 1932 radio segment of Douglas Stanley giving a voice lesson, using Nelson to demonstrate, can be heard on Mac/Eddy Series #JN 110, "The Early Years."
[19] Caesari's daughter Alma discussed Nelson and his Caesari studies with the author.
[20] Interviews with Marston's close friend Sarah Smith and others; interviews with Helen Jepson and Rose Bampton, 1989.
[21] Sybil Thomas to Diane Goodrich. Verified by a lady friend of Nelson's.
[22] Steber made this comment when asked about the album at a lecture given in New York, 1986.
[23] Author's taped interview with Stevens was done in an office at the Met.
[24] Details of these problems are discussed in *Sweethearts* and sourced from various people, including Nelson's mother.
[25] All this is fully detailed in *Sweethearts.* Dorothy Killgallen was one of the reporters in the know about Ann Eddy's demands. In 1995 reporter Mae Mann verified quotes attributed to her in *Sweethearts* re: the state of Jeanette's marriage.
[26] Contemporary letters; data coming from Isabel Eddy to her close friend.
[27] What data we know was filled in by Frank Laric, John Pickard and others; also two of Nelson's lady friends. Since Nelson's code name is unknown, the full documentation has not been released under the Freedom of Information Act.
[28] Author's interview with Tibbett, Jr. was done in his home, while a phone interview was done with his twin brother, Richard

[29] Author's phone interview with Uppman, 8/3/91.
[30] Their relationship verified by Harper McKay in a 1992 interview with the author, and other contemporaries. McKay was music arranger for the nightclub act and good friends with Gale Sherwood.
[31] In the movie treatment "Timothy Waits for Love," for example, Nelson has himself and Jeanette playing over-the-hill performers. While she has faithfully loved him for years, he's run off with a young blond (who was to have been played by Gale Sherwood). Due to the outrage over their age differences, he agrees to be cryogenically frozen and brought back to life when she is older – shades of Mel Gibson's movie *Forever Young.* But when Nelson wakes up he finds that he and Gale's character have nothing left in common, so he returns to the ever-loving and always forgiving Jeanette.
[32] Author's interviews with Charles Higham and others; newspaper accounts.
[33] Nelson's live nightclub act can be heard on Mac/Eddy Series #JN134.
[34] This written quote has been reprinted in several publications.
[35] Many instances of this are quoted from contemporary eyewitness reports in *Sweethearts.*
[36] Author's interview with Bampton at her home, 1989.
[37] RCA liner notes on a Jeanette operatic LP.
[38] Anna MacDonald letter to Jeanette's fan club.
[39] In a letter to her fans, the explanation was that she was sent home and put in bed due to a "very bad cold."
[40] From one of the "Isabel letters," 8/28/45.
[41] Jeanette's unpublished autobiography.
[42] Merrill's autobiography, *Between Acts.*

Index

L

M

N

O

P

R

S

Made in the USA